China, the United States, and Global Order

The United States and China are the two most important states in the international system and are crucial to the evolution of global order. Both recognize each other as vital players in a range of issues of global significance, including the use of force, macroeconomic policy surveillance, the non-proliferation of nuclear weapons, climate change, and financial regulation. In this book, Rosemary Foot and Andrew Walter, both experts in the fields of International Relations and the East Asian region, explore the relationship of the two countries to these global order issues since 1945. They ask whether the behaviour of each country is consistent with global order norms, and which domestic and international factors shape this behaviour. They investigate how the bilateral relationship of the United States and China influences the stances that each country takes. They also assess the global implications of national decisions, coming to the sobering conclusion that China and the United States tend to constrain rather than encourage more cooperative solutions to key global challenges. This is a sophisticated analysis that adroitly engages the historical, theoretical, and policy literature.

Professor Rosemary Foot is Professor of International Relations and John Swire Senior Research Fellow in the International Relations of East Asia at St Antony's College, University of Oxford. She is author of several books including *Human Rights and Counterterrorism in America's Asia Policy* (2004), *Rights Beyond Borders: The Global Community and the Struggle over Human Rights in China* (2000), and *The Practice of Power: U.S. Relations with China since 1949* (1995). Her co-edited works include *Order and Justice in International Relations* (2003).

Dr Andrew Walter is Reader in International Political Economy at the London School of Economics and Political Science. His previous books include *Governing Finance: East Asia's Adoption of Global Standards* (2008) and *Analyzing the Global Political Economy* (2009, with Gautam Sen).

For Nina and Tim

China, the United States, and Global Order

ROSEMARY FOOT
University of Oxford

ANDREW WALTER
London School of Economics and Political Science

CAMBRIDGE UNIVERSITY PRESS
Cambridge, New York, Melbourne, Madrid, Cape Town, Singapore,
São Paulo, Delhi, Dubai, Tokyo, Mexico City

Cambridge University Press
32 Avenue of the Americas, New York, NY 10013-2473, USA

www.cambridge.org
Information on this title: www.cambridge.org/9780521725194

First published 2011

Printed in the United States of America

A catalog record for this publication is available from the British Library.

Library of Congress Cataloging in Publication data
Foot, Rosemary, 1948–
    China, the United States, and global order / Rosemary Foot, Andrew Walter.
        p.   cm.
    ISBN 978-0-521-89800-3 (hardback) – ISBN 978-0-521-72519-4 (pbk.)
    1. United States – Foreign relations – China.   2. China – Foreign relations – United
    States.   I. Walter, Andrew, 1961–   II. Title.
    JZ1480.A57C647   2010
    327.51073–dc22   2010031324

ISBN 978-0-521-89800-3 Hardback
ISBN 978-0-521-72519-4 Paperback

Contents

Figures and Tables

Acknowledgements

The research and writing of this book owe a great deal to the assistance and inspiration offered by a number of colleagues and friends across three continents. Our editor at Cambridge University Press, Marigold Acland, has been particularly supportive, and her genuine interest in the project has been of great importance to us. We are also very grateful to those individuals who read parts of the manuscript and provided very helpful comments: Howard Davies, Evelyn Goh, Bruce Jentleson, Kathy Morton, Andrew Sheng, and William Walker. Thomas J. Christensen and Samuel S. Kim very kindly read the whole manuscript and provided comments that were both extensive and challenging; we are particularly grateful to them. We were fortunate in having Amitav Acharya act as discussant at a conference where we presented early forms of our ideas. Colleagues at the London School of Economics who attended a research-in-progress seminar offered many valuable ideas that helped to sharpen our thoughts on the research framework and its various applications. Jeffrey Chwieroth, Robert Falkner, and Uli Sedelmeier kindly followed up with additional suggestions and advice. At Oxford, Andrew Hurrell has been a constant source of encouragement, always showing interest in the progress of the project and asking thought-provoking questions about it. Jochen Prantl's various workshops and conferences – in China and at Oxford – on the theme of "effective multilateralism" have provided further very useful opportunities to test out ideas. We offer all of these people our grateful thanks, but we remain responsible for any errors or lapses in judgement.

Rosemary Foot would like to extend her warm thanks to Roham Ahlvandi, Tiang Boon Hoo, Nicola Horsburgh, Carlotta Minnella, and

Anna Schrimpf for help with the research for particular chapters. Hannah Ellermann deserves our special thanks for her painstaking work in checking the references and bibliography, and compiling the list of acronyms. Tim Kennedy has provided inspiration for the cover design, has produced the index with great efficiency and care, and has made many other valuable suggestions. Clare Hammond, Andrew Sheng, Wataru Takahashi, and Michael Yahuda helped to arrange interviews in Beijing, Shanghai, and Washington, DC, as did Evan Medeiros and Suzanne Yang, who also gave up a great deal of their own time. To those in China, Europe, and the United States who agreed to be interviewed, most on a confidential basis, we owe a huge debt of gratitude.

Our two institutions, the University of Oxford and the London School of Economics, have not only provided supportive intellectual environments but also the research funding required for our various trips abroad. During one of our trips to Beijing, we were accompanied by Nina and Tim. We dedicate this book to them in celebration of their friendship and for their ability to make this particular period of research both possible and especially enjoyable.

RF & AW
April 2010

Acronyms

ABA	American Bankers Association
ABC	Agricultural Bank of China
ABM	Anti-Ballistic Missile
ACDA	(US) Arms Control and Disarmament Agency
ACDD	(China) Arms Control and Disarmament Department
ACES	American Clean Energy and Security Act
ADB	Asian Development Bank
A-IRB	Advanced IRB
AOSIS	Association of Small Island States
AP	Additional Protocol
ARF	ASEAN Regional Forum
ASEAN	Association of Southeast Asian Nations
BASIC	Brazil, South Africa, India, China
BCBS	Basel Committee on Banking Supervision
BOC	Bank of China
CAR	Capital Adequacy Ratio
CBRC	China Banking Regulatory Commission
CD	UN Conference on Disarmament
CDM	Clean Development Mechanism
CDO	Collateralized Debt Obligation
CDS	Credit Default Swap
CNAO	Chinese National Audit Office
COCOM	Coordinating Committee for Multilateral Export Controls
COPs	Conference of the Parties

COSTIND	Commission on Science, Technology, and Industry for National Defence
CRS	Congressional Research Services
CTBT	Comprehensive Test Ban Treaty
DPRK	Democratic People's Republic of Korea
EPA	(US) Environmental Protection Agency
EPBs	(China) Environmental Protection Bureaus
EU3	France, Germany, and the United Kingdom
FDI	Foreign Direct Investment
FDIC	Federal Deposit Insurance Corporation
F-IRB	Foundational IRB
FMCT	Fissile Material Cutoff Treaty
FRBNY	Federal Reserve Bank of New York
FSA	Financial Services Authority
FSAP	Financial Sector Assessment Programme
FSB	Financial Stability Board
FY	Fiscal Year
GAO	United States Government Accountability Office
GATT	General Agreement on Tariffs and Trade
GCC	Global Climate Coalition
GCR2P	Global Centre for the Responsibility to Protect
GDP	Gross Domestic Product
GHG	Greenhouse Gases
HLP	High-Level Panel
IAEA	International Atomic Energy Agency
IAS	International Accounting Standards
ICBC	Industrial and Commercial Bank of China
ICCP	International Climate Change Partnership
ICG	International Crisis Group
ICISS	International Commission on Intervention and State Sovereignty
ICJ	International Court of Justice
IEA	International Energy Agency
IEO	Independent Evaluation Office, IMF
IFIs	International Financial Institutions
IFRS	International Financial Reporting Standards
IGOs	Intergovernmental Organizations
IIF	Institute of International Finance
IISS	International Institute for Strategic Studies
ILG	International Liaison Group

IMF	International Monetary Fund
IP	Intellectual Property
IPCC	Intergovernmental Panel on Climate Change
IPS	Inter Press Service Agency
IRB	Internal Ratings-Based Approach to Credit Risk Measurement
ISIS	Institute for Science and International Security
LTCM	Long-Term Capital Management
MEF	Major Economies Forum on Energy Security and Climate Change
MFN	Most-Favoured Nation
MID	Militarized Interstate Dispute
MNCs	Multinational Companies
MOFA	(Chinese) Ministry of Foreign Affairs
MRA	Market Risk Amendment
MRV	Measurable, Reportable, Verifiable
MTCR	Missile Technology Control Regime
NAM	Non-Aligned Movement
NBC	Nuclear, Biological, or Chemical
NBER	National Bureau of Economic Research
NCA	Nuclear Cooperation Agreement
NDRC	National Development and Reform Commission
NEPA	National Environment Protection Agency
NFU	No First Use of Nuclear Weapons
NGOs	Non-Governmental Organizations
NNPN	Nuclear Non-Proliferation Norm
NNWS	Non-Nuclear Weapons States
NPLs	Non-Performing Loans
NPR	Notice of Proposed Rulemaking
NPT	Nuclear Non-Proliferation Treaty
NSG	Nuclear Suppliers Group
NWS	Nuclear Weapons States
OCC	Office of the Comptroller of the Currency
OECD	Organization for Economic Cooperation and Development
OMB	Office of Management and Budget
OTS	Office of Thrift Supervision
P5	Permanent Members of UN Security Council
PAROS	Prevention of an Arms Race in Outer Space
PBOC	People's Bank of China

PIN	Public Information Notice
PLA	(Chinese) People's Liberation Army
PRC	People's Republic of China
PSI	Proliferation Security Initiative
PTBT	Partial Test Ban Treaty
QDR	(US Department of Defense) Quadrennial Defense Review
R2P	Responsibility to Protect
RGGI	Regional Greenhouse Gas Initiative
RMB	Renminbi
ROC	Republic of China (Taiwan)
SCO	Shanghai Cooperation Organization
SED	Strategic Economic Dialogue
S&ED	Strategic and Economic Dialogue
SEPA	State Environmental Protection Agency
SIPRI	Stockholm International Peace Research Institute
SOCBs	State-Owned Commercial Banks
SOEs	State-Owned Enterprises
SORT	Strategic Offensive Arms Reduction Treaty
START	Strategic Arms Reduction Treaty
TAN	Transnational Activist Network
UDHR	Universal Declaration of Human Rights
UNCED	United Nations Conference on Environment and Development
UNCHE	United Nations Conference on the Human Environment
UNEP	United Nations Environment Programme
UNFCCC	United Nations Framework Convention on Climate Change
UNGA	United Nations General Assembly
UNPKO	United Nations Peace Keeping Operation
UNSC	United Nations Security Council
UNTAET	United Nations Transitional Administration in East Timor
US DOD	US Department of Defense
USNSS	US National Security Strategy
VaR	Value at Risk
WBCSD	World Business Council on Sustainable Development
WMD	Weapons of Mass Destruction
WSO	World Summit Outcome
WTO	World Trade Organization

Introduction

Norms and Global Order

The United States and China are the two most important states in the international system. The global economic crisis of 2008–09 has, unusually in the post-1945 period, hurt the United States disproportionately in the short term and may accelerate an erosion of its military, economic, and cultural preponderance. Many now see China as the major beneficiary, but the longer-term consequences of this crisis are very uncertain. America's primacy in global politics and economics, including its position in many global institutions, remains considerable, and its impact on key global issues – either through its neglect of or participation in their management or resolution – will remain a central influence upon the evolving global order for decades to come.

At the same time, China's influence in global markets, its military modernization, and active diplomacy in all major regions of the world have demonstrated its growing potential to shape the global order of the twenty-first century and to reduce US preponderance in certain contexts. China is the state commonly viewed as most likely to be both willing and able to expand these areas of challenge in the future. There is a strong perception in both Beijing and Washington that they are each other's most important interlocutor on a range of crucial issues, arising as much from their interdependence as from the competitive nature of their relationship. Although it is uncertain as to how the global economic crisis will affect their long-run relative positions, it has reinforced the centrality of their bilateral relationship within the contemporary global order.

We argue for the importance of these two states and their bilateral state-to-state ties in what follows even though we acknowledge that the scope of world politics goes well beyond intergovernmental relations.

Significant as these two countries may be, they operate within a global order that contains spheres of authority beyond the actions and behaviour of states and governments. The global system is a contested arena that includes non-official actors and processes that do not always operate coterminously with the territorial spaces we associate with states (Rosenau 1997). In this conception, civil society actors, for example – both transnational and domestic – exert influence over policy choices. They may also affect each state differently: the US government is relatively open to civil society influence compared to China, but both states are often wary of transnational claims of authority. The ways in which the United States and China manage their relationship within this complex system of global order affects their attitudes towards the norms that influence its stability and evolutionary path.

This book asks three main questions. First, what factors shape the degree to which actor behaviour is consistent with global order norms? Second, what has determined the degree of Chinese and American consistency with global norms in different policy areas? Third, how has their bilateral relationship influenced those levels of consistency? This chapter sets out to provide a framework for responding to the first question. We answer the second and third questions by investigating five key areas of historical and contemporary importance: the use of force, macroeconomic policy surveillance, the non-proliferation of nuclear weapons, climate change, and financial regulation. The United States' and China's changing attitudes towards and behavioural consistency with regard to each of these issues are addressed in the next five empirically based chapters. This introductory chapter also provides further justification for our focus on the United States and China as actors that are central to any evaluation of the prospects for global order issues as well as for our decision to select these five particular global order issues and their associated norms, principles, rules, and standards. Finally, it provides a brief preview of our major findings.

1 What is Global Order?

As with many concepts in International Relations, that of global order is essentially contested. Our understanding of global order further complicates its application because we see order as dynamic and as a matter of degree. Over fifty different meanings of order have been noted (Alagappa 2003: 36); however, various authors have tried to distil what is essential to the concept. Steve Chan, for example, refers to definitions that range among "de facto patterns, normative ideals, and strategic conduct." These roughly correspond to order as an existing arrangement among relevant political actors; a vision that outlines a future, preferred set of relations; or actual policy conduct out of which we might discern a country's broad attitude to global order (Chan 1999: 197). Andrew Hurrell, who emphasizes patterns, distinguishes among minimalist, pluralist, and solidarist conceptions of order. The first relies on power, and occasional coincidences of interest rather than negotiated rules or common understandings to sustain some form of order; the second privileges the preservation of the society of states through mechanisms that acknowledge difference but seek to regulate the use of violence as a means of resolving the tensions that derive from difference; and the third requires a broad consensus on core principles among state and non-state actors with respect to the governance of global society, together with acceptance of the processes that are necessary to give effect to those principles (Hurrell 1998, 2007).[1]

Such classifications do not imply that only one definition provides an accurate description of reality. Within most countries, at the conceptual level, there are always competing ideas of what constitutes national interest, desirable foreign policy goals, and associated views of global order. These varying conceptions compete for policymakers' attentions and often coexist over long periods, including within the minds of individual policymakers. For example, in the 1990s, humanitarian arguments figured in some nine cases of conflict that came before the UN Security Council, although Council members debated possible responses on the basis of interest-based considerations as well (Roberts 2004: 81). Conceptions of order also evolve, and not necessarily in a progressive direction. G. John Ikenberry (2001), in his analysis of the "greater West" during the Cold War era, contrasts the pluralist order of coexistence between the West and East with a Western liberal order promoted via rules, institutions, and partnerships. This dualistic order gave way, he argues, to the emergence of a more solidarist liberal order in the post–Cold War era. Writing in 2005, however, he argued that the solidarist order of the 1990s may have given ground again in the George W. Bush era – this time to a more

---

[1] James Mayall defines pluralist and solidarist conceptions of international society more narrowly. Pluralist refers to "a society of sovereign states" with a commitment to territorial integrity and non-interference. Solidarist implies "a society of peoples in which sovereignty would not be regarded as absolute and where, when necessary, the international community would intervene for humanitarian reasons and to protect the victims of massive and sustained human rights abuse" (Mayall 2004: 121).

minimalist neo-imperial logic based on unipolarity and eroding norms of state sovereignty (Ikenberry 2005).

Our own position is closer to those of Ian Clark (2007) and Andrew Hurrell (2006, 2007). We do see some continuity between the Cold War and post–Cold War eras. US power, the maintenance of Cold War institutions, and the effects of globalization blur the differences that can be attributed to the systemic change of 1989–91. We would also argue that the development of global normative frameworks in a range of areas critical to global order provide some stability to the system, as shown by the inability of a materially powerful United States during the George W. Bush administration to reinterpret successfully the rules in areas such as climate change and use of force. As Hurrell points out, however, contestation is a persistent phenomenon in the global system, which remains characterized by inequality. As a result, where you stand on matters of order depends on where you sit in the global hierarchy. He notes the continuing "unhappy coexistence" between traditional pluralism, including the unequal power that underpins it, and liberal solidarism, which is often promoted by transnational actors or powerful states. For example, when the superpowers during the Cold War used the nuclear non-proliferation regime to restrict access to the nuclear club, some among the excluded saw this not as a global public good, but as a way of freezing the distribution of world power and maintaining hierarchy. While liberal solidarists in the post–Cold War era celebrated the increased opportunities to promote a set of core principles that intruded into traditional areas of state sovereignty, pluralists asserted a strong and continuing preference for sovereign equality, non-interference, and non-intervention.

These understandings of global order demonstrate both its evolutionary and contested nature and the complexities involved in any attempt to capture its contemporary essence. We still witness strong elements of pluralism where the role of great powers and international institutions remain prominent, and where mechanisms such as international law, the balance of power, and diplomacy that help to sustain a state-based order retain their relevance. The United States is notable for its often vigorous defence of the sovereignty of its national democratic institutions and their primacy vis-à-vis international institutions – witness its hostility to the International Criminal Court despite the various safeguards for national institutions that were built into its procedures. China's sense of itself as a formerly victimized state has prompted its vigorous support of pluralist norms to defend its policies from external demands for change. In other circumstances, China has used its growing economic and political leverage to assert its rights as a great power.

Yet, the normative and material processes associated with globalization have brought to the fore a wide range of issues beyond the capacity of individual states to regulate and have exposed the insufficiency of pluralist mechanisms for addressing them.[2] In order to deal with the demands these issues have thrown up, states in conjunction with other state-based and non-state-based institutions of a transnational and domestic kind have devised measures that are often intrusive in form and ambitious in their aims. Globalization has also led to an expansion of global norms in a range of areas, including human rights, self-determination, trade, finance, investment, and the environment. Technological advances in communication have provided opportunities to develop a global discourse of shared values. Some individuals and groups have found community in these values rather than in membership of a state, and see the promotion of a particular global or communal goal as their primary aspiration. Both intrusive rules as well as shared discourses have challenged the centrality of the state, in the former case through the devising of regulations that impact directly on the organization of domestic society, and in the latter through the development of new foci of loyalty. However, those same assumptions of interconnectedness can be overdone. Many states, and our two states in particular, retain autonomy in certain key areas of decision making, as we shall show in the empirical chapters that follow.

2 Order and its Constituent Parts

We accept, then, the argument that both pluralist and solidarist conceptions of order are present in uneasy coexistence. As Hurrell has put it: "We are ... not dealing with a vanished or vanishing Westphalian world, ... but rather with a world in which solidarist and cosmopolitan conceptions of governance coexist, often rather unhappily, with many aspects of the old pluralist order" (Hurrell 2007: 9). The challenge this mixed conception of order poses for the creation, course, and legitimacy of global order norms is considerable given the different perspectives on what should be preserved and how this should be done. Nevertheless, whether this uneasy coexistence necessarily spills over into systemic instability or portends a crisis for global order is a question that this book is in part aimed

---

[2] For one important analysis of Chinese debates on globalization, see Kim (2009).

at answering. To prefigure this part of our argument, we do not see such a crisis as imminent, but the nature of the contemporary global order is such that many crucial collective action problems are likely to remain unresolved.

One way of capturing more concretely and with greater precision the implications of the uneasy coexistence at the heart of the global order is to focus on certain specific issues and the norms associated with them.[3] We take norms to be both regulative and as Katzenstein has defined them, "collective expectations for the proper behavior of actors with a given identity" (1996: 5). Sometimes, but not always, these may be embodied in international rules and standards. We understand "international rules" to mean the specific prescriptive and proscriptive contents of international treaties. "International standards" are prescriptive technical solutions and best practice policy principles usually set by specialized international bodies and intended to apply across different political, regulatory, and legal jurisdictions; most often they are voluntary and lack treaty status. Both international rules and standards are usually associated with or assume adherence to more general global norms.

Our argument is that unpacking global order into a series of separate norms in specific issue areas allows us to explore more effectively the extent to which the United States and China challenge or support the evolving global order. This approach, we suggest, permits a more finely grained treatment of global politics and actor behaviour than that offered through the analytical lens of globalization. Importantly, it enables us to determine the extent of contestation and consensus between the United States and China about key global order norms.[4] If the levels of contestation between them are great, then, given the significance that we and

---

[3] We have chosen to situate our study within the literature on norms rather than on regimes. The work on regimes has tended to accept the central realist premise that power and interest are at the core of state behaviour. In addition, it has neglected the role of global actors other than states, as well as the social basis of world politics. See *International Organization*, Special Issue, 1982, for further elaboration of the concept of regimes.

[4] These differences in perspective are implicitly accepted by Western politicians who call on China to become a "responsible stakeholder." The term implies that Beijing does not yet, but should, accept the norms and associated rules that are allegedly adhered to by the more established powers. For discussion of the "responsible stakeholder" concept by US officials, see Zoellick (2005) and Christensen (2006a, 2009). As Christensen put it in 2009, after his return to Princeton University: "While China is still quite far from becoming the 'responsible stakeholder' that former deputy secretary Robert B. Zoellick envisioned in his famous speech in September 2005, China has made positive adjustments in its foreign policy that would have been hard to imagine just several years ago" (2009: 90).

others impute to them as global actors, we might expect growing conflict or a future radical revision of the norms and associated rules and standards.

It is worth underlining at this point that our three central questions are primarily concerned with elucidating the extent to which the behaviour of these two crucial states conforms to key global order norms. This is quite different from the concern of many constructivists with the question of whether norms constrain behaviour. Our study therefore fits with what has been described as the second and third waves of scholarship on norms and global politics (Acharya 2009). The first wave argued that norms matter for actor behaviour (Klotz 1995; Finnemore 1996). One criticism of this early literature was that norms "do not float freely" and that it is necessary to show how they "are attached to real physical environments and are promoted by real human agents" (Kowert and Legro 1996: 490). Later work made clear that anchoring global norms in particular domestic political structures can be important for their progress (Cortell and Davis 2000; Checkel 2001; Acharya 2009). We agree with these refinements but wish to push this further to uncover the wide range of conditions – both domestic and global and including the characteristics of the norms themselves – that promote norm-consistent behaviour. Our framework allows for the possibility that norms do shape behaviour, but also that other factors, sometimes operating in tandem with norms and sometimes not, may be more important determinants of behavioural outcomes. For this reason, we think it is artificial to divide the ideational from the material, and like other analysts find it unhelpful to impose barriers between materialist and constructivist approaches (Tannenwald 2007; Hurd 2008).

3 What Factors Shape Behavioural Consistency with Global Norms?

There is a large body of existing literature that throws light on this question, much of which we summarize later. Determining levels of behavioural consistency is complicated by at least three factors: norms may strengthen or weaken over time, may vary in terms of their specificity, and differ in the extent to which they are binding upon political actors. These features are likely to matter in a global order that contains contested understandings of what best contributes to that order and disagreement over whether particular norms should be viewed as legitimate. However, we show in each of our empirical chapters that it is possible to specify the core characteristics of key global order norms against which behaviour may be assessed.

In this section, we outline the domestic and global factors that might promote behavioural consistency. We recognize that this domestic/global distinction is artificial and that there is much interaction between the two levels, but this division is nevertheless analytically useful. We also discuss how particular features associated with the norms themselves may shape behaviour. Our objective here is not to offer a simple predictive theory of which particular factors promote behavioural consistency with global norms but instead to delineate those we see as worthy of investigation in our empirical chapters. We use our empirical investigations to determine which among these various factors have the greatest explanatory power.

The Domestic Level

Actor behaviour is most likely to be consistent with global norms when domestic institutions and actors reflect or share material interests, values, and causal beliefs that are broadly consistent with these norms (Underdal 1998; Checkel 2001; Acharya 2009). Should this sharing be supported by authoritative or valued global civil society groups, this consistency is likely to be reinforced. However, this need not mean that the global norms themselves directly influence these actors' values and hence behaviour.[5] Indeed, as Acharya notes, the direction of influence may run in the other direction: there are examples where external norms have adapted to meet local practices (Acharya 2009: 19).

In the absence of well-developed local norms, global norms may provide focal points for behaviour (Garrett and Weingast 1993). As we show later, they can also act as focal points for domestic debate and normative contestation, as in the case of the debate over Kyoto in US domestic politics. In this sense, states and other political actors can be seen to be "unavoidably embedded in social relationships and norms" (Hurd 2007: 196).

Crises may play an important part in dislodging or undermining existing local norms. In these instances, global norms sometimes provide

---

[5] For example, a norm of open trade will be more likely to be observed if domestic employer and labour organizations share a preexisting preference for open trade (as has been broadly true in countries in Scandinavia, as well as the Netherlands and Germany). On the other hand, if domestic social actors draw on global norms and point to the benefits of behavioural convergence to strengthen their influence over national policy, we can say that global norms have influenced state behaviour and promoted behavioural consistency (Keck and Sikkink 1998).

the basis upon which new "common knowledge," institutions and patterned behaviours are built (Culpepper 2008).[6] Constructivists have often emphasized that "deeper" socialization or norm internalization is more likely to occur in situations of uncertainty. As Cortell and Davis (2000: 75) put it: "*Ceteris paribus*, the absence of preconceptions and other unique national beliefs enhances the probability that the proponents of an international norm – domestic or transnational – can establish the legitimacy of the international norm in domestic discourse, laws, and institutions."

Policymakers may or may not share the normative beliefs of domestic and transnational social movements and policy entrepreneurs. Public officials may adopt policies consistent with global norms either to acquire a reputation as a generally reliable or responsible international actor, or to remain in power, or because they have been persuaded to change their beliefs. Persuasion may be more likely to happen when policymakers participate actively in a wide range of international institutions in which global norms are negotiated and embedded (Checkel 2001; Johnston 2008).[7] When policymakers are relatively autonomous of domestic interest groups and where the policy in question has ambiguous consequences for their political survival, global norms may provide a focal point for state policy. But the relationship between domestic societal interests and policymakers is not a one-way street in which the former only make demands upon the latter. Officials can also play off different societal groups against one another to achieve their own goals, and may also attempt to shape the preferences of these groups.

Domestic institutions will likely be important in shaping the degree of behavioural consistency with global norms, but they will not have a unidirectional effect. For example, behavioural consistency is more likely when global norms are consistent with the norms embedded in domestic institutions (Goldstein 1993), or when domestic institutions privilege the voice of groups that favour conformity. On the other hand, domestic institutions can also work against behavioural consistency with global norms, such as when they allow narrow but well-organized interest groups to block international cooperation (Milner 1997). Political constitutions

---

[6] There is disagreement in the literature on norms over the extent to which local norms are displaced, adapt, or themselves act to localize the global (Acharya 2009).

[7] Whether this will affect behavioural consistency will depend upon whether socialized public officials are in a powerful domestic policymaking position, and whether they are in a position to persuade other domestic political actors and social groups who are opposed to behavioural convergence.

that disperse political power can provide multiple veto points for actors who oppose policies aimed at producing behavioural consistency with global norms. This can also happen at the level of policy implementation, where the strength of institutions can affect the degree to which policies consistent with global norms are implemented.[8]

The Global Level

There is a range of global factors that conceivably can affect the level of actors' behavioural convergence upon global order norms. We divide these into two main groups: first, those that concern how the processes of global governance operate in relation to normative frameworks and, second, those that concern how the particular characteristics of global norms affect behavioural convergence.

In addressing the first question, we focus on three main groups of actors: those who are directly involved in the processes of global governance and who can be designated as "norm providers"; those who are "free riders" because they largely accept the outcomes of global governance processes but have not actively involved themselves in those processes; and "norm takers" who are excluded from these processes. We would expect behavioural consistency with global norms to be more likely for norm providers and free riders than for norm takers, because the first two categories of actors are more likely to view the processes of global governance as having an acceptable degree of "input" and "output" legitimacy (Scharpf 1999).

Hegemonic coalitions of norm providers – which may include states, international organizations, transnational activists, market actors, and even powerful private individuals – form to put new or revised norms onto the global agenda.[9] More importantly still, they will be in a position to determine to a considerable degree the specificities (treaties, rules, and

---

[8] For example, China's ability to abide by its commitments to impose nuclear export controls and to protect intellectual property have been limited by divisions within the party-state apparatus and by the sometimes weak enforcement capacity of the state. By contrast, relatively strong institutions enforcing competition law can favour conformity with the norm of open trade, as has occurred within the EU.

[9] There are clearly similarities between our idea of hegemonic coalitions and that of a transnational activist network (TAN) favoured by Keck and Sikkink (1998). These two authors use the term *networks* in order to "evoke the structured and structuring dimension in the actions of these complex agents, who not only participate in new areas of politics but also shape them" (Keck and Sikkink 1998: 4). Our preference reflects our desire to place more weight on power and hierarchy rather than on the notion of horizontal linkages. (For the Keck and Sikkink definition of which actors make up a TAN, see 1998: 9).

international standards) of global norms. For these norm providers and for free riders who share the values of the hegemonic coalition without contributing to the processes of global governance, behavioural convergence can often be thought of as "cheap moral action" because of a high value fit and low costs (Busby 2007: 254).

However, cheap moral action is unlikely to account for all forms of behavioural convergence on the part of norm providers and free riders. These actors may be constrained unintentionally because the establishment of global norms, even when intended primarily to constrain others, may also limit their ability to act inconsistently with them. This may be especially true for norms that have become embedded in domestic institutions and standard procedures. As noted earlier, these actors are not independent of the social relationships that the norms they have created embody (Hurd 2007: 196). Actors in the hegemonic coalition may also be constrained for more tactical reasons, such as a perceived need to ensure that global rules and norms enjoy a minimum degree of legitimacy in the eyes of others, a legitimacy that can be undermined by their own non-convergence.[10]

Norm takers are more likely to see existing global norms as biased and as entrenching the position of hegemonic values and interests, perhaps often because they have emerged into a global normative order established during a period in which their preferences were either ignored or suppressed. Such perceptions of bias in the global normative order may be shared by subordinate states, domestic societal groups, and transnational actors who oppose either the norm or its more specific manifestations. These actors may form anti-hegemonic coalitions that actively oppose behavioural convergence and may constrain the language and the prescriptions that pro-convergence actors are able to deploy. Where the norm providers display behaviour inconsistent with the standards they played a major part in establishing, norm takers' perceptions of injustice are likely to be magnified.

This can lead aggrieved actors to try to oppose or to change global norms and, in doing so, to attempt to become rule makers themselves. They are likely to try to do so when (a) there is a conflict between existing global norms and local norms; (b) existing global norms have at least some constraining effects that disadvantage these actors; and (c) they believe that they have sufficient power resources to challenge the legitimacy of existing norms and rules and to propose new ones. These power

---

[10] *International Politics*, Special Issue, 2007.

resources are unlikely to be only of the hard power variety, since successful rule makers must generally also persuade others that their preferred
norms have substantive legitimacy (Risse 2000; Nye 2004).

Norm Characteristics

The characteristics of particular global norms are also likely to affect the
stance of particular actors towards them. We identify and discuss here
the effects on behavioural convergence of norm longevity, domestic social
and political significance, specificity, norm "bindingness" and enforcement, and symmetry.

The longevity of some global normative frameworks implies reasonable levels of consensus and a diminution in the framework's association
with the dominance of a particular state or other actor. Both conditions are important to a norm's perceived legitimacy. Longevity does not
always work in this way, of course: the imperialist norm of the nineteenth
century only gradually became seen as illegitimate over the course of the
following century. It is also clear that many weaker countries associate
many of the current global order norms with Western dominance. Thus,
longevity by itself is unlikely to be an important factor producing behavioural consistency unless the norms themselves have substantial levels of
legitimacy amongst many actors in international society. In the absence
of this, as we discuss later, enforcement mechanisms may be required to
produce high levels of behavioural convergence.

The degree of domestic significance – that is, the extent to which the
content of global normative frameworks has direct implications for
domestic society and politics – is likely to have strong effects on actor
attitudes towards global order norms. Generally, norms with high levels of domestic significance will increase the relevance of the domestic
normative, institutional and interest configurations discussed previously.
High domestic significance is likely to constrain the ability of state leaders
to choose policies that are inconsistent with dominant domestic political
values, coalitions, and institutional constraints. This will often mean that
prospects for international cooperation are reduced, including for countries with authoritarian governments (Milner 1997: 12), unless there is a
high degree of consistency between domestic political considerations and
international norms, rules, and bargains (Putnam 1988).

The degree of specificity of normative frameworks is also likely to matter for the willingness of actors to conform to them. Other things being
equal, higher levels of specificity and detail are likely to reduce prospects for conformity. It is easier for actors to accept a very general norm

("protect air quality") than a very specific application of it ("reduce SO_2 pollution to X parts per million"). Global normative frameworks will normally contain a mixture of both broad principles and more detailed rules and behavioural standards, but the relative balance between these is likely to influence levels of behavioural convergence.

The extent to which global normative frameworks are binding on actors may also be important. Generally, normative frameworks that are more binding are associated with higher levels of behavioural convergence. The international relations literature has disagreed on how to explain this phenomenon, with some arguing for a greater role for persuasion and self-interest and others arguing that coercion is crucial. The "managerial" school focused on how compliance with international laws depends substantially on state capacity and how behavioural convergence often becomes routinized (Chayes and Chayes 1993). More recently, constructivists emphasized the role of actor persuasion and social learning in behavioural convergence (Underdal 1998; Checkel 2001; Johnston 2008). In contrast with both of these schools, realists more often argued that much behavioural convergence on the part of states with international laws and norms is trivial. When vital national interests are at stake, they suggested, states would prefer to diverge from such laws and norms unless strong international enforcement mechanisms prevent them from doing so (Downs, Rocke, and Barsoom 1996).

Most of the forces for behavioural consistency acting at both domestic and global levels fall between the extremes of consensual persuasion and involuntary coercion. It is difficult to think of any norm anywhere that is not seen as biased or illegitimate by some societal group. This means that behavioural consistency will often be generated by the persuasion of some actors and the inducement or even coercion of others. The relative importance of persuasion and coercion can also change over time. Initial behavioural convergence may involve "mimicking," in which actors behave in ways consistent with global norms for utilitarian reasons or simply because they have no strong reason to do otherwise. This need not involve the internalization of norms, but it may be a route to that stage. Where the global norm appears to have been accepted by others, a "novice" might feel the need to converge even though it has not yet come to believe in its rightness (Kent 2007; Johnston 2008).

Over time, such patterned behaviour may evolve into a standard operating procedure that becomes more deeply institutionalized. Actors may even come to rationalize this behaviour post hoc via cognitive adaptation to the global norm. Separating and assessing the importance of such post hoc rationalizations from processes of normative "learning" from peers can be very difficult. Moreover, the material benefits that may flow from behavioural consistency can reinforce this process of cognitive adaptation – we see no reason why social learning should not often be encouraged and accompanied by such material inducements (Culpepper 2008). But there is no strong a priori reason to believe that mimicking will always evolve into socialization, or that the process could not be reversed if conditions change.

There are certainly also likely to be occasions when coercive enforcement is the main source of behavioural convergence. On such occasions, the enforcement process itself may be seen by the target and various other societal actors as illegitimate, reinforcing a perception of bias in the global normative order. Over a longer time span, this could erode prospects for behavioural convergence.[11] Interventions in Iraq in 1990 and again in 2003 illustrate how different processes of enforcement can reinforce or undermine global norms – in these cases, relating to the use of force.

Enforcement mechanisms take various forms. They can range from positive or negative material inducements to more general considerations of reputation and image, where reputation relates to credibility of commitments with costs if this is undermined, and image is a social marker related to perceptions of one's own behaviour by oneself and others. Such inducements may be centralized through international organizations, or decentralized, as when market forces favour behavioural convergence. Various methods of enforcement are available for use, such as economic or political sanctions, military force, market forces, peer pressure, and public shaming. The effectiveness of these inducements will likely vary by issue area and will depend upon the degree of leverage of the external actor(s), the degree of vulnerability of the target, and the ease with which others can monitor behavioural departures from global norms (Walter 2008: Chapter 2). Sustained behavioural consistency with global norms and their associated rules and standards is more likely when the mechanisms promoting compliance are perceived to be consensual (based on persuasion) rather than coercive. Consensus is related to legitimacy both substantively and procedurally (Clark 2001: 191) and to the idea that the party that has been persuaded has been free in advance to consider a range of options (Finnemore 2003: 152–61).

---

[11] Examples might be military intervention by a dominant state in order to enforce a non-proliferation norm, International Monetary Fund (IMF) conditionality that forces the adoption of greater economic openness in a crisis-hit country, or the belief that private international investors can be prime beneficiaries of developing country financial crises.

The final characteristic of global normative frameworks that might affect the level of behavioural convergence is their degree of symmetry. More symmetrical frameworks that are designed to apply equally to all states or other actors and are seen as such may be more legitimate and thus more likely to encourage conformity. Examples include global norms and rules on human rights and use of force, though as these cases suggest, degrees of legitimacy may also depend on perceptions of symmetry of application and enforcement. However, as with other norm characteristics, there is unlikely to be a simple linear relationship between normative symmetry and behavioural convergence.

We should also recognize that the norm characteristics that we highlighted for analytical purposes are not generally independent of each other. For example, norms with high levels of domestic significance may be relatively loose and non-binding precisely because of the domestic sensitivity of the associated policy areas. Sometimes, high degrees of specificity may only be achievable if agreed standards are non-binding[12]; relatively binding rules may often only be possible if they allow sufficient ambiguity to permit actors to contest their meanings. Norm longevity, as already noted, may sometimes be associated with more established, legitimate, symmetric, and perhaps more legalized frameworks. In general, there is little we can do to control for such interdependence except to be aware of it in our analysis.

4 Why the United States and China?

Given the contested nature of global order, it could be profitable and interesting to examine the attitudes and policies of almost any country towards key global norms.[13] But doing so would not allow us to say much about their systemic significance. We argue that the United States and China are the two most important countries in the contemporary global order, that they have an important and evolving bilateral relationship, and that this has developed to become the most significant and complex bilateral state-to-state relationship in the global order. How much the global order affects the evolution of this relationship, and how much the relationship in turn reinforces or challenges this global order, are central questions for our time and for this study.

---

[12] One possible example, elaborated in Chapter 6, is financial regulatory norms set by technocratic institutions like the Basel Committee on Banking Supervision.

[13] As Mahoney and Goertz (2006) argue, one legitimate purpose of social science is to explain outcomes in individual cases.

At the other end of the spectrum of research possibilities, a large-N analysis might in principle be better suited to examining whether (for example) there has been a broad transition from pluralist to solidarist conceptions of global order. However, data constraints are substantial in this area, and one of the justifications for a more detailed qualitative investigation is that it is generally far from obvious how to describe national policies and attitudes towards global order.[14] Nor would a large-N analysis easily permit strong conclusions about the dynamic stability of the global normative order. Many, perhaps most, countries were opposed to key global norms relating to international finance and trade during the 1970s and 1980s, but this did not substantially threaten either the relative stability of the system or the norms themselves (Krasner 1985). In this instance, relative power mattered a great deal.

The complexity of the global order and the considerable degree of disciplinary uncertainty about the preconditions for its stability makes any case study choice open to question. Nonetheless, two propositions are relatively uncontroversial. First, some countries are more important than others in terms of their significance for global order. Second, the United States is the most important (state) actor within the system. It has the world's largest economy, its defence budget is larger than that of the combined spending of about the next twenty countries, and it is at the head (or expected to be) of most major negotiating fora. There was still some evidence of global deference to its leadership in the George W. Bush era, in spite of the extent to which such leadership was put into doubt (Hurd 2007: 204–5).

Relevant to this question of US leadership is America's own sense of uniqueness, which has given rise to what has often been described as an element of exceptionalism in its foreign policy. Ignatieff delineates three versions of exceptionalism in US foreign policy behaviour: "exemptionalist," when the United States exempts itself from the requirements of global treaties and norms it has earlier taken a lead in formulating; "double standards," in judging its own and friendly state behaviour in reference to global norms more benignly than that of its enemies; and privileging, in viewing its own domestic legislation as more legitimate than agreements negotiated at the global level (Ignatieff 2005: 3–9).

---

[14] There are some cross-country surveys of public attitudes towards global issues, such as the Pew Global Attitudes Project (http://pewglobal.org/). Although these can be revealing, they do not always map directly to particular global norms; nor do they necessarily reflect prevailing national policies.

Of course, the United States might not be alone here: many states exhibit tendencies towards hypocrisy and bias. Nonetheless, particular characteristics of American exceptionalism do make it relatively unique. As McDougall (1997) has argued, the original US conception of exceptionalism focused on the United States as a beacon to others and gave primacy to the protection of liberty at home. However, he shows how from the time of President McKinley, and especially after 1945, the United States mobilized its power to export the nation's ideals and make the world a better and a safer place. It is this "transformationalist" aspect of post-1945 American foreign policy, wedded to its related self-perception as the "ultimate custodian of international order" during this period (Reisman 1999–2000: 63–4), that has distinguished American exceptionalism and that has been particularly consequential for global order. This custodianship perspective has sometimes led American policymakers to argue the need to act extra-legally in defence of the existing global order, and on occasion to act as "norm revisionists" when existing norms are seen as incompatible with US needs (Dunne 2007: 720). For these reasons of power and expectations of leadership, both by itself and by others, the United States is an uncontroversial choice for a study of global order.

The case of China requires more justification. Our reasons for choosing China in addition to the United States should appeal to both materialists and constructivists. China is by many measures already one of a handful of great powers: it is a nuclear weapons state and has permanent UN Security Council membership and a growing development aid budget. It is also the world's most rapidly developing large economy and it is widely seen, alongside the United States, as a key driver of the global economy. China's influence is no longer merely regional; its trade, aid, and foreign policies are now of considerable consequence globally, including in Africa and South America. Some commentators even speak of China's rising soft power, at a time when many others believe that recent US policy has eroded America's own (Kurlantzick 2007; Yu 2008). The rapid forward momentum of this influence, though disputed in some of its aspects, has created a strong sense amongst commentators and policymakers that China is the country to be reckoned with after the United States.

China is also important, we contend, because of both the centrality of Beijing and Washington to one another and the centrality of the bilateral China-US relationship to the global order itself. China's entry into global society would not have been so extensive without the Sino-American rapprochement of 1972 and the normalization of US-China relations in 1979. Both of these events have had major consequences for global order with normalization in particular facilitating China's policies of economic reform and opening introduced by Vice-Premier Deng Xiaoping in late 1978. Those policies, in giving primacy to China's growth and development via integration into the global economy, required the People's Republic of China (PRC) to learn new ideas and to participate in international and transnational institutional environments that embodied global norms. From that period onwards, and more particularly from the early 1990s, the Chinese leadership which signalled it had rejected revolutionary confrontation in favour of integration, and struggle in favour of stability. It was therefore faced with the task of evaluating the benefits that adherence to global norms might bring to the fulfilment of its newly articulated goals.

Those reform policies formed the catalyst for China's resurgence to the point where the United States now sees China as its most important strategic interlocutor and as the most important long-term threat to its economic, political, and military hegemony (US Department of Defense 2006: 29). From 1972 to the end of the Cold War, security was at the core of the bilateral US-China relationship; from the 1990s, human rights and economic issues became increasingly important and more strongly connected with security factors. Japan's lasting economic slowdown after 1990, the Asian crises of the late 1990s, and China's entry into the World Trade Organization (WTO) in 2001 reflected and enhanced the centrality of the bilateral economic relationship (Lieberthal and Sandalow 2009: 13). It has become commonplace to note the importance of the US market for Chinese exports and the importance of Chinese holdings of US debt in the bilateral relationship. That exchange rate and climate change issues have now moved to the top of the bilateral agenda which underlines the increasing complexity of the relationship. It would be wrong to claim that the relationship approaches one of "deep integration" (as, for example, may apply to the relationship between France and Germany), but "complex interdependence" is now a reasonable descriptor. Although we borrow this term from Keohane and Nye (1977), we do not wish to imply that the growing importance of economic, environmental and social aspects of the US-China bilateral relationship has necessarily entailed a diminution of military and strategic competition.

Managing this complex interdependence has been difficult for both sides, and mutual strategic distrust remains a critical feature of those ties (Lieberthal and Sandalow 2009: 14). During the George W. Bush administration, a "Strategic Economic Dialogue" and "Senior Dialogue" were established to discuss some of the economic and strategic issues of central relevance to the relationship and to global and regional order.[15] One Bush administration response to China's rise was to demand that China "must act as a responsible stakeholder" if it wanted to work successfully with the United States (US National Security Strategy 2006: 41–2). This phrasing was deemphasized in the Obama administration, and the language of common interests initially given greater play, but that focus on cooperation has been difficult to maintain as the United States and China have faced up to critical bilateral and third-party issues such as currency values, US arms sales to Taiwan, climate change, and sanctions against Iran.

As for China, it has long seen the United States as the critical state in the global political and economic order, and US policies as variously either key constraints upon or enablers of China's rise (Deng 2001; Foot 2006: 80–4). Overall, Beijing more than Washington has had to weigh the consequences of thwarting the US demands placed upon it. This has not been easy when these demands have conflicted with its key interests, but it has also been difficult to finesse when they have been in tension with China's definitions of certain global order norms.

The global financial and economic crisis of 2008–09, because it has been centred on the United States, has further reduced the asymmetry in the bilateral relationship while reinforcing its centrality. The extraordinary spending commitments made by the US government have made it more dependent than ever on the continued willingness of foreigners, including China, to purchase ever larger amounts of US Treasury debt. The crisis has also reduced US self-confidence in the validity of its economic model and its willingness to "lecture" Chinese officials in bilateral meetings. In contrast, China's model has seemed relatively robust and its government appeared capable of taking decisive actions to maintain growth. Various commentators argued that the crisis would advance the date by which China overtakes the United States in economic size.[16] Meanwhile, China emphasizes that its main contribution to global economic recovery should be to maintain rapid Chinese growth, and it has resisted demands

[15] The fourth Strategic Economic Dialogue (SED) in June 2008, for example, led to the signing of a ten-year energy and environment cooperation framework. It involved five US cabinet agencies and seven from China. Obama has continued with a similar format, but has rolled the two separate dialogues of the Bush era into one (now called the Strategic and Economic Dialogue, or S&ED) and it operates at a higher ministerial level.

[16] Jim O'Neill, "China Shows the World How to Get Through a Crisis," *FT.com*, 23 April 2009; Gideon Rachman, "How the Bottom Fell out of 'Old' Davos," *Financial Times*, 2 February 2010.

that it accept more extensive international responsibilities (including, for example, substantial currency revaluation and making much larger contributions to still unreformed international financial institutions).

The perception on both sides of this bilateral relationship of the critical strategic importance of the other is driven, in part, by the perceived diminished importance of other actors in particular areas and issues, including Europe and Japan. Again, the crisis of 2008–09 reinforced this perception in both Beijing and Washington. It is also a product of the relative passivity of the European Union (EU) and Japanese foreign policies and their strategic dependence upon their own bilateral relationship with the United States.[17] Russia's difficult relationship with the West under President and then Prime Minister Putin, its continuing status as a nuclear power, and its importance as an energy exporter still give it considerable leverage, but it lacks China's economic importance and is increasingly overshadowed in American eyes by China's increasing force-projection capabilities. India, though also of rapidly increasing importance, is still far from matching China's impact on the United States and the rest of the world.

In our focus on the central role of the United States and China in the international system, we are not claiming that the global order is approaching a condition of "bipolarity," as it did during the Cold War. Neither are we convinced, mainly for this reason, as well as reasons relating to procedural legitimacy, of the viability of proposals for the creation of a "G2." Today, the United States, as the preeminent even if diminished global power, has a range of important bilateral relationships, including with Europe, Japan, Russia, and India. The recent global economic crisis has also increased the importance of various large emerging countries besides China. The trend towards more rather than less inclusive forms of global governance is exemplified in the political eclipse of the G7/8 by the G20. China's relations with these other emerging or resurgent countries have also deepened substantially since about the mid-1990s. In Asia itself, there are several powerful states with differing conceptions of regional order, as reflected in the evidence of a degree of rivalry between China, India, and Japan (Emmott 2008), the continuing role many states allocate to the United States as security guarantor, as well as the debates over which states should be included in various of the regional groupings.

---

[17] The EU is the world's major trading power, but it is not a great power in the same sense as the United States and China, given its long-standing difficulties in framing a collective foreign and security policy.

Nor are we claiming that, while China's aggregate economic size in 2010 just eclipsed that of Japan (IMF figures), it is dominant across all major indicators –Table 1.1 shows that it is not. What we do claim is that China's rapid growth, its economic size and population, its prominence as a global trader, its significance as an international creditor, together with the pace of its increasing influence in regional and global politics in the security, energy, and environmental areas, make it of central importance to the United States and to the global order.

In short, the United States and China are, on a plausible reading, the current hegemonic state and prospective challenger, respectively, which makes their bilateral relationship of central importance in any assessment of the dynamic stability of the global order (Gilpin 1981). We argue that this holds even though the global order is much more than a system composed of states. This view does not imply that a major war between these two states is probable, or that there is a plausible case to be made for a foreseeable future in which "China rules the world," as some versions of power transition theory claim. Policy choices are there to be made, and policy adjustments between hegemonic power and putative challenger can be and have been negotiated. Neither is it certain, until policies with respect to global order norms are investigated in detail, that one particular state in this dyad should be seen as the status quo power and the other as a revisionist, or that one is a satisfied state and the other dissatisfied (Chan 2008). However, we do argue that China's resurgence and the impact that this is having on the US global role has important implications for global order that require closer examination.

5 Case Selection and Chapter Outlines

How should we assess China and America's relationship to and impact upon the global order? In this book, we examine the evolution of US and Chinese policies and attitudes towards a limited range of key global order issues and related normative frameworks. Our working assumption is that the attitude of both countries towards global order norms will differ depending upon the case and that these attitudes may also evolve over time. It would be uncontroversial to expect, for example, the Chinese government to be relatively hostile towards norms favouring the protection of civil and political rights, though rhetorically and to some extent behaviourally this hostility has diminished over time. Conversely, we might expect the US executive branch to be relatively hostile towards the norm of non-intervention and for the level of this hostility to change

TABLE 1.1. *Benchmarks for US Preponderance: Measures of Relative Importance*

	US	China	EU[a]	Japan	India	Russia	Brazil
Economic size relative to US, current dollars and market exchange rates 2009	100%	33%	113%	35%	9%	9%	10%
GDP per capita relative to US, current exchange rates 2009	100%	8%	67% (2007)	85%	2%	19%	17%
GDP per capita relative to US, PPP exchange rates 2009	100%	14%	66% (2007)	71%	6%	32%	23%
Real GDP growth, 1990–2009 p.a. average	2.5%	9.9%	1.9%	1.1%	6.3%	1.6%	2.5%
Population 2007, proportion of US	1.00	4.37	1.65 (2006)	0.42	3.73	0.47	0.63
Share of world merchandise exports, 2008, excluding intra-EU exports[a]	10.6%	11.8%	20.4%	6.5%	1.5%	3.9%	1.6%
Trade to GDP ratio, 2004–06 (excluding intra-EU trade for EU)	25.9%	69.0%	20.2%	28.8%	41.8%	55.8%	26.4%
Share of world CO_2 emissions from energy consumption, 2007	20.1%	21.0%	15.7%	4.2%	4.7%	5.6%	1.3%
Share of world military spending in US$ 2009	43.0%	6.6% (est.)	11.0% (EU3)	3.3%	2.4%	3.5% (est.)	1.7%
Deployed and other nuclear warheads, 2010[b] (all figures approximate)	9,600	240	525 (UK, France)	0	60–80	12,000	0

[a] EU27, except where otherwise indicated.
[b] The estimated figures for Pakistan and Israel are 70 and 90, respectively.
Sources: Rows 1–5, IMF, *World Economic Outlook Database*; EU, *Eurostat Database*. Rows 6–7, WTO. Row 8, US Energy Information Administration. Rows 9–10, Stockholm International Peace Research Institute (SIPRI) *Yearbook 2010, Military Expenditure Database; World Nuclear Forces*.

in relation to America's evolving military preponderance. The attitudes of both countries towards a norm like open trade might also be expected to evolve in line with their perceptions of its costs and benefits.

Our case selection choices were driven above all by our concern to address topics of central historic and contemporary relevance for global order. As noted earlier, these are use of force, macroeconomic policy surveillance, nuclear non-proliferation, climate change, and financial regulation. In making these choices, we wanted to address a sufficiently broad range of issue areas as well as to bridge a common divide between security and economic issues, drawing on our own academic specializations in order to do that. Certainly, the addition of chapters on, for example, trade and human rights would make the book more comprehensive, but not necessarily more useful analytically. These two areas have also been covered extensively elsewhere (e.g., Kent 1999; Pearson 1999; Foot 2000; Lardy 2002; Cass, Williams, and Barker 2003; Ignatieff 2005), and we consider how our results can be generalized in the concluding chapter.

More importantly, we have taken a range of methodological considerations into account in selecting our five cases. The immediate methodological challenge that arises from addressing any set of issue areas important to global order is that they inevitably vary in multiple ways across a range of possible criteria. This makes it difficult and probably impossible to select cases that vary on only one particular explanatory variable. For this reason, we think it is important to be transparent about the main elements of variation across a range of potential cases and to draw on these variations in our analysis. This will also facilitate comparisons between our own empirical findings and those of other scholars who have worked on these and different cases.

It is self-evident that a key premise of this book is that the United States and China are both crucial to the global order. As for any great power, they are far from "normal" countries in terms of their relationships to key elements of the global order. Because of their power, size, and importance, their attitudes to and behaviour towards a range of global normative frameworks affect these frameworks and the global order of which they are a part. That is, the global order and the attitudes and behaviour of these two important states are a mutually constitutive social phenomena. The global order cannot be taken as given and relates reflexively to all the actors within it, but this property of mutual constitution is especially important when considering the most important actors within it.

In taking this approach, however, we are confronted with yet another methodological complication: the relationship of both countries to the global order is also affected by their bilateral relationship. As we have already noted, both countries have increasingly seen their own relationship to various global normative frameworks through the lens of their bilateral relationship. This is not true, however, for all issue areas. Nor is it true that in the post-1945 era the bilateral relationship with China was always a significant influence on America's attitude towards particular global order norms, though the same may not be true for China. In order to discern the influence of the bilateral relationship on both countries' attitudes towards global order norms, it is therefore important that we ensure there is variation across our cases on this factor. As Table 1.2 summarizes, the bilateral relationship was initially of generally low importance in some of our cases but has steadily become crucial in these same cases over time (climate change and international macroeconomic surveillance). For one case, financial regulation, the bilateral relationship has never been an important consideration for either side, and for another, nuclear non-proliferation, it has always been reasonably high. This variation gives us greater analytical leverage on the question of how the US-China bilateral relationship affects the stance of each country towards the global order.

This variation is important, but it is not the only one. Table 1.2 shows that global normative frameworks also often differ in terms of their longevity, their degree of domestic social and political significance, their degree of specificity, the extent to which they are binding on states, and their degree of symmetry. As discussed already in Section 3 of this chapter, all of these factors might plausibly affect the relationship of major states to global order norms.

We have already argued that the effects of norm longevity on legitimacy are ambiguous. However, the matter of empirical variation in this dimension is fairly straightforward: for example, the normative frameworks pertaining to the use of force and human rights in modern times are associated predominantly with the creation in 1945 of the United Nations; the International Monetary Fund and the General Agreement on Tariffs and Trade date back to the 1940s; the nuclear non-proliferation framework began to accelerate in the late 1950s; and the global climate protection and global financial regulatory frameworks date back to the 1970s at the earliest. Although some of these issues were prefigured in earlier eras, our main analytical focus is on the post-1945 period.

The degree of domestic significance also varies across our empirical cases and sometimes also varies over time. Nevertheless, it seems fairly

TABLE 1.2. *Variation Across Cases: Characteristics of Normative Frameworks*

Case	Longevity of Global Order Frameworks	Salience of Bilateral Relationship	Degree of Domestic Social Significance	Degree of Specificity of Normative Framework	Degree of Bindingness of Normative Framework	Degree of Symmetry (for China & US)
Use of force	1945 (UN Charter); R2P 2005	Changes from high to medium	Low (where force is limited)	High (Articles 2[4], 51); low-medium (R2P)	Mixed	High
Macroeconomic policy surveillance	1940s (Bretton Woods)	Changes from irrelevant to very high	High	Mixed: some aspects low, some medium	Mixed: some aspects low, some medium	Low
Non-proliferation of nuclear weapons	1950s (1963 PTBT, 1968 NPT)	Generally high to medium	Low	Mixed: medium to high	Mixed: medium to high	High
Climate change	1972 (Stockholm)	Changes from very low to very high	High	High (specific CO2 equivalent targets)	Mixed: some aspects low, some medium to high	Low
Financial regulation	1974 (Basel Committee on Banking Supervision)	Remains low	Medium	Medium to high	Low	Medium
Human rights	1948 (UDHR)	Low to high	High	Mixed	Low to medium	High
International trade	1940s (GATT)	Changes from very low to high	High	High	Medium before 1994; high after	Medium
Foreign direct investment	Late 1950s (early BITs and regional integration agreements)	Changes from very low to medium	High	Mixed	Mixed: some low, some high (binding BITs treaties, FTAs, etc.)	Low

Note: The empirical areas italicized in the final three rows of this table are not covered in this study but are included for purposes of comparison. BITs are bilateral investment treaties; FTAs are free trade areas.

clear that areas like macroeconomic policy surveillance and climate change are directly related to domestic economic growth, income, and employment, whereas non-proliferation and the use of limited force are for the most part relatively traditional areas of foreign policy that impinge less directly on everyday domestic social life and politics. In these more traditional areas, national leaders will normally enjoy a greater degree of autonomy from domestic political constraints.

The degree of specificity within our normative frameworks – that is, the extent to which they contain relatively detailed obligations – also operates at different levels across our cases. Frameworks that contain the most specificity include those on international financial regulation, nuclear non-proliferation, and climate change; most others tend to be less specific in content.

Some of our norms are binding where they have been incorporated into legal obligations through international treaties: for example, the use of force, nuclear non-proliferation, and climate change. Sometimes, normative frameworks create legally binding obligations in some policy areas but not in others, as with the international macroeconomic policy surveillance framework which mainly creates specific legal obligations for exchange rate policy. In an increasingly large number of areas, norms are elaborated only in the form of voluntary, non-binding standards (notably financial regulation, Nuclear Suppliers' Group export standards).

Finally, our norms can also be categorized as either symmetric or asymmetric based on whether their demands apply to all or only to some states. For example, the climate change framework is asymmetric since it is more demanding of the United States, categorized as an advanced economy, than it is for China, currently categorized as a developing country.

The rest of the book is organized as follows. The next five chapters address the nature of the global normative framework in the five issue areas listed in this chapter. Each chapter then proceeds to examine the rhetorical and behavioural relationship of China and the United States with the global norm before assessing the factors that best explain the evolving levels of behavioural consistency exhibited by each country. (Generally, we place the country with the longest relationship with the norm first, except where the length is similar, when we deal first with China's position.) The chapters also address how the bilateral relationship between China and the United States has shaped their relationship to each normative framework. Here, we provide brief summaries of each of the five global frameworks we have chosen and our reasons for doing so.

Chapter 2 considers the use of force, a critical pillar of global order. It sets out the normative prohibition on the use of force and the evolution in thinking on the conditions under which the use of force might be justified. It focuses in particular on understandings of self-defence and humanitarian military intervention, the latter now transformed into the concept of "The Responsibility to Protect." It takes the UN Charter, the UN General Assembly, and the Security Council as the major sources for understanding the normative framework relating to force and then examines and explains Chinese and US adherence to the various components of a norm subject to some variety in interpretation and development. In summary form, China has come to adopt policies and rhetoric that to some degree have been self-binding. It has moved to support a restrictive interpretation on when force might be used. The United States for most of the post-1945 era, on the other hand, has adopted wide definitions of self-defence and has been reluctant to allow others to determine the conditions under which it might use force, including for humanitarian purposes. As Permanent Members of the UN Security Council, and as states in direct conflict at earlier stages in their history, their perspectives have been consequential for these debates and their practical outcomes. But their positioning on the two core components of the use of force norm has not been as directly influenced by the bilateral relationship over the last two decades or so, compared with earlier periods. In the US case, domestic values and capacities have been critical to its positioning; for China domestic values have been indirectly aligned with its regional and global preferences and have been important in shaping convergence with ideas on when force might legitimately be used.

Chapter 3 addresses the global framework for the surveillance of macroeconomic policy. International macroeconomic surveillance was one of the key norms of the Bretton Woods system created in the mid-1940s, which presupposed that national macroeconomic policies should be subject to international, peer-based surveillance and constraint. A second though more contested norm was that responsibilities for adjustment to international payments imbalances should be shared symmetrically between surplus and deficit countries. We show that both norms were in tension with increased national macroeconomic policy activism and that this growing degree of domestic significance has been reflected in a relatively soft policy surveillance framework. The United States has had an especially asymmetric approach to multilateral surveillance, seeing it mainly as applying to the policy choices of other countries and one means among many of shifting the costs of international adjustment onto others. Over time, it focused on strengthening the framework in the area of exchange rate surveillance, placing pressure on surplus countries to accept currency revaluation or measures to boost domestic demand. China, a latecomer to international surveillance, began by seeing its relationship with the surveillance framework as relatively unproblematic, but over the past decade China has come to view it as increasingly constraining for its domestic policy choices and development objectives. Bilaterally, the issue became increasingly difficult to manage for both sides and we argue that the global economic crisis of 2008–09 has not produced a new consensus.

Chapter 4 focuses on the normative framework that constrains the proliferation of nuclear weapons, an important underpinning of global order in the Cold War era that has latterly appeared to many commentators to be a norm that is in serious retreat with potentially dire consequences for global survival. China's decision to acquire a nuclear capability was important in helping to convince the US government of the need to create a non-proliferation norm and associated legal frameworks. Beijing at first described that norm as discriminatory and as reflective of US and Soviet hegemony in the global system. US elaboration of the norm over subsequent decades, comprising in particular a focus on the control of nuclear-related exports, placed specific new demands on China that it found difficult, and sometimes was unwilling, to meet. Over time, however, as a consequence of US use of various carrots and sticks, as well as the influence of ideas transmitted by other global political actors that Beijing values, China's beliefs and behaviour converged with the norm. Ironically, as China became more supportive, the United States appeared to be diverging from the norm's universal underpinnings. Washington, at a time of external shocks and changing domestic preferences, emphasized counter-proliferation over non-proliferation and adopted a more particularist interpretation. US attempts at norm reinterpretation destabilized the normative framework as previously understood. Currently, there are attempts to restabilize the non-proliferation framework, but the outcomes of this effort are uncertain.

Chapter 5 deals with climate change and the evolving norm of global climate protection. It argues that neither state has been a particularly supportive player in the advancement of a normative framework that has high domestic significance and that raises highly contentious and unresolved questions of fairness in the distribution of abatement costs. China has adhered to the specifics of the normative framework more fully than has the United States, but only because the demands on it as a developing country participant in norm creation and elaboration have been far less onerous than those required of an advanced country like America. In addition, the evolutionary nature of the science behind the general norm of climate protection and the ambiguous and long-term costs it implies have provided these reluctant players with additional room for manoeuvre. The bilateral relationship has acted as an important constraint on both governments' policies in this policy arena: their attitudes towards climate change negotiations have been strongly affected by each others' stances on the issue. Matters of allocating responsibility, and other related questions of equity, have been particularly prominent in influencing their public positions, but relative power concerns have also been a significant part of the argumentation in this policy area.

Chapter 6 addresses financial regulation, another topic of considerable contemporary importance. From the mid-1970s, the major developed countries agreed on general principles for financial regulation in the Basel Committee on Banking Supervision, and elaborated a range of voluntary standards relating to various aspects of financial sector supervision and regulation that have achieved global significance. We focus on the evolving framework of banking regulation, paying particular attention to the norms of financial stability, competitive equality through international harmonization, and the more recent norm of self-regulation by market actors. The United States has played a crucial and often decisive role in the evolution of the Basel framework, but we show how the increasingly polarized domestic politics of financial regulation has also limited its ability to implement Basel standards. Paradoxically, we show that China's status as a norm taker in this area has not prevented a growing level of behavioural consistency with the Basel framework. In marked contrast to most other areas we discuss, the US-China bilateral relationship has to date played relatively little role in shaping the behaviour of each towards the global framework of financial regulation.

In concluding the book, Chapter 7 summarizes the variations in behavioural consistency addressed in each of the major chapters across issue areas and by country. It draws together the explanatory framework of the study, showing how we can make sense of the complex patterns of behaviour across these and other areas of importance for global governance. We also discuss the implications of our analytical argument for the scholarly debate over the relationship between norms and actor behaviour in the global order. Finally, it outlines the implications of the analysis for our understanding of global order and its prospects.

We find that, in broad terms, China's levels of behavioural consistency with global norms have generally improved since the early 1980s, admittedly from a low starting point prior to that. The United States, on the other hand, does not exhibit a trend in either direction but is much more selective in terms of its behavioural conformity. Three elements are of particular importance in explaining these levels of consistency: first, they depend on the domestic social and political significance that the normative framework has for each country; second, they depend on the extent to which the process of norm creation and elaboration is perceived as procedurally legitimate and, in substantive terms, provides for a reasonably fair distribution of material and social costs and benefits across countries; and third, they depend on how this distribution of costs and benefits is seen to affect the global power hierarchy within which the bilateral US-China relationship has become increasingly integral.

The larger implications of this study for understanding the relationship between global norms and state behaviour are that rarely is it the norm itself, operating autonomously, that performs the work of shaping the behaviour of these two states. Domestic interests, values, and institutional configurations are often the primary determinants of the level of behavioural consistency with global norms. However, it is also clear just how central to the landscape of global politics norms have been: serving as focal points for debate, as benchmarks for measuring behaviour, as devices useful in signalling state identity, and as means to undercut or bolster the legitimacy of state action. That global norms can perform this range of functions suggests that they are a fundamental constituent of global order and that they add an important layer of influence when states consider how closely to conform to them.

Our study also demonstrates that both countries are embedded firmly in but also contribute significantly to an evolving global order that is situated uncomfortably between pluralism and solidarism. The relationship of both countries to this global order, shaped in part by their own increasingly important bilateral relationship, has paradoxically reinforced both the limits to solidarism and the inadequacies of pluralist understandings of global order. Neither state, we suggest, has yet found a way to effectively deal with this complexity and to provide solutions in a period of world politics marked by transition and uncertainty.

2

Use of Force

In this first substantive chapter, we engage with a global norm that is central to global order. We take the global normative framework associated with the use of force to be built predominantly around the UN Charter – particularly Article 2(4) and Article 51 – and including the critical role it gave the UN Security Council in responding to threats to international peace and security.[1] In our later discussion of humanitarian intervention, we include the initiatives of the UN Secretaries General and the General Assembly culminating in the World Summit Outcome (WSO) document of September 2005 and its references to the "Responsibility to Protect." Reference to the Charter or WSO document is not meant to imply that the use of force norm has been free from contestation over interpretation, or that the thinking on the conditions under which force might be used has not evolved. However it may be interpreted, this prohibitive normative framework nevertheless has some longevity and is symmetric in the sense that it is meant to apply to every state in the global system. And while the Sino-American bilateral relationship has clearly played some role in certain of their most important decisions about when to use force – the Korean and Vietnamese wars being the most pertinent – concerns about force have become more diffuse in the bilateral relationship. The relationship is not as directly prominent as in several of our other normative areas, or as prominent in the last three decades as was the case before then.

[1] Various regional agreements have also been developed to regulate the use of force. For example, in 1976 member states of the Association of Southeast Asian Nations (ASEAN) established the Treaty of Amity and Cooperation, subsequently amended to allow accession to states from outside the ASEAN area.

The chapter first sets out the general normative prohibition on the use of force and the evolution in thinking on the conditions under which force might be used. It then examines and explains Chinese and US adherence to the various components of a norm that has been subject to some variance in interpretation. Finally, it assesses the extent to which their own relationship has affected their positions on the use of force. As Permanent Members of the UN Security Council, and as states in direct conflict at earlier stages in their history, their perspectives have had influence on these debates, the constitutive features of the norm, and on their own bilateral relationship.

As is shown later in this chapter, global debate on the conditions under which force can be used in international politics has been reinvigorated in the last two decades. The ending of the Cold War, and a belief in some capitals that the global threat environment required fundamental reassessment, together with stark evidence of governmental involvement in mass killings of their own peoples, spurred on these arguments. One result has been a more pointed debate over the meaning of self-defence and whether it could be said to encompass preemptive and preventive uses of force. Another dimension has dwelt on the controversial matter of using military force for humanitarian purposes – humanitarian intervention – which now has evolved into a concept that generates a wider degree of international consensus (for reasons to be explained later): the "Responsibility to Protect." These two issues are the prime focus of this chapter.

1 Normative Development

Normative standards designed to circumscribe the use of force in international relations developed markedly after the late nineteenth century and were set at a high level after 1945. Two centuries earlier, war had been depicted as a virtuous and honourable occupation, but by the second half of the twentieth century many uses of force had been deemed illegitimate and permissible only as a last resort in exceptional circumstances (Finnemore 2003: 19). The idea of warrior as hero and war as heroic had well and truly "died ... in Flanders field" (Rengger and Kennedy-Pipe 2008: 898). The blood-letting, degradation, and exploitation associated with the industrialized nature of late nineteenth- and twentieth-century warfare propelled forward the normative prohibition on uses of force except in self-defence. After the Second World War, states moved to support a UN Charter stipulating that it would be the UN Security Council, rather than individual governments, that would step in to promote collective arrangements designed to sustain or reestablish international peace and security. These understandings served to legitimate multilateral over unilateral uses of force, except in the initial stages of self-defence, and to elevate non-intervention and territorial integrity as foundational principles of international order.

The influence of these understandings was reflected in the changing objectives for which war was fought. Whereas between 1648 and 1945 about 80 percent of conflicts involved territorial redistribution, this percentage dropped to 23 percent between 1945 and 1996 (Zacher 2001; Finnemore 2003: 126). Gradually a consensus built that states should not use force to resolve irredentist claims, the Indian annexation of Goa being a partial exception to this understanding (Gray 2000: 49). In the more favourable international political circumstances of 1990, there was near unanimous denunciation in the United Nations of the Iraqi invasion of Kuwait, including by both the United States and the Soviet Union. What followed was a rapid collective response to Iraqi aggression, with only China among the Permanent Five abstaining on the resolution authorizing the use of force to effect an Iraqi withdrawal. And while there have been several major inter-state conflicts since 1945, the prohibition against the use of force has been accepted as "not only a treaty obligation but also customary law and even *ius cogens*" (Gray 2008a: 25). Despite violations of this prohibition, major legal judgements have concluded that these should be treated as breaches of the rules, and not as the basis for the establishment of new rules.[2]

The most powerful statement of this constraint on the use of force is made in Article 2(4) of the UN Charter, which calls on all member states to "refrain in their international relations from the threat or use of force against the territorial integrity or political independence of any state." That Article has to be read in conjunction with Article 51, which acknowledges a state's "inherent right of individual or collective self-defence if an armed attack occurs against a Member of the United Nations." Crucially, however, unilateral acts of self-defence are permitted only "until the Security Council has taken measures necessary to maintain international peace and security." That right of self-defence includes the requirement that any force used be both "necessary and proportionate"

---

[2] Gray draws on the International Court of Justice (ICJ) judgement in the Nicaragua case to illustrate this point (2000: 19).

(Gray 2008b: 94). Article 2(3) proffers a blanket appeal to all member states to "settle their international disputes by peaceful means."

Inevitably, these formulations do not remove contentious issues of interpretation. The United Nations was never able to create the standing army that potentially would have allowed it to exercise its prescribed monopoly on the use of force (Roberts 2008). When conflicts ensued in the context of a bipolar Cold War world order, the veto system effectively prevented the Security Council from acting under its Chapter VII provisions.[3] Moreover, the Charter was written with the experience of major inter-state war in mind, whereas many of the conflicts after 1945 were to be civil in origin or mixed in form,[4] immediately raising the issue of whether and how those Articles might apply in these cases. Anti-colonial movements involved in civil conflicts claimed a right to use force to achieve self-determination and to accept outside assistance to further their cause against aggressor occupying powers. When occupying powers claimed they were using force against these movements in self-defence, their critics disavowed the validity of these claims on the grounds that such states' operations were based on illegal policies. Other states raised questions about the narrowness of the definition of what constituted force: whether the force prohibition related only to armed conflict or additionally covered economic coercion (Gray 2000: 15; 2008b: 87, 93).

Thus, determining the scope of self-defence has always been particularly difficult. The use of the word "inherent" in Article 51 sparked legal debate as to whether self-defence should be interpreted as reflecting wider customary law or had been given a new and restricted definition in the 1945 UN Charter. There were also debates on the thorny concept of anticipatory action against an imminent attack, and on whether force could be used to protect nationals under threat overseas, with those assuming a relationship between Article 51 and customary international law arguing that these actions had previously been deemed legitimate uses of force. Later on, and especially after the terrorist attacks on the United States in September 2001, some saw previous interpretations of imminence to be overly restrictive, resulting in an attempt to expand the notion of anticipatory self-defence to encompass preventive action to halt the further

---

[3] Technically, the UN action in Korea in 1950 was an instance of collective security, but Security Council agreement was reached only because the Soviet Union was temporarily boycotting the Council as a result of the failure to allocate the UN seat to the People's Republic of China.

[4] See the Uppsala Conflict Data Program at http://www.pcr.uu.se/research/UCDP/, accessed 18 March 2010.

development of a serious threat (e.g. Bobbitt 2008; Doyle 2008). After 9/11, UN Security Council Resolutions 1368 and 1373 identified terrorism as a threat to international peace and security and self-defence as a rightful response.[5] These resolutions implied that force legitimately could be used against non-state actors and, thus, consequently, the states that hosted them.

The US-led 2003 intervention in Iraq, without a specific enabling UN resolution, proved the most controversial of developments in reference to interpretations of self-defence. The UN sanctions regime against Iraq had been eroding, the fear that Iraq was stockpiling weapons of mass destruction was high in key Western capitals, and Saddam Hussein continued to obstruct the work of UN inspectors. Nevertheless, neither the legal nor the political case for intervention in Iraq and replacement of the regime was strong, as UN debates in the run-up to the war demonstrated. The UN Secretary General described this period as a "fork in the road" for the United Nations, and as a result he established a High Level Panel (HLP) on Threats, Challenges and Change. The HLP Report that ensued, entitled *A More Secure World* (UNGA Document 2004), summarized the three most difficult questions that had arisen out of recent practice and that needed to be resolved: "first, when a State claims the right to strike preventively, in self-defence, in response to a threat which is not imminent; [and] secondly, when a State appears to be posing an external threat, actual or potential, to other States or people outside its borders, but there is disagreement in the Security Council as to what to do about it." The third question (discussed in the next paragraph) related to humanitarian intervention: that is, "where the threat is primarily internal, to a State's own people" (UNGA Document 2004: 54). The HLP's response was to set out five criteria for determining when the use of force would be regarded as legitimate. These were seriousness of the threat, proper purpose, last resort, proportional means, and the balance of consequences. The HLP invited debate over these criteria in the hopes of obtaining greater consistency in state behaviour in unsettling global circumstances.

The third of the "difficult questions" that the HLP raised had been posing a particular challenge since the ending of the Cold War, an event that had provided greater political space for addressing humanitarian intervention. Although there is reference in the UN Charter, including in its preamble, to human rights protections, there is no mention of the possible use of force to address a humanitarian catastrophe inside a

---

[5] S/RES/1368, 12 September 2001; S/RES/1373, 28 September 2001.

member state of the UN. Yet events in Somalia, Haiti, and Bosnia and Herzegovina, and especially the failure to act in Rwanda in 1994 as well as NATO action in Kosovo in 1999 without a mandatory UN resolution, prompted the desire to flesh out some kind of authoritative collective response. These conflicts, all of which involved massive human rights violations, led to consideration of the use of military force – not always solely, but often including, for humanitarian purposes. Preferably, this action would be endorsed or authorized by the UN Security Council, but would not be reliant on the consent of those authorities who were manifestly guilty of abusing their populations.

Over the course of the 1990s, in fact, the Council regularly demonstrated a willingness to recognize humanitarian disasters inside a state's borders as a threat to international peace and security and subject to Chapter VII provisions of the UN Charter, with some nine cases raising these matters quite distinctly (Roberts 2004: 81; Wheeler 2004: 32–3). The involvement in Somalia in 1992–93 was the first occasion when military intervention was authorized under Chapter VII "without the consent of the sovereign government *and* for solely humanitarian reasons" (Welsh 2008: 539).

UN Secretaries General Boutros Boutros-Ghali and Kofi Annan were important in stimulating this evolution in thinking and behaviour. Annan, in particular, demonstrated a willingness to argue that humanitarian disasters represented a threat to international peace and security, that "another Rwanda" had to be prevented, and that sovereignty had to mean more than the recognition of the sovereign rights of other states.[6] In several of his writings and speeches, and particularly in his September 1999 statement to the UN General Assembly, Annan emphasized that the global community could not stand idly by watching gross and systematic violations of human rights, that state sovereignty was being redefined to encompass the idea of individual sovereignty, and that the contemporary reading of the UN Charter meant we were "more than ever conscious that its aim is to protect individual human beings, not to protect those who abuse them" (Annan 1999).

In response to Annan's call, the government of Canada led the establishment of a twelve-person International Commission on Intervention and State Sovereignty (ICISS). Its report, produced in December 2001 and entitled "The Responsibility to Protect" (R2P) – showing obvious

---

[6] Note also that in *An Agenda for Peace* (1992) Boutros Boutros-Ghali wrote: "The time of absolute and exclusive sovereignty, however, has passed."

sensitivity to the unease caused by the term humanitarian intervention – launched a debate on where that responsibility lay.[7] ICISS commissioners were in no doubt that when states were "unwilling or unable" to protect their own citizens from humanitarian catastrophe, then that responsibility had to be borne "by the broader community of states." The methods to be used might include "political, economic or judicial measures" and "only in extreme cases" they might also involve military action, it stated (ICISS 2001; MacFarlane and Khong 2006: esp. Chapter 5).

Much controversy followed the publication of this report with widespread ICISS consultations afterwards highlighting considerable governmental hostility towards what had become the predominant interpretation of humanitarian intervention (Bellamy 2008b: 621). However, the World Summit Outcome document of September 2005 accepted a cautious version of R2P ideas, with all UN member states agreeing to adopt the R2P language in paragraphs 138 and 139 and promising to act "in accordance with the Charter, including Chapter VII, on a case-by-case basis and in cooperation with relevant regional organizations as appropriate, should peaceful means be inadequate and national authorities are manifestly failing to protect their populations from genocide, war crimes, ethnic cleansing and crimes against humanity" (UNGA Document 2005). UN Security Council Resolution 1674, which passed unanimously on 28 April 2006 and focused on the "Protection of Civilians in Armed Conflict," also contained an endorsement of R2P. And Security Council Resolution 1706 that year relating to the crisis in Darfur reaffirmed the language, suggesting some institutional embedding of the R2P idea.[8]

Moreover, this debate was not only held at elite levels. The idea of a "Responsibility to Protect" started to find support among a number of publics, beyond the vocal and active domestic and transnational human rights organizations that had been pressing for higher standards of protection against abuse. One multinational study based on sample interviews in twelve countries found that a majority in eight of them and a plurality in four accepted that the UN Security Council had a "responsibility [not just a right] to authorize the use of force to protect people from severe human rights violations such as genocide, even against the will of their own government" (World Public Opinion.org 2007). Undoubtedly, use

---

[7] Important antecedents include Francis Deng et al. (1996) and, notably, the 2000 Constitutive Act of the African Union, which recorded the "right of the Union to intervene in a Member State pursuant to a decision of the Assembly in respect to grave circumstances, namely: war crimes, genocide, and crimes against humanity."

[8] S/RES/1674, 28 April 2006; S/RES/1706, 31 August 2006.

of the word "genocide" may somewhat have skewed the results, but the levels of support were strikingly high at between 64 percent and 76 percent – even discounting for the use of this terminology – in China, the United States, and among Palestinians and Israelis.[9]

Nevertheless, closer examination of these discussions of self-defence, prevention, preemption as well as R2P shows that the changes in interpretation may not have gone as far as these generalized points suggest. This is certainly so if one looks beyond the practice and perceptions of some of the most powerful states. Gray concludes in reference to the self-defence arguments that "in practice these fundamental doctrinal differences were not (until recently) of decisive significance as to the legality of the use of force except in a few isolated, though much discussed, instances." She goes on: "States using force against another state almost invariably invoke self-defence; in the vast majority of such claims this has not given rise to any doctrinal issues or to any divisions between states as to the applicable law" (Gray 2008a: 114). And the use of an argument of anticipatory self-defence she finds to be "in practice ... rare." States much "prefer to rely on self-defence in response to an armed attack." Overall, they would rather take a wide view of what constitutes an armed attack than make an open anticipatory self-defence argument, because "they know [that it] will be unacceptable to the vast majority of states" (Gray 2008a: 161).[10]

Gray notes, too, that when the HLP Report stated it was "well-established that Article 51 allowed pre-emptive forcible action in the face of an imminent threat," this assertion attracted the disapproval of many states, including the Non-Aligned Movement, and it was left out of the 2005 WSO document (Gray: 2008b: 97). With respect to preventive uses

[9] Some 76% of the Chinese public supported this, followed by Americans at 74%, Palestinians at 69%, and Israelis at 64%. A 2003 study of elite attitudes by the US Brookings Institution, involving workshops with officials, scholars, and legal and military experts from Europe, Russia, China, Latin America, South Asia, the Middle East, and sub-Saharan Africa, generated somewhat different results. European, African, and American participants believed force was appropriate when used to end or prevent widespread humanitarian disasters, and they supported the idea of R2P. Mexicans, South Asians, and Russians saw R2P as an "unwarranted interference in the internal affairs of states." Discussions with scholars from China "demonstrated movement from a stance of strict non-interference toward a more pragmatic evaluation of China's strategic interests" (Daalder 2007: 3), of which more later. Note, however, Donald Steinberg's valid cautionary comment in reference to US views that it is "difficult to tell a pollster that America should stand by and watch while genocide takes place" (2006).

[10] Arend and Beck (1993: Chapter 10) disagree that such prohibitions are in place and argue that a self-help paradigm more accurately reflects current conditions.

of force, supported in several George W. Bush administration statements,[11] and occasionally in the United Kingdom, France, and Russia (Daalder 2007: 5–6), the HLP's remarks on the issue were qualified. It stated that, if there were "good arguments for preventive military action, with good evidence to support them," any action based on those arguments had to be made subject to UN Security Council authorization – that is, unilateral preventive attacks were illegitimate in its view but action authorized by a collective body such as the Security Council was acceptable. In one of its most telling passages with respect to this distinction it stated: "in a world full of perceived potential threats, the risk to the global order and the norm of non-intervention on which it continues to be based is simply too great for the legality of unilateral preventive action, as distinct from collectively endorsed action, to be accepted" (UNGA Document 2004: 55). Where the HLP qualified the argument for preventive uses of force, the more authoritative and consensual 2005 WSO document went much further: it left this discussion of prevention out of that document entirely, preferring to terminate the debate and "reaffirm that the relevant provisions of the Charter are sufficient to address the full range of threats to international peace and security" (UNGA Document 2005: para. 79), a clear example where attempted norm reinterpretation failed to make headway.

Finally, although that HLP Report claimed that there is an "emerging norm that there is a collective international responsibility to protect, exercisable by the Security Council authorizing military intervention as a last resort, in the event of genocide and other large-scale killing, ethnic cleansing or serious violations of international humanitarian law which sovereign Governments have proved powerless or unwilling to prevent" (UNGA Document 2004: 57, para. 203), in fact the emerging norm came to be far more circumscribed than this 2004 statement implied. As noted earlier, the language of Responsibility to Protect was taken up in the 2005 WSO document and in UN Security Council Resolution 1674, but several reformulations narrowed the original intentions behind this idea. This was hardly surprising. As the UN Secretary General, Ban Ki-Moon, subsequently put it, the legacy of the 1990s had been unhelpful in that it "posed a false choice between two extremes: either standing by in the face of mounting civilian deaths or deploying coercive military force to protect the vulnerable and threatened populations" (UNGA Document 2009).

---

[11] The US National Security Strategy documents of 2002 and 2006 and their coverage of prevention will be discussed in later sections of this chapter.

Thus, in the WSO document of September 2005, the conditions spark-
ing R2P became more exacting in terms of the violations requiring an
international response – genocide, war crimes, ethnic cleansing, and
crimes against humanity, together with their incitement. Gone were the
broader references to "large-scale killing," or "serious violations of international humanitarian law."[12] These more specific conditions potentially
were less controversial because they were "firmly based on existing international law" (Luck 2008: 4). The initial reference to a state's inability
or unwillingness to act became in the Outcome document (with both US
and some developing country support) "the stronger hurdle of 'manifest
failure'" (Welsh 2008: 558). In addition to raising the just cause threshold,
the Outcome document gave the host state a primary role in the responsibility to protect, diminishing the prominence of the HLP's reference to
a "collective international responsibility." In turn, that reference to collective responsibility in the HLP Report became in the WSO document,
"we are prepared to take collective action, in a timely and decisive manner, through the Security Council, in accordance with the Charter." The
Outcome document also removed all reference to the five criteria outlined
in *A More Secure World*, as well as dropping a paragraph that called for
debate of the criteria (Bellamy 2006: 166–8).[13] Notably, China, Russia
and the United States all opposed adopting criteria for intervention.[14]

The UN General Assembly debate in July 2009 of the UN Secretary
General's Report "Implementing the Responsibility to Protect" (UNGA
Document 2009) similarly put emphasis on ways of preventing abuse
and the state's responsibility to protect its population from the four
crimes (state responsibility being referred to as Pillar I of R2P). It also
suggested ways in which the international community could help states
build capacities to prevent atrocities (Pillar II), thus drawing attention
away from the knottier questions of reaction and response to evidence of
atrocities (Pillar III). As far as Thomas Weiss, the former research director
of the ICISS, is concerned, these kinds of developments ducked some of

---

[12] Apparently, these linkages to specific crimes were suggested by Pakistan's ambassador to
the UN (Luck 2009: 13, note 6). Edward C. Luck is the UN Secretary General's Special
Adviser on R2P.

[13] Luck is not against this omission, arguing that too open-ended a conception of R2P
"would be impossible to operationalize or institutionalize. It would become one more
case of the United Nations stretching a relatively discrete and well-defined concept until
it loses its shape, clarity, and meaning" (Luck 2008: 5).

[14] The US government took this stance because it did not want its freedom of action to be
limited (Luck 2009: 11); the Chinese and Russian governments, because they believed it
might lead to circumvention of the UN Security Council (Bellamy 2008b: 626).

the central dilemmas, turning the WSO version into "R2P-lite" (quoted in Wheeler and Egerton 2009: 123). However, it is a formulation of the emerging norm that generates a far wider global consensus.

In sum, the global normative framework on use of force still shows strong attachment to non-intervention and non-interference as key components of international order; a preference for multilateral rather than unilateral uses of force; and demand for a UN Security Council role as the authorizing body. There is also widespread agreement on the illegitimacy of using force to effect territorial redistribution, even covering irredentist claims. Despite the fears among a number of major states about new sources of threat, there is not much latitude given to states that want to be able to engage in either preemptive or preventive uses of force in dealing with these threats. Instead, there is a distinct preference for a more conservative interpretation of the scope of the self-defence norm.

In respect of military intervention for humanitarian purposes, this part of the normative framework suggests there has been some reinterpretation of the state sovereignty norm. Many political actors – state and non-state – have more firmly endorsed a concept of security that focuses on protecting the individual from abuse and have accepted that state sovereignty cannot function as a shield behind which governments commit gross violations of human rights. But the use of force for these ends has been set at a high bar in the WSO consensus document. For all its potential, that document has not helped states decide what should be done where an anticipated or actual use of a Permanent Member's veto prevents the Security Council from acting in cases of supreme humanitarian need.[15] The consensus position behind the WSO document is that the threshold for intervention should be set at a high level, both in deciding when there should be an international response to atrocities, and when a state should be judged to have failed in offering protection for its people. Military means should only be used as a last resort when other methods such as mediation, threat of international criminal prosecution, or sanctions have been tried and have failed. The international debate over R2P emphasizes the first and second pillars of the R2P idea: that is, acceptance of the idea that it is a state's responsibility to prevent abuses from developing, and the international community's duty to build capacities inside states so that atrocities do not occur in the first place. Force for

---

[15] In the July 2009 General Assembly debate, more than thirty-five states called upon Permanent Security Council members to refrain from using their veto in situations that had been identified as evoking R2P (GCR2P 2009).

humanitarian ends, the R2P debate implies, should only be used *in extremis* and with full UN Security Council authorization.

2 China and the Use of Force

Ask most Chinese about the relationship between China and the use of force and they would declare the country to have long been pacific, non-threatening and desirous of maintaining peaceful relations with its many neighbours in order that it can get on with the job of developing the society and economy. Peaceful coexistence, peaceful rise, peaceful development, harmonious society, and harmonious world have been prominent in the elite discourse in the last two decades or more, reinforced in specific areas by reference to doctrines such as "no-first-use" of nuclear weapons, and the labelling of China's military doctrine as based on "active defence." Cultural traditions linked to Confucius and the military writings of Sun Zi have regularly been drawn upon to explain an alleged "predisposition to seek non-violent solutions to problems of statecraft" (Scobell 2003: 1–2).

Few scholars have been willing to leave the debate on China's predispositions at that point. Those who have used calculations based on social science datasets[16] have shown the PRC to have been involved in a large number of disputes, especially in the years between 1954–58 and 1964–68 (Johnston 1998: 10), and despite its limited force projection capabilities. This neither implies Beijing was the initiator in all cases, nor always the aggressor. Almost half of these quarrels have related to territorial issues. Alastair Iain Johnston, in his observations of PRC behaviour over the period 1949–92, records that, "in general China has been more dispute-prone than many other major powers (except the United States)" (Johnston 1998: 17). Using another dataset, Johnston also reports PRC involvement in eleven foreign policy crises between 1949 and 1985, eight of which resulted in force being used (72 percent). These uses of force, as described in the dataset, were "high intensity," involving "serious clashes" or "full-scale war" (quoted in Johnston 1996: 252). Most were located along China's borders and contained some territorial element.

---

[16] Johnston based his analysis on the Militarized Interstate Dispute (MID) dataset, put together by the University of Michigan's Correlates of War research group, in the version covering cases from 1815 to 1992. A MID is defined as the "threat, display or use of military force short of war by one member ... explicitly directed towards the government, official representatives, official forces, property, or territory of another state" (quoted in Johnston 1998: 5). For a larger discussion, including the problems of this and another similar dataset, see Fordham and Sarver (2001).

Six particular disputes involving policy or sovereignty questions have tended to result in violence. As M. Taylor Fravel indicates, these six have led China to use force on sixteen occasions, with conflict against India, Taiwan, and Vietnam making up most of those instances of violence (2007/08: 53; 2008a: 63).[17] The status of Taiwan has been a particularly contentious issue, a problem for Beijing that combines concerns about disputed territory with the critical issues of national unity and national identity.

Participation in these conflicts, the availability of economic means to modernize its armed forces, as well as observation of other major uses of force – such as the US-led intervention in Iraq in 1990 – have had considerable influence on China's military doctrine. "People's War" became "People's War under Modern Conditions." After 1993 the focus was on "limited wars under high-technology conditions." Later still, this became "high-technology" and "informationization" (China's Defence White Paper 2006). Chinese strategists project these limited wars as "sudden, intense, and destructive thus requiring China to develop new operational capabilities stressing joint operations, rapid response, and offensive strikes to deter such local wars from arising or to win them if they do erupt" (Fravel 2008b: 126). Beijing has allocated double-digit growth rates in the Chinese defence budget since the early 1990s. Indeed, over the period 1998–2007, China's military spending in real terms has been estimated to have increased by 202 percent (SIPRI 2008: 177) and in 2009 it was up another 15 percent over the previous year (IISS 2010a). Only in 2010 did this start to slow with a projected rise for that year of 7.5 percent.[18] As in earlier decades, this more recent military doctrine does not rule out the preemptive or preventive use of force in conditions where the People's Liberation Army (PLA) believes it needs to gain the initiative at the early stage of any conflict.

Beyond potential uses of force in limited wars, the PLA has begun to develop new competencies in space, on land, and at sea, including a burgeoning submarine deployment programme to enhance sea denial and sea control operations.[19] It has also begun the development of a

---

[17] His definition of use of force (rather than solely involvement in disputes) also follows the Correlates of War project and "includes occupation of territory or a blockade, raid, clash, or war" (Fravel 2007/08: 53).

[18] Kathrin Hille, "China eases rise in defence spending," *Financial Times*, 5 March 2010.

[19] In Robert S. Ross's view, this "access-denial capability is not a war-winning capability; the United States retains overwhelming maritime superiority in the western Pacific Ocean. But China's submarines make vulnerable U.S. surface ships, especially aircraft carriers, operating near the Chinese coast." It is then, a "limited deterrent capability" which "considerably complicates the operations of the U.S. Navy" (Ross 2009: 59).

power-projection capability and plans to acquire an aircraft carrier or carriers. China's armed forces now more readily engage in non-combat missions – for example, participating in UN peacekeeping operations and sending two destroyers to escort Chinese merchant ships through the pirate-infested Gulf of Aden for the first time in January 2009.[20] These new roles are partial fruits of the military modernization that has ensued particularly after 1989. They are also responses to President Hu Jintao's call for the PLA to "perform new historic missions" including responding to natural and man-made disasters (Gill and Huang 2009: 4).

However, military doctrine and deployments are only one component of a broader Chinese foreign policy strategy that, especially from the mid- to late-1990s, has placed greater emphasis on the strategic reassurance of neighbours and the need to promote regional and global stability. That broader strategy has led to a convergence of Beijing's rhetoric and behaviour with the use of force norm as articulated in the UN Charter. For example, China's response to international political debates after 2001 on preemptive or preventive uses of force against terrorist groups has been to argue that this does not fit comfortably with the self-defence doctrine. President Jiang Zemin is on record as stating in September 2001 that such an attack required "conclusive evidence, specific targets, compliance with the UN Charter, and a role for the Security Council" (Kramer 2007: 104).[21] Disputed territorial issues on its western borders with India and the Central Asian states have been approached somewhat differently from that of the Maoist era, Beijing agreeing to various confidence building measures, settling claims where it could, and in the early twenty-first century embarking upon joint military exercises with these states. Tensions over the dispute with India undoubtedly are high, and resolution of the rival territorial claims seemingly remains a distant prospect, but some attempt at creating a framework designed to prevent escalation has been put in place. The six-nation Shanghai Cooperation Organization (SCO), committed to the removal of "separatism, extremism, and terrorism" in these territories, also has been part of a strategy to develop coincidences of interest and stabilize relations among China, Central Asia, and Russia. Stability concerns seem uppermost: despite a

[20] Apparently, it took the Ministry of Foreign Affairs (MOFA) two months to persuade China's armed forces to send this naval fleet to Somalia (ICG April 2009: 26). One effect has been to stimulate "mass interest in an aircraft carrier" (Ross 2009: 63).

[21] Given Al Qaeda's threat in October 2009 to target Han Chinese in reaction to the repression of Uighurs in Xinjiang, this particular prohibition might be tested at some later date.

meeting of the SCO at the time of the crisis in Russian-Georgian relations in 2008 and despite some sympathy for Russia's position in this dispute,[22] China stuck to its line developed from the start of the fighting that the main task was for the "parties concerned … to call for a ceasefire, show restraint, and avoid actions that would escalate the crisis or further damage the region's peace and stability."[23]

Beijing's sovereignty disputes in the South China Sea have been managed rather than resolved via the signature by China and ASEAN in 2002 of a "Declaration on the Conduct of Parties in the South China Sea," which rules out the use of force for settling these sovereignty issues and attempts to impose some constraints on the occupation of presently uninhabited islands and reefs.[24] Beijing signed ASEAN's Treaty of Amity and Cooperation in 2003 (the first major Asian state outside ASEAN to do so), which mimics the UN Charter in its emphasis on the non-use of force for resolving issues in dispute. Between 2002 and 2006, China and ASEAN members exchanged more than seventy high-level defence visits, plus eleven naval goodwill visits (Thayer 2007), and these exchanges continue as a part of Beijing's military reassurance strategy.

Finally, Beijing has become a supportive player in the various formal and informal multilateral security mechanisms that have been a feature of the post–Cold War Asia-Pacific. In doctrinal terms, China developed what it calls a "New Security Concept," not dissimilar from the five principles of peaceful coexistence it first enunciated (with India) in 1954, but with an emphasis on the language of cooperative and common security: mutual interest, trust-building via dialogue, and the peaceful settlement of disputes. In 2002, in its "Position Paper on the New Security Concept" issued at that year's ASEAN Regional Forum (ARF) meeting, its foreign minister provided an overly positive gloss on recent

---

[22] Author interviews, Beijing, September 2008.

[23] China's UN Security Council statement of 8 August 2008 is available at http://www. china-un.org/chn/xw/t464029.htm, accessed 18 March 2010.

[24] For one pessimistic assessment of this declaration given difficulties among the Philippines, Vietnam, and China in 2008, see Mark Valencia, "The South China Sea Hydra" at http://www.nautilus.org/fora/security/08057Valencia.html, 24 July 2008. Valencia states: "the South China Sea disputes are resurfacing and the temporary cooperative arrangements are unravelling. ASEAN's efforts to entangle China in a legally binding Code of Conduct for the South China Sea have come to naught." But Fravel contends that despite improvements in China's naval capabilities, China has not moved to occupy any additional features in the Spratlys (2008a: 298). The year 2009 saw increased Chinese patrolling of these waters in light of perceived "foreign intrusions" into territory Beijing claims, and in 2010 a somewhat ominous official statement that sovereignty over this area represented a "core" Chinese interest.

developments but nevertheless publicly reaffirmed China's commitment to peaceful resolution of sovereignty questions: "As for the outstanding disputes and issues, China has reached consensus with the parties concerned to maintain peace and stability in the disputed areas and resolve the issues through peaceful means. Disputes over territorial land and water are no longer an obstacle for China and its neighbors to develop normal cooperation and good-neighborly relations and jointly build regional security" (quoted in Foot 2007: 108–9). Since it first published a White Paper on "Arms Control and Disarmament" in 1996, it has produced Defence White Papers on a two-yearly cycle. These have become less opaque about China's strategic goals and defence planning priorities.

The combined effect of these policies has been to constrain a military doctrine of "active defence," that allows for preemptive uses of force, instead tipping the balance in favour of approaches that stress interdependence, the pursuit of common goals, and the peaceful resolution of disputes. Above all, they bring Chinese rhetoric and much of its behaviour in line with the use of force norm as articulated in the UN Charter: non-use of force for settling issues in dispute except in self-defence (Taiwan excepted for reasons already given).

Chinese policies in response to interventions that include a humanitarian mandate have also suggested some willingness to participate. Its contribution to UN Peace Keeping Operations (UNPKOs) has increased 20-fold since 2000, and at the end of 2008 it had more personnel involved in these operations than Russia, the United Kingdom, or the United States. Most of these peacekeepers are concentrated in the region of greatest need: that is, Africa. In August 2007, a Chinese General was appointed for the first time to be force commander of the UN mission in Western Sahara (Gill and Huang 2009: 1, 3).[25] China prefers to offer only police, medical, and engineering contingents for the UN operations. Nevertheless, the mandates now involve something far more extensive than keeping warring parties apart: they are intrusive in nature and often include the requirement to establish the conditions for the holding of elections, to demobilize fighting groups, to promote human rights, and to build institutions to create a rule of law. The PKO of 1991 in El Salvador was the first to include a human rights division, but almost all PKOs have since maintained that profile (Roberts and Zaum 2008: 54). Chinese

---

[25] This mission is not in an area that appeals to China's interest in natural resources, illustrating that there are broader motivations than material interest behind China's UNPKO participation.

Ambassador Liu Zhenmin acknowledged the complexity of PKOs in the twenty-first century, noting "the basic parameters of peacekeeping – consent, impartiality and the non-use of force – should remain intact ... [however] the Security Council is now facing new challenges in crafting peacekeeping mandates, especially as countries began asking for the inclusion of new duties, such as the protection of civilians."[26]

Debates in the UN since the 1990s over the potential use of force in response to evidence of humanitarian disaster have posed far greater dilemmas than participation in peacekeeping – even with their more complex mandates – for a state concerned to protect the norms of state sovereignty and non-interference in internal affairs. However, as the UN has moved to broaden its understandings of the conditions that can cause a breakdown in international peace and security, including humanitarian crises, Chinese officials have been required to reconsider their position. Generally, they have acquiesced in UN action but have been keen to claim that precedents have not been set, that host state consent had been sought and (mostly) given, and that regional states were supportive of the action. China's 2005 paper on UN Security Council reform puts its position succinctly: that is, "when a massive humanitarian crisis occurs, it is the legitimate concern of the international community to ease and defuse the crisis. Any response to such a crisis should strictly conform to the UN Charter and the opinions of the country and the regional organization concerned should be respected ... Wherever it involves enforcement actions, there should be more prudence in the consideration of each case" (China's Position Paper, 2005).

Thus, Beijing joined other permanent members of the Security Council (P5) in authorizing military action in Somalia in 1992 under Chapter VII provisions of the UN Charter, remarkable in that the enforcement mission was mandated to "use all necessary means to establish as soon as possible a secure environment for humanitarian relief operations" in the country.[27] Moreover, the use of force was justified solely to deal with the "magnitude of the human tragedy caused by the conflict in Somalia" (quoted in Welsh 2008: 541). China also supported one of the key resolutions on Haiti in 1993 that referred to the "incidence of humanitarian crises, including the mass displacements of population," as well as – even more extraordinarily – resolution 940 whereby the

---

[26] UN Press Release, Special Committee on Peacekeeping Operations, GA/PK/199, 23 February 2009.
[27] SC/RES/794, 3 December 1992.

Security Council showed a willingness to authorize force to replace one state government with another.[28]

Certainly, Beijing was very critical of developments in Kosovo in 1999, especially once the Security Council had been circumvented, and NATO's aerial bombing had begun. Its anger intensified when China's Belgrade embassy was hit a few months later. It also voted, with Russia and Namibia, in support of a Russian-sponsored draft resolution that called for an "immediate cessation of the use of force against the Federal Republic of Yugoslavia." Nevertheless, a short while later, and having initially held back its consent, it voted in support of both UN Resolutions that authorized robust intervention in East Timor. And although there is no explicit reference in the UN Charter to the international administration of war-torn territories, such an authority was established in Timor and permitted to exercise "supreme executive, legislative and judicial authority" in the territory for a limited period (Roberts and Zaum 2008: 55). China further indicated its support by deploying a few civilian police to the UN Transitional Administration in East Timor (UNTAET) mission (Carlson 2006: 227).

However, in each of these instances, Beijing also found a way to make the intervention more palatable to it and more compatible with its preferences: on Somalia, it argued that it agreed to intervention because there was no responsible governmental authority to give consent (Welsh 2008: 541); on Haiti, China and others stated that "prior action" on the part of the Organization of American States as well as the General Assembly provided the enabling context that "'warrant[ed] the extraordinary consideration of the matter by the Security Council and the equally extraordinary application of measures provided for in Chapter VII'" (quoted in Welsh 2008: 542). East Timor was made easier for Beijing when the Indonesian President gave his grudging consent to a UN-mandated operation and by the fact that China had never recognized the 1975 Indonesian takeover of East Timor in the first place.[29]

China has been unwilling to support UN Security Council sanctions against Burma/Myanmar during times of humanitarian need in that country. It even went so far as to use its veto in January 2007, "the first time since 1973 that Beijing vetoed any matter unrelated to Taiwan" (Kleine-Ahlbrandt and Small 2008: 42). However, even in this instance, it has tried to straddle a preference for non-intervention with a commitment

---

[28] SC/RES/841, 16 June 1993; SC/RES/940, 31 July 1994.
[29] Author interviews, Beijing, September 2008.

to offer some response to a humanitarian crisis. For example, its veto was followed by acquiescence in the passage of a condemnatory resolution in the UN Human Rights Council. It also supported a UN Security Council statement that "strongly deplore[d] the use of violence against peaceful demonstrations in Myanmar" and pressed the Burmese government to receive the UN special envoy, Ibrahim Gambari (Holliday 2009: 490). Beijing additionally called for meaningful efforts by the regime to reconcile with its domestic opposition groups and minority ethnic factions: as Vice President Xi Jinping told the Burmese leader, Than Shwe, in December 2009, he hoped to see "political stability, economic development and national reconciliation."[30]

Another major controversy has involved China's relationship with Sudan, where, like Burma, it has energy and other interests that it wishes to promote. As with Burma, it has adopted a guarded stance but still has tried to do more than simply obstruct international action. In April 2006, Beijing abstained on UN Security Council resolution 1672 imposing targeted sanctions on four Sudanese officials,[31] while also affirming that it endorsed "the idea that those responsible for the serious violations of international humanitarian law and international human rights must be brought to justice" (quoted in Teitt 2009: 220–1). By September that year, Beijing had started to put pressure on the Sudanese government to accept a hybrid African Union-UN peacekeeping force, and in November its UN ambassador "made crucial interventions to secure the Sudanese government's agreement to the plan" (Kleine-Ahlbrandt and Small 2008: 42; Christensen 2009: 94). During President Hu Jintao's visit to Khartoum in February 2007, he privately put pressure on his Sudanese counterpart to comply with this hybrid force deployment, and China itself committed to send engineering troops. That pressure for full deployment was to continue into the following year, during which Chinese oil workers came under serious threat, with some kidnapped and killed (ICG 2009: 20–1). In an unusual move, Beijing also engaged some of the non-governmental

---

[30] Wai Moe, "China Tells Than Shwe It Wants 'Stability, National Reconciliation'," *The Irrawaddy*, 21 December 2009. This became particularly urgent from August 2009 when attacks on the minority Kokang armed group caused 37,000 to flee over the border into China. For evidence of Chinese planning and preparations for dealing with the Kokang refugee crisis, see Thompson (2009). He describes Chinese actions as averting "one of the largest refugee and security crises to occur on its borders since 1979" (Thompson 2009: 11).

[31] Teitt notes that China argued that sanctions would not work, that they would victimize civilians, and that the timing was bad because the resolution came a week before the deadline on the Abuja peace talks sponsored by the African Union (Teitt 2009: 220).

lobbies involved in the issue in an attempt to explain what it was trying to do to address the conflict (ICG 2009: 22).

Beijing has also joined in the deliberations that led to the R2P references in the 2005 WSO document and voted in support of UN Security Council Resolution 1674 that used the idea of R2P in the context of the protection of civilians in armed conflict. Here too it tried to draw a fine line between not obstructing the debate, and making sure that the agreements reached were "prudent" in what they advocated. China was one of the states that set out to tame the language of the HLP Report before the World Summit of 2005, suggesting that the Security Council should put the emphasis on action designed to prevent the abuses from occurring in the first place. Once R2P had been defined to its satisfaction in the WSO document, it stuck firmly to it: thus, initially it refused to endorse UN Resolution 1674, until that resolution reflected the language of R2P as described in the 2005 document (Teitt 2008: 8). During the July 2009 UN General Assembly debate on implementing R2P, it stressed again the importance of the consensus that underlay the WSO document's interpretation of R2P, and the central role that states must play in taking on the responsibility for protecting their own people. Positive as that support for Pillar I of R2P was, Beijing offered little or nothing in the way of ideas about the kinds of measures that might prove helpful to implementing the concept, and it was sceptical about the idea of establishing an early warning system unless it could operate with "neutrality ... fairness and transparency."[32]

Thus, Beijing is a conservative force in the R2P debate, but it is neither blocking discussion outright, nor trying to unpick the 2005 WSO consensus, nor refusing to accept the need to consider action in cases of supreme humanitarian need.[33] It has confirmed that it regards such crises as a "legitimate concern of the international community."[34] The Chinese government, while emphasizing its continuing support for the norms of state sovereignty and non-interference, has found ways of supporting international action for UN operations that have linked humanitarian

---

[32] "Statement by Ambassador Liu Zhenmin at the Plenary Session of the General Assembly on the Question of 'Responsibility to Protect'," 24 July 2009 at http://www.mfa.gov.cn/ce/ceun/eng/hyyfy/t575682.htm, accessed 18 March 2010.

[33] One knowledgeable interviewee in New York in October 2009 confirmed that China had kept silent about the position it would take in that R2P debate until the last moments. This interviewee found no evidence that it had tried to influence other delegations to support its cautious position.

[34] China's Position Paper (2005).

catastrophe to threats to international peace and security (Teitt 2008). Both officials and elites have begun to debate not how best to "defend the principle of non-interference" but to assess the "conditions under which intervention is justified" (Kleine-Ahlbrandt and Small 2008: 39).

Chinese scholars, in particular, have responded to the political elite's need to provide possible justifications (Carlson 2006: 225–31).[35] Zhang Tuosheng, for example, has suggested that China accepts that "legitimate intervention in a country's internal affairs may occur ... when a country suffers a large-scale humanitarian disaster and its government has no control or rescue capacity; when a country experiences significant domestic turbulence and chaos that undermines regional peace and stability," but he added, this was "only subject to judgment of the United Nations Security Council" (Zhang 2010: 33, 45).

By some measures, Chinese public attitudes might be more advanced than those of the elites. Public opinion polling in several countries, including China, showed that when a sample were asked "whether the UN Security Council 'has the responsibility to authorize the use of military force to protect people from severe human rights violations, such as genocide, even against the will' of the government committing such abuses" the highest level of support came from the Chinese public (76%), followed by the American public at 74 percent (World Public Opinion.org 2007). The questioning of focus groups in China bore out these results (Brookings Institution Panel 2007) as did discussions with some Chinese scholars, even eliciting the somewhat dubious statement that, if Kosovo had arisen in 2006 rather than in 1999, "China would have supported military intervention" (Daalder 2007: 3).[36]

In sum, China's positions on the use of force have shifted quite markedly. In the first two decades after 1949, in particular, the Chinese were dispute prone, predominantly over territorial issues. Moreover, Mao Zedong believed in the positive benefits of struggle and conflict, supported an argument associated with just war that could be found elsewhere in the Third World and in other socialist states, and called for revolutionary insurgency

---

[35] Author interviews, Beijing and Shanghai, September and December 2008. According to Pang (2008: 43) and in reference to R2P, "some Chinese analysts worried that this concept would be used to justify unwarranted military intervention by the United States or some European powers, but gradually they recognized that R2P could be used to bridge the divide between supporters of 'humanitarian intervention' and supporters of state sovereignty and non-intervention" through the imposition of certain conditions on intervention.

[36] This more flexible position on Kosovo was not borne out in our interviews in Beijing in September 2008.

including in the territories of China's neighbours. This took Beijing well beyond the generally accepted norm of non-interference, and Maoist ideas on insurgency have taken a long time to live down with neighbouring Southeast Asian states. At that time, Beijing justified its own uses of force, even preemption, as defensive in nature and rightful because of the imperialist nature of the opponent. Its exclusion from the United Nations until 1971 meant an inability to play a direct role in debates in this institutional environment on justifications for and limitations on uses of force.

In the last decade or so, there has been an evolution in China's position on the use of force concerning some of its outstanding sovereignty questions and other policy differences with neighbouring states. It has adopted positions and rhetoric that have placed some constraints on any use of force to deal with matters that it could claim as domestic sovereignty questions (Taiwan excepted) and thus has converged with the global normative framework. On the question of preemptive or preventive uses of force, it has rhetorically aligned itself with the WSO conclusion that the UN Charter remains preeminent, Article 2(4) remains adequate, Article 51 does not need reinterpretation, and a role for the UN Security Council must be protected. With respect to events that question an absolutist interpretation of the norm of state sovereignty, and the evolving if as yet unconsolidated global norm of R2P, Beijing has shown a capacity to shape and constrain the pace at which this norm has developed, although this has not meant that it has blocked elaboration and the potential for consolidation entirely.

Explaining Levels of Behavioural Consistency

The PRC was undoubtedly dispute prone in its early years, and was often involved in the use of force. Undoubtedly, in the absence of (re)unification, it is highly unlikely ever to renounce the possibility of attack on Taiwan (a domestic matter in its view where it would seemingly have no compunction in diverging – if necessary – from the perspective that irredentist claims should be settled by negotiation). That threat of force is part of its deterrence strategy in what it views as a critical matter of unity and identity.

However, its generally more pacific behaviour, which has led to convergence with common understandings of Article 2(4) over the last decade or so, requires explanation. Processes influencing that alignment show both the coincidence of domestic interests and values with global norms, as well as the power of international institutional mechanisms, especially those that retain legitimacy for a state such as China, to move even reluctant states along paths they otherwise might not have taken. Moreover, regional and global organizations have acted as platforms to expose forms of behaviour that attract the approval or disapproval of authoritative political actors. There is an important feedback process in play in which evolving domestic interests and beliefs become linked with international processes, and these work to reinforce each other.

We attempt first to explain China's earlier dispute-ridden behaviour, and to assess how that period helps elucidate its latterly more pacific behaviour. As noted at the start of this chapter, wars to effect territorial redistribution declined dramatically after 1945, as did approval of the use of force to resolve such claims. However, many of China's conflicts have involved territorial issues, and in its early decades in order to consolidate the new state and to complete its national unification project it was willing to risk war to make good on its claims. Geo-strategic factors heightened China's interest in the stability of and control over its vulnerable border regions. The PRC has the longest land borders in the world (about 14,000 miles) and since the breakup of the Soviet Union direct land frontiers with fourteen countries. It also has a number of maritime frontiers (Gill 2007: 106). Ethnic minorities dominate in these land-border regions, raising particular issues of loyalty, subjugation, or control. Fravel notes that "of the 135 [Chinese] counties adjacent to China's international frontiers, 107 are ethnic autonomous regions" (Fravel 2005: 60, note 40). Although most of these borders have now been successfully demarcated, a number of its sovereignty disputes still remain unresolved: with Japan over ownership of energy-rich islands in the East China sea, with some ASEAN members over the islands and atolls in the South China Sea, and with India over their land border. The inability to resolve these issues should make us circumspect in discussion of China and the use of force; but in the twenty-first century – a time of growing Chinese military power – Beijing has not resorted to force to resolve these questions. Instead, it has utilized both peaceful mechanisms and some coercive diplomacy in an attempt at resolution or management.

Two explanations for the Chinese resort to force over many of these matters in the past have rested on arguments in the scholarly literature that pay no heed to the potential regulatory effects of prohibitive norms or the alignment between domestic and global values; rather, they emphasize relative power considerations. First, the Chinese leadership is said to operate on the basis of what can be described as trend analysis, or "windows of opportunity": that is, when military or political conditions appear likely to turn against Beijing, then leaders believe that early use of force is better than waiting (Christensen 2006c: 51). Fravel's finding, in respect of territorial disputes, on the other hand, stresses that "negative shifts" in bargaining power best explain China's resort to force.[37] He goes on: "China has used force against adversaries that possess military forces capable of contesting its control of disputed land. China has also used force in conflicts where it has occupied little or none of the land that it claims. When China has faced an adversary seeking to increase the amount of disputed territory that it occupies or to improve its position in the local military balance, China has usually responded with force to signal resolve to maintain its claims, or, at times, to seize part of that territory" (2007/08: 47).[38] Neither of these positions, then, offers an opportunity for normative constraints on the use of force to affect calculations in Beijing, either in the past or future; nor do they dwell on domestic reasons for the shifts in behaviour and attitudes towards security observable in recent decades. However, they imply that as the number of such disputes has declined, China's behaviour is able to conform more closely to the global prohibitions on the use of force.

Another major explanation for China's past resort to force is mainly doctrinal or ideological. During Maoist times, Beijing argued that war with imperialist states was inevitable, and that wars of national liberation were just wars which therefore should be viewed as defensive because of the aggressive nature of colonial occupation. In that latter case, the PRC was in tune with the use of force norm as articulated by some members of the Non-Aligned Movement and local leaders in many colonial and post-colonial states. In addition, Chinese leaders emphasized the military doctrine of "active defence": defined by Mao himself as "offensive defense, or defense through decisive engagements" (quoted in Whiting 2001: 105). This does not rule out the idea of a first strike.[39] Indeed,

---

[37] Fravel argues that the "windows of opportunity" approach is an alternative explanation to the one he advances, meaning "when one state enjoys a sudden and favorable increase in the local military balance in a dispute" (2007/08: 78). But it is worth underlining that Christensen's "windows" includes force used against superior foes. As Christensen puts it, "CCP leaders have used force – sometimes against superior foes or their allies – because they feared that, if they did not, the PRC's strategic situation would only worsen further" (2006c: 51).

[38] Note also Fravel's other findings in respect of China's territorial disputes where he demonstrates that it has settled seventeen of its twenty-three territorial disputes since 1949, "usually receiving 50% of the contested land" (Fravel 2005: 46). His 2008 book offers a fuller discussion of this argument.

[39] As China's Defence Minister, Peng Dehuai, put it in 1957: "when we are expecting an imminent large-scale offensive attack by the enemy against our country, are we permitted

according to Allen Whiting, "students of Chinese military affairs" have found that "seizing the initiative is embedded in doctrine as a preferred course of action" (Whiting 2001: 105). "Active defence" (still relevant to Chinese military thinking in the twenty-first-century Scobell suggests [2003: 34]) actually implies not only acceptance of preemption, but also of the need for preventive uses of force – striking before actual physical provocation occurs.

However, as noted earlier, despite elements of continuity, Chinese military doctrine has evolved and crucially this has involved rejection of Mao's emphasis on the inevitability of major war. This, then, points to a fundamental source of change in China's relationship with the global use of force norm: a shift in domestic beliefs, together with consolidation of the Chinese state. Deng Xiaoping, an authoritative political actor around which other political actors coalesced, argued that world war was not inevitable, peace and development were the dominant trends of the era, and economic reform and opening, together with greater international involvement, should be China's way of showing its desire to support and benefit from those trends (Deng 1987: 116).[40] From the 1980s, China emerged with a government focused on economic development, one that offered the promise to its citizens that only the Party-State could offer social and political stability and improvement in the material quality of their life.[41] President Jiang Zemin argued at the 16th Party Congress in 2002 that the first twenty years of the twenty-first century were a time

to act first and launch an offensive strike against enemy territory or not? We may consider this unacceptable. Yet, in such a situation, the chief criminal culprit is the enemy who originally schemed to launch the war." He went on to suggest that if, in these circumstances, China struck first: "In this case our war in defense of the motherland would be completely just" (quoted in Scobell 2003: 35).

[40] Of course, it must be remembered that Deng authorized the major inter-state war with Vietnam in 1979, and there were several subsequent skirmishes with Vietnam in the 1980s. But in a 1985 speech, he stated "The danger of world war still exists. Because of the arms race between the two superpowers the factors making for war will increase. But the people want peace and oppose war, so the world forces for peace are growing faster than the forces for war.... As long as the forces for peace continue to expand, it is possible that world war will not break out for a fairly long time to come, and there is hope of maintaining world peace." He went on: "China must concentrate on economic development if it wants to become a modern, powerful, socialist country. Therefore we need a peaceful international environment and are striving to create or maintain one" (Deng 1987: 116).

[41] These ideas were intimately connected in Deng Xiaoping's view. As he put it on 13 January 1987, "Opening to the outside world is no simple matter, and reform is even more difficult. None of these endeavours can succeed in the absence of stability and unity" (Deng 1987: 169).

of "important strategic opportunities, which we must seize tightly" in order for China to be able to achieve its goal of building comprehensive national strength.[42] Beijing thus came to emphasize the need for policies that ensured a peaceful regional and global environment in order that it not be diverted from this central task. This firm linkage of domestic values and interest with external relations helped cement the more pacific and less disruptive approach to global and regional order that has prevailed in the last two-to-three decades and that has brought closer alignment with the global norm.

Economic reform transformed China's relationship with the global political economy and therefore its understandings about how instabilities could be generated. Many of China's elites acknowledge that the country has benefited from economic globalization, and that any disruption of trading and investment patterns would have dire consequences for its growth rates, its social and political stability, and the stability of neighbouring countries (Kim 2009). As China's President of the China Institute of Contemporary International Relations has put it: "China's [e]mergence with economic globalization accelerated after the mid-1990s" and it became "a noticeable beneficiary and key proponent of the system." He went on: "though the negative impact of globalization on China is real ... three decades of history authoritatively conclude that China's growing relationship with the world has largely been benign and the interaction mutually stabilizing" (Cui 2008: 9). Fu Ying, when Director-General of the Department of Asian Affairs in China's foreign ministry, placed emphasis on the benign political and security benefits for others of China's late twentieth century resurgence, arguing that globalization and regionalization now made it impossible for a rising power to exploit and bully other countries. She went on: "Every large country needs stable and prosperous frontiers, 'to enrich its neighbours', and move forward together on the development path. China is not an exception. Time has made a choice for China" (Fu 2003: 307). The architect of "peaceful rise," Zheng Bijian, concluded that "striving for national aggrandizement by relying on territorial expansion and military aggression is doomed to failure" (quoted in Glaser and Medeiros 2007). China's 2008 Defence White Paper, published in January 2009, stated: "the future and destiny of China have been increasingly closely connected with the international community. China cannot develop in isolation from the rest of the world,

---

[42] Jiang Zemin, "Build a Well-off Society in an All-Round Way and Create a New Situation in Building Socialism with Chinese Characteristics," 8 November 2002, at http://english. peopledaily.com.cn/200211/8/eng20021118_106983.shtml, accessed 20 February 2009.

nor can the world enjoy prosperity and stability without China" (China's Defense White Paper 2009).

On the other hand, China's reform and opening strategy has been so successful that its resurgence has created something of a security dilemma (Zhang and Tang 2005). Where once leadership goals were encapsulated in the protection of national unity and territorial integrity, together with the socialist revolution at home and promoting revolution abroad (if mostly only rhetorically), the requirements now are much greater. Unity and territorial integrity, alongside protection of the political regime, undoubtedly remain paramount, but as a major trading nation with growing resource needs China now has maritime interests to protect.[43] Its citizens working abroad in often unstable locales have been subject to kidnapping and violence, and Chinese expectations are that the Chinese state will offer them protection. Nationalist sentiment inside China is undoubtedly fuelling its naval and other military ambitions, with some-what unpredictable consequences (Ross 2009).[44] With increased capacity, greater need for resources, and higher expectations among its citizenry, use of force decisions will be subject to influences of several different kinds and the leadership's interpretations of self-defence could well alter.

This enhancement in capacities has already changed the nature of its foreign relationships, especially with its neighbours (Shambaugh 2005). Yet, any excessive use of its various forms of leverage, let alone a use of force in its own neighbourhood, not only would be disruptive economically but would generate sufficient unease that local states' security strategies, based on hedging in response to China's resurgence, would likely harden. Beijing witnessed the speed with which life could be breathed into the "China Threat" theory through its use of coercive diplomacy against Taiwan in 1995 and 1996, and its occupation of Mischief Reef in late 1994 – territory in the South China Sea claimed by Taiwan and the Philippines (Deng 2006; Fravel 2008a: Chapter 6).[45]

---

[43] China's 2006 Defence White Paper puts it thus: the military's goals are to "stop separation and promote reunification, guard against and resist aggression, and defend national sovereignty, territorial integrity and maritime rights and interests" (quoted in *China Daily*, 29 December 2006). Lampton notes that in 2002, 84% of China's oil imports came on foreign flagships and about 80–85% of these imports "flow through the vulnerable Straits of Malacca" (2007: 245).

[44] See also "Challenge US Dominance, A Report of Senior Colonel Liu Mingfu's Book *The China Dream*," which argues that China should build the world's strongest military. *Reuters*, 1 March 2010.

[45] A great deal of attention became focused on this seizure because it was the first time that China had "actively asserted itself against a claimant other than Vietnam, destroying the myth that China would only act aggressively towards Vietnam and leave other claimants

The leadership's responses to these dilemmas arising from the enhancement of its relative power have been three-fold: first, to undermine the argument that China's rise is threatening and destabilizing; second, to emphasize that its priorities are basically domestic and revolve around sustaining economic development in a globalized economy; and third, to show by its diplomacy that it is a responsible regional and global political actor that adheres to UN norms on the use of force. A number of these commitments are solely discursive. Some involve minor behavioural shifts, such as military-to-military exchanges and more active participation within regional multilateral security institutions. Some officials and analysts – especially those regularly participating in security cooperation with ASEAN states via the ARF – may even have altered their beliefs about how security is best achieved (Johnston 2008: 177–8). Whatever the broader status of that claim for internalization of new ideas on security, certainly violation of these agreements and doctrines would impose serious costs on China, probably leading states of the region and beyond to develop political and security policies that would increase China's levels of insecurity. As David Lampton has aptly put it: "how China deals with its neighbors will be taken as an indicator of how it will employ its growing strength more broadly. China's neighbors are the proverbial canaries in the mine for the rest of the world" (Lampton 2007: 166).

Important to the prominence of this reassurance strategy has been the institutional lead taken by the Ministry of Foreign Affairs with central leadership backing. The leadership's adoption of the term "peaceful rise," later labelled "peaceful development," was perceived as an important counter to the idea that China's resurgence represented a threat. Apparently, initially, it attracted the disapproval of the PLA because the emphasis on "peaceful" was seen as diminishing their role in protecting the state.[46] The PLA also emerged as a major institutional sceptic with regard to the new role of international peacekeeper that more latterly had been thrust upon it, some in the armed forces believing the activity not to be a "top priority" and only of "marginal importance" compared with its mandate of protecting national security (ICG 2009: 26–7). Thus, important to the outcome of Chinese involvement in post–Cold War PKOs with their expanded and intrusive mandates has been the role played by the

---

alone" (Valencia 1995: 6–7). In 1992, China passed a law for the territorial sea, which reiterated its sovereign rights over the South China Sea and authorized the use of force to make good on those claims, if need be. See also note 24 above.

[46] Author interview, Shanghai, December 2008.

MOFA[47] (ICG 2009: 26), backed by President Hu Jintao who called on the PLA to use the opportunity to develop "new historic missions."

With respect to UNPKOs in particular, Chinese leaders have seen the PLA's increasing involvement in these operations as a particularly useful way of signalling its changing normative stance on use of force issues. Growing involvement in PKOs allows Beijing "to cultivate the image of a *responsible great power, and cultivate the image of [a] state which protects international peace*. It also wants to improve the image of the Chinese and the Chinese military" (quoted in Suzuki 2008: 56, emphasis added). Such participation allegedly "has been a public relations success ..., has given the PLA an important boost domestically, and helped massage its image internationally" (ICG 2009: 13) (although it is important to underline that Chinese peacekeepers have been engaged in "civilian" rather than combat-related activities).

Yet clearly the MOFA has not always been able to dominate the decision-making environment. While concern about international image in the cases of Burma and Sudan, together with a threatened boycott of the "Genocide Olympics," brought about some moves to respond to the humanitarian disasters inside these two countries, China's commercial and energy interests have made it problematic for image concerns always to be determinative. As in other issues areas, institutional interests are not coordinated on these questions; instead, the competition between ministries tends to be mediated on a case-by-case basis (ICG 2009: 16).

Broadly, though, international institutions, such as the UN Security Council, have operated in ways that are supportive of MOFA positions. Chinese analysts and officials have referred to the UN as a body that derives its authority from the fact that it represents an international procedural consensus: there is nothing else available to play this role, so many Chinese commentators aver.[48] In order to demonstrate that it is a responsible great power, privileged to hold a permanent UN Security Council seat, Beijing has stated a firm willingness to respect the UN Charter and its prohibitions on the use of force except in certain defined

---

[47] Author interview, Beijing, September 2008.

[48] As former Chinese Foreign Minister Qian Qichen put it, the UN is the "most universal, representative and authoritative international organization in the world" (Qian 2004). China's Position Paper on UN reform of June 2005 repeats this: "the UN plays an indispensable role in international affairs. As the most universal, representative, authoritative inter-governmental international organization, the UN is the best venue to practice multilateralism, and an effective platform for collective actions to cope with various threats and challenges."

circumstances. China's response to the international political debates on the conditions that might allow for preemptive or preventive uses of force has been to argue against these more expansive definitions of self-defence, because they are disruptive of world order. President Jiang Zemin is on record as stating in September 2001 that any attack on terrorist targets required "conclusive evidence, specific targets, compliance with the UN Charter, and a role for the Security Council" (Kramer 2007: 104), a view Beijing reflected in the WSO debate in 2005.

Involvement in the institutional environment of the Security Council has also been a major factor behind China's somewhat more relaxed interpretations of state sovereignty and the concept of intervention. Undoubtedly, China's preferred position in response to humanitarian crises is to remain focused on non-coercive means for dealing with these and on building the capacity of states so that violations of human rights are not at a level that would attract the attention of other political actors. If intervention is seriously contemplated, then its preference is that the UN Security Council must authorize any operation, wherever possible there should be host state consent, and force should only be used when all other options have been tried and have manifestly failed. China's actions in this issue area are designed to ensure the R2P's conservative application.

However, while China has worked to ensure a constrained interpretation of R2P, it has not acted as a blocking force in the debate over its further development and implementation. Instead, it has placed itself at the conservative end of the spectrum of R2P interpretation: that states do have a responsibility to protect their own people from the four crimes of genocide, war crimes, ethnic cleansing, and crimes against humanity, as listed in the WSO document; that the 2005 consensus is not open to being renegotiated; and that emphasis should be given to preventive action (GCR2P 2009; Foot 2009b). Pang Zhongying is probably right when he argues that compromise in Beijing's position has come because it came gradually to recognize that "R2P could be used to bridge the divide between supporters of 'humanitarian intervention' and supporters of state sovereignty and non-intervention" (2008:43), but it was those debates within the institutional context of the UN that led to the exploration of this idea and that realization.

In light of internal unrest, continuing sovereignty disputes, the de facto independence of Taiwan, and uncertainties surrounding the future relationship with the United States, Chinese uses of force cannot be ruled out. However, changes in domestic belief about the inevitability of war, and its overwhelming interest in growth and development through integration into the global political economy, have undoubtedly constrained China's potential for the unilateral use of force. In reference to the use of force for humanitarian purposes, China has found itself in reasonably close alignment with the evolving norm's focus on preventive mechanisms rather than military intervention in response to gross violations of rights. Certainly, Beijing will not be prominent in moving that norm in a more solidarist direction – indeed R2P might turn out to be an instance where a norm retreats rather than advances. On this particular issue, China has been able to help shape that norm's interpretation and content, relatively sanguine in the knowledge that its more conservative approach to R2P will find support among other UN member states.

3 The United States and the Use of Force

The US government played a leading role in negotiating constraints on the use of force that resulted in passage of Article 2(4) of the UN Charter (Luck 2006). However, noted in passing in the previous section is that only one state has been more dispute prone than China, and that is the United States. The caveat has to be made that this says nothing about whether the United States is the aggressive party in the disputes in which it is involved. Although different datasets code in different ways under different definitions – serious inter-state disputes, displays of military power for political reasons, and the like – one coding exercise using an expansive definition records 506 incidents in which the United States resorted to a military option between 1870 and 1995,[49] and another dataset notes 395 cases between 1946 and 1995 (Fordham 2004: 636–7). From 1989 to 2001, the United States intervened using "significant military force on eight occasions: once every 18 months."[50] As one author has concluded, "possession of a very sharp sword indeed appears to have been a source of temptation" (Fordham 2004: 652).

The US blade is certainly very sharp. With over 1.5 million in the armed forces, almost one million in the reserves, one quarter of a million permanently stationed abroad at over 700 military bases, and many thousands deployed overseas in actual operations, the US military presence has been ubiquitous. The United States stands preeminent in controlling

[49] This calculation included both "physical changes in the disposition of military forces" for political ends, as well as actual "'martial' uses of force" (Fordham and Sarver 2001: 462).

[50] Ivo H. Daalder, "The Next Intervention: Legitimacy Matters," *The Washington Post*, 6 August 2007.

the sea and air lines of communication. America has been preponderant since 1945, as Melvyn Leffler accurately has put it (Leffler 1992), a preponderance that was particularly marked in the late twentieth and early twenty-first centuries. In 2008, the US defence budget stood at $607 billion, representing 41.5 percent of the world's total spending on defence (SIPRI 2009: 11). Over the course of fiscal years 2001–07, SIPRI calculated that US military expenditure increased by 59 percent in real terms (2008: 179).[51] The Clinton administration's final strategy paper, *A National Security Strategy for a Global Age*, affirmed that the goal remained to have the "best-trained, best-equipped, most effective armed forces in the world" able "to respond to the full spectrum of threats." That full spectrum included the "physical security of the American homeland and the territories of our allies, the physical safety of American citizens at home and abroad, the protection of our infrastructure, including energy, banking, finance, transportation, and water systems, and the protection against the proliferation of weapons of mass destruction" (quoted in Leffler 2005: 403–4). The underlying goal remains in place.

Elaborate legal justifications have often accompanied America's frequent uses of force, more so than most other governments have offered in similar circumstances (Gray 2008a: 11). For Ian Hurd, who gives more weight to rhetoric than to behaviour, this illustrates the extent to which states – even the most powerful among them – are social actors embedded in normative frameworks (Hurd 2007: 196). However, Washington has not always convinced the intended audiences. The Soviet Union during the Cold War tended to put forward legal justifications that were "unexceptionable in themselves," but controversial with regard to the interventions to which the legal doctrines were applied – for example, Hungary 1956, Czechoslovakia 1968, and Afghanistan 1979 (Gray 2008a: 12). The United States, on the other hand, justified intervention in Indochina in the 1960s and Nicaragua in the 1980s on the grounds of collective self-defence. Its wide interpretation of self-defence, referencing Article 51, was used to explain intervention to protect nationals in places such as the Dominican Republic, Iran, Grenada, and Panama, as well as reprisal raids against Libya in 1986, and Iraq in June 1993 (because of its alleged involvement in an assassination attempt on former President

---

[51] *The Military Balance* figures put the US Department of Defense (US DOD) budget at $675 billion in 2008 and $664 billion in 2009. It states that between 2000 and 2009, that budget rose by around 75% in real terms. (IISS 2010a: 22–3). Secretary of Defense Robert Gates has requested $708 billion for 2011. *The Economist*, 6 February 2010: 47.

George H. W. Bush in April that year). Attacks on a training camp in Afghanistan and pharmaceutical plant in Sudan in 1998 were justified as self-defence in response to the targeting of US embassies in Kenya and Tanzania that same year (Gray 2008a: 196–7). As Gray notes, not all of these reprisal actions attracted the widespread condemnation of other states, but "those who refrained from condemnation or expressed support were careful not to adopt the US doctrine of self-defence" (Gray 2008a: 197).

Most controversial of all has been the US attachment to preemptive and preventive uses of force, controversial whenever US administrations have articulated such ideas, but particularly so when articulated in the first term of the George W. Bush administration. President Harry S. Truman may have once stated: "We do not believe in aggression or preventive war. Such a war is the weapon of dictators, not of free democratic countries like the United States" (quoted in Shue and Rodin 2007: 1); but as Leffler has argued, the idea of preventive war has deep historical roots. President Theodore Roosevelt favoured taking preventive action in the Caribbean and Central America – using military force to establish an order sufficient to "preclude European powers from having any excuse for inserting their forces on America's periphery" (Leffler 2005: 398). And reducing the PRC's power in Asia, even if it risked war, appeared in Eisenhower-era strategy documents (Leffler 2005: 399).

The early post–Cold War era saw further evidence of this US attraction to prevention. In December 1993, the US Secretary of Defense, Les Aspin, announced the "Defense Counterproliferation Initiative" as the Clinton administration's central response to new threats. In April 1996, US Secretary of Defense William Perry raised the spectre of a world in which "rogue states" were immune to deterrence calculations and thus had to be crippled before they could act.[52] The Presidential Decision Directive 39 of June 1995 that focused on the countering of terrorism made clear that the United States would do all it could to develop the capabilities to "detect, prevent, defeat, and manage the consequences of nuclear, biological or chemical (NBC) materials or weapons used by terrorists." There was "no higher priority than preventing the acquisition of this capability from terrorist groups potentially opposed to the U.S." (quoted in Leffler 2005: 404).

These earlier initiatives became a more fully developed doctrine in the first term of the George W. Bush administration, arising mainly from the

---

[52] In 1999, Perry and Ashton Carter published *Preventive Defense: A New Strategy for America*.

terrorist attacks of September 2001. The Bush Doctrine, as it came to be called, and as outlined in the US National Security Strategy (USNSS) document of September 2002, elevated the case for preemption, or more accurately preventive action, to a security doctrine rather than a series of responses to particular threats. With that doctrinal status, it gave far greater prominence to similar ideas articulated under Clinton.

The USNSS document disturbed other states because it was produced by an administration that had little respect for international law, overwhelming military power, and deep ambivalence about multilateral action. That document stated in part: "The United States has long maintained the option of preemptive actions to counter a sufficient threat to our national security. The greater the threat, the greater is the risk of inaction – and the more compelling the case for taking anticipatory action to defend ourselves, even if uncertainty remains as to the time and place of the enemy's attack. To forestall or prevent such hostile acts by our adversaries, the United States will, if necessary, act pre-emptively." In attempting to tie this to a legal argument, the document noted: "For centuries, international law recognized that nations need not suffer an attack before they can lawfully take action to defend themselves against forces that present an imminent danger of attack. Legal scholars and international jurists often conditioned the legitimacy of pre-emption on the existence of an imminent threat – most often a visible mobilization" of armed forces. It went on: "We must adapt the concept of imminent threat to the capabilities and objectives of today's adversaries" (USNSS 2002: Section V).

The Bush Doctrine, in committing the fallacy of determining "general doctrine" from "a few hard cases," undermined the non-intervention norm "more directly than was necessary" (Roberts 2004: 145), and it stretched the self-defence norm well beyond what other states were willing to tolerate. For Hurd, it was a "profoundly revisionist" move and "expressly designed to delegitimize the existing practices around pre-emption and institutionalize a new norm based on a different understanding of imminence" (Hurd 2007: 199). When, in 2002 and 2003, UN member states came to debate the basis for any military intervention in Iraq, it is likely that many had the Bush Doctrine in mind when determining their positions, rather than the claim that Iraq was in violation of previous UN resolutions and therefore merited punishment.

Thus, despite a more multilateralist stance and more vigorous attempts at engagement in international diplomacy during the last two years of the second Bush administration, the effects of that first term in office were to associate the United States strongly with a revisionist position on the normative prohibition on the use of force. In his early years in power, Bush had gone against the grain of global opinion on this normative framework and broadly found that he was unable to legitimate his administration's particular interpretations of the norm.

The Obama administration's NSS of May 2010 has tried to retreat somewhat from the Bush era's positions, downplaying preemption and prevention, emphasizing the need to build international consensus, and making clearer distinctions between wars of choice and wars of necessity. In addition, the State Department has produced a "Quadrennial Diplomacy and Development Review": a deliberate attempt to underline this shift in emphasis by matching the quadrennial review regularly produced by the Defense Department. Clinton has also promised to promote "development as an equal pillar of our foreign policy, alongside defense and diplomacy."[53]

At the same time, US behaviour in important instances does not match this new rhetoric. While US forces remain in Iraq, the United States has stepped up its involvement in fighting in Afghanistan and Pakistan, including the decision to deploy an extra 30,000 US troops. Moreover, and controversially, the Obama administration has increased the use of unmanned aerial vehicles (drones) in operations designed to kill alleged terrorists.[54] While President Obama might have preferred to move closer to the international consensus regarding self-defence and to move away from prevention, the fact of US involvement in fighting has made that move more difficult to execute.

US positions in relation to the evolving humanitarian intervention norm, especially in its more intense development from the early 1990s, have been complex and variegated. During the Cold War, the United States was generally in tune with the prevailing preference for denying humanitarianism as a legitimate basis for uses of force. It preferred the term "self-defence" rather than humanitarian action when it intervened to protect its nationals overseas. Despite the atrocities committed by Pakistani forces in East Pakistan in 1971, America's Ambassador to the

---

[53] Hillary Rodham Clinton, "Remarks on Development in the 21st Century," 6 January 2010 at http://www.state.gov/secretary/rm/2010/01/134838.htm, accessed 15 January 2010.

[54] *The Wall Street Journal* stated that Pakistan and Yemen had both given permission for these drone operations, adding: "Even if they hadn't, the U.S. would be justified in attacking enemy sanctuaries there as a matter of self-defense." "The Drone Wars," 9–10 January 2010. *National Journal* magazine reported the Obama administration "ordering a record 50 drone strikes on suspected terrorists in 2009 compared with 31 the year before" (Kitfield 2010).

UN, George H. W. Bush, stated that the Indian intervention represented a case of "clear cut aggression" and represented a blatant attack on the territorial integrity and sovereignty of Pakistan (Wheeler 2000: 65–9). President Carter's Ambassador to the UN, Andrew Young, had to explain US criticism of the Vietnamese intervention in Cambodia, even though it had the effect of removing the murderous Khmer Rouge from power. He chose to morally censure a regime that had a human rights record rivalling that of the Nazis, but affirmed that Washington remained "equally adamant that a commitment to defend human rights could not justify breaching the rules of non-intervention, territorial integrity, and non-use of force" (Wheeler 2000: 91).

With the ending of the Cold War, those refusals to intervene in support of the abused became more difficult to justify. As President, George H. W. Bush reluctantly came to agree to the provision of "safe-havens" for the Kurds of Iraq – even though initially he categorized the violence as an "internal struggle" or "civil war" that was up to the Iraqis to resolve (Wheeler 2000: 147–52). The US intervention in Somalia in 1992 after a UN Chapter VII resolution (passed unanimously), and the unprecedented seeking of UN authority for it to use force within its own hemisphere, suggested that the United States had begun to test the post–Cold War political possibilities for promoting democracy and humanitarian intervention via the United Nations.

The US attitude towards the use of force for humanitarian purposes, however, did not follow a linear path. A failure to act in Rwanda in 1994 was followed by vigorous military intervention in Kosovo without a UN mandate, and then the circumspect treatment of Sudan when faced with the humanitarian disaster in that country. The Obama administration's ambassador to the United Nations, Susan Rice, before her appointment to the US government in 2009 was on record as stating that the Sudanese government should be given an ultimatum to accept an effective and robust international force or risk "air strikes targeted at the aircraft, the airfields, and the other assets that have been involved in the genocide itself" (Brookings Institution Panel, April 2007: 19). Yet, the official Sudan strategy announced in October 2009 has continued with a more cautious approach promising "frank dialogue," and various incentives and disincentives (Sudan Strategy 2009).[55] In addition, the large-scale loss of civilian life in the Tamil areas of Sri Lanka in May 2009, while

---

[55] See also "Statement of President Barack Obama on Sudan Strategy," http://www.state. gov/p/af/rls/rm/2009/130710.htm, 19 October 2009, accessed 21 November 2009.

they did lead President Obama to call for a halt in the fighting and for steps to alleviate the humanitarian crisis, nevertheless did not lead him to authorize much beyond putting some economic pressure on the government via delaying an IMF loan. Neither did he urge the UN to act under the doctrine of R2P.[56]

This is not to imply there has been no support for the concept of R2P under Obama.[57] During the July 2009 debate over the UN Secretary General's report on R2P, the US representative, Rosemary A. DiCarlo, emphasized the need to develop an early warning system as well as the tools and resources to prevent the eruption of the types of conflicts that lead to wide-scale violations of human rights. She also underlined that "only rarely, and in extremis" would collective measures include the use of force.[58] Secretary of State Clinton's speech on promoting development also focused on prevention, emphasizing the links between violence and poverty.[59] Thus, the Obama administration has placed itself as a supporter of R2P but on the side of preventive action wherever possible. The recognized need to maintain a low profile in the debate in light of the widespread and negative association of the United States with unauthorized military intervention for alleged humanitarian purposes in part explains this caution[60]; but the US military is overcommitted, and the complexity of the issues at stake and cross-cutting interests involved also point towards circumspection.

The US position on elaborating the terms of reference for R2P began in cautious mode during the George W. Bush years, supportive of the

---

[56] US Embassy, Sri Lanka "Remarks by Ambassador Robert O. Blake at his Final Press Conference as U.S. Ambassador to Sri Lanka and Maldives," 20 May 2009 and "Obama Calls for Halt in Sri Lankan Fighting," 13 May 2009 both at http://srilanka.usembassy.gov/, accessed 21 November 2009.

[57] Susan E. Rice, Ambassador, US Permanent Representative to United Nations. "Respect for International Humanitarian Law in the Security Council," 29 January 2009 at http://www.usun.state.gov/briefing/statements/2009/january/127018.htm, accessed 26 August 2009; and "UN Security Council and the Responsibility to Protect," address given at the International Peace Institute Vienna Seminar, 15 June 2009, USUN Press Release 126(09).

[58] Rosemary A. DiCarlo, U.S. Alternate Representative for Special Political Affairs. General Assembly Debate on the Responsibility to Protect. 23 July 2009. http://www.usunnewyork.usmission.gov/press_releases/20090723_146.html, accessed 26 August 2009.

[59] Hillary Rodham Clinton, "Remarks on Development in the 21st Century." Washington DC. 6 January 2010. http://www.state/gov/secretary/rm/2010/01/134838.htm, accessed 15 January 2010.

[60] Interviews in New York October 2009. When the intervention in Iraq in 2003 came eventually to be justified on humanitarian grounds, scepticism of US motives increased.

high-bar phrase "manifest failure" and the circumspect language of paragraphs 138 and 139 of the WSO document (Steinberg 2006; Wheeler and
Egerton 2009: 122).[61] The Obama administration has offered support for
the concept, but that caution remains in place.

Explaining Levels of Behavioural Consistency

US emphasis on an admittedly expanded definition of self-defence as the
major explanation for its decisions to use force shows some ability of
the legal enshrinement of the use of force norm to constrain – if only at
the rhetorical level – the most powerful state in the global system. It also
demonstrates some recognition that Articles 2(4) and 51 (defined earlier) are important global order principles to protect. The United States,
despite its material power, does continue to seek legal justification for its
actions. Yet, it would be seriously misleading to suggest that US behaviour has shown high levels of consistency with this norm as others in the
global community have interpreted it.

Explanations for this lack of behavioural consistency with the global
norm are over-determined in the US case. US possession of a "very sharp
sword" gives its government a range of coercive options that other states
do not have. Relative power, in this sense, clearly matters in explaining inconsistency. Preponderant military power, with ever-more special-
ist capabilities, has also had institutional consequences: the US Defense
Department has emerged as a powerful institutional actor and thus its
officials' views are accorded high respect in both the legislative and
executive branches of government. For some scholars, this has led to the
emergence after World War II of a country with unnecessarily overwhelming military power, best epitomized as a "national security state" and associated with an all-pervasive "military-industrial complex" (Leffler 1992:
Hogan 1998).

Nevertheless, while these power and domestic institutionalist arguments
have some potency, great wealth does not necessarily have to translate
into great military capacity; neither does that power have to be put in
service of an expansive definition of what constitutes self-defence, or used
to deny a primary role for the UN in determining how to respond to
international threats. Underlying these decisions is the sense of US special

---

[61] USUN Ambassador John Bolton, appointed just before the September 2005 World
Summit, described R2P in his memoirs as "a moveable feast of an idea that was the High
Minded cause du jour" (Bolton 2007: 207). Apparently, he objected to language in an
early draft of the WSO document that suggested the Security Council had a legal obligation to intervene when atrocities were occurring (Wheeler and Egerton 2009: 122).

responsibility for world order deriving from its exceptionalist impulse. W. Michael Reisman has put this belief pithily: "The United States functions as the ultimate custodian of international order, the actor of last resort in matters of fundamental importance to contemporary international politics" (1999–2000: 63). If the United States perceives the need to act preventively before dangers gather, then it believes it has a responsibility to do so, not simply for its own security but for global order principles as it defines them.

Some presidents have been more exceptionalist than others; some might better be described as "exemptionalist" rather than "exceptionalist" (Ruggie 2005). However, both understandings draw on the presumed resonance between US national values and universal values, a perspective promoted particularly strongly after 1945 (McDougall 1997:174). Echoing Presidents McKinley and Wilson, President Truman claimed that "God has created us and brought us to our present position of power and strength for some great purpose" (quoted in McDougall 1997: 169). When his administration first threw its weight behind Article 2(4), that was largely because there was this presumption of a direct correspondence between US and global values (Luck 2006: 65).[62] The Kennedy administration also had no doubt about the intimacy of that relationship, President Kennedy stating for both a domestic and international audience that America would "pay any price, bear any burden, meet any hardship, support any friend, oppose any foe, in order to assure the survival and the success of liberty." During the Reagan era, the ambassador to the UN, Jeane Kirkpatrick, put that global role more prosaically, describing the UN Charter position on the use of force as broadly sensible, but "hardly in itself a sound basis for either US policy or for international peace and security" (quoted in Gray 2008a: 29). The Clinton administration's ambassador to the UN, Madeleine K. Albright, spoke of the United States as the "indispensable nation" that stood tall and saw "further into the future" than other governments. USNSS 2002 in its introduction noted that America possessed "unprecedented – and unequaled – strength and influence in the world" but went on to underline that this possession came with "unparalleled responsibilities, obligations, and opportunity."

While the United States has sometimes accorded Israel special license to interpret the self-defence doctrine quite broadly, when other governments have tried this or to assert a world order role, US administrations

---

[62] As US Secretary of State Stettinius said to Truman: "the standards of conduct of this country permit us to assume this obligation with no hesitation" (quoted in Luck 2006: 65).

have usually given them short shrift. During the 1956 Suez crisis, Britain and France claimed, among other things, to be acting as a "police force" in the international interest only to be admonished by an Eisenhower administration critical of its allies' undermining of the UN Charter. US overt intervention in 1965 in the Dominican Republic on the basis of an alleged need to protect its nationals and at the express invitation of a government that it actually went on to overthrow did not later constrain its criticism of the Soviet intervention in Afghanistan in 1979. Then, Moscow claimed to be acting on the basis of collective self-defence because the government it had recently put in power had invited Soviet support to deal with foreign aggression. President Carter described this act, instead, as a violation of the UN Charter. Israel's attack in June 1981 on the Iraqi nuclear reactor elicited US condemnation of this preventive attack of an "unprecedented character."[63] And lest these be seen as proclivities associated with Cold War politics, even after the 11 September 2001 terrorist attacks, US exceptionalism continued to manifest itself. Washington claimed a right to act preemptively and preventively where it found evidence of terrorist activity, but when Russia used a self-defence argument to bombard Chechen positions in Georgia in response to terrorist attacks by Chechens on Russian soil, the United States "deplored the violations of Georgian sovereignty and spoke of bombings by Russian aircraft *'under the guise of* antiterrorist operations'*, even though it acknowledged that Georgia had not been able to establish effective control over the eastern part of the country and accepted a link between the Chechen forces and Al Qaida" (Gray 2008a: 230–1).

This US tendency to proclaim a custodial role for itself received allied support during the Cold War in part because of the inability of the UN Security Council to function as intended in response to threats to international peace and security. However, US positions during the first years of the twenty-first century have been deemed far more controversial, and some have attracted a great deal of hostility. This was so because the Bush administration between 2001 and 2008 married exceptionalism with a set of neo-conservative beliefs that suggested total "moral clarity about [the] forces of good and evil" in world politics; and the certainty that others would find beneficial a world where the United States had both "strategic and ideological predominance" (Khong 2008: 256). That administration had strong faith in the wisdom of putting US military force in service of

---

[63] Discussion of these cases can be found in the compilations available in the *American Journal of International Law*, various years, "Contemporary Practice of the United States Relating to International Law."

these goals and an equally strong conviction that "international law and institutions" were ineffective as a means to obtain either peace or justice (Khong 2008: 258).[64]

Under Obama, there have been some adjustments to these earlier beliefs. As the President put it in response to a question about American exceptionalism, his national pride did not "prevent him from 'recognizing that we're not always going to be right, or that other people may have good ideas, or that in order for us to work collectively, all parties have to compromise ... And that includes us'" (quoted in Broder 2009: 898). However, exceptionalist arguments and beliefs, together with contemporary US involvement in major conflicts, will continue to challenge a more consensual interpretation of the self-defence norm, and the general prohibition on the unilateral use of force.[65]

With respect to the concept of humanitarian intervention, now circumscribed and more strictly defined within the idea of the Responsibility to Protect, three major forces appear to have shaped US attitudes. Contemplation of such action was undoubtedly easier after the ending of the Cold War when it was assumed that national security goals did not always have to trump the call to "save strangers." However, the intensity or otherwise of domestic civil society pressures, the power of competing interests, and the retention of control over strategic decision making appear to have been influential in determining the US relationship with the use of force for humanitarian ends. President George H. W. Bush's support for the "safe havens" in Iraq in 1991 only came when Turkey expressed concern about the Kurdish refugees flooding across the border, and especially after pressure from the US public and Congress. The US Secretary of State, James Baker, informed Bush that the administration had to change course. Even then, the President needed to be convinced that the operation would be temporary, and could rapidly be handed over to the United Nations (Wheeler 2000: 147–52). In the case of Somalia, it was seen as an operation that would be over quickly at low cost and might provide the outgoing Bush administration with the legacy it desired – "a glittering humanitarian success" (Wheeler 2000: 190).[66]

---

[64] As President Bush put it on 11 December 2003, "International law? I better call my lawyer ... I don't know what you're talking about by international law" (quoted in Sands 2005: 205).

[65] The 2010 *Quadrennial Defense Review Report* promised "whenever possible" use of force within an "internationally sanctioned coalition," but repeated US commitment to "the ability to act unilaterally and decisively when appropriate" (US DOD 2010: 10).

[66] That the norm of humanitarian action in support of "strangers" can be perceived as capable of offering a "glittering success" is instructive.

The subsequent loss of life of eighteen US Rangers in a firefight, and the dragging of a Ranger's body through the streets of Mogadishu, led to a US unwillingness to act in response to the atrocities in Rwanda. As Clinton put it in May 1994, the United States had no vital interests that it needed to defend in Rwanda. His National Security Adviser, Anthony Lake, reported that there was not enough non-governmental organization (NGO) noise for US-supported action to occur. And although Clinton later apologized for US inaction in response to the genocide, it became clear that his administration would not act solely for humanitarian reasons: US security interests had also to be engaged (Wheeler 2000: 229; Power 2002). Kosovo in 1999 was one such case where action was called for: the West had to stop the terrible atrocities but US interests were also at stake in protecting NATO credibility and Europe as a stable and democratic space (Wheeler 2000: 266). In the 2000s, Sudan has loomed large. Yet, while there have been genuine humanitarian concerns, while various quarters in the United States have persuaded the administration to adopt a more forceful posture towards the government in Khartoum, and the Bush administration labelled the conflict there as tantamount to genocide, it has not used coercive military action to stop the atrocities.[67] The complexity of any solution to the problems in Sudan, together with a US focus on anti-terrorism, as well as the over-extension of the US military in Iraq and Afghanistan, have served to constrain the use of force option.

Finally, there is protection of the domestic sovereign right to determine strategic decisions. The US government has long found it unacceptable that its freedom to decide on action involving the use of force can be circumscribed legally or otherwise by outsiders. Hence, there has been an unwillingness ever to place its armed forces under UN Command, even when the United Nations has endorsed or supported a military operation in which US troops have been involved. In addition, because of its overwhelming military and logistical capabilities, together with its vocal civil society, the US government knows full well that it will often be pressed by others to take action in circumstances where it would rather not be drawn in. Thus, it has sometimes stood with China and Russia – if for different reasons – in criticizing UN attempts to codify the circumstances under which the international community might be required to intervene for humanitarian purposes, and remains keen now to give support to the preventive pillars of R2P.

---

[67] For one critical analysis of this failure to act see Williamson (2009).

Two main factors explain US behavioural inconsistency with the global norm: its available military capacity, and belief that its national goals correspond closely with the interests of global society. However, its frequent attempts to argue that it is legally compliant with Article 2(4) of the UN Charter – an Article that it played a large role in establishing – has exposed the divergence between its position and a more consensual understanding of the global norm. The United States thus sometimes has had problems in persuading other actors of the legitimacy of its positions.

4 The Bilateral Relationship and Behavioural Consistency

The Sino-American relationship has played a role in shaping each state's understandings of the role of force in international relations. Unlike the US relationship with the Soviet Union, within five years of the ending of World War II, China and America found themselves as adversaries on the Korean battlefield. This direct experience solidified their mutual enmity at that time, underpinned for both sides the legitimacy of certain uses of force, and helps to account for continuing strategic distrust in the contemporary era. America's two major Cold War conflicts – Korea and Vietnam – were motivated by the need to contain an allegedly expansionist and aggressive Communist China disruptive of world order. Washington argued it was operating on behalf of the "free world" to halt the communist menace. Indeed, the United States went through the UN General Assembly in 1951 to label the PRC (and North Korea) aggressors in the Korean conflict and therefore ineligible for UN membership, a position that voting rules allowed it to uphold until 1971 in Beijing's case.

China's own participation in these conflicts (the first using the fiction of a volunteer army and the second intervention by covert means), on the other hand, was avowedly to halt imperialist aggression, in support of just war principles, and to protect China's territorial integrity. A major consequence was the US attempt until 1972 to contain Beijing's alleged expansionist tendencies through diplomatic isolation, basing arrangements, regional military alliances, and economic sanctions. Until the improvement in relations in the early 1970s, the prospects for violence between them remained an ever present prospect, given their opposing world order perspectives.

The status of Taiwan has also long been another point of contention between the two states, particularly during the Cold War. Chinese coercion towards Taiwan and the Offshore Islands in 1954, 1958, and

1995–96 were in part a determination to signal – at times of increased levels of US support for the island's authorities – that China would use force to prevent any legal separation of the territory from the mainland. The US goal was to signal that China would not be permitted to use forceful means to resolve this matter. And in that mutual signalling, both governments have been able to provide some clarification of where the line on using force has been drawn in both capitals. This clarification has been of use in constraining violence as a means of effecting a resolution of China's outstanding territorial claim to the island (Ross 2000). However, Taiwanese de facto independence and US support for the island have been significant drivers behind China's military modernization plans. The issue has long been volatile and has required continued careful handling by all three protagonists to prevent periodic crises erupting into war.

Undoubtedly, since the 1972 rapprochement in Sino-American relations and intersection of the 1979 normalization in ties with China's reform and opening, the prospects for direct conflict between these two states have diminished. Beijing has for a decade or more described its approach to the United States as "developing cooperation and avoiding confrontation" (quoted in Medeiros 2009: 98). Paradoxically perhaps Beijing's strategic distrust of the United States has helped to promote more pacific Chinese foreign policy rhetoric and behaviour. Beijing initially used the development of its "New Security Concept" stressing common security to form the basis for criticism of the United States' continued use – and even strengthening in the case of Japan – of "old-style bilateral military alliances" with their Cold War characteristics (Foot 2006: 85). Beijing's improvement of ties with most of its neighbours, while central to its goal of an orderly region that allows a focus on domestic economic development, has also been linked with its aim to ensure that any US attempt to constrain its resurgence will be unsuccessful.[68] As Huang Renwei of the Shanghai Academy of Social Sciences put it in 2006: "The United States has never given up its efforts to establish a 'small-sized NATO' and has been trying its best to build a strategic balance of power in Asia using Japan and other regional powers to pin down and to use against China" (quoted in Medeiros 2009: 54).

US intervention in Kosovo in 1999 and its use of force against Iraq in 2003, outside the remit of the UN Security Council, reinforced China's strong vocal commitment to reserving a central place for the Council

[68] Author interviews, Shanghai, December 2008.

in responding to international threats to peace and security.[69] Similarly, when the George W. Bush administration emphasized preventive uses of force to deal with new threats, this induced a clarification of the Chinese position on this attempted normative reinterpretation. In Beijing's view, UN Charter principles were adequate to the task and needed no revision: thus, it was one of the states that supported an end to the debate that had been raised directly in the HLP report on prevention and preemption, topics that eventually were left out of the WSO document entirely.

China's conservative positions on preventive uses of force and on R2P are encapsulated in its preference for a Westphalian interpretation of state sovereignty that stresses non-interference in internal affairs. However, the staunchness of this support and general unease about interventionist practices come less from a fear of direct US intervention on Chinese soil and more from a suspicion that the United States might attempt the strategic encirclement of China.[70] China's caution relates to its perception that a United States seemingly unrestrained by UN Charter rules might have no compunction in moving in a way detrimental to Chinese interests – whether in Burma, the Democratic People's Republic of Korea (DPRK), or elsewhere.[71]

The rapprochement between China and the United States and the subsequent resurgence of Chinese power has resulted in a more mixed outcome for America. While relations have been far easier to handle and beneficial strategically overall since 1972, US adjustment to China's rising power and presence has not been easy for it, and we cannot be sure that serious clashes between these two states will not occur at some time in the future, perhaps over matters involving freedom of the seas.[72] The US Department of Defense's Quadrennial Defense Review (QDR) of 2006 stated that: "Of the major and emerging powers, China has the greatest potential to compete militarily with the United States and field disruptive

---

[69] Li Xuejiang, writing in *Renmin Ribao*, offered one of the staunchest criticisms: "the United States opposes any constraints, despises the United Nations, violates international law, obstructs democratic principles, and disobeys the will of the people in the whole world against war. It upholds the supremacy of force, pursues free unilateral action, and openly advocates imperialist rule of the world," *Foreign Broadcast Information Service, Daily Report, China (FBIS-CHI-2003–0728)*.

[70] Of course, China is incensed by global and US criticism of its heavy-handed methods of dealing with internal unrest, especially in minority ethnic areas.

[71] This view is hardly unknown elsewhere in the world. See Hurrell (2006).

[72] A standoff in the South China Sea in March 2009, when Chinese ships harassed a US navy surveillance ship, the USNS *Impeccable*, is indicative of the areas where "rules of the game" urgently need to be established.

military technologies that could over time offset traditional U.S. military advantages absent U.S. counter strategies" (US DOD 2006: 29). A clarification of the requirements of the alliance with Japan including air base rights, improved relationships with India and Indonesia, and access for US aircraft carriers to the Changi naval base in Singapore relate in part to China's rise. With these improved alignments in place, the expectation is that, were relations with Beijing to deteriorate, then the United States would have the option of responding with a range of tools from coercive diplomacy to military force, in concert with other states. Or, as the QDR of 2006 baldly put it: "Should deterrence fail, the United States would deny a hostile power its strategic and operational objectives" (US DOD 2006: 30).

However, while it is the case that strategic distrust continues to characterize this bilateral relationship, it is also recognized that involvement in direct conflict would be severely costly for both sides and for their partners and allies. This recognition has helped to stabilize ties and provided incentives to note common as well as competitive interests. On R2P, both states have taken a stance that affords some basis for reconciliation of their positions even if those positions are based on different motivations and beliefs. The normative framework associated with the use of force speaks directly to the question of world order; for the time being at least it is a far less direct matter of concern in their bilateral relationship than was the case in the 1950s and 1960s.

5 Conclusion

Both China and the United States have recognized the value of the legal enshrinement of the use of force norm within the UN Charter and both have given rhetorical support to this global normative framework. US supportive rhetoric has relied predominantly on the use of an expansive definition of self-defence for itself, and on statements exhorting others to respect the demands of the Charter. Even at the time of its 2003 military intervention in Iraq, in the end an intervention based on a limited coalition of the willing, it had been persuaded to attempt prior UN legitimation of its action. China, in recent years, has similarly tried to signal a level of respect for the norm, but in discursive terms predominantly by signing regional agreements that have ruled out the use of force for settling issues in dispute and by offering staunch verbal support for the UN Charter and the central role of the Security Council in dealing with threats to international peace and security.

However, when it comes to the actual behaviour of the two states in respect of a norm that is symmetric in form – that is, it should apply equally to both states – we begin to see divergence. China's behaviour has become more pacific in the last two to three decades as the state has consolidated, boundary agreements have been signed, and its territorial disputes have reduced markedly in number. In its own region, it has sought to underline this shift towards what it has described as responsible great power behaviour primarily through enhanced support for multilateral security frameworks, and engagement with modest confidence building measures. Globally, it has begun to contribute to UNPKOs, currently offering the second largest contribution of all P5 members. Underlying this shift in behaviour has been a central objective to ensure a peaceful regional and global environment in order that Beijing can concentrate on its economic development goals. Beijing, and particularly the MOFA, has also understood the requirement of attending to its image: it must attempt the difficult task of reassuring its neighbours that there is no threat to be had from a resurgent China. This has become especially challenging at a time when increased economic power has resulted in a sizable modernization of its military programme with defence budgets that over several years have often outstripped levels of economic growth.

This sensitivity to international perceptions has also influenced China's positions on potential uses of force for humanitarian purposes and R2P. Wary of breaches of the non-interference norm and protective of its interests in states that stand accused of abusing the rights of their peoples, China has been constrained by the development of the R2P idea and its associated commitments. Debate of these issues within what it projects as an authoritative UN body – the Security Council – has heightened its awareness of trends in opinion at both the individual state and regional organizational levels. Even though China is no supporter of R2P, neither is it blocking its advancement, in part because it perceives as legitimate the procedure that led to the World Summit Outcome document and R2P, and very few other states are stopping discussion of the concept either.

US behaviour with respect to the global norm has been far less constrained, however. Its military capacity, the high degree of latitude that it enjoys when it contemplates strategic action, together with its presumed custodial role when it comes to the interpretation of the needs of global order, have resulted in frequent divergence from common understandings of the global norm of self-defence. Neither do US political elites accord the United Nations as high a degree of procedural legitimacy as does China or some other states.

While there have been many instances, especially during the Cold War, when US military actions gained the support of its major allies, America has been less successful in generating support in the post–Cold War era for its arguments in favour of a role for the preventive use of force. However, that lack of international approval has mattered to some US administrations more than others, depending on their attitudes towards international law and the United Nations.

On humanitarian intervention and R2P, while the United States is sympathetic to arguments made on humanitarian grounds, its position also reflects a long-standing concern that others will press it to take action when its priorities lie elsewhere, or its interests are not also significantly engaged – thus, a concern about distributive fairness. In response to the current debate over R2P, the Obama administration has indicated its support for ways to prevent atrocities from occurring in the first place, and prevention clearly mitigates concerns about distributive questions. This stance on R2P is not strongly at odds with views voiced in Beijing, even if different values underpin their convergent position.

Force and its prospective use defined the Sino-American relationship in significant ways at the height of the Cold War. But more recently the bilateral relationship has not influenced their respective positioning with regard to the normative framework as directly as in the case of nuclear non-proliferation, climate change, or macroeconomic surveillance. It is the case that China's staunch support for a conservative reading of the UN Charter, the prominent role it gives to forging a UN Security Council consensus on use of force questions, and the determination to stabilize its relations with its neighbours are in part dictated by its fears of US strategic encirclement. But those fears do not determine every aspect of the relationship, and both sides have made some effort to stress the interests they hold in common.

3

Macroeconomic Policy Surveillance

Macroeconomic policy "surveillance," as James Boughton (2001: 67) points out, did not become part of the formal language of the International Monetary Fund until the Second Amendment of its Articles of Agreement in 1977. The revised Article IV (Section 3a) set out two distinctive forms of policy surveillance: "multilateral surveillance," requiring the Fund to "oversee the international monetary system to ensure its effective operation," and "bilateral surveillance," requiring it to "oversee the compliance of each member with its obligations under Article IV, Section 1."[1] Article IV is concerned with member state "obligations regarding exchange arrangements," though it also contains general language on each member state's obligations to "endeavor to direct its economic and financial policies toward the objective of fostering orderly economic growth with reasonable price stability."[2] The IMF's general surveillance function thus stems from an assumed mutual responsibility to collaborate in the setting of macroeconomic policies, with, as we shall see, particular emphasis on countries' exchange rate policy obligations (IMF 2006c). The primary objective of such surveillance "is, through thorough analysis, candid discussions, and a peer-review mechanism, to promote the domestic and

---

[1] Bilateral surveillance by the IMF over individual member country policies is conducted mainly through "Article IV consultations," which are typically held annually. The main instruments of multilateral surveillance are the semiannual World Economic Outlook and Global Financial Stability reports. In a general sense, even "bilateral" surveillance is associated with multilateralism, the idea of institutionalized interstate cooperation based on norms and principles of conduct (Caporaso 1992: 600–1).

[2] "Articles of Agreement of the International Monetary Fund," http://www.imf.org/external/pubs/ft/aa/index.htm, accessed 20 March 2010.

external stability of members' economies and thereby the stability of the international monetary system as a whole" (IMF 2009d: 3).

As a normative principle, international macroeconomic surveillance can be traced back to the system established at Bretton Woods in 1944, and it developed over the following decades. It was founded on the recognition, borne of the painful experiences of the 1920s and 1930s, that global economic stability required a minimal degree of consistency in the macroeconomic policy choices of (at least) the most important countries. This was most obvious in the area of exchange rate policy, when in the wake of the breakdown of the restored international gold standard in the early 1930s a number of countries engaged in beggar-thy-neighbour currency devaluations that increased political tension and further reduced international trade. By the time of the Bretton Woods agreement, there was also growing acceptance by the major industrialized democracies of the newer Keynesian idea that fiscal and monetary policy should be oriented towards the stabilization of the domestic economy. This new policy priority raised difficult questions about how domestic macroeconomic activism was to be reconciled with the goals of global monetary order and open international trade. IMF surveillance was meant to reconcile these domestic and external priorities by fostering sufficient policy consistency among countries to promote stability of exchange rates and to prevent the reemergence of large international payments imbalances that had proven such a fatal flaw of the system in the 1920s (James 1996: Chapter 1).

The ambitions and dilemmas of international surveillance over macroeconomic policies raise issues that have been central to global order over the past century and remain so today. It also reflects the tensions in a hybrid system of global order with which we are concerned in this book. First, global macroeconomic stability has public good characteristics for most actors in the system, but the growing pressures on governments to respond to domestic societal demands for growth in incomes and employment make this difficult to achieve. These domestic pressures have made it very difficult to make international surveillance concrete by agreeing to specific, binding rules that constrain domestic policy choices in ways that are widely perceived as legitimate. Second, although the IMF was intended to be the dominant locus of surveillance in the global economy, various other organizations and ad hoc groupings dominated by the major developed countries have come to supplement and sometimes to detract from its role. Third, as the multilateral organization in which formal rules are most developed,[3] the IMF's surveillance mechanism has often been ineffective in constraining the policy choices of its most influential members, to the detriment of its global stabilization objectives. By contrast, weaker states – especially those that borrow from the IMF – have often perceived IMF policy constraints to be both substantial and illegitimate. This perceived illegitimacy has been enhanced by the long-standing dominance of the major developed economies, and the particularly privileged position of the United States, within the IMF (Woods 2006). For all of these reasons and more, contentious debates about reform of the surveillance system have persisted ever since the multilateral framework was established.

These debates reached a new peak in recent years in the wake of increasingly large and frequent financial and economic crises, persistent and widening imbalances in international payments, and the rising importance of non-Western countries in the global economy. Some critics argue that IMF surveillance has been most ineffective in constraining policies in the major emerging countries, above all China, and have asked whether the post-1945 multilateral framework can be sustained in the face of this challenge (Goldstein, 2007; Bergsten, 2008; Wolf, 2008). Although the history of IMF surveillance shows that this problem is in fact not at all new, growing US frustration with Chinese "monetary mercantilism" has threatened to disrupt the burgeoning trading relationship – and even the broader political relationship – of the two countries. For China, the increasing contentiousness of international surveillance has become problematic for its broad strategy of membership in and conformity with major global institutions. For other key actors in the global economy such as the EU, the "global imbalances problem" became seen as being characterized primarily by large US payments deficits and Chinese surpluses and thus as an essentially bilateral US-China issue.[4] This position underestimates the global dimensions and impact of the imbalances problem, but the centrality of the United States and China to it has become increasingly clear.

The normative framework of international macroeconomic surveillance has some key features relevant to our discussion. First, it has

---

[3] At a regional level, the European Union's internal processes of macroeconomic policy coordination and surveillance may be more extensive and well developed, although similar problems of coordination and enforcement arise.

[4] Author discussion with official from the Directorate-General for Economic and Financial Affairs, London, 30 November 2009.

very high levels of domestic social and political significance because, as mentioned previously, it directly concerns areas of policy that affect incomes and employment at the aggregate level and income distribution within societies. Second, the rules and procedures of the framework distribute adjustment costs differently across countries. As we discuss later in this chapter, the framework places more specific constraints on countries' exchange rate policy choices than on the fiscal and monetary policy choices of countries that are not IMF borrowers. Third, this bias reflects the historic dominance of the major developed countries and particularly the United States within the various processes of international surveillance and in the Fund itself. Mainland China is a relative newcomer to international macroeconomic surveillance and has not enjoyed anywhere near the level of influence over the development of the surveillance framework as the United States or major European countries. Fourth, the relative lack of consensus among economic experts over the causes and consequences of international payments imbalances has hampered the further development of the norm and the procedural legitimacy of surveillance itself.

The first section of this chapter explores in more detail the framework of international surveillance and its evolution over time. The second and third sections address the evolving degree of behavioural consistency of the United States and China, respectively, with its main norms and rules. It then explores why the United States came to take a relatively critical and ambivalent stance towards the framework that it had played such an important role in establishing and why China has much more recently done so. A fourth section asks how the bilateral US-China relationship has affected the stance of each country towards the multilateral framework. We argue that the bilateral trade and financial relationship between China and the United States has become increasingly central to the future of the international surveillance framework, but the difficulties of managing this relationship have weakened rather than strengthened the commitment of both countries to this framework.

1 The International Macroeconomic Policy Surveillance Framework

The first norm of the international surveillance framework is that national macroeconomic policies should be subject to international, peer-based surveillance and constraint. This core norm has its origins in the international monetary negotiations of the early 1940s, which culminated in the Bretton Woods agreement of September 1944. The large international payments imbalances in the years after World War I became seen as important contributors to the instability and eventual collapse of the international gold standard and the international trading system. This convinced officials in the United States and the United Kingdom that a new global monetary framework, involving institutional and regulatory innovations, would be a necessary condition of a more stable and prosperous post-war global economic order. This system also had to reflect the new and explicit desire of governments to pursue domestic macroeconomic stabilization policies (Ruggie 1982; Ikenberry 1992; James 1996: 22–30).

The institution made responsible for maintaining the stability of the global monetary system, the IMF, would oversee the agreed system of pegged exchange rates and advise governments when changes in par values were required to correct fundamental disequilibria in international payments. However, Article 1(i) of its Articles of Agreement put the IMF's oversight role in very vague terms, stating that the Fund would provide "machinery for consultation and collaboration on international monetary problems." Another purposeful ambiguity in the Bretton Woods framework was that the concept of a "fundamental disequilibrium" was left undefined, though it was intended to mean a persistent surplus or deficit on a country's balance of payments that was either incompatible with the maintenance of approximate full employment and price stability domestically or created unsustainable strains at the global level.

Since unsustainable payments deficits imply counterpart surpluses elsewhere in the global economy, IMF surveillance would apply to both sides of such imbalances. John Maynard Keynes, then the world's most famous economist and also the leading British policymaker in this area, argued strongly that a deflationary bias within the gold standard stemmed from the fact that deficit countries were under much more pressure than surplus countries to adopt costly adjustment policies.[5] This was because persistent deficits led to a loss of monetary reserves to surplus countries, with the result that deficit countries suffered weakening currencies that they were compelled to defend via fiscal and monetary contraction. Surplus countries such as the United States and France in the 1920s could comparatively easily block costly adjustment by "sterilizing" the impact of gold inflows through central bank operations that broke the link between gold

---

[5] For an analysis of the deflationary bias of the gold standard system, see Eichengreen (1992).

acquisition and domestic inflation. Not least because Britain expected to face continuing large external deficits and America large surpluses after World War II, Keynes believed that it was crucial to ensure that the new international monetary order placed symmetrical adjustment pressure on both deficit and surplus countries through a system of monetary fines.

Although the US Treasury's negotiating team, led by the economist Harry Dexter White, was largely convinced of this Keynesian principle, it was substantially constrained by the desire of the administration and Congress to use America's now dominant financial and strategic position to its advantage (Boughton 2002). This domestic constraint meant that the establishment of a multilateral institution with the power to direct or constrain economic policy choices in surplus countries was out of the question. However, the Treasury team did feel able to make a small concession to the British demand by offering in December 1942 what became the "scarce currency clause" in Article VII (3). In principle, this clause provided for IMF-authorized sanctions, mainly in the form of temporary exchange restrictions, on countries whose large persistent surpluses produced a shortage of their currency in the Fund. In practice, the system of weighted voting on the IMF's Executive Board and the large share of votes controlled by the United States meant that it could always block such a move.

Thus, although the significance of the scarce currency clause remains a matter of debate, it reflected a second, albeit weaker norm of international surveillance: that countries running persistent current account surpluses had an obligation to contribute to the international adjustment process. This second norm was also implicit in the agreement that the IMF could provide loans to countries experiencing temporary payments deficits so as to avoid the need for excessively deflationary policies. As it turned out, the scarce currency clause was never invoked even during the decade or so of persistent "dollar shortage" after the end of the war, when the Truman administration ceased the financial assistance to its two major allies associated with the Lend-Lease programme. In practice, large persistent deficits in Europe were financed by Marshall Aid from 1948 and later by the substantial US government military-related outflows that followed the outbreak of the Korean War. Devaluations by most western European countries of about 30 percent against the US dollar in the late 1940s were also an important contribution to the eventual restoration of approximate international payments equilibrium.

These developments in the early Cold War period were also indicative of a general tendency for the United States and its allies to deal with international economic issues outside of the formal framework of IMF-based surveillance, which inhibited its further development. By the late 1950s, dollar shortage had turned into dollar glut, and new surplus countries such as West Germany absorbed large amounts of dollar-denominated foreign exchange reserves. This shifted the focus and the politics of surveillance. By 1961, mutual surveillance had been adopted by the G10 group of industrialized countries as one of its core responsibilities.[6] G10 macroeconomic surveillance was conducted not within the IMF but in the more exclusive developed country club, Working Party 3 (WP3) of the Organization for Economic Cooperation and Development (OECD). WP3's remit was to "analyze the effect on international payments of monetary, fiscal and other policy measures, and ... consult together on policy measures, both national and international, as they relate to international payments equilibrium" (quoted in James 1996: 181).

Before the late 1960s, the US position was that appropriate adjustment mechanisms included fiscal and monetary policies but *not* exchange rate policies, because of a desire – which they shared with the British – to keep the international roles of the dollar and sterling off the surveillance agenda (James 1996: 183). This position, however, did little to promote international surveillance and policy coordination because national fiscal and monetary policy choices were broadly seen as too sensitive to be negotiated at the international level. In any case, the US position changed as its current account surplus eroded sharply in the late 1960s, and the current surpluses of West Germany and Japan continued to grow. Although the United States did not record its first annual current account deficit in the post-1945 period until 1972, US policy towards the major surplus countries had already shifted substantially. By the end of late 1960s, the United States and the United Kingdom demanded that the major surplus countries, particularly West Germany and Japan, revalue their currencies against the dollar, a demand consistent with the second norm of the Bretton Woods system. The perceived reluctance of these surplus countries to undertake sufficient adjustment measures was a major reason for the growing dissatisfaction within US officialdom with the Bretton Woods system generally and the system of international surveillance specifically (Solomon 1982: 166–75; Gowa 1983; Walter 1993: chapter 6).

---

[6] The G10 began as a group of creditor countries that provided an additional source of liquidity to the IMF in the form of the General Arrangements to Borrow in 1961. Switzerland joined it in 1964.

The difficulty on both sides with the existing framework was that there was no agreement as to what policy measures were required by the general norm of international surveillance, and particularly how the costs of adjustment should be distributed. The surplus countries resisted full acceptance of the second norm that they should share equally in adjustment; instead, they largely sought to blame international imbalances on irresponsibly expansionary macroeconomic policies in the deficit countries, especially the United States (Walter 1993: chapter 6; James 1996: 194–5). Before 1969, the German coalition government was deeply split on the question of what measures should be taken, but the refusal of important elements within it (led by Finance Minister Strauss) to contemplate damaging German export interests was a key barrier to a solution. Nor did the major reserve currency countries accept any significant responsibility for adjustment. The United States saw its own persistent payments deficits largely as a "residual" of other countries' demand for dollar foreign exchange reserves and of policies in surplus countries (US Treasury 2008b: 3). In the absence of agreement over the distribution of adjustment responsibilities, rising levels of short-term capital mobility virtually ensured that the system of pegged exchange rates between the major countries was bound to collapse, which it duly did during 1972–73 (Solomon 1982: 166–75; James 1996: 203–27). The IMF's international surveillance function had patently failed to achieve its basic objectives.

Somewhat surprisingly to many contemporary observers, the divide between the developed surplus and deficit countries persisted in spite of the adoption of floating exchange rates by the major developed countries. The G5 club (which later became the G7) succeeded the G10 as the main forum for debate between the main deficit and surplus countries from the mid-1970s. This permitted these major countries to share information informally about their macroeconomic policy choices without ceding more authority to the IMF on surveillance. During the 1970s, the United States argued that the surplus countries should accept either continued currency appreciation or domestic macroeconomic expansion to increase imports. If domestic fiscal and/or monetary expansion was too politically sensitive, then currency appreciation should take the lion's share of adjustment. Other European countries sometimes supported this position. They often ran bilateral deficits with Germany and shared the goal of encouraging it to accept more domestic expansion, as did the IMF, subject as ever to American influence (James 1996: 291).

The IMF surveillance regime continued to be ineffective in reducing international payments imbalances, which widened considerably in the second half of the 1970s. The United States had made a series of formal proposals in the early 1970s to raise the costs for persistent surplus countries, much as Britain had proposed in the 1940s (James 1996: 247–51). But it was no longer in a position to achieve these goals without surplus country support. In collaboration with France, however, the United States did succeed in obtaining agreement on the legalization of floating exchange rates and the formalization of surveillance for all Fund members at a special meeting of the IMF in Jamaica in January 1976. This agreement was subsequently elaborated in the Second Amendment of the Articles of Agreement in 1977, which further narrowed the focus of surveillance upon exchange rate issues. Article 3(b) of the amended Articles stated that "The Fund shall exercise firm surveillance over the exchange rate policies of members, and shall adopt specific principles for the guidance of all members with respect to those policies." The Amendment obliged member countries to cooperate with the IMF in its surveillance function and an associated policy decision further stipulated that: "A member shall avoid manipulating exchange rates or the international monetary system in order to prevent effective balance of payments adjustment or to gain an unfair competitive advantage over other members."[7] The US–French compromise at the basis of this agreement thus strengthened the focus of surveillance on exchange rate policies but did little to impose new multilateral disciplines on monetary and fiscal policies (James 1996: 272–3).

For the major countries, IMF surveillance in practice was limited to annual Article IV consultations of little real consequence and the provision of background papers and data to G7 deputies. Nor was it only fiscal and monetary policies that proved too politically sensitive for international surveillance. Exchange rates proved so politically sensitive that they increasingly were left off the agenda of Article IV consultations as well, even though they provided their formal rationale after 1977 (Sobel and Stedman 2006: 6; Mussa 2007: 1–2). As for the G7, it too produced little in the way of systematic policy coordination, with the exception of a few isolated attempts with mixed results (Funabashi 1989; Webb 1995; Sobel and Stedman 2006). Over the course of the late 1980s and 1990s, the trend towards central bank independence, national inflation targeting, and medium-term fiscal frameworks largely pushed macroeconomic policy off the centre stage of G7 meetings. The major developed countries

---

[7] IMF, "Surveillance Over Exchange Rate Policies," Decision No. 5392-(77/63), 29 April 1977: http://www.imf.org/external/pubs/ft/sd/index.asp?decision=5392-(77/63).

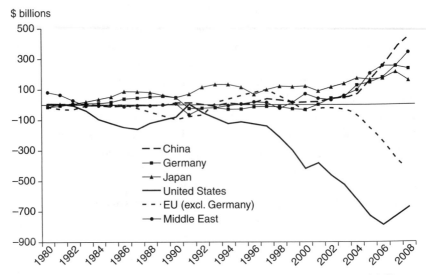

FIGURE 3.1. Current accounts, major countries/regions, 1980–2008, US$ billions. *Source*: IMF, *World Economic Outlook* database. 2008 figures are estimates as of October 2008.

had learned to live with floating exchange rates, and G7 finance minister and central bank meetings in the 1990s were relatively quiet affairs compared to the more controversial debates of the 1970s and 1980s. Only towards the late 1990s did international payments imbalances begin to reemerge as a subject of discussion, mainly due to an increasingly large US current account deficit. The economic optimism that prevailed in America during this period, however, meant that the old concerns about currency manipulating surplus countries were subdued.

This changed as the world economy recovered from the slowdown of 2000–01. US current account deficits continued to grow rapidly, while a few other important countries and regions moved towards substantial surplus positions (Figure 3.1). Germany and the oil exporting countries had returned to surplus positions, and Japan's surplus also began to rise again. A number of Asian developing countries had responded to the financial crisis of the late 1990s by maintaining current account surpluses and building their foreign exchange reserves as insurance against future crises. China did not initially stand out among these Asian emerging markets, but during 2004–05 it suddenly emerged as a major surplus country. By 2006, it had surpassed Germany and Japan as the single most important surplus country, at a time when the US current deficit reached unprecedented levels.

These developments had important implications. Although the G7 had never managed payments imbalances between its own members effectively, it was increasingly clear that its exclusivity made it poorly equipped to deal with what had become a global problem. The G7/G8 grouping[8] was reluctant to expand further its permanent membership, and its experimentation with ad hoc invitations to major developing countries from 2000 appeared increasingly unsatisfactory (China attended from 2003). G7 finance ministers and central bank governors reiterated the norm of collective adjustment responsibility, but in a global rather than a purely G7 context at their April 2006 meeting: "the adjustment of global imbalances [is a] shared responsibility and requires participation *by all regions* in this global process."[9] From the perspective of some developing countries, this looked like a request that they accept responsibility without representation.

Difficult for China was the growing consensus among the major developed countries that the renminbi (RMB) was becoming steadily more undervalued and that this was a serious threat to the stability of the global economy. RMB undervaluation was increasingly regarded as an important (though not the only) cause of rising global imbalances, and in particular of America's large current account deficits and China's growing surpluses.[10] In February 2005, G7 finance ministers and central bankers called on unspecified countries to accept that "more flexibility in exchange rates is desirable for major countries or economic areas that lack such flexibility to promote smooth and widespread adjustments in the international financial system."[11] The choice of language was deliberately diplomatic ("greater exchange rate flexibility" rather than currency revaluation), but it was clear to all what it meant. As detailed later, China did permit a very gradual appreciation of the RMB from July 2005 (Figure 3.2), but its current surpluses continued to grow rapidly. As a result, the United States and some other G7 governments argued that much more was needed. In April 2006, the G7 called explicitly for the

[8] Russia joined the grouping to create the G8 in 1997, but G7 finance ministers and central bank governors often continued to meet in the narrower grouping to discuss economic matters.

[9] Statement by G7 Finance Ministers and Central Bank Governors, Washington, DC, 21 April 2006. All G7 statements can be found at the following site: http://www.g8.utoronto. ca/finance/index.htm. (Italics added.)

[10] For early contributions to the debate, see Dooley, Folkerts-Landau, and Garber (2003); Obstfeld and Rogoff (2004); Bernanke (2005); Cooper (2005); IMF (2005a: chapter 3).

[11] Statement of G7 Finance Ministers and Central Bank Governors, London, 4–5 February 2005.

FIGURE 3.2. Dollar exchange rate indexes: euro, yen, and RMB, January
2000 through July 2010 (3 January 2000 = 100).
Source: US Federal Reserve Board currencies database.

further appreciation of the RMB: "In emerging Asia, particularly China,
greater flexibility in exchange rates is critical to allow necessary apprecia-
tions, as is strengthening domestic demand, lessening reliance on export-
led growth strategies, and actions to strengthen financial sectors."[12] As
we discuss later, the United States was crucial to this initiative, though
the EU and Japan were willing to provide some support because dollar
depreciation after 2002 meant that they perceived growing costs for their
own economies from RMB undervaluation.

The evident shortcomings of the G7/8 process also shifted attention
back to the possibilities of the more formal processes of IMF surveillance.
During 2006–07, the IMF convened a special set of multilateral consultations on global imbalances that brought together IMF members deemed
to be "systemically important": China, the euro area, Japan, Saudi Arabia,
and the United States (IMF 2007). These discussions, however, produced
few concrete results. China committed itself to "further improving the
exchange rate regime," the European Union to improving internal market
flexibility, and the United States to "fiscal consolidation over the medium
term" and "tax incentives to support private saving" (IMF 2007). In all
cases, these policies had already been announced unilaterally, though

[12] Statement by G7 Finance Ministers and Central Bank Governors, 21 April 2006.

during the period 2005–08, the RMB appreciated against the US dollar by 18 percent, and slightly less in real effective terms (it *depreciated* against the euro over the same period). After the consultations were completed in April 2007, the IMF itself projected that global imbalances – in particular the current account deficit and surplus of the United States and China, respectively – would continue to widen in the foreseeable future, which was hard to reconcile with its claim that the consultations had been a "success."[13]

The Independent Evaluation Office (IEO) of the IMF reached the unsurprising conclusion in 2007 that IMF surveillance of exchange rates had often been ineffective (IEO 2007). Notably, this study found that the levels of understanding of and commitment to exchange rate obligations by member states were often low, and that many countries were strongly of the view that surveillance was not even-handed. The major countries themselves were to a considerable extent to blame for this failure, but by this time they had come to see the weakness of IMF surveillance as a problem. The G7's dominance of the IMF Executive Board proved useful in pushing through an initiative to strengthen the language on currency manipulation set out in the 1977 Amendment. In June 2007, the Executive Board approved the *Decision on Bilateral Surveillance over Members' Policies*, which replaced the 1977 rules as the guiding document on bilateral (i.e., IMF–member state) surveillance. This Decision put the focus of bilateral surveillance on the question of whether a country's policies promoted "external stability." Although this modification of the surveillance mandate in principle included all relevant macroeconomic policies, the main focus of the revised rules remained on exchange rate policies:

The 2007 Decision provides that a member would be "acting inconsistently with Article IV, Section 1 (iii)," if the Fund determined it was both engaging in policies that are targeted at – and actually affect – the level of the exchange rate, which could mean either causing the exchange rate to move or preventing it from moving; and doing so "for the purpose of securing fundamental exchange rate misalignment in the form of an undervalued exchange rate" in order "to increase net exports."[14]

China, along with a few other developing countries, voted against this revision, which was unusual for a board that normally operates by

[13] IMF, World Economic Outlook database (estimates in April 2007, October 2007, and April 2008).
[14] "IMF Surveillance – The 2007 Decision on Bilateral Surveillance," http://www.imf.org/external/np/exr/facts/survo7.htm, accessed 5 March 2008.

consensus.[15] Some prominent American commentators openly expressed the hope that it would allow the IMF to be more robust in its exchange rate surveillance by downgrading the apparent need to prove "intent to manipulate" and by allowing the Fund to make the less politically charged finding of "fundamental misalignment" (Goldstein and Lardy 2007: 38). Many were highly critical of the Fund itself, arguing that it was shirking its global responsibility by refusing to declare China in breach of its legal commitments.[16] The IMF's own *Triennial Review of Surveillance* identified various weaknesses in the surveillance process, including the lack of analysis of linkages between macroeconomic and financial sector developments, but it also noted a continued resolve to integrate exchange rate analysis into the surveillance process (IMF 2008). The 2007 Decision also specified seven indicators that would serve as "triggers" for exchange rate surveillance, with the stated goal of decreasing the subjectivity of IMF judgements and the political sensitivity of the process. These triggers included protracted and large-scale one-way intervention in exchange markets, the use of capital controls, fundamental exchange rate misalignments, and large and prolonged current account deficits or surpluses. Thus, although the 2007 Decision did not openly discriminate between member countries with floating and pegged exchange rates, it raised the risk that any country with an exchange rate target and consistently positive net exports could be judged in breach of multilateral rules.

The US government was active in interpreting the 2007 Decision as strengthening the IMF's exchange rate surveillance mandate. According to the US Treasury (2009c: Appendix 2), "[t]he 2007 Decision restored exchange rate surveillance's position at the core of the IMF's mandate." This underlined the continued relative laxity in multilateral constraint over other macroeconomic policies and reflected the interests of the major developed countries, who had long since prioritized monetary and fiscal policy autonomy over exchange rate stabilization. It was less consistent with the interests of many developing countries, who have a strong revealed preference for exchange rate targeting (Reinhart and

---

[15] Interviews, Chinese officials, Beijing, September 2008.

[16] Mussa (2007: 2, 40) argues that international surveillance withered on the vine over the course of the 1990s and that the IMF has never found any member country in breach of its obligations under the currency manipulation rule. However, there were two cases of special IMF consultations with individual countries in the 1990s after US and German complaints of currency manipulation by the Republic of Korea and Sweden, respectively (Sanford, 2006: 41). The currency manipulation clause may also have had some deterrent effect on other countries, though this is difficult to substantiate.

Rogoff 2002; Reinhart and Reinhart 2008). There are various reasons given for this preference, notably the view that pegged and undervalued exchange rates promote economic development and can substitute for a range of institutional weaknesses common to developing countries (Broz 2002; Rodrik 2008). China, so often untypical of developing countries, is more typical in this regard. Even so, it remained unclear how much difference the 2007 Decision would make in practice. As the IEO evaluation of IMF exchange rate policy surveillance concluded, "The reduced traction [of IMF surveillance] with advanced economies is in danger of being extended to large emerging market economies, and beyond" (IEO 2007: 35).

The global economic crisis of 2008–09 had the paradoxical effect of pushing negotiations on global imbalances off the agenda of international surveillance in the short term whilst strengthening the argument that global imbalances needed to be tackled more effectively in the medium term. In mid-2008, China returned to a policy of a fixed peg against the US dollar, which strengthened during the initial stages of the crisis and weakened after March 2009 (Figure 3.2). As we discuss later, this reflected China's unwillingness to continue RMB appreciation as its exports fell, as well as a perception that other major countries now had more important concerns than the value of China's currency. Nevertheless, there was a growing consensus in Western economic policy circles that the emergence of persistent large imbalances in international trade and finance was an important factor in the unsustainable boom that preceded the global financial crisis of 2008–09 (Dunaway 2009; FSA 2009: 32; IMF 2009a; Brender and Pisani 2010).[17] The IMF Executive Board agreed in October 2008 on a statement of surveillance priorities to guide surveillance through 2011, among which was a commitment to promote an "orderly reduction of global imbalances."[18] Under considerable pressure from the United States and other developed countries, the G20 leader's summit which succeeded the G7 as the key informal body responsible for global economic policy coordination during the crisis, also pledged to address global imbalances more effectively in the future. Within the G20, only two countries (China and Saudi Arabia) retain explicit exchange rate targets, though some other countries continue to deploy capital controls and to intervene in foreign exchange markets to smooth fluctuations.

---

[17] For a dissenting argument, see Dooley, Folkerts-Landau, and Garber (2009).
[18] "IMF Executive Board Adopts Surveillance Priorities for 2008–2011," IMF Press Release No. 08/238, 8 October 2008.

At the Pittsburgh summit in September 2009, G20 leaders accepted a collective "responsibility to ensure sound macroeconomic policies that serve long-term economic objectives and help avoid unsustainable global imbalances" and to a strengthened process of multilateral review and consultation supported by the IMF.[19]

For its own part, the IMF has recommitted itself to be – in Keynes's phrase – a "ruthless truth-teller" in the wake of the crisis. Dominique Strauss-Kahn, IMF Managing Director since November 2007, persistently criticized China's "undervalued currency" and called for a return to a policy of RMB appreciation.[20] The other main cause of global imbalances he identified was the general one that developing countries preferred to accumulate national foreign exchange reserves instead of relying on an IMF that they felt did not sufficiently represent their interests.[21] Elsewhere, the IMF has also argued that the United States and other major developed countries must also contribute to the reduction of global imbalances through medium-term fiscal consolidation (IMF 2009a: 35–7). So far, however, "ruthless truth-telling" with respect to global imbalances has remained largely consistent with the post-war norm, in that undervalued exchange rates appear to be the main concern of the IMF's senior management.

To summarize, the norm of international macroeconomic surveillance was central to the Bretton Woods regime. In practice, however, there was a strong emphasis on the prevention of unfair exchange rate policies and an expectation that international surveillance would not seriously impinge on the national fiscal and monetary policy decisions of countries that refrained from borrowing from the IMF. This norm persisted after the advent of floating exchange rates between the major developed countries. In legal terms, the norm was institutionalized and deepened in 1977 and in 2007, when the IMF Executive Board agreed to tighten the legal obligations of member countries to avoid "manipulating" their currencies to the detriment of other countries and to the stability of the global economy. Important parts of the international surveillance framework, however, remained highly contested. Some surplus countries contested the second Bretton Woods norm that they, with deficit countries, had an equal responsibility to undertake adjustment to reduce global payments

---

[19] "Leaders' Statement: the Pittsburgh Summit," 24–25 September 2009, http://www.pittsburghsummit.gov/mediacenter/129639.htm, accessed 9 October 2009.

[20] "Statement by IMF Managing Director Dominique Strauss-Kahn at the Conclusion of his Visit to China," IMF Press Release No. 09/411, 17 November 2009.

[21] "IMF Chief Renews Call for Currency Reform," *FT.com*, 2 October 2009.

imbalances. Many developing countries also felt that the international framework imposed highly asymmetric constraints on developed and developing countries, since it was the latter who were the main borrowers from the Fund and thus subject to relatively intrusive macroeconomic and microeconomic policy conditionality. They were also much more likely than developed countries to retain exchange rate targets after the early 1970s, so that the legal obligations of IMF membership even for non-borrowers appeared to constrain their policy choices considerably more than those of developed countries. Meanwhile, IMF surveillance seemed not to present a serious constraint on the fiscal and monetary policy choices of the major developed countries.

2 The United States and International Surveillance

As previously noted, in marked contrast to its position in the 1920s and 1930s, the United States came to accept an international obligation to pursue macroeconomic policies that were broadly stabilizing during and after World War II. At the Bretton Woods conference in September 1944, the US delegation supported the general norm of international surveillance of national macroeconomic policies. It also took some important steps towards accepting the second norm that surplus countries – of which it expected to remain by far the most important – had a responsibility to share the burden of international adjustment (Solomon 1982: 18). This represented a major shift from the US stance in the interwar period, which denied any such surplus country responsibility.

As noted earlier, the practical importance of the scarce currency clause remains in some doubt. But some in the administration did accept the need for the world's largest surplus country to adjust: Harry Dexter White personally favoured a substantial reduction in the large US holdings of gold after the war finished (James 1996: 45; Skidelsky 2000: 251–2; Boughton 2002). The Truman administration was well aware that the argument that America could usefully tie its own hands via an internationally binding agreement would be unacceptable to Congress. When the administration decided in mid-1947 that it needed to provide emergency financial assistance to Western Europe, it chose to bypass the Bretton Woods institutions and the scarce currency clause entirely by providing such assistance directly as Marshall Aid from 1948 to 1951 (Solomon 1982: 14–18). Nevertheless, this policy can still be seen as broadly consistent with the norm of surplus country responsibility, as can the US tolerance of large European devaluations in 1949 and of Europe's continuing exchange and trade discrimination against US exports.[22] By the early 1950s, these policies, combined with the large US foreign military expenditures precipitated by the Korean War and outward foreign direct investment (FDI) by American companies, had already begun to eliminate the overall US payments surplus[23] that had dogged the global economy since 1919. Thus, after World War II, the US government accepted to a much greater degree than before (and perhaps any surplus country since) that surplus countries had a responsibility to contribute to the reduction of international payments imbalances.

The consistency of the US government with the first norm of international macroeconomic surveillance is, however, more ambiguous. US efforts to reduce international payments imbalances after the war were, as noted earlier, unilateral and avoided the very multilateral processes that America had played such a central part in establishing. In fact, the US government had always intended that international surveillance would apply mainly to other countries. The main concern of the US delegation in the Bretton Woods negotiations had been to impose multilateral discipline on *deficit* countries, much to the annoyance of the British (Gardner 1980: 96). Implicit in the Marshall Aid programme was the belief that it was other countries' policies that needed monitoring, not those of the United States, whose macroeconomic policy choices remained essentially off-limits for multilateral oversight. The Federal Reserve Act was not modified in response to Bretton Woods, as no multilateral constraint over US monetary policy was either accepted or foreseen. Nor did Congress, which eventually passed the Bretton Woods Act in July 1945 in the face of considerable opposition from farming and banking interests, indicate that it had any intention of accepting multilateral constraints on US taxation and spending policies (Gardner 1980: 129–43).

In short, both branches of the US government saw the new multilateral constraints as applying to others rather than to America. This reflected the new form that American exceptionalism took in the post-1945

---

[22] Some British officials saw the United States' unwillingness to invoke the scarce currency clause in the late 1940s as a betrayal of their commitment to Keynes in the Bretton Woods negotiations. Britain also tried, unsuccessfully, to strengthen the scarce currency clause in the late 1950s, when West Germany had become the main surplus country (James 1996: 108).

[23] Note that the US current account balance remained positive until the early 1970s. From the early 1950s, larger capital account deficits produced an overall deficit that was financed by reductions in US official gold holdings and by foreign accumulations of US government debt (as foreign exchange reserves).

period: US power would be used to transform the world through multilateral institutions. Periodically, the United States itself would need to accept responsibilities for international adjustment and stabilization, but such responsibilities should be freely chosen by US policymakers, not imposed by international institutions. In this conception, other countries of concern fell into two main categories: first, those that borrowed from the IMF, and second, those countries pursuing unfair exchange rate policies. The US government never expected to have to borrow from the Fund and was therefore mainly concerned to limit its own financial obligations to it and to ensure that borrowers repaid IMF loans (Gardner 1980). Although the government was strongly committed to the principle that exchange rates should be fixed, exchange rate decisions came to be seen as relevant only to other countries that chose to peg their own currencies to the dollar. America's main exchange rate obligation under the Bretton Woods system became that of maintaining the dollar's peg to gold, but even this was seen as a matter of national (US) sovereignty.

As the US current account surplus eroded steadily after the late 1950s, and some of America's key allies emerged as the main surplus countries, the tables gradually turned. By the late 1960s, the US government became increasingly frustrated with the apparent refusal of surplus countries like West Germany to accept substantial adjustment responsibility (Solomon 1982: 170). In the Nixon administration, this frustration began to trump the preference of the foreign and defence policy establishment for refraining from disrupting overall relations with key allies. The policy of demanding currency revaluations from West Germany and other surplus countries reached a peak during 1970–71. At the same time, however, the US government consistently refused to accept that it had special responsibilities to adjust as the country running the world's largest overall payments deficit. Instead, it argued that these deficits were a residual, the product of other countries' strong and growing demand for dollars as reserve assets and not, as some European countries insisted, a product of US fiscal irresponsibility (Walter 1993: 168–9).

In August 1971, the Nixon administration decided to force surplus countries to accept their adjustment responsibilities by closing the so-called Treasury gold window and by imposing a temporary 10 percent tariff on US imports (Gowa 1983). When George Shultz became Treasury Secretary in 1972, the United States increasingly viewed floating exchange rates as a means of using market pressure to force Germany, Japan, and others to accept stronger currencies. The United States was also a key mover behind the Second Amendment of 1977, which as we have seen mainly strengthened the legal obligation on IMF members to avoid currency undervaluation (James 1996: 270–7). Through bilateral negotiations and in the G5/G7, the United States achieved some modest successes in encouraging West Germany and Japan to accept some currency appreciation and, at certain points (notably at the Bonn, New York, and Paris summits of 1978, 1985, and 1987, respectively), macroeconomic expansion as a contribution to reducing global imbalances (Funabashi 1989).

But this success came at the cost of breeding substantial resentment among some of America's major allies and of further eroding the legitimacy of the norms of international surveillance and surplus country responsibility. Allies' resentment was enhanced by the fact that the United States refused to accept a different principle – advocated most in Europe – that reserve centre countries had special responsibilities to run "responsible" macroeconomic policies (meaning close-to-balanced budgets and monetary policies consistent with low inflation over the cycle) (Walter 2006a). It was also due to the obvious power imbalance in these negotiations. The domestic politics of fiscal policy everywhere meant that governments found it difficult to make international adjustment commitments (Sobel and Stedman 2006), but the United States seemed to be saying that other countries should accept the lion's share of the domestic political costs. The Reagan administration was not the first to point out – though few needed to do so as explicitly – that America's fiscal and external deficits were partly products of the United States' willingness to bear a disproportionate share of the costs of collective Western defence.

Nor did the United States see the 1977 Amendment to the IMF Articles as having practical application to itself. Even in periods of dollar weakness, such as 1977–78, 1987, and periodically since 2002, US governments were unwilling to accept that this could amount to a breach of America's multilateral obligations. US Treasury officials sometimes even engaged in "talking down" the value of the dollar to put further pressure on surplus countries to accept currency appreciation or domestic reflation (as did Treasury Secretary Blumenthal in 1978). Provisions in the 1988 Omnibus Trade and Competitiveness Act were indicative of this position. Under this legislation, Congress required the Treasury to report biannually on whether particular countries were guilty of currency manipulation and if so for the Treasury Secretary to negotiate with them to remove the practice. This part of the US law is based upon the IMF's currency manipulation rules of 1977, the language of which is carefully crafted so as to deter both persistent under- and overvaluation. However, the clear intent of the US Trade Act was to target countries that pursued deliberate *undervaluation* at the expense of American firms and workers.[24]

This unilateral stance also reflected a Congressional belief that the IMF's enforcement of its currency manipulation rules had been weak and needed to be bolstered by US muscle, and the view that the US administration's own hand needed strengthening. There has always been disagreement within the United States over the respective merits of constructive diplomacy and more aggressive, unilateral actions. Historically, the executive branch has more often favoured the former, in part because of its greater concern with the maintenance of the overall diplomatic relationship with major surplus countries, whereas the legislative branch has seen more merit in unilateralism. But this distinction can be overdrawn. Presidents have sometimes been willing to opt for unilateralism, notably Nixon and Reagan in the case of Japan in the 1980s. Also, Congress has sometimes used unilateral measures of the kind deployed in the 1988 Trade Act as a means of strengthening the administration's bargaining position without necessarily intending to derail broader relations with US partners (Taiwan and Korea were both cited for currency manipulation in 1988). Over time, both tactics became part of the standard repertoire of US economic diplomacy, including vis-à-vis China in the 1990s (see Section 4).

The United States has periodically recognized that its emphasis on the responsibilities of surplus countries can generate perceptions of double standards and weaken incentives for other countries to accept international norms. In February 2007, for example, the Bush administration accepted language along with other G7 countries that: "To be more effective [IMF] surveillance must be applied equally and even-handedly, focused on external stability, and subject to a clear accountability framework, without creating new obligations."[25] As the latter clause emphasized, however, the focus of such surveillance would remain firmly on exchange rates, a position that was subsequently confirmed in the 2007 Decision of the IMF's Executive Board, which the George W. Bush administration strongly supported.[26] There appeared to be a hope that a strengthened IMF would be able to do what US administrations

---

[24] 22 U.S.C. 5304, section 3004.

[25] G7 Finance Ministers' Statement, Essen, 9–10 February 2007.

[26] US Treasury (2008: 2, 6); author interviews, London, November 2008 and Washington, DC, April 2009.

themselves had generally been unwilling to do: explicitly name China and perhaps other countries as undermining external stability by policies serving to undervalue its exchange rate. If so, this hope was soon disappointed. A US Treasury Report in 2008 assessing the impact of the 2007 Decision argued that the IMF had not fully followed through on the commitments the Decision entailed:

For the IMF to retain its central role in the international financial system, it must strengthen its efforts to exercise clear surveillance over IMF members' exchange rate policies and it must not shy away from the job of making tough judgments, especially when these policies are undertaken by large countries and have systemic implications. (US Treasury 2008b: 2)

As regards surveillance over the United States itself, the IMF had argued that the dollar needed to fall further to reduce the external deficit. The George W. Bush administration did not openly dispute this argument, but viewed it as of little policy relevance to a country with a market-determined exchange rate. The IMF also argued for fiscal deficit reduction during these years, but it was very wary of arguing for tax increases to an administration and Congress that were unwilling to listen to such arguments.[27] In G7 meetings from 2005, Washington did accept language calling for US fiscal consolidation as part of a multilateral effort to reduce global payments imbalances. But the emphasis was firmly on spending reductions, and tax increases were not mentioned. In retrospect, it is also clear that before 2008 IMF staff had failed to identify US financial regulatory policies as an important threat to domestic and external stability – in contrast to some other international institutions such as the Bank for International Settlements (see Chapter 6). In these ways, the relative weakness of the IMF vis-à-vis its most important member has substantially reduced both the practical impact of international surveillance and its overall legitimacy.

After the global economic crisis of 2008–09, the Obama administration accepted the G20 language cited earlier that appeared to accept the need to enhance the role of international surveillance so as to prevent the reemergence of large global payments imbalances. The US Treasury also argued that "[e]nhanced multilateral surveillance by the IMF is crucial for both recovery from this crisis and prevention of future economic instability" (US Treasury 2009c: Appendix 2). Whether this reflected a fundamental shift in the United States' stance towards surveillance norms

---

[27] For example, see Rodrigo de Rato, "Global Imbalances and the Transatlantic Relationship," speech at the European Institute, Washington, DC, 10 November 2005.

was, however, unclear. There did seem to be a greater US tolerance for IMF criticism of US policies. In the 2009 Article IV consultation with IMF staff, the Fund reiterated its concerns about the medium- to long-term sustainability of US fiscal policy and noted that the Obama administration's budget projections were based on a number of optimistic assumptions. In addition, in contrast to the mid-2000s, the IMF staff also explicitly recommended tax increases in the medium term to stabilize the government's fiscal position – to which the administration did not openly object (IMF 2009a: 34–5). But it remains unclear how much difference such criticism, with which many American economists and commentators agree, will make in practice.

The historic tendency to see surveillance as applying mainly to others also diminished somewhat in the depths of the crisis. Tim Geithner, Obama's choice as Treasury Secretary, stated in his nomination hearing that the new President believed that China did manipulate its currency, but the administration quickly backtracked from this position. During the nadir of the crisis, the administration assiduously resisted raising the issue directly with China, including in the renamed bilateral Strategic and Economic Dialogue, despite the fact that the Chinese government had re-fixed its currency against the dollar from mid-2008 at the rate of 6.82 RMB per dollar (US Treasury 2009c: 15). In its semiannual report on exchange rate policies in October 2009, like the Bush administration before it, the new administration refrained from naming China as a currency manipulator although it signalled its concern over China's exchange rate policies (US Treasury 2009c). As the global economy began to recover in the second half of 2009, however, with China in the lead of this rebound, the administration also began to argue that it had "serious concerns" about the value of the RMB and that further appreciation was needed.[28] By early 2010, tension over the currency issue had become a major threat to the administration's goal of achieving a positive and stable relationship with China. In April 2010, the administration decided to delay the publication of its semiannual report on foreign exchange rate policies on the grounds that it preferred to allow the G20 and S&ED processes more time to produce new commitments from surplus countries, including China.[29] By the time this report was finally released in July 2010, the Chinese government had decided to revise its exchange

[28] "US Hardens Stance on Renminbi Rigidity," *FT.com*, 16 October 2009.
[29] "Statement of Treasury Secretary Geithner on the Report to Congress on International Economic and Exchange Rate Policies," US Treasury Press Release, TG-627, 3 April 2010.

rate regime, permitting the administration to avoid designating China as a currency manipulator.

Explaining Levels of Behavioural Consistency

What accounts for the persistently lop-sided attitude of the United States towards international surveillance? The vigorous US promotion of such surveillance from 1942 can only be explained by a combination of domestic and international factors, including learning from the experiences and policy mistakes of the interwar period, America's rise to global preeminence during World War II, and the role of Keynesian ideas among key policymakers in the US Treasury. Domestic factors, especially the New Deal thinking in the administration and in the Treasury in particular, were crucial in this global leadership strategy. But so was America's unparalleled creditor and strategic position, which gave it the opportunity to achieve ambitious objectives to remake the world (McDougall 1997: 177). The objective was explicitly not to reform America by binding it to new international treaties and institutions.

By the end of World War II, domestic political support for the New Deal was on the wane, and Congressional resistance to the notion of the United States acting as paymaster for irresponsible policies abroad remained considerable. This was most clearly reflected in the very contentious bilateral negotiations with the British for a large balance of payments loan at the end of 1945. It was also reflected in the view that international surveillance of economic policies was intended mainly for IMF borrowers, who might not otherwise be trusted to repay what was, after all, mainly US taxpayers' money. It was also intended to prevent countries from engaging in unfair currency policies that could endanger US firms and jobs. These asymmetric understandings of international surveillance were the only basis on which Congress could have been convinced to ratify the Bretton Woods Act and to contemplate considerable financial assistance to the IMF, to other international financial institutions, and to the British in 1946 (Gardner 1980: 129–43).

US power has been another important factor from the beginning. The US position towards the international surveillance regime has been asymmetric in part because it could be. The United States provided by far the largest financial contribution to the IMF and would be the dominant player on its executive board; there was no intention that the United States would ever become a borrower. During the Cold War it was the senior alliance partner of the main surplus countries of the time and could bring its unequalled leverage to bear on them. As Webb (1995) has explained, this ability to shift adjustment costs onto others accounts for both the ad hoc nature of G7 cooperation in macroeconomic policy and its asymmetry. Late in the Cold War era, US power was reflected in and reinforced by domestic legislation, in which Congress demanded that the administration enforce IMF currency manipulation rules. The main target by the 1980s was Japan, but Asian developing countries were also seen increasingly as benefitting disproportionately from America's strategic deployments and relatively open markets. The large size of this market for foreign imports was an important source of US leverage, first over Europe and Japan and later over developing countries.

The United States was much more willing to accept the principle that surplus countries should share responsibility for international adjustment – and more so than most surplus countries (Boughton 2002). But the crucial practical policy moves associated with this were the launch of Marshall Aid, later substantial defence-related outflows, the encouragement of large European currency devaluations against the dollar in 1949, continued tolerance of exchange and trade restrictions that discriminated against American exports, and the encouragement of private capital outflows by US firms (Solomon 1982: 18).

It is doubtful that these policies had much to do with the deep internalization of the norm of surplus country responsibility among key US policymakers after 1947, though this was the case for Harry Dexter White and other Keynesians in the US Treasury (Ikenberry 1992). The shift in policy that occurred from mid-1947 instead can be explained mainly by the changing strategic incentives provided by the Cold War, which strengthened the Truman administration's hand compared to business sector and Congressional sceptics of multilateralism. Without the Cold War and the associated strategy of containment, it is unlikely that Congressional opposition to foreign devaluation and protectionism could have been overcome (Gaddis 1982).

Once again, however, it is the combination of American power in a changing global strategic environment and the peculiarities of its domestic values and institutions that best explains these outcomes. Marshall Aid was not just a product of a new containment strategy; it also reflected the particular form that American exceptionalism took in this period, especially the urge to remake post-war Europe in the American image. As Raymond Aron commented, the particularities of the Marshall Aid programme were also driven by

[t]he American propensity to consider their own system exemplary ... After 1945, the Europeans had more to learn than to teach. The Americans, by virtue of their

philosophy, considered it a matter of course to teach others the secret of their own success. (Aron 1974: 191)

As America's European and East Asian allies recovered and prospered in the 1950s and 1960s, concerns about free riding on the part of the beneficiaries of US generosity revived and began to exert greater influence over US policy outcomes. The constitutional importance of Congress in trade policymaking and its susceptibility to domestic interest group pressures made it especially sensitive to business and labour complaints about unfair trade and exchange rate policies in other countries. As allies like West Germany, the Netherlands, and later Japan began to accumulate large trade surpluses and dollar reserves, it became increasingly difficult for administrations still focused on containing communist expansion to ignore exchange rate policies in these countries. These strong domestic institutional incentives to try to deter foreign economic policies that are perceived to put American firms and workers at a disadvantage have been reinforced from time to time by perceptions of relative economic decline. Such perceptions played an important role in the more aggressive unilateralism of the Nixon and Reagan administrations.

US policymakers have had even less compunction in demanding that China revalue its currency more recently. What is puzzling, perhaps, is why this objective was not more aggressively pursued given the uncertainty surrounding China's strategic intentions towards the United States and, since the early 2000s, its extraordinarily large bilateral trade surplus with America. Domestic business and labour interests, working primarily through Congress, have on balance favoured a relatively tough stance on Chinese exchange rate policy. Unions and firms in exposed sectors such as steel and textiles have lobbied hard to have China named as a currency manipulator.[30] So too have some prominent academics and think tanks. Morris Goldstein of the influential Peterson Institute for International Economics has argued consistently that the evidence of Chinese currency manipulation was overwhelmingly strong by the mid-2000s:

China has been engaging in large-scale, one-way, sterilized intervention in exchange markets for the better part of four years. The Chinese authorities continue to assert that they do not accept the concept of currency manipulation, and they

---

[30] See, for example, the membership of the Fair Currency Coalition (until 2008, it was called the Chinese Currency Coalition), which has since 2004 favoured immediate economic sanctions on China: http://faircurrency.org/members.html, accessed 17 November 2009.

have accused the IMF of "meddling" in China's exchange rate policies ... [This] raises doubts about China's intention to become a responsible stakeholder in the international monetary and trading system. (Goldstein 2007: 2–3)

Two main factors have pushed against a more aggressive economic policy towards China. Many large, internationalized US firms benefit from Chinese access to the US market and could lose from RMB revaluation and more generally from a deterioration of the bilateral trade relationship. The US-China Business Council, an industry body representing US firms doing business in China, has publicly favoured RMB revaluation but argued in favour of a diplomatic approach rather than unilateral sanctions.[31] Broader strategic considerations have also favoured a more diplomatic approach. The growing complexity of the bilateral relationship with China has made it difficult for administrations to treat the currency issue in isolation, a factor we discuss in Section 4. The Clinton and George W. Bush administrations also concluded that quiet diplomacy rather than aggressive unilateralism was more likely to produce a positive response from China, a tactic that the Obama administration also appears to accept.[32]

The global economic crisis of 2008–09 also diminished the leverage that the United States has historically enjoyed in this area of international diplomacy. In particular, the crisis significantly increased America's perceived dependence on Chinese financing of its now much larger fiscal deficits. In her inaugural visit to China, Secretary of State Clinton thanked China for its continued purchases of US Treasury bonds and noted the two countries' mutual interdependence. "By continuing to support American Treasury instruments, the Chinese are recognizing our interconnection. We are truly going to rise or fall together" (quoted in Glaser 2009: 2). This statement was perceived in the United States as a mistake, giving the impression that the United States depended significantly on Chinese generosity rather than self-interest; and Secretary of State Clinton and other members of the Obama administration did not repeat it.[33] The crisis also generally weakened US perceptions of policy superiority and increased the influence of the major developing countries in global economic

[31] Wal-Mart is well known as China's major global customer, but high-tech manufacturers such as Apple, Dell, and HP all operate global supply chains in which China-based assembly often represents the final stage. See testimony of John Frisbie, President, the US-China Business Council, Hearing on US-China Economic Relations Revisited, Senate Committee on Finance, 29 March 2006.

[32] Communication to authors from former US administration official.

[33] Communication to authors from former US administration official.

governance, which has in turn increased the pressure on the developed countries to agree to the reform of institutions such as the IMF. Indeed, the United States played an important role in promoting the G20 as the key grouping within which to manage the global economic crisis, with the conscious objective of increasing the voice of emerging countries. The perceived need to maintain consensus within the G20 on policy responses to the crisis also weakened the United States' ability to single out particular countries for criticism. Nevertheless, we argue later that in other ways the global crisis has sharpened the bilateral focus of macroeconomic and currency diplomacy and increased the likelihood of further conflict with China on these issues.

In summary, the United States' stance towards international surveillance is best explained by a complex and evolving interaction between domestic values, economic interests, and political institutions on the one hand and US power on the other. The relative balance of these factors has changed over time with different administrations, although partisanship seems not to have played a decisive role either in the executive branch or in Congress. The balance between these domestic and external considerations has also shifted in response to the changing global strategic environment. US power and normative exceptionalism have combined to ensure that the norm itself, and the international institutions and groupings with which it is associated, have exerted relatively little influence on US domestic policy outcomes. Instead, the United States has viewed international surveillance primarily as a mechanism to constrain the policy choices of others. The effect of this asymmetric stance towards international surveillance, however, has been to inhibit its development and to reduce its effectiveness.

3 China and International Surveillance

China is a relative latecomer to international surveillance and to IMF membership (see Jacobson and Oksenberg 1990: chapter 3). The Republic of China (ROC) was a founding member of the Fund and, because of its political importance to the United States, was granted the fourth largest quota in it. After the Kuomintang relocated the ROC to Taiwan in 1949, communist mainland China was excluded from the Bretton Woods institutions. As Jacobsen and Oksenberg (1990: 62–6) point out, mainland China considered joining the Bretton Woods international financial institutions (IFIs) in the 1970s but decided that doing so would compromise its policy of self-reliance, especially avoiding foreign borrowing, and the principle of sovereign equality.

Deng Xiaoping was well aware that Western countries, above all the United States, dominated the IFIs, but he saw Chinese membership as a means of strengthening the domestic reform process, of raising China's international status at Taipei's expense, and of obtaining access to concessional finance. China joined both IFIs in 1980, having negotiated an increase in its quota share (which had shrivelled under Taiwan's membership) that by 1983 was the ninth largest in the Fund, giving it a single seat on the Executive Board (Kent 2007: 107).

The objective of self-reliance remained strong, however. China indicated that it would obtain project-related financial and technical assistance from the World Bank but did not intend to borrow for balance of payments purposes from the Fund. While China did in fact borrow twice from the Fund in the early years of its membership (in 1981 and 1986), there is no indication that the policy conditionality attached to these loans was inconsistent with the government's own economic stabilization policies.[34] China also became a large consumer of IMF technical assistance, another indication of the constructive working relationship it developed with the Fund, which established a representative office in Beijing in 1991. China appears to have found technical assistance useful rather than intrusive, at a time when it was undertaking the wholesale reform of its monetary policymaking framework and domestic financial sector. However, it continued to criticize the Fund's underrepresentation of developing country interests and concerns (Kent 2007: 131–5). China's gradualist approach to reform inevitably produced some inconsistencies: it maintained a dual exchange rate from 1986 to January 1994, and it only accepted its full Article VIII obligations (which require the avoidance of restrictive practices on current account transactions) in December 1996.[35]

The Asian financial crisis of the late 1990s certainly strained relations between the IMF and other countries in East Asia, but China's strong economic performance through this crisis, its low exposure to international

---

[34] Author interviews, Beijing, September 2008.

[35] Kent (2007: 136) claims that China's continuing use of capital account restrictions was also inconsistent with IMF norms. This is wrong in that Article VIII still permits member countries to use capital controls, though the major developed countries and key Fund staff were, by the late 1990s, increasingly convinced that this provision should be removed (see Chwieroth 2010).

bank lending, and its continuing current account surplus and strong FDI inflows meant that there was never any threat that it too would be forced to go to the Fund. The Asian crisis did, however, demonstrate to all in the region that IMF policy advice could be destructive of both economic as well as political stability. It also confirmed the view in Beijing that the IMF was still dominated by Western countries and particularly the United States. But throughout the crisis and until 2004–05, China's relationship with the Fund remained good.[36] In the first published notes on the IMF Executive Board annual Article IV consultation with China in 2000, the Board commended China on its handling of the crisis and supported its monetary and fiscal policy stances, though it signalled that China should consider introducing greater exchange rate flexibility (IMF 2000). The equivalent report the following year (IMF 2001) had a broadly similar tone, though it noted that the Board thought there was a need "to gradually reduce the fiscal deficit further over the medium term" in view of banking sector weaknesses and a need to build and extend the social safety net. But these were criticisms that did little to constrain China's policy autonomy, which was underpinned by its robust growth and continually improving creditor position; moreover, the Chinese leadership was well aware of these issues and shared this reform agenda.[37]

The tone of China's Article IV consultations began to change over the next few years in ways that were less to Beijing's taste. In 2003, the Board recommended a tighter monetary policy as well as a gradual move in the direction of exchange rate flexibility, though "most directors" felt that there was "no clear evidence that the renminbi is substantially undervalued at this juncture" (IMF 2003). In 2004, for the first time, the Executive Board discussion of China's annual Article IV consultation moved to an increasingly clear emphasis on the part of some countries on the desirability of RMB revaluation, noting that "[s]everal Directors stressed that greater exchange rate flexibility should also be helpful in contributing to an orderly resolution of global imbalances." In response, the Chinese authorities signalled that they intended to introduce greater currency flexibility, but emphasized that they would do so at their own pace and at a time of their own choosing (IMF 2004a). A few months later, China permitted, for the first time, the publication of the staff report associated with this consultation (IMF 2004b). This showed that IMF staff raised the issue of greater RMB flexibility, but emphasized that this would benefit

---

[36] Author interviews, Beijing, September 2008.
[37] Author interviews, Beijing, September 2008.

China by permitting it greater monetary policy autonomy; its potential effects on global imbalances were not emphasized at this point, at least in the published document. Indeed, IMF staff at this time reiterated their view of a year earlier that "it is difficult to find persuasive evidence that the renminbi is substantially undervalued" (IMF 2004b: 3, 14).

By 2005, bilateral surveillance was becoming increasingly constraining for China and relations with the IMF were beginning to become more fraught. By the time the 2005 Article IV consultation and Executive Board discussion were published, China had already agreed to permit a very modest appreciation against the dollar. But as China's external surplus and foreign exchange reserves continued to grow rapidly, more Executive Board countries and, by this time, IMF staff encouraged the government to move more decisively in the direction of a more market-determined exchange rate and more rapid appreciation (IMF 2005a, 2005b, 2005c). In the 2006 bilateral surveillance consultation, the IMF staff argued explicitly that the gradual nominal appreciation of the RMB since mid-2005 had failed to compensate for the rapid increases in Chinese export competitiveness due to high productivity growth (IMF 2006b: 17). IMF staff again "urged the [Chinese] authorities to increase exchange rate flexibility," made clear their view that the RMB was significantly under-valued and stated "that this undervaluation has increased further since last year's Article IV consultation" (IMF 2006b: 17). The published dialogue between IMF staff and the Chinese authorities during 2005–06 is fairly robust and demonstrates considerable Chinese resistance to IMF arguments (IMF 2005c: 15–17; IMF 2006b: 18–20). In retrospect, it is perhaps remarkable that the Chinese government permitted these reports to be published (any member state may choose to prevent publication, as China did in the past). It may indicate the government's willingness to accept the principle of international surveillance, particularly at a time when China was accepting the need for RMB revaluation.

By this point, however, China's relationship with the IMF and with international surveillance was breaking down. From Beijing's perspective, the growing public attention given to the RMB exchange rate encouraged growing amounts of speculative capital inflow into China, as investors were attracted by the probability of continued RMB appreciation. This negated one of the benefits that the IMF claimed would follow from greater currency flexibility: the restoration of monetary policy autonomy. Instead, it seemed to be promoting dangerous speculative inflows and consumer and asset price inflation. Thus, after Beijing took the decision in June 2005 to partially liberalize the exchange rate, China increasingly came to see international surveillance as worsening rather than assisting its adjustment process.

IMF staff arguments were increasingly seen as part of a general coordinated strategy on the part of the United States to obtain more rapid and substantial RMB revaluation through both bilateral and multilateral mechanisms. It also coincided with claims from various US politicians and some prominent think-tank economists that China's gradualist approach to RMB appreciation and sustained intervention in foreign exchange markets to prevent the RMB from rising more rapidly demonstrated conclusively that China was manipulating its currency and in clear breach of its multilateral obligations.[38] Fred Bergsten (2008) is representative of this position in arguing that "[i]nducing China to become a responsible pillar of the global economic system (as the [United States and European Union] are) will be one of the great challenges of coming decades – particularly since at the moment China seems uninterested in playing such a role ... In numerous areas, [China] is pursuing strategies that conflict with existing norms, rules, and institutional arrangements."

In fact, China was deeply reluctant to accept publicly that its currency was still seriously undervalued and that an accelerated pace of RMB appreciation was necessary. From Beijing's perspective, China had demonstrably accepted that greater exchange rate flexibility was needed, but the major developed countries, especially the United States, were now demanding accelerated appreciation that jeopardized China's economic and social stability. Chinese officials argued that such public pressure made it more rather than less difficult to achieve a consensus within the leadership on currency revaluation. There was also a growing sense that the international surveillance process itself was biased and unfair. In response to the arguments of Fund staff in 2005, Chinese officials argued that

[A] resolution to the problem of global imbalances required a concerted effort by all major countries, led first by credible action in the United States to reduce its fiscal deficit and increase national savings. While acknowledging that China had a role to play, they stressed that China alone could not solve this problem. They noted that growing protectionism against Chinese exports and stepped-up international pressures for an exchange rate change have complicated the decision-making process. (IMF 2005c: 15)

[38] Indeed, Morris Goldstein of the Peterson Institute of International Economics in Washington had argued as early as 2004 that the RMB was seriously undervalued and that the Chinese government was engaging in currency manipulation (Goldstein 2004). See also Morris Goldstein and Nicholas Lardy, "China's Revaluation Shows that Size Really Matters," *Financial Times*, 22 July 2005; Goldstein (2007).

This Chinese complaint echoes a general concern among some IMF members that an IMF decision to identify individual countries' exchange rate policies as systemically harmful risks "stigmatizing" such countries (US Treasury 2008b: 1). The published IMF documents on China do not broach the issue of currency manipulation directly, but it is clear that charges of currency undervaluation produced increasing frustration in Beijing. For example, in a speech to the US Chamber of Commerce in Beijing in May 2005, Premier Wen Jiabao reiterated the argument that external pressure on China to change its policies was counterproductive and that China's exchange rate system and its appropriate level were both matters of national sovereignty.[39] On the face of it, this position was inconsistent with China's IMF obligations, though Wen made the remark to a US Chamber of Commerce delegation and may have been referring to pressure from other countries rather than from the IMF.[40] China has certainly been willing to dispute the right of other countries to demand RMB revaluation outside of the formal process of IMF surveillance. In response to US Congressional pressure on Chinese currency policy, the Chinese Foreign Ministry responded in early 2007 that "On the question of the renminbi exchange rate, we have consistently adopted the principle of responsibility and independence."[41] In April 2007, the deputy governor of China's central bank did argue that the IMF "should respect its member countries' core interests and actual economic fundamentals" and said that its advice ignored the need to maintain domestic economic stability in China.[42] But this evidence of growing Chinese frustration with the surveillance process is less conclusive on the question of whether China has been in breach of its multilateral commitments and legal obligations. A clearer sign of a break was the Chinese government's decision to suspend annual Article IV bilateral surveillance by the IMF in 2007 and in 2008; these were only resumed again in 2009 (China still participated in the multilateral consultations on imbalances in 2006 and early 2007).

The difficulty for China was that the circumstantial evidence that it was in breach of its IMF obligations grew steadily during 2005–06. By 2005, China's surplus had become unprecedented in absolute terms and

[39] "RMB Exchange Rate a Sovereignty Issue of China: Premier," 17 May 2005, Embassy of the People's Republic of China in Australia, http://au.china-embassy.org/eng/xw/t195926.htm.

[40] Goldstein's (2007) evidence is fairly circumstantial on this score (he cites a *China Daily* article from 2007: "IMF Meddling Disturbing," *China Daily*, 17 April 2007).

[41] "China Urges Respect, Not Threats, from US on Yuan," *Reuters*, 29 March 2007.

[42] "Central Bank Rejects IMF Yuan Advice," *China Daily*, 16 April 2007.

Current account, % GDP

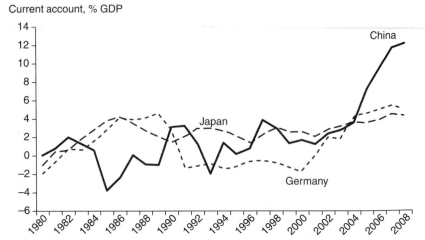

FIGURE 3.3. Current accounts of major surplus countries, percentage of
national GDP, 1980–2008.
Source: IMF, *World Economic Outlook* database. 2007 and 2008 figures are
estimates as of October 2007.

in relation to China's total economic size – even by historical comparison
with Japanese and German surpluses (Figure 3.3). China's extraordinary
and steady accumulation of foreign exchange reserves indicated massive
and sustained foreign exchange intervention (IMF 2006a: 15–16; Mussa
2007: 23–4). On this score, however, Chinese officials reasonably replied
that sustained intervention had been necessary to counteract the hot
money inflows triggered by the international debate over the value of the
RMB. More problematic for the Chinese case was that the growing capital intensity of investment and production in China also indicated serious currency undervaluation for a labour-abundant country, as does the
growing capital intensity of exports and substantial import substitution
away from capital-intensive imports.[43]

Chinese officials tried to refute these and related claims, but in doing
so they did not always strengthen their position in the debate. They
argued that global imbalances reflected not RMB undervaluation but low
US savings, although most economists, including those from the IMF,

---

[43] Heavy investment in industries such as steel, automobiles, and semiconductors belies
China's comparative advantage in labour-intensive sectors and has had the perverse
effect of producing very slow employment growth in a rapidly expanding economy
(employment growth slowed from 2.5% p.a. between 1978 and 1993 to just over 1%
between 1993 and 2004, when heavy investment in capital-intensive manufacturing took
place) (Bergsten et al. 2008: 110).

argued that both could contribute (IMF 2006b: 18; Vines 2006). Another common argument was that the global production strategies of MNCs concentrated final assembly production in China and explained its growing export surplus, though this overlooked that currency undervaluation could contribute to large inward investment flows. Another was that currency revaluation could hurt China's fragile banking sector, though this ignored the possibility that the large sterilization[44] of dollar purchases by the People's Bank of China (PBOC, the central bank) might itself contribute to financial sector fragility (IMF 2006b: 18–20; Yu 2006: 25–6; Prasad 2007a: 11). Nor were all of these arguments consistent with each other, notably the claim that RMB appreciation would not help to reduce global imbalances but could have serious negative effects on Chinese growth, employment and social stability (IMF 2004b: 3; 2006b: 18). The Chinese government was clearly willing to engage arguments for currency revaluation, but seemed unwilling to be persuaded – at least in public – that they had any merit.

Taken together, these Chinese objections suggested that the Chinese leadership had adopted an exchange rate policy after June 2005 – one that permitted gradual appreciation – that balanced a range of competing domestic interests, and they were very reluctant to renegotiate this policy decision in response to renewed foreign pressure. After all, from Beijing's perspective, they had already agreed to show good faith by responding to demands for RMB revaluation, something that US officials acknowledged (Taylor 2007: 299–300). Having done so, however, the United States only seemed to want more. The Chinese government's main objection was not so much to the need for greater exchange rate flexibility – this they had conceded in discussions with the IMF and in bilateral discussions with the United States even before mid-2005. Rather, they argued that the United States and other developed countries did not have the right to dictate the pace and timing of RMB revaluation.[45] In their debate with IMF staff on currency policy in 2006, the Chinese government "agreed that greater flexibility was needed over the medium term, but stressed that exchange rate reform would proceed in a gradual and controlled manner" (IMF 2006b: 3). As the leadership's stated goal of achieving more balanced growth appeared increasingly unlikely to be achieved, a slight increase in the rate of RMB appreciation was permitted in 2007–08, but the gradualist strategy remained intact.

---

[44] "Sterilization" generally refers to actions by the central bank (usually the issuance of bonds) that serve to counteract the increase in the domestic currency money supply that results from its purchases of foreign currency.
[45] Author interviews, London, November 2008.

As regards the second Bretton Woods norm that surplus countries should accept equal responsibility with deficit countries for adjustment to global imbalances, China has not demonstrated a high degree of acceptance, as is true for most other surplus countries. Chinese officials argue that their willingness to respond to international demands for RMB revaluation during 2005–08 indicates acceptance of this norm, but as we argue later, the primary drivers of this policy were domestic rather than international. Many Chinese officials do accept that greater exchange rate flexibility should be a medium-term objective, but this indicates limited concern with the large global imbalances that have emerged in the recent past. Most importantly in terms of official policy, in 2006, the National Development and Reform Commission (NDRC) in its eleventh five-year plan also adopted the goal of achieving a balanced current account within five years. But it is unclear how serious this policy goal really is; on current projections, it has no chance of succeeding.

China's response to the debate about the role of global imbalances in producing the 2008–09 global financial crisis has been revealing in this respect. Chinese officials have strenuously disputed in public the view that global imbalances, and China's large surplus in particular, were an important cause of the crisis (as opposed to poor financial risk management and regulation in the advanced countries).[46] In the view of most Chinese officials and economists, high savings (and related current account surpluses) are associated with virtue, whereas deficits are associated with debt-fuelled over-consumption and lax financial regulation. Countries strongly associated with the latter, moreover, are seen as the main culprits behind both global imbalances and, more recently, the global financial crisis. After mid-2008, when the RMB was re-fixed to the US dollar, Chinese officials also repeatedly brushed aside any suggestions for renewed RMB appreciation and instead emphasized that China's main contribution to global economic recovery was the large fiscal stimulus to domestic investment and growth, and its decision not to *devalue* the RMB when its exports collapsed.[47] This position was maintained during and after China's return to the annual bilateral surveillance process with the IMF in 2009, when both the IMF and some executive board countries (including the United States) continued to argue that further RMB appreciation

---

[46] "US Fumbling for a New China Tone," *FT.com*, 16 November 2009.
[47] "Premier Wen Jiabao Meets the Press," 14 March 2010, http://www.fmprc.gov.cn/eng/zxxx/t673753.htm#, accessed 20 March 2010.

was a necessary part of China's contribution to global adjustment and financial stabilization (IMF 2009c).

One difficulty with China's position was that it's large fiscal stimulus, three-quarters of which was delivered through the state-controlled banking system in the form of increased lending to local authorities, was heavily focused on raising investment. This is likely to increase already substantial levels of overcapacity in some sectors, doing little to boost domestic consumption and raising the incentive to export surplus production (European Chamber of Commerce in China 2009; Prasad 2010: 6). Another difficulty was that China's new pegging policy persisted even after the dollar began to weaken against other major currencies from March 2009, which once again produced substantial devaluations against the euro, yen, and many developing country currencies.[48] By early 2010, rapidly rising asset prices and the reemergence of consumer price inflation led some Chinese officials to conclude that a return to a policy of gradual appreciation against the dollar was needed. In March 2010, Zhou Xiaochuan, PBOC governor, suggested that the return to a fixed dollar peg in mid-2008 was part of a temporary package of measures to combat the global crisis from which China would at some point exit.[49] Finally, on 19 June 2010, on the eve of a G20 summit in Toronto, China's leadership announced that it would enhance the flexibility of the RMB exchange rate regime, though the PBOC stated clearly that given the declining current account surplus "the basis for large-scale appreciation of the RMB exchange rate does not exist."[50] Thus, the arguments for and against a return to RMB appreciation became more finely balanced as economic recovery was consolidated, but the Chinese leadership evidently remained unwilling to jeopardize that recovery and has been willing to weather renewed international criticism about its exchange rate policy.

To summarize, from 1980 through about 2004, China had a reasonably good relationship with the IMF and showed a fairly normal degree of acceptance of its responsibilities under the bilateral surveillance process. Until that time, there was no strong consensus within international institutions like the IMF that the Chinese currency was substantially undervalued. This relationship significantly worsened from 2005 with the emergence of large Chinese current account surpluses and as international

---

[48] "Geithner Lauds Stance on Exchange Rates," *FT.com*, 12 November 2009.
[49] "Beijing Studies Severing Peg to US dollar," *FT.com*, 6 March 2010.
[50] "Further Reform the RMB Exchange Rate Regime and Enhance the RMB Exchange Rate Flexibility," People's Bank of China Press Release, 19 June 2010.

pressure on China to accept substantial and rapid currency appreciation increased. China's government did in fact decide to accept a significant revaluation of the RMB during 2005–08, though it became increasingly concerned that the public diplomacy over the exchange rate issue undermined one of its key objectives, that of restoring domestic monetary stability. In addition, China believed that it was being asked to accept an unreasonably large share of the burden of international adjustment to reduce global imbalances. The 2007 Decision on Bilateral Surveillance by the IMF Executive Board was seen as the culmination of a US-led international campaign, which China unusually voted against. It withdrew from the bilateral surveillance process during 2007–08 in response. This casts considerable doubt on China's commitment to the evolving rules of the international surveillance regime, which it has seen as unbalanced and biased against its interests. China only returned to bilateral surveillance in 2009, after the global crisis had broken and when other issues had displaced exchange rates at the top of the international agenda. Finally, China seems reluctant to accept, as a new surplus country, that it has equal responsibility for international adjustment to global imbalances to deficit countries, though in this respect it is hardly unusual.

Explaining Levels of Behavioural Consistency

The most important reason for China's increasingly problematic relationship with the international surveillance framework is the strong priority given by the government to domestic growth. In the first two decades of China's relationship with the international surveillance process, it was not perceived by the Chinese leadership as a substantial constraint upon this growth priority. On the contrary, both IMF (and even more, World Bank) membership was seen as consistent with the leadership's domestic economic reform project. By 2005, macroeconomic surveillance had become seen as increasingly problematic because it posed demands on China that complicated and even jeopardized the process of domestic macroeconomic management. China's large external surpluses and the demands for currency revaluation that they generated among its major trading partners, almost certainly unexpectedly for the government, increased the tension between China's growth model and the multilateral obligations it assumed three decades ago. Not only did it come to threaten China's strategy of joining and benefitting from international institutions such as the World Trade Organization, it also appeared to threaten the very basis of China's post-1980 economic development.

By 2004–05, the leadership was grappling with understanding the causes and consequences of the weaknesses and imbalances in China's growth model. Demands for currency revaluation were strongly resisted by interests associated with the export sector, seen as a key driver of economic growth. In its 2004 surveillance consultation with the IMF, the government's response was clear: "The authorities agree in principle on the need for greater exchange rate flexibility, but are concerned about the impact of a potential appreciation of the renminbi on the domestic economy, particularly with respect to employment growth" (IMF 2004b: 3). There can be little doubt that the promotion of exports was an important policy priority for China in recent decades and that this has been seen as a key plank of employment creation and social stability. From mid-2008, when export growth collapsed and many thousands of Chinese firms in this sector were faced with bankruptcy and workers with redundancy, the government decided to halt its gradual appreciation against the dollar entirely. The rapid expansion of exports and associated foreign and domestic investment in export capacity and import-substituting industry created a powerful lobby that strongly resisted significant RMB revaluation. This included the finance and commerce ministries and many local party officials in the eastern provinces.[51] Export interests are also well represented at the highest levels of economic policymaking, including in the NDRC.[52]

Yet these are not the only voices in economic policymaking in China. Since the mid-2000s, the senior Chinese leadership has been increasingly explicit in arguing for the need to rebalance the economy towards domestic growth, higher consumption, and a balanced current account. Implicitly, this position accepted the need for RMB revaluation as part of this general process of rebalancing. The PBOC in particular favoured more rapid currency appreciation as the dilemmas of managing monetary policy under the constraint of a managed exchange rate became more acute, but it was far from the most powerful actor within the Chinese policymaking system. The government appeared uncertain about how to achieve these multiple objectives with its existing policy tools. Even when inflation was rising during 2007–08, the government announced an annual urban job creation target of 10 million, which was probably unachievable without real GDP growth of 10 percent

---

[51] Author interviews, Beijing, September 2008, and Washington, DC, April 2009.
[52] Author interviews, Beijing, September 2008, and Washington, DC, April 2009.

or more and which thus reduced the credibility of its commitment to reduce inflation.[53]

As in many other policy areas, the leadership's gradualist approach to change offered a middle way between these competing objectives and debates, with the overriding objective of not jeopardizing rapid growth. During 2003–05, when growth was high, inflation low, and exports boomed, the pro-export lobby had the upper hand. By mid-2005, when the domestic and external costs of the dollar peg were becoming increasingly apparent, the Hu-Wen government decided that a significant appreciation of the currency was needed but that it must be achieved gradually. The price of this caution was a ballooning current account surplus by 2005 and over-accumulation of foreign exchange reserves, which had growing costs for China's economy and its relationship with the IMF and the major advanced countries.[54] Within limits, these appear to have been costs that the leadership was willing to bear. China's revaluation strategy from 2005 to 2008 seems to have been judicious in that it was sufficient to deter the credible threat of a sharp protectionist response from its main developed country trading partners whilst maintaining rapid growth. It was not, however, sufficient to remove the imbalances and weaknesses in the Chinese growth model that were of increasing concern to the leadership. As inflation accelerated during 2007–08 and external pressure for more rapid RMB appreciation also increased, the leadership accepted more rapid appreciation. But when export growth collapsed during 2008–09 and concerns about preventing a broader economic collapse came to the fore, the leadership chose to halt appreciation completely.

Although concerns about balancing domestic growth and inflation objectives have been the dominant factor in exchange rate policymaking and in the leadership's attitude towards the international surveillance framework, it would be wrong to assume that international factors have played no role. We have already suggested that external pressure coincided with arguments from important domestic actors – arguments to which the leadership has clearly been sensitive – that RMB appreciation

---

[53] See Michael Pettis, "More, or Less, RMB Appreciation?," 7 March 2008, http://piaohaoreport.sampasite.com/blog; Victor Shih, "China's credit boom," *Asian Wall Street Journal*, 21 February 2008; Shih (2008); "China Lets Yuan Appreciate a Bit Faster," *China Daily*, 29 December 2007.

[54] See IMF (2006b); Michael Pettis, "More Warnings on Inflation Vigilance in China," 28 February 2008, http://piaohaoreport.sampasite.com/blog; Vines (2006); Yu (2006); Prasad (2007a, 2007b).

would help to improve domestic monetary control, rebalance growth, prevent dangerous over-accumulation of foreign exchange reserves, and prevent a disruption in China's trade relationships with the developed countries. This makes it difficult, given the problems of gaining access to the highest levels of decision making in China, to discern whether external factors tipped the balance in mid-2005 in favour of currency appreciation. However, some insiders argue that a combination of foreign persuasion and pressure, coordinated through a range of bilateral and multilateral mechanisms, did reinforce domestic arguments in favour of appreciation and played an important role in this policy shift.[55] Furthermore, it is almost certainly the case that the mid-2008 decision to halt the gradual appreciation of the RMB was due to the external shock of the global financial crisis. As this case demonstrates, however, external forces generally interact with domestic political and social factors in ways that make them difficult to disentangle.

The relationship between external forces and China's level of consistency with international surveillance norms is also non-linear. We have already noted that Chinese officials commonly argue that public demands from the United States, European Union, or IMF to accept greater adjustment responsibilities make it more rather than less difficult for China's government to fall into line, lest it be seen by domestic nationalists as overly deferential to foreigners. Another common complaint was that despite professions to the contrary (European Commission 2007b; Paulson 2008), foreigners cared too little about China's economic, social, and political stability.[56] A more extreme but far from uncommon response was that foreign demands for substantial RMB revaluation were part of a conspiracy to "keep China down."[57] All of these arguments can be useful negotiating tactics, but they are in line with other Chinese concerns about the process of international surveillance. In particular, the Chinese government came to see the process of international surveillance as not only taking insufficient account of domestic concerns, but also being procedurally biased and distributionally unfair.

Out of the glare of public diplomacy, many Chinese officials had come to accept that RMB appreciation was necessary, even if the decision to do so in mid-2005 was in retrospect belated. But the intensification of

---

[55] Taylor (2007: 291–300), and author interviews, Beijing, September 2008 and Washington, DC, April 2009. See also Keidel (2008).
[56] "Central Bank Rejects IMF Yuan Advice," *China Daily*, 16 April 2007. See also IMF (2006b: 20); Yu (2007: 11).
[57] "Wen Rails at 'Unfair' Renminbi Pressure," *FT.com*, 30 November 2009.

international pressure after the decision to accept gradual appreciation had been taken convinced many Chinese that the developed countries, particularly the United States, used the process of international surveillance to push most of the costs of adjustment onto China (IMF 2005c: 15). From China's perspective, there was little in the IMF or G7 processes and mechanisms that placed equivalent pressure on these countries to accept politically costly adjustment measures. In 2003, well before international pressure on China to revalue became important, Li Ruogu, then Assistant Governor of the PBOC, called on the IMF to "tighten its surveillance of the macroeconomic and financial policies of the major industrial countries" (quoted in Chin and Yong 2010: 3). Chinese officials were well aware of the long history of the United States using its privileged position in the global political economy to push adjustment costs onto other countries. The view that the United States forced Japan to accept a large and rapid appreciation of the yen in the late 1980s that led to a collapse of Japanese economic growth may be mistaken, but it is often said to be an important negative example that the Chinese leadership wanted to avoid (Yu 2006: 28).

Moreover, escalating international pressure on China to accept more rapid currency revaluation after mid-2005 was not connected with credible commitments by advanced countries, and especially the United States, to accept equivalently costly adjustment policies. This is clear from the Chinese government's response to the IMF's argument that RMB revaluation could contribute to the reduction of global imbalances: "They [Chinese officials] stated that the problem of global imbalances was caused in large part by the United States and should be dealt with primarily by the United States taking appropriate policy actions" (IMF 2006b: 19–20). From Beijing's perspective the IMF was not acting as a neutral arbiter of international policy surveillance and coordination, but as an instrument of US influence. The efforts by the main developed countries to use their dominance of the IMF Executive Board to push through the 2007 Decision on Bilateral Surveillance reinforced these views, since it seemed directed towards gaining further concessions from China without correcting the bias in international surveillance that favoured the developed countries. In February 2008, Wen Jiabao made clear China's view that the slow process of internal reform of the Fund needed to be accelerated.[58]

---

[58] "Premier Wen Jiabao Meets IMF Chief," 14 February 2008, http://www.china-embassy.org/eng/gyzg/t407374.htm, accessed 25 November 2009.

Thus, the domestic growth priority of the Chinese leadership and the growing perception that the international surveillance process gives insufficient weight to this priority has made China's relationship with this global normative framework increasingly difficult. China almost certainly paid little attention to the implications of international surveillance when it first joined the Bretton Woods institutions. Only recently did it come to see the second norm of surplus country responsibility as relevant to it, and in the absence of significant multilateral constraints on the United States and other developed countries, it saw this norm as problematic. China had shown that it was willing to accept, albeit cautiously, some responsibility for international adjustment after July 2005, but its leaders came to believe that it was being asked to bear a disproportionate share of the international adjustment costs and this threatened the domestic growth priority. Its withdrawal from bilateral surveillance during 2007–08 reflected these concerns.

As noted earlier, once the global economic crisis of 2008–09 broke and inflation ceased to be a major concern of China's policymakers, the domestic growth priority was reasserted with a vengeance and RMB appreciation ceased. Within the G20, China's strong rejection of the claim that global imbalances and surplus countries in particular were partly responsible for the crisis has also hampered the emergence of a deeper consensus on international surveillance and policy coordination. China's main concern seems to have been preventing the emergence of a G20 consensus that would place a significantly higher share of the adjustment burden on the main surplus countries. Along with other emerging market countries in the G20, China has been uncomfortable with the concept of "peer review" of macroeconomic policies promoted by the United States and others; not least, this sounded too close to the process of IMF peer review.[59] The Pittsburgh G20 compromise was instead to initiate "a cooperative process of mutual assessment of our policy frameworks and the implications of those frameworks for the pattern and sustainability of global growth."[60] China has no substantive interest in internationalizing its policy choices by linking its exchange rate and other macroeconomic policy choices to pressing global issues of international imbalances, financial stability, and trade policy. Rather, the G20 is more likely seen as a useful source of protection against overly intrusive surveillance of the old kind, but also as a potential means of

---

[59] Author interviews, Beijing, September 2008, London, March 2010.
[60] Pittsburgh G20 Summit, Leaders' Statement, 24–25 September 2009.

developing a more balanced process of international policy surveillance in the future.

China's decision to return to the process of annual IMF bilateral surveillance in 2009 may have been driven in part by the consideration that being outside of the surveillance process was inconsistent with the enhanced global position of the G20 and China's role within it. It may also have been driven by the consideration that China was now also in a much stronger position to resist external pressure to alter its policies – the IMF made it clear in 2009 and 2010 that it still believed the RMB to be "substantially undervalued."[61] However, in contrast to the 2004–06 period, further documentation connected with the 2009 Article IV consultation was not released, suggesting substantial lingering Chinese sensitivity about IMF surveillance. Chinese officials continue to criticize the still limited representation of developing countries in the IMF Executive Board and the lack of even-handedness in the surveillance process and have called for a further thorough review of the 2007 Decision.[62] Even after the revisions of the weighted voting on the IMF Executive Board agreed upon in early 2008, China's voting share will reach only 3.81 percent in 2010, smaller than that of France and the United Kingdom (at 4.29 percent), and the United States at 16.73 percent (though the G20 agreed to a further rebalancing in voting shares in the future).[63]

These considerations suggest that the new role of the G20 and the slight enhancement of China's voice in the IMF have not fundamentally changed its attitude towards the international surveillance framework. The emergence of a growing consensus within the G20 by June 2010 on the need for RMB revaluation, just as in the G7 in mid-2005, may have contributed to China's decision to announce a reform of its currency regime.[64] But domestic factors are likely to remain most important in determining Beijing's future exchange rate and macroeconomic

---

[61] In February 2010, Dominique Strauss-Kahn, IMF Managing Director, also announced that Zhu Min, a deputy governor at the PBOC, would become one of his special advisers. Along with the appointment of Justin Yifu Lin as chief economist at the World Bank in 2008, this was seen as an indication of China's rising importance in the major international financial institutions ("Chinese Official Named as Top IMF Advisor," *FT.com*, 24 February 2010).

[62] Yi Gang, Deputy Governor of the PBOC, "Global Cooperation, China's Economy and the IMF," remarks at the twentieth meeting of the International Monetary and Financial Committee of the IMF, Istanbul, 4 October 2009.

[63] "IMF Executive Board Recommends Reforms to Overhaul Quota and Voice," IMF Press Release, No. 08/64, 28 March 2008.

[64] "Geithner Harnesses G-20 to Push for Yuan Revaluation," *Bloomberg.com*, 23 April 2010.

policy choices. International factors, including the international surveillance norms themselves, are very unlikely to be important motivators of Chinese policy choices if these push against the domestic norms and interests that have dominated policy outcomes. In early 2010, as international pressure on China to resume RMB appreciation increased, the leadership strenuously resisted foreign demands and gave the strong impression that the decision to permit further revaluation of the RMB – even after the June 2010 decision to increase its "flexibility" – would depend on domestic circumstances rather than China's highly contested "international responsibilities."[65]

4 The Bilateral Relationship and Behavioural Consistency

For both the United States and China, their bilateral relationship initially had very little to do with their respective approaches to international surveillance and their levels of behavioural conformity with it. For the United States, its relationship with European countries and then later Japan (and to some extent the smaller Asian tigers) dominated its global macroeconomic diplomacy. As many of these countries, perceived to have benefitted substantially from American largesse, developed trade and payments surpluses, this steadily reinforced the US perception that the international surveillance framework needed to be strengthened and that surplus countries in particular needed to accept greater policy constraint. For China, international surveillance for its first two decades was largely viewed in terms of its bilateral relationship with the IMF, which was largely positive and barely constraining.

The long-standing tendency in US policy to place adjustment pressure on other countries can be seen in its bilateral economic diplomacy with China since the early 1990s. Under the terms of the 1988 Trade Act, the Treasury recommended negotiations with China on its currency for the first time in November 1990 and cited China for actual currency manipulation in the first half of 1991 and for the following five 6-month periods. It seems likely that domestic political pressures were important in this decision, since the economic case for RMB undervaluation was then weak (Lardy 1994: 86–90). After China unified its formerly dual exchange rate regime in early 1994, China was not formally cited for

[65] "Premier Wen Jiabao Meets the Press," 14 March 2010, http://www.fmprc.gov.cn/eng/zxxx/t673753.htm, accessed 20 March 2010.

currency manipulation under the 1988 Act, though it was closely moni-
tored (GAO 2005; Frankel and Wei 2007). For the most part, the George
H. W. Bush and Clinton administrations remained more interested in
maintaining good political relations with China and did not yet see it as
a major economic threat.

Despite the reputation of the George W. Bush administration for
unilateralism, no Treasury citation occurred during Bush's tenure despite
the large increase in China's current surplus after 2004 and in its bilateral surplus with the United States (Frankel and Wei 2007). For some
of its critics, the George W. Bush Treasury appeared to bend over back-
wards to find excuses not to cite China for currency manipulation by
emphasizing the difficulty of proving "intent" to manipulate in both the
IMF rules and US legislation.[66] Since it is difficult to imagine any government openly admitting to currency manipulation, this position struck
critics as evasive and not serious about pressing China on this issue.
However, behind the scenes, the United States engaged in more quiet
diplomacy aimed at encouraging China to see the need for RMB appreciation, for the sake of both its own domestic monetary management
and to promote stability in China's international economic relations. In
this, George W. Bush administration officials believed that this policy of
quiet diplomacy was successful, culminating in the decision to begin the
process of gradual RMB appreciation against the dollar in mid-2005
(Taylor 2007: 291–300).

As we have seen, this situation changed significantly by 2005 as
Chinese surpluses grew suddenly and as China became seen by US critics
as inheriting the mantle from Germany and Japan of the most important,
and recalcitrant, surplus country. The growing importance of the bilateral
relationship in the currency and surveillance debate thus in part reflected
economic reality: by 2006, China had become the world's major surplus
country and the United States was by far the largest deficit country. The
bilateral trade imbalance between the two countries was also the world's
largest and fuelled domestic demands within the United States for action,
making it difficult for policymakers on both sides to keep these issues off
the agenda of Chinese–US relations.

---

[66] See McCown, Pollard, and Weeks (2007), and Mark Sobel, Treasury Deputy Assistant
Secretary, Testimony on Currency Manipulation and Its Effect on US Businesses and
Workers, hearings before the Committee on Ways and Means Subcommittee on Trade,
the Committee on Financial Services, Subcommittee on Domestic and International
Monetary Policy, Trade and Technology, and the Committee on Energy and Commerce,
Subcommittee on Commerce, Trade and Consumer Protection, 9 May 2007.

Henry Paulson, Treasury Secretary from 2006 to 2009, was portrayed as a "China heavyweight" whose personal influence in China might allow patient bilateral diplomacy to work its magic, notably in the form of the bilateral US-China Strategic Economic Dialogue. The US Treasury (2007: 2) report in December 2007 outlined America's multipronged approach:

China should significantly accelerate the appreciation of the RMB's effective exchange rate in order to minimize the risks that are being created for China itself as well as the world economy, of which China is an increasingly critical part. Treasury reinforces the need for China to rebalance growth, including reform of the exchange rate regime, with Chinese authorities at every available opportunity and will continue to do so. China's exchange rate regime has been a prominent feature of the U.S.–China Strategic Economic Dialogue (SED), G7 discussions with China, and G20 and IMF Board deliberations.

John Taylor, Undersecretary of the Treasury for International Affairs during this period, claimed that achieving RMB appreciation was a policy priority for the Treasury from 2005 (Taylor 2007: 291, 294), though others felt that the administration saw market opening in China as a greater priority and that the SED became a valuable source of political protection for Beijing against its most vociferous US critics.[67] The Schumer–Graham Senate bill of early 2005 would have authorized a 27.5 percent tariff on Chinese imports if negotiations with China did not result in the elimination of the assumed equivalent undervaluation of the RMB. However, this bill, like others that followed it, was never brought to a formal vote, and was probably intended mainly to demonstrate Congressional activism and to spur the executive branch. A version of this bill obtained a substantial majority in the Senate in March 2005, but a final vote was deferred on the understanding that the Treasury would take action to ensure concrete change in China's currency policy (Henning 2007: 789).

There are some signs of evolution in the US position on these issues since the 2008–09 crisis. After 2008, some US commentators and officials argued that global imbalances were one important cause of the global financial crisis and that this strengthened its claim that surplus countries, in particular China, needed to accept currency appreciation and the expansion of domestic demand. The incoming Obama administration was widely expected to take a more aggressive stance on China's currency policy than

---

[67] Author interviews, Washington, DC, April 2009.

its predecessor, but it had also signalled that it would be more multilateralist too. The unexpected severity of the 2008–09 global economic crisis in practice pushed the currency issue off centre stage; it may also have raised the administration's concerns that a more aggressive bilateral policy towards China on this issue was risky given the rapid growth of US fiscal deficits and the perceived dependence on continued Chinese purchases of Treasury debt. During Treasury Secretary Geithner's visit to Beijing in June 2009, he stressed that the Obama administration was committed to the long-term sustainability of the US fiscal position, whilst encouraging Beijing "to continue progress toward a more flexible exchange rate regime" as part of a broader contribution to a more balanced global economy.[68] In the first bilateral China – US S&ED in July 2009, China asked the United States to cut its large fiscal deficit to prevent inflation and protect the long-term value of China's dollar assets. The Obama administration tried to reassure China that it would pursue a strong dollar policy and that it would achieve a sustainable fiscal position by 2013.[69]

The problem is that the Chinese assign little credibility to US government reassurances about their fiscal position; the economic crisis has greatly exacerbated these long-standing Chinese concerns. Just as American fiscal conservatives fear that the George W. Bush and Obama administrations have placed the United States on the path to fiscal ruin, so too the Chinese government worries that the consequences of US fiscal profligacy for China will be serious and potentially catastrophic. As noted earlier, the IMF and G20 surveillance processes are very unlikely, in Chinese eyes, to substantially constrain US fiscal policy choices in the coming years. The willingness of the George W. Bush and Obama administrations to give China a greater say in global institutions like the IMF and G20 is therefore not especially reassuring to China. Beijing has signalled publicly in various ways in recent years that it wishes to reduce its over-reliance on dollar assets through diversification, but the leadership is well aware that this can only be done very gradually and that dollar reserves will likely continue to take the preponderant share of its foreign reserve portfolio for years to come. Given the limited leverage enjoyed by the IMF, G20, China, or anyone else over US fiscal policymaking, much may depend on whether the private bond markets and the credit rating agencies threaten the US government with rising bond yields in the coming months and years.[70]

---

[68] "Geithner Calls for Closer Ties with China," *FT.com*, 1 June 2009.
[69] "China Hopes US Will Cut Budget Deficit," *China Daily*, 28 July 2009.
[70] In March 2010, for example, Moody's analysts argued that the "distance to downgrade" for US federal debt had substantially diminished as a result of the crisis and the absence

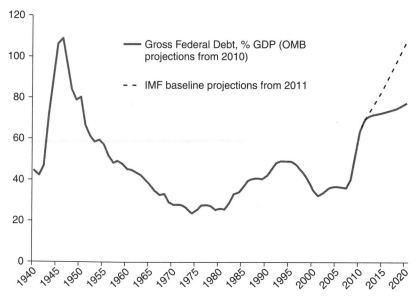

FIGURE 3.4. US gross federal debt outstanding as percentage of GDP, 1940–2009, with projections from 2010 to 2020 (US Office of Management and Budget and IMF).
Sources: US Office of Management and Budget (OMB) and Celasun and Keim (2010).

The Obama administration has repeatedly pledged to reduce the US fiscal deficit over the medium term, but its projections are based on a number of optimistic assumptions; in January 2010, it projected that the fiscal deficit will stabilize at 4 percent of GDP by 2014, but that US public debt levels will continue to rise. Meanwhile, the IMF's new-found truth-telling increased China's (and others') concerns about US fiscal deficits: IMF staff predictions of both fiscal deficits and outstanding federal debt in 2009 and 2010 have been substantially higher than those of the Obama administration and suggest that without further politically unpopular actions, by 2020 US public debt will reach levels last seen during World War II (Figure 3.4).[71] To the extent that the US recovery is weak and high levels of unemployment persist, the political difficulty of reducing deficits is likely to be high. It is also clear to the Chinese

of a credible deficit reduction strategy ("Moody's Warns U.S. Debt Could Test Triple-A Rating," *New York Times*, 15 March 2010).

[71] The picture is substantially worse if sub-federal government debt is included (in its World Economic Outlook of April 2009, the IMF projected that this more inclusive estimate of US public debt would reach 98% of GDP by the end of 2010).

leadership that both Presidents and Congress have been largely unwilling to tackle the longer term fiscal problems posed by rapidly rising "entitlement" spending in areas such as health and pensions.[72]

Faced with such a scenario, the Chinese leadership fears that it will be locked into additional, long-term financing of US fiscal deficits and the possibility of extraordinarily large capital losses at some point in the future. These potential future paper losses for China might not be particularly worrying except that the government appears to fear that nationalist public opinion in China might apportion much of the blame for large losses on the leadership. From the Chinese perspective, the US government, along with the European Union and IMF, are already demanding that China accept such losses: RMB revaluation against the dollar, of course, itself reduces the value of China's dollar foreign exchange reserves.

There is a potential bilateral deal to be made between the United States and China: credible US fiscal consolidation in return for renewed Chinese currency appreciation. But there are few signs so far that such a deal is likely. The Obama administration did appear to have concluded in its first year of office that accepting a greater degree of US responsibility for imbalances might encourage China to accept more exchange rate flexibility. It publically accepted to some degree the legitimacy of Chinese concerns about the United States' large fiscal deficits, its loose monetary policy, the value of China's holdings of US government debt, and the sustainability of the US commitment to open trade.[73] As Michael Froman, Deputy National Security Adviser for international economics, said before the Pittsburgh G20 summit in September 2009, "[w]e hope to reach agreement on a framework for balanced growth, for agreeing on how to address the imbalances that led to this crisis and on some process for holding each other accountable."[74] One obvious problem with this is that China rejects the notion that imbalances, rather than US regulatory failures, were at the root of the crisis. Nevertheless, this approach appeared to bear some fruit in the US–China bilateral summit of November 2009, in which both sides agreed that:

China will continue to implement the policies to adjust economic structure, raise household incomes, expand domestic demand to increase contribution of

---

[72] The successful passage of a healthcare bill by Congress in March 2010 may reduce the growth in healthcare costs, but the Obama administration had already assumed that this would be achieved in its budget of January 2010.

[73] "US Fumbling for a New China Tone," *FT.com*, 16 November 2009.

[74] "Deal on Global Imbalances Sought at G20 Summit," *FT.com*, 17 September 2009.

consumption to GDP growth and reform its social security system. The United States will take measures to increase national saving as a share of GDP and promote sustainable non-inflationary growth. To achieve this, the United States is committed to returning the federal budget deficit to a sustainable path and pursuing measures to encourage private saving. Both sides will also pursue forward-looking monetary policies with due regard for the ramifications of those policies for the international economy.[75]

However, this agreement fell short of obtaining a clear Chinese commitment to further RMB revaluation. It is possible that the emollient approach of the Obama administration was perceived in Beijing as reflecting weakness and a desire to secure China's commitment to support continued deficit financing (Prasad 2010: 2, 9). But the simplest explanation is that the Chinese leadership simply does not trust the US government to deliver on its promises of fiscal consolidation (nor, it seems, does the IMF). If US fiscal policy promises are empty words, then any such deal, from Beijing's perspective, amounts to yet another American attempt to push the costs of adjustment onto other countries. For the Chinese leadership, these costs, both in growth and political terms, may be too high. Only a month after the US-China summit, Wen Jiabao reiterated Beijing's strong opposition to either bilateral or multilateral pressure in this area of policy: "We will not yield to any pressure of any form forcing us to appreciate."[76] This resistance made it more difficult for the US administration to continue to fend off domestic pressure to take more aggressive action against Beijing, even if it believed that such a shift would be counterproductive and potentially destabilizing. If US unemployment remains high, Beijing's reluctance to accept substantial RMB appreciation risks being seen as a central obstacle to the Obama administration's economic recovery efforts (which include a doubling of US exports by 2015, mainly to developing Asia).[77] This risk is compounded by the fact that although the US trade deficit has fallen after the crisis, the bilateral deficit with China now accounts for nearly two-thirds of the total deficit, up from one-third in 2008 (Prasad 2010: 3).

In early 2010, pressure built on the administration to cite China as a currency manipulator unless China took action to change its currency policy. As in the past, some prominent US economists and a number of

---

[75] "US–China Joint Statement," 17 November 2009, Beijing, http://beijing.usembassy-china.org.cn/111709.html, accessed 6 December 2009.

[76] "Beijing Studies Severing Peg to US Dollar," *FT.com*, 6 March 2010.

[77] Secretary of Commerce Gary Locke, "National Export Initiative Remarks," 4 February 2010, http://www.commerce.gov/NewsRoom/SecretarySpeeches/PROD01_008893, accessed 8 March 2010.

members of Congress called for urgent action to be taken by the administration against China.[78] Many doubt whether China could seriously contemplate significantly reducing its holdings of US government debt in the face of increased American pressure to revalue, though it should be noted that China's total holdings of such debt probably only amount to about 17 percent of net US Treasury debt (Prasad 2010: 7).

Managing this issue is made more difficult by the fact that tensions over the bilateral exchange rate also interact with other aspects of what has always been a sometimes volatile relationship. For example, the Obama administration's policies on arms sales to Taiwan and towards Tibet and the Dalai Lama make it more difficult for Beijing to make concessions on currency policy. In March 2010, Obama urged China to adopt a "more market-oriented exchange rate"; Wen Jiabao's response was that it was wrong to ask "other countries to appreciate their own currencies solely for the purpose of increasing one's own exports."[79] One Commerce Ministry official openly called upon American multinational companies (MNCs) with Chinese interests to lobby the Obama administration to persuade it to avoid trying to resolve the currency issue by taking further trade protection measures against Chinese imports.[80] However, a spokesperson from the US Chamber of Commerce, which has in the past played an important role in persuading politicians to avoid a tougher stance against China, claimed that the pro-trade business community was finding it increasingly difficult to resist the emergence of a more aggressive policy towards China: "I don't think the Chinese government can count on the American business community to be able to push back and block action [on Capitol Hill]."[81] The Obama administration's decision to delay a decision on the RMB in April 2010 offered the advantage of relying more heavily on the growing concern in the rest of the G20 about RMB undervaluation than on the increasingly problematic bilateral option.

5 Conclusion

Neither China nor the United States has been unambiguously committed to the international surveillance framework, but paradoxically it

---

[78] "China Hits Back at Currency Criticism," *FT.com*, 12 March 2010.
[79] Michael Pettis, "How Will an RMB Revaluation Affect China, the US, and the World?," 17 March 2010, http://mpettis.com/2010/03/how-will-an-rmb-revaluation-affect-china-the-us-and-the-world/, accessed 24 March 2010.
[80] "China Asks US Groups to Back It on Currency," *FT.com*, 16 March 2010.
[81] "China to Lose Ally Against US Trade Hawks," *FT.com*, 21 March 2010.

has become increasingly central to their bilateral relationship over the past decade. In marked contrast to China, the United States has been by some distance the most important norm and rule maker in this area of global ordering. But its position towards the surveillance framework has always been ambivalent, seeing its norms and rules as constraining the macroeconomic policies of other countries rather than itself. The main exception to this generalization was its remarkable if qualified adherence to the second norm of international surveillance, that surplus countries and deficit countries had an equal responsibility to contribute to international adjustment. Since it ceased to be the major surplus country in the early 1970s, the US commitment to this second norm – and to its asymmetric understanding of the first norm – has strengthened over time. So too has its related insistence that persistent surplus countries accept substantial currency appreciation and/or domestic demand expansion to reduce global imbalances and promote US growth and employment. Its achievements in this respect have been mixed though still considerable.

China has been a relative latecomer to international surveillance and played little role in its establishment. For almost two decades after it joined the IMF in 1980, the Chinese leadership could easily accept the basic norm of international surveillance and oversight over macroeconomic policy because it expected little practical constraint on its macroeconomic policy decisions from the Fund, an expectation that was largely borne out. The leadership was almost certainly taken by considerable surprise in the mid-2000s when it discovered that its commitment to the multilateral framework conflicted with its exchange rate policy preferences. By mid-2005, there were some domestic reasons for accepting a modest degree of currency appreciation against the dollar, and these grew more compelling over the following two years. But it is also likely that external pressure, which the United States and other major countries ensured was linked to China's IMF obligations, played some role in the government's decision to permit RMB appreciation.

This does not mean that China's level of commitment to the international surveillance framework is much greater than that of the United States. The United States' commitment to the norm of surplus country responsibility is probably unrivalled, but it has not been matched by a corresponding commitment to subject its own fiscal and monetary policy choices to serious multilateral constraint. China has seen America's persistent focus on surplus country responsibilities and the related rule discouraging currency manipulation as reflecting deep biases within the multilateral framework that have been shaped by US power. This "stigmatization" of China has reinforced Beijing's reluctance to treat the main norms and rules as universally observed and legitimate and to opt instead for policies that are driven mainly by its growth imperative. Thus, Chinese exchange rate policy has been driven more by the evolving balance between domestic growth and inflation concerns, tempered by assessments of the probability of a foreign protectionist response. There has been no deep internalization of regime norms on either side. Nor did the crisis of 2008–09 change this, despite the likelihood that basic weaknesses in the international macroeconomic policy surveillance framework contributed to the build-up of global financial fragility before 2008.

4

The Non-Proliferation of Nuclear Weapons

We turn next to consideration of an issue that directly affects the survival and security goals of global society. This global normative framework relates to a traditional foreign policy area, the negotiation of which has only a diffuse impact at the domestic level. It is a less contested policy area within the broader society than others we discuss in this book, although political elites have disagreed about its value and about some of its requirements.

The nuclear non-proliferation norm has a number of associated dimensions of a voluntary and mandatory nature. The normative idea that the spread of these weapons is dangerous to global order has come to be legally enshrined in a core treaty (the Nuclear Non-Proliferation Treaty [NPT]),[1] but the status and legitimacy of that treaty is complicated by the unequal bargain between nuclear and non-nuclear weapons states (NNWS) that is at its heart. This unequal bargain was supposed to be resolved by the eventual disarmament of the nuclear weapons states (NWS), and mitigated by the provision of access to nuclear energy for peaceful, civilian use. Other aspects of the normative framework cover nuclear export regulations (some voluntary and others mandatory), together with international verification mechanisms and physical security of nuclear material.

Since the NPT acknowledges both China and the United States as NWS, the global norm affects them in equal measure. However, the bilateral relationship to some extent undermines that symmetry in that the United States has enjoyed a strategic advantage over China in this area for several decades, Beijing entered into the normative framework after

[1] The NPT opened for signature in 1968 and came into effect in 1970.

the creation of its core elements, and the United States used various forms of leverage over Beijing to persuade it to adhere with greater behavioural consistency with the non-proliferation norm as Washington defined it. Thus, China has often been in reactive mode and has carefully weighed the associated costs and benefits of norm adherence against its strategic position and international image.

The overall strength of the normative framework has come into question in the last decade or so. Examined through a wide lens, and as one historian of this regime has argued, non-proliferation has "developed into a well-respected global norm" (Gavin 2010: 415). Evidence for this stance includes the low numbers of states that have acquired nuclear weapons, the high levels of accession to the NPT, the thousands of International Atomic Energy Agency (IAEA) inspections of nuclear facilities that have been carried out, as well as the elaboration of other global rules designed to prevent the acquisition of nuclear weapons by state and non-state actors that do not already possess them.

Yet, some of those writers who focus predominantly on the post–Cold War era have claimed the non-proliferation regime to be in tatters (Joseph 2009: 79). Jonathan Schell, for example, has argued that the bomb has lately "outgrown its parochial Cold War breeding ground" and has taken up "residence in every part of the globe" (2007: 4). Former US officials have been vocal in arguing that the world is at a nuclear tipping point, only likely to be reversed if there were serious efforts made to abolish nuclear weapons.[2] The evidence for these assessments is also strong. Three new states have become NWS, India and Pakistan testing their weapons in 1998, with the DPRK joining them in 2006 and 2009. Israel remains a covert NWS, and Iran is making steady progress with a uranium enrichment programme. North Korea withdrew from the NPT in 2003, and neither India, Pakistan, nor Israel has moved any closer to joining the treaty regime. The monitoring of governmental opinion in NNWS suggests that, in the absence of serious moves towards nuclear disarmament, these states have become far more resistant to efforts to curtail proliferation (Choubey 2008). This is particularly disturbing because renewed interest in nuclear power – in a period of turbulence in global energy markets and concern about climate change – means that access to nuclear technology and trading in nuclear-related materials

---

[2] George P. Shultz, William J. Perry, Henry A. Kissinger, and Sam Nunn, et al. "A World Free of Nuclear Weapons," 4 January 2007, and "Toward a Nuclear-Free World," 15 January 2008, both in *The Wall Street Journal*.

have become more valuable. Already, several countries have announced an interest in developing or expanding enrichment programmes to meet the demand for nuclear fuel.[3]

As NWS and members of the NPT, Chinese and US actions in this policy area matter significantly to the prospects for this global regime. China is believed to have been modernizing its nuclear weapons at a time when the United States has been qualitatively upgrading its arsenal, even while reducing the number of warheads (Twomey 2008: 4–5). While there is no nuclear arms race between the two states, these two programmes, to some degree, are "framed with the other in mind" (Twomey 2009). Both states have a history of blocking discussion of a Fissile Material Cutoff Treaty (FMCT) for a decade or more at the UN Conference on Disarmament (CD) because of a bilateral dispute over arms control priorities (Kent 2007: 90–1). Only after 2009 has there been some movement in these negotiations (Johnson 2009). Both are closely involved in dealing with Iran's putative and North Korea's actual weapons programme, not always adopting positions that are in close alignment.[4] Neither state has ratified the Comprehensive Test Ban Treaty (CTBT), Chinese nuclear policy specialists stating privately that China is waiting for the United States to move first.

This chapter investigates the life cycle of a norm that came to be expressed in a legal treaty framework (especially the NPT) and has been elaborated through the creation of global and domestic institutions that have constrained nuclear exports and have developed rules on inspection of nuclear-related activity. Given the low number of states with nuclear weapons, broadly these efforts have been highly successful, and the norm could be said to be consolidated. However, because of shifts in beliefs and policies, together with breakouts from the regime, there is widespread agreement that this norm is under challenge despite earlier apparent consolidation. The different dimensions of this norm, together with the variation in its hold on behaviour in different historical periods, complicates attempts to evaluate US and Chinese levels of normative consistency, but because of the strong elements at its core, these attempts will be made in what follows. The chapter will also highlight the significant ways in

---

[3] The danger this poses is contested. In an independent 2008 report for the IAEA some of the Commissioners thought that the safety and security risks associated with nuclear energy were being exaggerated (IAEA 2008). See also Pomper 2009.

[4] Many analysts see these two issues as a litmus test of future non-proliferation efforts (e.g., Yuan 2007: 180).

which the bilateral relationship has affected each individual country's attitude and behaviour towards the norm, including in its contemporary unstable manifestations.

1 The Nuclear Non-Proliferation Norm

The legal centrepiece of the Nuclear Non-Proliferation Norm (NNPN) is the NPT, which opened for signature in 1968 and entered into force in 1970. This treaty has spurred the development of other agreements and activities that have bolstered its objectives. These have included bilateral nuclear arms control agreements between the two leading NWS the Anti-Ballistic Missile (ABM) Treaty of 1972, the CTBT of 1996, and the treaties that have promoted nuclear-weapons-free zones in regions such as Central Asia, Southeast Asia, Africa, and Latin America.[5] The NPT itself was designed primarily to prevent proliferation but also eventually to remove the reliance of the original five NWS on these weapons as a means of managing security threats. And although the treaty did not require signatories to adopt nuclear export rules, it spawned sets of regulations designed to constrain these exports, and to inspect and account for nuclear materials.

The 1950s saw the first efforts to develop criteria to govern nuclear exports, later to include the establishment of bodies such as the Nuclear Suppliers Group (NSG) in 1975, which now has forty-five members – including China, Russia, and the United States. These states have agreed on a voluntary basis to coordinate their export controls on civilian nuclear material and related equipment to NNWS inside and outside the NPT. Arguably, this has contributed to "an emerging international standard for an export control system" (Anthony et al. 2007: 112). The IAEA, established in 1956, developed into a mechanism for verifying that nuclear material is only put to peaceful use in NWS. These facilities have to be declared to the IAEA and to be opened to inspection and monitoring. Following its reform in the mid-1990s, the IAEA's remit has been expanded to include the detection of clandestine activities.

---

[5] Other treaties could be added to this list including the Partial Test Ban Treaty (PTBT) of 1963. Even though it dealt with the outlawing of nuclear tests in the atmosphere, it was a part of the trail leading towards the NPT and later still the CTBT. Within two months of the PTBT opening for signature, more than one hundred countries had signed it (Reiss 1988: 18). For a Chinese perspective on what the non-proliferation norm embraces, see Li (2003: 51).

The external threat environment prompted the creation of this norm. The commitment to non-proliferation came from reactions to the United States' dropping of two atomic bombs on Japan at the end of World War II, Washington's thwarted initial desire to try to maintain its monopoly on the weapon, and eventual realization in both the Soviet Union and the United States that they had a common interest in preventing horizontal proliferation. The Soviet Union was particularly concerned about potential West German acquisition of the bomb, a reasonable supposition given British, French, and Soviet nuclear weapons status. The United States was especially exercised by China's march along the nuclear path, also a reasonable supposition given the number of occasions that China had been threatened with a nuclear strike and its strongly negative attitude to the superpowers' nuclear monopoly (Foot 1995: 167). The Cuban missile crisis of October 1962 further concentrated minds, as did the first Chinese test in October 1964, convincing both Moscow and Washington that they needed to make nuclear arms control and non-proliferation a priority in their relationship and for the world at large.

William Walker has described the Cold War nuclear order that emerged in the 1960s as being based on two characteristics: "a managed system of deterrence, whereby a recognised set of states continued (for the time being) to use nuclear weapons to curb enmity and maintain stability but in a manner that was increasingly controlled and rule-bound" and "a managed system of abstinence, whereby other states abandoned their sovereign rights to develop, hold and use such weapons whilst retaining rights to develop nuclear energy for civil purposes in return for economic, security and other benefits" (Walker 2004: 25). Extended deterrence protected US and Soviet allies and was in part designed to diminish their incentives to go the nuclear route, as was the agreement to allow access to civilian nuclear technology including the fuel cycle in exchange for submitting facilities to international inspections. Finally, there was the long-term promise that the original five NWS would eventually disarm, built into the NPT under Article VI, important in any effort to retain the commitment of others to abstinence.

Moral and legal discourse reinforced this bargain. Sweden worked initially for a treaty eliminating nuclear weapons entirely rather than for the more modest NPT (Krause 2007: 486–7). The Irish Republic, having introduced UN resolutions each year from 1958 to 1961, was finally successful in winning the approval of the UN General Assembly for a resolution calling for an international agreement that prevented the transfer and acquisition of nuclear weapons (Mackby and Slocombe

2004: 196). In 1964, members of the Non-Aligned Movement (NAM) pledged not to produce, acquire, or test any nuclear weapons, and the Organization of African Unity announced an intention to introduce non-proliferation resolutions at the UN (Seaborg and Loeb 1987: 133; see also Paul 2009: 162). When the 1968 NPT opened for signature, sixty-two states immediately signed up, alongside the two superpowers and the United Kingdom, and it entered into force in March 1970. Subsequently, nearly all UN member states have acceded to the treaty. This high level of accession signals a strong global consensus behind the goal of preventing nuclear proliferation.

Societal forces were also to play critical roles in developing this normative framework, especially in the democratic world. Anti-nuclear weapons activists were instrumental in keeping the opposition to nuclear weapons prominent, voicing arguments on both moral and prudential grounds. Hiroshima was the host city in August 1955 of the "First World Conference Against the Atomic and Hydrogen Bombs," and the movement against atmospheric weapons testing was especially active over the course of the 1950s (Wittner 1997: 9 and passim). Nina Tannenwald makes the valid point that the "nuclear taboo" that delegitimized the use of the weapon also reinforced the non-proliferation norm: it was not simply deterrence that prevented the weapon's use and thus encouraged others to refrain from seeking nuclear status, but also the stigmatization of nuclear weapons that took place over the postwar era – often with the anti-nuclear movement linking up with weaker states to take the lead in that effort (Tannenwald 2007).[6]

Treaty making and treaty requirements provided opportunities for the further consolidation of the norm. The 1995 NPT Review Conference agreed that, rather than maintain the original twenty-five-year span of the treaty, it would be extended indefinitely, and at the Treaty Review Conference of 2000, all 188 NPT signatories (out of a UN membership of 191 states at that time) affirmed the thirteen steps that needed to be taken to achieve disarmament, including ratification of the CTBT, the placement under safeguards of fissile materials, and the preservation and strengthening of the ABM Treaty. Negotiation of the 1996 CTBT itself sent two important messages: first, at century's end NNWS largely still accepted

---

[6] Paul (2009: Chapter 2) challenges aspects of the taboo argument, preferring the phrase "tradition" of non-use. However, he agrees with Tannenwald that "the activism of non-nuclear states ... along with scientists, strategists, and nongovernmental organizations such as peace movements" helped to create the tradition (Paul 2009: 160).

that there should not be horizontal proliferation and, second, those with nuclear weapons status, in refraining from open testing, would seemingly not be placing a priority on modernizing their nuclear weapons – thus suggesting the diminished political and military significance of these parts of their weapons arsenal.[7]

Perhaps some of the most powerful signals of this widespread acceptance of the norm came when former vigorous critics of the treaty, China and France, signed the NPT in 1992. This meant that all permanent members of the UN Security Council had finally come on board. Elsewhere, diplomatic negotiation with several states actually persuaded them to reverse or give up their nuclear ambitions, including Argentina, Brazil, South Africa, and later Libya. After the breakup of the former Soviet Union, Belarus, Kazakhstan, and Ukraine also gave up their claims to any nuclear weaponry stationed on their soil. Although there have been breakouts from the regime, President John F. Kennedy's fear voiced in 1963 that there would be fifteen to twenty nuclear powers by 1975 has not yet come to pass (Gavin 2010: 400).

However, most if not all normative frameworks are subject to interpretative weaknesses and are likely to be challenged by external shocks or fundamental shifts in perspectives on the sources of security and insecurity. The structural weaknesses inherent in the non-proliferation normative framework, apparent over the course of the creation of the NPT and its associated bodies, relate to its discriminatory nature, technical imperfections, and inadequate policing powers. As Daniel Joyner has put it with respect to policing, "zero proliferation" was never going to be a reality given that "borders are too porous, corruption at both high and low levels is too rampant ..., and both legitimate commercial and illicit-trafficking in WMD [weapons of mass destruction]-related and dual-use items and technologies are too big a business for states to hope to control it completely" (Joyner 2005: 518).

Moreover, the NPT's asymmetrical provisions have facilitated the initial five NWS keeping their weaponry. Certainly, those five signatories, many had assumed, had agreed under Article VI to abandon nuclear weapons over time, had offered protection in the meantime through extended deterrence either through alliances or collective security provisions, and had asserted in Article IV that they would provide help for the civilian use of nuclear energy subject to states' full compliance with

---

[7] Of course, some NWS then and subsequently were able to take advantage of developments in computer simulation that reduced the need for explosive testing.

the Treaty's other rules. Yet such provisions were double-edged – necessary to reaching the bargain that was struck in 1968, but in particular circumstances capable of being interpreted as reinforcing the need to retain nuclear weapons, or contributing to offering the technical know-how that would make that decision viable at some later date.

Some forty years after the NPT's entry into force, complete nuclear disarmament has not occurred, and possibly all or most signatories to the treaty had never expected that it would. But the fact that it has not occurred has provided a "ready-made alibi" for those few states that have been in quest of nuclear weapons status (Hassner 2007: 463) and a boost to those who argued that preventing nuclear proliferation was legal and normative cover for the NWS to maintain technological and military superiority.

Beyond those hard-nosed interpretations, the privileged position accorded the original NWS has caused resentment among those who hoped or believed that nuclear disarmament would eventually occur (Choubey 2008). Hierarchy in this aspect of global order has been the source of much discontent, especially after 1995 when it was assumed that the agreement to an indefinite rather than limited extension of the NPT rested on an explicit determination by the nuclear haves to move towards elimination of their arsenals. States such as South Africa would probably not have renounced nuclear weapons without such commitments being formalized at that crucial 1995 Review Conference.

Above all, this failure to disarm has prevented full legitimization of the norm of non-use of nuclear weapons.[8] India, and thus Pakistan, refused to join the NPT (Israel – an undeclared nuclear weapons state – is also not a member) and claimed this refusal rested on the grounds of the asymmetries built into the treaty. They still refuse to join despite renewed pressure after their open testing of weaponry in 1998. One other glaring weakness built into the original treaty is that national security concerns are given priority over collective security with the provision for withdrawal on three months' notice if a state's security was ever deemed to be at stake. North Korea was the first state to make use of this provision when it decided to withdraw from the NPT in January 2003.

---

[8] Rebecca Johnson puts it thus: "The policies and utterances of the nuclear-armed states conveyed … that nuclear weapons are indispensable for security and essential for deterrence, provide insurance against unknown future threats, and make their possessors much more important than anyone else in their regions" (2010: 434).

The technical provisions of the NPT have also been open to potential abuse. The pursuit of civilian nuclear technologies readily led to the development of several nuclear-threshold states since the technologies involved in both civilian and military uses were "almost indistinguishable" (Anthony et al. 2007: 7–11; Ruhle 2007: 513). Yet, several countries would have refused to join the NPT without those civilian nuclear use provisions. The Federal Republic of Germany, for example, stated that it would not sign the treaty unless it could remain free to engage in nuclear research and development to preserve its civilian nuclear industry and maintain its competitive commercial position in the field.[9] It was also concerned about industrial espionage by the multinational team of IAEA inspectors. This weakened the treaty's initial inspection powers (Seaborg and Loeb 1987: 293; Mackby and Slocombe 2004: 198–9). Although the Additional Protocol (AP) to the IAEA is intended to strengthen the safeguards regime by including surprise inspections, some states are baulking at contemplating such action and have held back from ratification. The May 2010 NPT Review Conference rejected language that would have made the AP an integral element in the safeguards system (Albright and Stricker 2010). Thus, inspection powers remain weak and sanctions for breaking the rules left undefined and heavily reliant on UN Security Council follow-up action.

Post–Cold War and Post-9/11 Challenges

These long-standing weaknesses associated with the non-proliferation framework have been further exposed in the last decade or so. Expectations were high with the ending of the Cold War that the NNPN would receive a considerable boost. And, indeed, there were some reasons to be optimistic in the early post–Cold War period, a number of which have been detailed already. Both the United States and Russia negotiated a series of significant arms reduction agreements. South Africa's President announced in 1993 that his country previously had developed a small nuclear arsenal but had decided to dismantle and destroy it on its accession to the NPT in 1991. Several other states joined the NPT in the late 1980s and 1990s. Apart from France, South Africa, and China,

---

[9] As the West German Chancellor, Willy Brandt, put it in 1967: "Germany's role and its future influence will be determined by whether or not we shall succeed in holding the front line economically and scientifically in matters of technology and quality, or even reaching the top. In this matter, a nonproliferation treaty must not be an obstacle – and this is a really vital matter" (quoted in Clausen 1993: 87).

this included all states of the former Soviet Union (Russia was already a member) together with Argentina and Brazil, which acceded to the treaty in 1995 and 1998, respectively. The 1995 indefinite renewal of the NPT, and promises made at the Review Conference that year – especially the reaffirmation of the goal of nuclear disarmament and the adoption of the NSG standard that nuclear energy supply would require acceptance of full-scope safeguards – was an important part of the context for the apparent deepening of the norm. So too was the conclusion in 1996 of the CTBT's negotiation (which began in 1993) with all five of the original NWS signing the treaty. Even if neither China nor the United States went on to ratify it, 151 states have ratified as of the end of 2009, and 182 states have signed it.

However, other developments over the same and later periods underlined the weaknesses in the regime's detection and enforcement capacities, and the power of external shocks to lead to a recalculation of the norm's capacity to contribute to national and global security. The IAEA discovery of the North Korean separation of plutonium from spent fuel followed hard on the heels of revelations of extensive bomb-making activity inside Iraq. Libya's decision to abjure its nuclear weapons programme in 2003 completed evidence on a trio of cases of state members of the NPT that had acquired nuclear technology, primarily based on imported items. Open testing of five nuclear devices by India and then the same number by Pakistan in May 1998 delivered a direct blow to the norm. Iran's refusal to suspend its uranium enrichment programme, or to cooperate fully with an investigation by the IAEA of that programme, has heightened suspicion that Tehran is determined to acquire nuclear weapons capacity.

Moreover, these attempts to contain Iran's programme were undermined by the striking of a cooperative deal in the civilian nuclear field between India and the United States in 2005 and 2006. One critic has described this agreement as "overturning more than a quarter century of American non-proliferation policy," and as actually "aiding" India's nuclear ambitions (Carranza 2007: 464, 475).[10] President George W. Bush signed an act permitting civilian nuclear cooperation with New Delhi that awards India open access to the United States' and other

[10] For further evidence of the damage such a deal might have inflicted, see Choubey (2009: 32) who reports a Brazilian reluctance to adhere to the AP of the IAEA safeguards system. As one of its diplomats stated: "The first victim of the India deal is support for the AP in Brazil. We have done everything right, the Indians have not, but they have gotten the better result. We are not taking on any more obligations."

countries' nuclear fuel and reactors as well as to US nuclear technology. The deal also accepted the Indian position that only some of its nuclear facilities would be placed under IAEA safeguards, despite NSG guidelines which required its members to allow nuclear transfers only to those states with comprehensive safeguards in place (Potter 2005: 344; Carranza 2007: 470–3). After strong Bush administration lobbying, in September 2008, the consensus view of the NSG was that the global ban on nuclear trade with India should be lifted – an exception to the rules that opens the opportunity for others (notably Pakistan) to argue for similar exceptions in their cases.[11] This NSG decision did not introduce "clear rules for general application" but reflected particular US political, economic, and strategic preferences (Anthony 2008: 16). Neither was the agreement with India made conditional on any compensatory measures, such as Indian signature of the CTBT.

The external shock of terrorist attacks on the United States in 2001 dramatically sharpened Americans' sense of vulnerability. Counter-proliferation, although it did not originate with Bush, became far more central to US strategic thinking than non-proliferation amid heightened fears that terrorist groups would acquire nuclear weapons capability. When it was discovered that A. Q. Khan, head of the Pakistani government's nuclear programme, had been at the centre of a worldwide nuclear supply network providing technology and designs to Libya, North Korea, and Iran, this added to the sense of nuclear danger (Cortright 2007). This network, in order to escape detection, developed a range of contacts in several different countries from whom separate parts could be bought. The original design for the Pakistani bomb, as well as 50 kg of weapons-grade uranium (as discussed later), apparently came from China, so Khan has stated.[12] But the subsequent supply of nuclear

---

[11] Not everyone interprets the deal as a threat to the non-proliferation norm. Paul and Shankar (2007/08: 115) argue that India is a "responsible nuclear-weapons state" as opposed to Pakistan, Iran, and North Korea, which they contend are not. Other arguments advanced in support of the deal are that it finally makes India a "stakeholder" in the non-proliferation regime; and it meets the country's growing energy and development needs, reducing India's contribution to global warming (reported in Anthony 2008). On the other hand, an ISIS report by Albright and Brannan (2008) states: "In assessing India's nuclear procurement practices, ISIS found several incidents where India conducted illicit nuclear trade and leaked sensitive nuclear information."

[12] In accounts given to *The Washington Post*, A. Q. Khan stated that in 1982 China "gave us drawings of the nuclear weapon" and enough weapons-grade uranium for two atomic bombs. See R. Jeffrey Smith and Joby Warrick, "A Nuclear Power's Act of Proliferation," *The Washington Post*, 13 November 2009. For further details on Khan's claims see Albright, Brannan, and Stricker (2009).

weapons-related technology involved purchases from many individuals and entities in South Africa, Switzerland, Dubai, Malaysia, South Korea, Turkey, Britain, and Germany (Schell 2007: 47).

Despite these signs of severe strain on the non-proliferation framework, from the time of its inception in the early 1960s, legal, moral, and strategic arguments have allowed it to achieve a remarkable level of rhetorical and behavioural consensus at both state and societal levels, and there is frequent endorsement of the non-proliferation norm in global venues. Some 111 states sponsored the proposal to indefinitely extend the NPT at the 1995 review conference, suggesting that, although it is discriminatory in nature, "its existence [has been] widely held to be a global good" (Tannenwald 2007: 346). In 2004, the UN Security Council unanimously passed Resolution 1540 that mandates a legally binding obligation on all states to enact strict export controls on components that might contribute to the manufacture of WMD by terrorist groups – a major step towards the development of an international standard for an export control regime. The UN General Assembly in September 2008 offered a general resolution of support for the CTBT with 168 countries voting in favour, three abstaining, and only one casting a no vote – the United States (Joseph 2009: 89). And at a UN Security Council Summit in September 2009, chaired by President Obama, Council members unanimously endorsed Resolution 1887 and its goal of bringing about a world without nuclear weapons.[13]

In sum, the central elements of this global norm are gradual nuclear disarmament by the nuclear "haves," an agreement to eschew the nuclear route by all other states, the facilitation of the use of nuclear energy for civilian purposes provided there is agreement to international inspection, and the agreement on rules of trade in nuclear materials and dual-use items. If all elements of this bargain were to be adhered to – admittedly, a significant challenge in global governance — this would represent a strong and solidarist normative framework. We turn now to the role that the United States has played in the creation and elaboration of a demanding framework that has become more specific in its compliance requirements over time.

2 The United States and the NNPN

Although it is vital to remember the societal and middle-state pressure designed to contain the nuclear threat and numbers of nuclear weapons

---

[13] S/RES/1887, 24 September 2009.

states, the United States did play a key role at particular stages in the development and elaboration of this normative framework. William Walker, in reference to the US role in first creating nuclear weapons and then in establishing some form of nuclear order (an overarching concept of which non-proliferation is a component) has noted that Washington adopted positions that were "pastoral and monarchical, proactive and managerial." Walker adds, "substituting WMD for nuclear weapons, this observation remains as valid today as it did in the years after 1945" (Walker 2004: 29).

One part of the US domestic response to weapons' development was to create, in 1961, the Arms Control and Disarmament Agency (ACDA). That agency promoted arguments for nuclear restraint against the views of those in the US military and Atomic Energy Commission who favoured reliance on nuclear weaponry (Tannenwald 2007: 244). China's test of a nuclear device in 1964 aided the ACDA efforts and prompted a more sustained turn towards halting proliferation now that it had become clear that nuclear capability would not be confined to the developed world or to superpower allies (Seaborg and Loeb 1987: 117). The US President, Lyndon B. Johnson, primarily in response to China's developing nuclear capacity, established an expert group led by a Wall Street lawyer and former Undersecretary of Defense, Roswell Gilpatric. He brought together serving and former US government officials, advisers, and scientists. The Gilpatric Committee, as it came to be known, was tasked to come up with recommendations as to how best to prevent the spread of nuclear weapons (Gavin 2004/05: 108).

This committee came into existence at a time of great uncertainty and sense of foreboding with respect to nuclear weaponry. Its expert standing, together with presidential backing, made it likely that its conclusions would carry weight. However, its response was not pre-ordained. It began its work at a time when US allies were considering a nuclear sharing agreement within NATO and in a period when proliferation seemed likely to be rapid. In response, the Committee considered a wide range of options from sanctions against emerging NWS to preemption. One briefing paper sent to the Committee raised the question as to whether it would actually be in the United States' interest to halt proliferation in all cases. In fact, the US Secretary of State, Dean Rusk, questioned whether the United States would be "prepared to have a general non-proliferation agreement without the participation of China" and noted that Washington might well want India and Japan to develop nuclear weapons capacity, once China had finally tested a nuclear device

(Seaborg and Loeb 1987: 132). The US Secretary of Defense, Robert McNamara, asked the Committee to challenge the assumption – perhaps based on instinct rather than analysis, he said – that a world without further proliferation of nuclear weapons "was more desirable" (National Security File document quoted in Seaborg and Loeb 1987: 139). However, the Committee's conclusions were unclouded: "preventing the further spread of nuclear weapons is clearly in the national interest, despite the difficult decisions that will be required." Multilateral agreements were recommended as a means to prevent that spread, together with the use of US influence with individual states considering the nuclear option, and the US setting of an example in this policy area (Seaborg and Loeb 1987: 141).

The US Secretary of State remained unconvinced: in Rusk's view, "non-proliferation [was] not the overriding element in U.S. relations with the rest of the world" (Gavin 2004/05: 114). However, this opposition did not stop President Johnson, as well as the ACDA, from backing the report. Eventually, it was determined that non-proliferation should be universally promoted and not just with respect to enemy states.

Later on, the US Congress played a role in advancing this normative framework, its involvement increasing in the 1970s as a result of India's 1974 explosion of its "peaceful nuclear device" at a time of poor Indo-American relations.[14] One result was a more sustained Congressional focus on nuclear export policy with the passage in Congress in 1976 of the Symington Amendment that prevented US military and economic assistance to countries importing enrichment technology and refusing full-scope safeguards, and in 1977 the Glenn Amendment that covered reprocessing activities. That Indian test also prompted Congress, with support from the Carter administration, to pass the 1978 Nuclear Non-Proliferation Act requiring all states to renegotiate their nuclear cooperation agreements with the United States, including acceptance (among other things) of the condition that countries in receipt of US nuclear exports had to agree to full-scope IAEA safeguards on all their nuclear facilities (Carranza 2007: 466; CRS 2010b: 5).

Even governments far closer to US administrations than that of India were subject to constraint. In the 1970s, the United States sought to prevent Taiwan, South Korea, and Pakistan from acquiring commercial

---

[14] President Nixon was engaged in his rapprochement with China in which Pakistan had played a constructive role. Nixon's tilt towards Pakistan during the 1971 Indo-Pakistani War also created serious hostility between New Delhi and Washington.

reprocessing facilities on the grounds that these programmes would be strategically destabilizing, although they were permitted by the NPT (Tannenwald 2007: 335–9). Pakistan was of particular concern to the US Congress, and in 1985 Congress passed the Pressler Amendment, which required the US President to certify each year that Pakistan did not have a nuclear weapon (Riedel 2008: 110).[15] President George H. W. Bush tried to coerce India and Pakistan into signature of the NPT, stopping all economic and military aid to Pakistan because the executive branch could not fulfil the terms of the Pressler Amendment (Carranza 2007: 467).

Certainly, there were instances in this earlier period where the United States applied the non-proliferation rules arbitrarily, most notably with respect to Israel. Once it became plain that active US efforts in the 1960s to contain the Israeli programme were going nowhere, it opted for secrecy about its findings, accepted Israel's nuclear weapons status as a fait accompli, and developed a tacit understanding with Tel Aviv that Israel would neither deploy nor overtly test (Clausen 1993: Chapter 5).[16] Similarly, with respect to Pakistan itself, and despite Congressional legislation, President Reagan decided to overlook the country's moves in the 1980s to develop the bomb, certifying "against the objections of many in the intelligence community" that Pakistan was still a non-nuclear weapons state (Levy and Scott-Clark 2007: 116; Riedel 2008: 110). This was a time when the two governments were allies in the fight against the Soviet presence in Afghanistan.[17]

The US government did, then, apply this policy in arbitrary ways. Nevertheless, it did commit to the adoption of a universal non-proliferation policy in the 1960s culminating in the NPT, even against the advice of senior officials within the State Department, and at some political cost to its relations with allies. Over time it tried to bolster the strength of that normative framework by adding to its restraining features. Senatorial involvement, as the US Constitution requires, in treaty consent as well as Congressional passage of related legislation imposed some restraints at times on the range of the executive branch's arbitrariness on proliferation

[15] Levy and Scott-Clark argue that the Pressler Amendment was in fact a "pro-Pakistan initiative" submitted by a sympathetic Republican Senator and designed to undercut a tougher response (2007: 116).

[16] Clausen states that it was in 1968 that the CIA concluded that Israel had the weapon (1993: 108).

[17] As a State Department classified memorandum put it three weeks after President Reagan was sworn into office: "Pakistan is a front-line state under heavy Soviet pressure ... crucial to our larger interests in the region" (quoted in Levy and Scott-Clark 2007: 79).

matters. The US record of nuclear non-use after 1945, and its role in promoting the domestic and international institutionalization of non-proliferation meant that Washington played a generally positive leadership role in developing and supporting a norm designed to constrain the nuclear ambitions of many states in the global system, including those of a number of its allies. However, over this same period, the United States did little to advance Article VI of the NPT that required the NWS to move gradually to disarm, or to reduce the significance of nuclear weapons in its security strategy. The norm was to constrain others, not the United States itself.

The US Challenge in the Post–Cold War Era

The post–Cold War era was to be a time of considerable flux in US attitudes towards the NNPN. US assistance in consolidating the norm came initially when the United States, in negotiation with Russia, began to reduce the size of its nuclear forces in conformity with the Strategic Arms Reduction Treaty of 1991, as well as – indirectly – Article VI of the NPT. The prevention of horizontal proliferation received a boost with US support for strengthening various supplier regimes that served non-proliferation objectives, including the Missile Technology Control Regime (MTCR), the Nuclear Suppliers Guidelines, the Zangger Committee trigger lists, and the Wassenaar Arrangement, the latter promoted as the successor to the Cold War Coordinating Committee for Multilateral Export Controls (COCOM) arrangement (Andreani 1999–2000: 48). The Clinton administration actively participated in the 1995 and 2000 NPT Conferences, consented to strengthening the language of the NPT's disarmament pledges, and signed the CTBT in 1996. Its intense efforts in the 1990s to dismantle the North Korean nuclear programme before it reached the stage of weaponization, as well as support for the UN-sanctioned IAEA inspection and elimination regime designed to counter the nuclear ambitions of Iraq, showed a similar commitment to the prevention of proliferation in the 1990s.

That broad evidence of US convergence with the NNPN began to break down in the latter part of that decade, however, particularly marked by a steady shift in emphasis from non-proliferation to counter-proliferation and the new role Washington allocated to its nuclear weapons. The ACDA also lost its status as an independent agency, becoming fully merged into the US State Department in 1997. The Iraqi and North Korean breakouts from the regime clearly encouraged the emphasis on counter-proliferation, but there were other influences contributing to this shift. The change reflected four main developments in the beliefs of US political elites: that neither reliance on deterrence nor on verification were any longer suitably robust guarantees of security, and that dangers were coming from new often non-state quarters, and from chemical, biological, and nuclear weapons (Walker 2007: 441–3). President Clinton signed a top secret presidential directive in 1997 that allowed for a nuclear reply to any attack that involved chemical or biological weapons,[18] "the first formal adjustment of targeting policy in sixteen years" (Tannenwald 2007: 331).

Those beliefs were reflected in hostile Senate attitudes towards ratification of the CTBT, although clearly many Republicans additionally desired to punish a President that they had come to "distrust and despise" (Kimball 1999). President Clinton did gain support for ratification from four former chairs of the US Joint Chiefs of Staff. In addition, the UK Prime Minister, the German Chancellor, and the French President published jointly an opinion piece in *The New York Times*, appealing for Senate support. Nevertheless, the treaty was rejected in October 1999 by a vote of 51 to 48 – a number well short of the two-thirds majority in the Senate required to pass it.[19] According to Gilles Andreani, non-proliferation had "always been a careful balancing act between international consensus-building, on the one hand, and the development of punitive and defensive options to protect one's security should non-proliferation fail." But, in his view, that balance was to be lost in the latter part of the 1990s with "presentations of the proliferation threat as unamenable to deterrence or political persuasion." One result was "a growing appetite for military options designed to counter proliferation once it ha[d] occurred; and a distinct scepticism of treaty-based arms control, and especially of international verification" (Andreani 1999–2000: 43).

These beliefs were further accentuated under the presidency of George W. Bush. Conservative US strategists argued that traditional arms control treaties took too long to negotiate, were unnecessarily restrictive on the United States, and could not be satisfactorily verified (Medeiros 2007: 192). Unlike the Strategic Arms Reduction Treaty (START), for instance, the Strategic Offensive Reductions Treaty (SORT) contained no instruments of verification at American insistence.

---

[18] The United States eschewed retaliation in kind to chemical or biological attacks – thus, one reason for its rejection of No-First-Use (NFU) of nuclear weapons.

[19] "Remarks by the President after the Senate Voted Not to Ratify the Comprehensive Test Ban Treaty," White House Transcript, 13 October 1999, http://www.fas.org/nuke.control/ctbt/text/101399clintonstatement.htm, accessed 16 November 2009.

One of the George W. Bush administration's first acts was to announce withdrawal from the ABM Treaty and to signal that ballistic missile defence systems would be pursued with renewed vigour. The thirteen steps of the 2000 NPT Review Conference were disavowed, and the Bush government delivered a snub to the 2005 NPT Review Conference when it downgraded its representation at that meeting to Assistant Secretary level. It refused to seek ratification of the CTBT, and cut funding to the CTBT Organization. Congress was asked to approve a shortening of the period before a nuclear weapon could be tested (Joseph 2009: 81–2), and the administration also began research on the development of new types of nuclear weapons for counter-proliferation and bunker-busting assignments (the 'Robust Nuclear Earth Penetrator'). The 2001 Nuclear Posture Review argued for a more "flexible" US approach to its nuclear arsenal and the bringing together of nuclear and non-nuclear capabilities to make military force "a more useable instrument of policy" (Alagappa 2008: 7). The first of the administration's NSS documents of 2002 committed the United States to using force preventively against any hostile actor deemed to be acquiring nuclear, chemical, or biological weaponry.[20]

Having divided the world into hostile and non-hostile forces, the administration made clear distinctions in the way that it treated their nuclear ambitions (Potter 2005: 345). The Iranian issue was to be tackled via UN Security Council and bilateral sanctions, the implied threat of a military strike, as well as a negotiating process that involved the United States, China, and Russia joining the EU3 (France, Germany, and the United Kingdom). However, over this same period, the Bush administration struck a civilian nuclear deal with a nuclear-armed, if friendly, India.

Agreements such as the 2003 Proliferation Security Initiative (PSI), involving interdiction of ships or planes possibly carrying WMD-related materials from or to "states of proliferation concern" – that is Iran and North Korea – (Valencia 2005: 7; Hadley 2008) similarly showed a preference for selective targeting rather than universal constraint.[21] The Bush administration position reflected the idea that horizontal proliferation

---

[20] As the 2002 National Strategy to Combat Weapons of Mass Destruction put it: "Because deterrence may not succeed, and because of the potentially devastating consequences of WMD use against our forces and civilian population, U.S. military forces and appropriate civilian agencies must have the capability to defend against WMD-armed adversaries, including in appropriate cases through preemptive measures." Available at www.whitehouse.gov/news/releases/2002/12/WMDStrategy.pdf, accessed 16 November 2009.

[21] For further discussion of the international legal implications of the PSI, see Joyner (2005). The PSI has faced problems of legitimacy, and several key states – notably China, India, and Indonesia – have been reluctant to participate (Foot 2009a).

was to be thought of as a "limited challenge ... dependent on regime type" (Reiss 2006) and that vertical proliferation – that is, the modernization and further development of its nuclear weaponry – had to become a necessary part of America's security policy.

Under Obama, however, that pendulum has swung back to a rhetorical emphasis on treaty-based agreements and multilateral action, marked in 2010 by a vigorous effort to achieve a final document based on a consensus at the NPT Review Conference that year (Albright and Stricker 2010). Early in his administration, the President had committed himself to reducing the role of nuclear weapons in US national security strategy, in a major speech in Prague in April 2009 announcing he would pursue ratification of the CTBT; seek a new FMCT; strive to make the PSI a more legitimate, universal, and "durable" institution; and work to strengthen the NPT.[22] In September 2009, Obama took the symbolic step of chairing the UN Security Council Summit on "Nuclear Non-Proliferation and Nuclear Disarmament," the first time a US President has taken on this particular role as chair. His assistant secretary, Rose Gottemoeller, stated in May 2009 that "[u]niversal adherence to the NPT itself – including by India, Israel, Pakistan and North Korea – ... remains a fundamental objective of the United States."[23] However, it is an objective that is very difficult to reach and little or no progress has been made with these states as yet. Moreover, there are no signs that the deal with India will be rethought or any attempt made at its renegotiation.

Obama has made progress with the disarmament arm of this norm when he reached a new arms control treaty with the Russian government in April 2010, which replaces the START I treaty of 1991. The new treaty, which has to be ratified by the US Senate, aims to reduce the number of deployed nuclear warheads from 2,200 to 1,550 within seven years of the treaty coming into force. It also places limits on delivery vehicles, dropping numbers from the current 1,600 to 800.[24] The hope is that US

---

[22] "President Obama's Visit to Prague," 5 April 2009, http://prague.usembassy.gov/obama. html, accessed 13 July 2009.

[23] "President Obama's Visit to Prague," 5 April 2009; Rose Gottemoeller, "Opening Statement at the Third Session of the Preparatory Committee for the 2010 Nuclear Non-Proliferation Treaty," New York, 5 May 2009, http://www.state.gov/t/vci/rls/122672. htm, accessed 6 May 2009. Obama did signal that India would come under greater pressure to sign treaties that support the NNPN, but that will be difficult to deliver. And since these states are NWS it is not clear as to the mechanism by which they could become NPT members.

[24] Peter Baker, "White House Presses Senate to Approve Russia Arms Pact," *New York Times*, 18 May 2010; "New START Provides for Significant Arms Cuts," *Strategic Comments*, 20 April 2010, IISS.

leadership on matters such as disarmament, CTBT ratification, and the like will strengthen the non-proliferation regime by reducing its asymmetric elements. This in turn could legitimize US policy towards the two countries of particular proliferation concern to Washington (as well as being of concern to several other states) – Iran and North Korea.

Thus, while the NNPN has weakened in the last decade or so, it could be revived were one or more of these US policy objectives to be successfully fulfilled.[25] This is not because norms bend to US power, but because the Obama administration has accepted that the satisfaction of certain US security objectives will remain elusive when US administrations attempt to rewrite norms that have commanded considerable global legitimacy.[26]

Explaining Levels of Behavioural Consistency

The United States has played a crucial role in norm creation in this issue area and especially in its legal elaboration. Where nuclear weapons are concerned, it has maintained what Walker described as a "pastoral and monarchical" role (2004: 29) – another example of what we have referred to elsewhere in this book as America's exceptionalist impulse and its perceived role as custodian of global order. In view of its leadership position, its actions have had both norm-promoting as well as norm-weakening effects, however Washington itself might have interpreted its behaviour. External incentives, domestic institutional creation, presidential beliefs, and distinct roles for the executive and legislative branches are important to explaining the levels of US consistency with this global normative framework. The framework itself has provided the focal point around which policies are debated, imposing some limits on what can be proposed and what is perceived as most likely to generate domestic and external support.

The most important of the external stimuli that led the United States to support a non-proliferation regime was undoubtedly the nuclear arms race with the Soviet Union which both Washington and Moscow realized, particularly after the Cuban Missile Crisis, was raising the stakes of Cold War contestation to unacceptable levels. The advancement in nuclear

---

[25] The opposite also holds: a further weakening of the non-proliferation norm if few or none of these conditions are actually met.

[26] Brooks and Wohlforth, on the other hand, see legitimacy as a "highly contingent and malleable constraint on U.S. security policy." For their larger discussion on legitimacy as a constraint, see Brooks and Wohlforth (2008: Chapter 6).

weapons capacity had also attracted the ire of a powerful grassroots anti-nuclear weapons movement that, in the 1950s, linked up with weaker states in the global system to focus largely on a halt to nuclear testing.[27] A nuclear inferior Soviet Union could make use of that sentiment, especially the criticisms levied by the NAM and newly decolonized nations, who were also calling for a halt to the nuclear arms race. This aspect of Soviet-American rivalry prompted the United States to respond with arms control policies of its own which were often debated at the primary institutional setting for these issues – the Eighteen Nation Disarmament Committee and its successor, the UN Disarmament Conference (CD), first made up of NATO and Warsaw Pact members plus, in 1961, eight non-aligned states. Those eight placed both superpowers under pressure to conclude a test ban, an important initial step in the move towards a non-proliferation treaty.[28]

However, a coincidence of strategic interest between Moscow and Washington also helped to promote the non-proliferation framework. Evidence of a burgeoning Chinese nuclear weapons programme, together with similar agitation elsewhere in the world, led to more determined efforts on both sides to halt the spread of such weaponry. Moscow stopped its support for the Chinese programme in the late 1950s, promising Beijing a reliable nuclear umbrella instead, while the United States debated whether to extinguish the embryonic Chinese programme entirely. Both Moscow and Washington also turned, however, to the creation of normative and legal constraints.

The external environment was to be critical again in shaping policy at the end of the Clinton period, but especially in the George W. Bush era after the terrorist attacks of 2001 and as a result of China's resurgence, which fuelled Beijing's military modernization programme. The linking of terrorist threats with the proliferation of WMD was important to attempts at norm reinterpretation – that is, the emphasis on counter-proliferation and on selective rather than universal application. Both these elements were present – counter-terrorist objectives and balancing China's resurgence – in the US decision to sign a nuclear agreement with India. The US ambassador to India in George W. Bush's first administration and a principal advocate

---

[27] As President Dwight D. Eisenhower put it in reference to a proposed halt in testing in August 1958: "the new thermonuclear weapons are tremendously powerful; however, they are not … as powerful as is world opinion today in obliging the United States to follow certain lines of policy" (quoted in Rublee 2009: 36).

[28] Both the United States and the Soviet Union proposed draft treaties to the CD in 1965. As at 2010, there are sixty-five members of the CD. (See also Paul 2009: 160.)

of the agreement (Robert Blackwill) could not have put the China case more plainly: there were he said "no two [other] countries which share equally the challenge of trying to shape the rise of Chinese power" (quoted in Schell 2007: 77).[29] Ambassador Blackwill's former senior advisor, Ashley Tellis, became special assistant to the President on the National Security Council staff and senior director for strategic planning and Southwest Asia. In November 2005, he argued before the House Committee on International Relations that Washington and New Delhi were "happily confronted by an unprecedented convergence of interests, values, and inter-societal ties in a way never experienced before," adding that these common interests included "[p]reventing Asia from being dominated by any single power that has the capacity to crowd out others and which may use aggressive assertion of national self-interest to threaten American presence, American alliances, and American ties with regional states."[30]

However, while the external stimuli were key to the decision to legalize the norm and later on to attempted reinterpretation of it, the domestic level was vital in determining which route would be chosen and how it would evolve. Domestic institutional developments, including the creation of the Gilpatric Committee and the ACDA – both of which rivalled the power of a more sceptical State Department – propelled forward the NPT. So too did high presidential interest in the non-proliferation question in the early to mid-1960s: the President not only put ACDA officials in charge of implementing the Gilpatric recommendation but also gave them direct access to the White House (Gavin 2010: 407). In a political system as fragmented as is the one in the United States, this presidential commitment was highly significant.[31]

The US State Department had been concerned about the negative impact of this decision on West Germany, India, and Japan. In addition,

---

[29] China returned to US nuclear planning in 1998 "after a long absence" and was also given a prominent place in the Bush administration's 2001 Nuclear Posture Review. (See Lewis 2007: 143.)

[30] Ashley J. Tellis, "The US-India 'Global Partnership': How Significant for American Interests?" Testimony before the House Committee on International Relations, 16 November 2005, http://www.carnegieendowment.org/publications/index.cfm?fa=view& id=17693, accessed 16 November 2009.

[31] Clausen argues that Johnson's commitment to non-proliferation owed much to his interest in promoting superpower détente and in reducing criticism of his policy towards the Vietnam War (1993: 98). Nevertheless, many of the arguments in favour of the NPT in the United States were based on globalist interpretations of security rather than solely on national interest. Moreover, when the Gilpatric Committee was set up (November 1964), Vietnam had not yet become a political millstone for Johnson. However, the NPT was a useful means of promoting superpower détente.

it did not believe there would be meaningful negotiations with the Soviet Union on non-proliferation questions. But the ACDA's direct access to the President undercut the force of its objections. Thus, although both the Kennedy and Johnson presidencies considered destroying China's burgeoning nuclear weapons capabilities (Burr and Richelson 2000–01), in the end a universal basis to the non-proliferation issue emerged, even though it generated tensions in relations with some of America's allies and within the bureaucracy.[32]

Beliefs held within the executive branch were to be important again in later years in shaping the US relationship with the normative framework. For example, under George W. Bush, there was a generally negative attitude towards international law and scepticism of its ability to deliver any security benefits to the United States. These beliefs, combined with those in a powerful Defense Department led until November 2006 by Donald Rumsfeld, resulted in a more obvious break from the universal features of the NNPN.[33] That position was to be reconsidered when the Obama administration entered office, articulating beliefs and outlining policies that suggested a desire to rebuild the legitimacy and constraining power of the global normative framework. This was worth doing, it was believed, not only for reputational reasons but also because it was thought likely to help advance US interests, including those with respect to Iran and North Korea. The fact that as of early 2010, little significant progress has been made in policy towards these two states has thwarted the ambition of Obama's proposals.

The US legislative branch has also played a critical role in elaborating the non-proliferation framework. However, at other times its actions have weakened it, especially when those generally hostile to multilateral treaties were in ascendance. Particularly after India's 1974 explosion of a nuclear device, the US Congress became active in developing legislation to curtail nuclear exports. The US constitutional division of powers provided the opportunity for an activist Congress to pass domestic legislation that hemmed in or supported various aspects of executive branch policies, or forced it to find creative ways to circumvent legislative constraints. Even where administrations tended to prevail over Congress, as

[32] As one West German official complained, the United States' attempts to work with the Soviets on non-proliferation were leading to "concessions from the wrong side and to the wrong address" (quoted in Gavin 2010: 396–7).

[33] The US-India nuclear deal owed much to Bush's own dismissal of the prospects for universalism and determination to pass a bill that he thought would cement bilateral relations with a major democratic state (Pant 2009: 283).

was often the case during the Reagan years – an administration that put more store by nuclear sales, and anti-Soviet policies than broader proliferation threats – the existence of that legislation carried some domestic political costs when the executive tried to overwhelm its requirements, as in reference to Pakistan.

Conversely, Congress played a role in diminishing support for the normative framework from the late 1990s, most powerfully reflected in the 1990s Senate debate on the CTBT. This debate failed to prioritize the ways in which this treaty could support non-proliferation objectives, preferring instead to focus on the treaty's potential to restrict the modernization of US nuclear capabilities, and to question the reliability of its verification provisions (Andreani 1999–2000: 42).

Moreover, later on Congress allowed its strong initial doubts about the nuclear deal with India to be overcome (Pant 2009: 280–1; CRS 2010b: 7). Of some significance in widening the coalition in support of that agreement were the presumed economic benefits it would bring to firms such as Westinghouse and General Electric. The Indian government apparently hired two major lobbying firms (the President of one firm was Robert Blackwill), and spent $1.3 million on a campaign to win support from the Congress.[34] Other groups, such as the US-India Business Council, the US-India Friendship Council, and the US-India Political Action Committee also weighed in "blanketing Capitol Hill with receptions, meetings and briefings."[35] Lobbyists raised expectations of more than $100 billion in future sales, and possibly tens of thousands of jobs, in the US nuclear industry.[36] Few legislators, in the end, were willing to stand out against this prospect, linked as arguments were with the strategic need to improve ties with democratic India at a time of China's growing power, and the support New Delhi could offer to US counter-terrorist policies in South Asia.

The US Senate has a prominent part to play once again as President Obama strives to gain the necessary sixty-seven votes to support

[34] Senator Hillary Clinton was a known supporter of India and had co-founded the first ever India caucus in the Senate. US Senator Barrack Obama also voted for the nuclear deal.

[35] Ghoshroy, Subrata, "Business Lobby Triumphs in U.S.-India Nuclear Deal," *Alternet*, 28 October 2006, http://www.alternet.org/module/printversion/43531, accessed 8 March 2009.

[36] This may well be difficult to realize given the United States' requirement that India pass laws covering liability and patent protection – legislation not required by either France or Russia. See "Despite Historic Pact, U.S. Firms are Hampered in Setting up Reactors in India," *The Washington Post*, 21 January 2009.

ratification of the CTBT and to fulfil other of the nuclear non-proliferation commitments he has made. The global normative framework will be pitted against the polarities apparent in the Senate and divergent interpretations of US strategic needs. The outcome, given persistent suspicions among both Democrats and Republicans of international treaties, raises serious questions about the likely success of this part of the administration's attempt to reconverge with a norm that it perceives as having legitimating properties.

3 China and the NNPN

China became a nuclear weapons state with its successful test in October 1964. Its decision to acquire nuclear weapons rested on three main motives: it was a response to Washington's nuclear threats of the 1950s, it represented a desire for greater strategic autonomy especially after its uncomfortable experience of being allied with the Soviet Union, and it rested on its concerns to boost its national and international esteem. As Mao Zedong put it in 1956: "if we are not to be bullied in the present day world, we cannot do without the Bomb"; adding later in 1958, without the bomb "others don't think what we say carries weight" (quoted in Foot 1995: 167–71).

Beijing's initial stance towards nuclear non-proliferation efforts was hostile, determined by the preferences of Chairman Mao and developed in the absence of a willingness or ability to participate in international non-proliferation debates. In its view, efforts to prevent proliferation were designed to ensure a continuing superpower monopoly over nuclear weaponry, and Beijing affirmed it would have nothing to do with them (Li 2003: 58–60). Uncertainty with regard to the security consequences of proliferation led to a number of contradictory statements. On the one hand, its declaration after its first atomic test introduced ideas that were in some small way to contribute to nuclear non-use and thus non-proliferation. It stated that it would never be the first to use nuclear weapons in war, that it had developed these weapons solely for defensive purposes, that its broader aims were to break the nuclear monopoly of the "self-ordained nuclear overlords," and that it would work to eliminate all nuclear weapons (Foot 1995: 177).[37]

---

[37] In a personal communication to the authors, William Walker has suggested that these statements, together with the No-First-Use pledge, may have been motivated in part by a desire to diminish the incentives of its East Asian neighbours (including Japan and Taiwan) to contemplate acquisition of these weapons.

On the other hand, breaking the superpower monopoly in advance of US and Soviet nuclear disarmament implied support for the proliferation of these weapons into the hands of other states, particularly those in the developing world. Indeed, one government statement in 1963 went beyond that grouping and supported any socialist country that wanted to become a nuclear weapons state: this would "better the guarantees for world peace" against imperialist nuclear blackmail (quoted in Medeiros 2007: 34).[38] Matters other than socialist solidarity also influenced China's proliferation decisions: Beijing's support for the Pakistani nuclear programme began soon after India's 1974 "peaceful nuclear explosion."[39]

China became more active in nuclear-weapons-related and conventional arms control institutions from the 1980s. Beijing entered the CD in 1980, joined the IAEA in 1984, and in 1987 became a member of the latter's board of directors. To make its IAEA membership credible, it had to announce support for the principle of nuclear non-proliferation (Li 2003: 61), as well as to permit international monitoring of its civilian nuclear facilities. However, over a similar period China apparently stepped up its support of Pakistan's nuclear programme, A. Q. Khan reporting the transfer in 1982 of technical drawings and weapons-grade uranium.[40]

Nevertheless, membership of such bodies like the IAEA and CD had a more positive influence on Beijing's policies. They required the development of an expert cadre that could understand, for example, the nature of the international standards on safe nuclear commerce (Medeiros 2007: 214–15), or ideas about verification. In order to develop a fuller range of specialists, the Ministry of Foreign Affairs used the CD as a training ground, including rotating officials from China's defence industry through the Geneva-based body. The MOFA also successfully argued in 1985 for the creation of an ambassador for disarmament, although it

---

[38] As Li (2003: 59) has put it: China "maintained that once the opponents of imperialism and their partners had achieved nuclear weapons, the imperialists and their partners would never be arrogant, the policies of nuclear blackmail and nuclear threats would be ineffective, and the possibility for the complete prohibition and total destruction of nuclear weapons would be more real."

[39] According to A. Q. Khan, the terms of a nuclear exchange agreement were set in a conversation between Mao and Prime Minister Bhutto in 1976. See R. Jeffrey Smith and Joby Warrick, "A Nuclear Power's Act of Proliferation," *The Washington Post*, 13 November 2009. Mao died that year and must have been seriously ill when this conversation with Bhutto allegedly took place.

[40] R. Jeffrey Smith and Joby Warrick, "A Nuclear Power's Act of Proliferation," *The Washington Post*, 13 November 2009.

took until 1997 before this led to the establishment of an Arms Control and Disarmament Department (ACDD) with separate status from the International Organizations Department in the MOFA. However, once established, Sha Zukang, who became the vocal head of that new department, emerged as the "primary official voice on multilateral arms control issues" (Johnston 2008: 54–5), including statements relating to nuclear non-proliferation. The expertise it demonstrated undercut much of the legitimacy of the earlier Maoist rhetoric in this policy area (Johnston 2008: 72).

More significant participation in international negotiation relating to the normative framework came in the 1990s. In 1990, China attended the fourth NPT Review Conference, although not yet an NPT signatory (Li 2003: 61). China finally signed the NPT in 1992 and moved on to support the indefinite renewal of that treaty in 1995. It added its signature to the CTBT in 1996, worked with the United States to draft UNSC Resolution 1172 which condemned the Indian and Pakistani tests of 1998,[41] and called on the two South Asian states to join the NPT and CTBT (Medeiros 2007: 88). It joined the Zangger Committee in 1997 and the NSG in 2004.

China also developed several sets of detailed export control regulations in the period after 1994,[42] leading one analyst to conclude that, with respect to China's export of nuclear-related goods and technologies in the early twenty-first century, these have become "few in number, dual-use in character, and under safeguards" (Medeiros 2007: 2). Various governmental moves designed to control exports suggest a desire to further tighten their scope, including periodically working with European, American, and Australian partners to discuss control measures.

China's signature of the CTBT in 1996 required a number of sovereignty and strategic sacrifices. Signature meant agreement to on-site inspections, as well as stopping further testing of its nuclear weaponry (Kent 2007: 77). Indeed, Johnston catalogues the extent to which the testing and weapons communities in China considered it a security sacrifice to sign the CTBT (Johnston 2008: 107), a position reinforced during our interviews in Beijing in September 2008.

Thus, we have witnessed a fairly lengthy but reasonably linear Chinese integration into the normative framework from supportive rhetoric, domestic institutional creation, domestic legal development,

---

[41] S/RES/1172, 6 June 1998.
[42] A comprehensive list up to 2005 can be found in Kent (2007: 94).

and behavioural change. Chinese scholars and top leaders now argue in different venues in support of non-proliferation. General Pan Zhenqiang has gone further than most. As he put it in a scholarly article in 2008, the immorality and illegality of nuclear weapons had to be established and nuclear disarmament and non-proliferation had to prevail via a reduction in the role of such weapons in nuclear weapons strategies and the strengthening of export controls (Pan 2008: 68–9). President Hu Jintao, at the UN Security Council Summit in September 2009 on "Nuclear Non-Proliferation and Nuclear Disarmament" called (among other things) for fulfilment of the nuclear disarmament clause of the NPT, the bringing into force of the CTBT, the start of negotiations for a FMCT, and the conclusion of a legally binding international instrument outlawing the use or threat of use of nuclear weapons against non-nuclear-weapon states or in nuclear-weapons-free-zones.[43]

In sum, "China has joined numerous nonproliferation treaties and agreements, narrowed the scope and content of its sensitive exports, institutionalized its commitments in national laws and regulations, and built a cadre of nonproliferation specialists both within and outside government circles" (Medeiros 2007: 240). Moreover, it made some effort to promote the normative framework beyond its own territory – a particular kind of commitment that brings the norm into competition with other of its state-to-state interests. Especially after 2000, non-proliferation became a part of Beijing's bilateral and multilateral diplomacy (Medeiros 2007: 89) – for example, as shown by its more active role in the Six Party Talks involving North Korea's nuclear programme from 2003 and its helping to draft a UN Sanctions resolution directed at Pyongyang in 2006 (Christensen 2009: 93).

However, China has important interests that sometimes conflict with the non-proliferation norm, and these have demonstrated the limits of its support for the normative framework. It has abjured, for example, sustained coercive policies against either the DPRK or Iran and has continued to aid Pakistan with a civil nuclear energy programme, even though Islamabad resists full international safeguards. Despite these limitations in support of the norm, on balance, its rhetoric, domestic legislation, and much of its international behaviour lead to the reasonable conclusion that

---

[43] The full statement is at http://ww.mfa.gov.cn/ce/ceun/eng/hyyfy/t606550.htm, accessed 16 November 2009. Some of our interviewees have suggested that China privately is reluctant actually to advance the negotiations on the FMCT because its fissile material stockpile lags significantly behind that of Russia and the United States.

Beijing has understood the security drawbacks of horizontal nuclear proliferation. In Medeiros' comprehensive assessment, he describes Beijing's
support for non-proliferation as "both substantial and enduring." But he
perhaps puts it too strongly when he avers that "preventing the spread of
nuclear weapons and all the attendant complexities is widely accepted and
firmly ingrained in the calculations of Chinese policymakers" (Medeiros
2007: 2 and 96). Full compliance is clearly not in place, and China can
be seen to be weighing a number of competing interests in certain of its
non-proliferation decisions. Nevertheless, it has signed the core treaties,
has placed constraints on its nuclear-related exports, and has borne some
economic and strategic costs in doing so.

Explaining Levels of Behavioural Consistency

How do we explain China's higher levels of behavioural consistency
with a norm that in the Maoist era was dismissed and depicted as being
underpinned by a superpower desire to retain US and Soviet monopoly
over nuclear weaponry? The three factors that seem of most importance
in promoting the degree of internalization that we noted previously are
predominantly international in origin, though they have led to domestic
institutional and domestic legal change that has helped to lock in the
rhetorical as well as the behavioural commitments. Strategic, political,
and economic incentives emanating from the international level – both
material and international image-related – encouraged treaty signature
and entry into international institutions with non-proliferation objectives. Participation in international institutions led to domestic institutional creation and the learning of new ideas. This eventually resulted in
domestic behaviour in closer conformity with the global norm.

Domestic institutional reorganization relevant to this issue area
accelerated in China, especially after Beijing had joined the CD. China's
MOFA played a critical role in reforming the policy-making apparatus,
spreading areas of professionalization, and encouraging the development
of scholarly research on nuclear strategy and non-proliferation issues.
Particularly crucial was the establishment of an independent voice from
within the Ministry of Foreign Affairs – the ACDD – able to argue its case
in competition with those arguments that emerged from the Ministry of
Foreign Trade and Economic Cooperation and China's Atomic Energy
Agency (Yuan 2001). As Johnston convincingly demonstrates, the MOFA
met resistance to its policy positions on a number of occasions, not least
because its concern to promote China's international image as a "responsible great power" could sometimes be seen to clash with the core policy

of promoting economic development, or with more direct concerns about the strategic costs to China (Johnston 2008: esp. Chapter 3).

As regards the economic costs, nuclear-related export controls, for example, were not always desired by a nuclear industry undergoing painful restructuring including a reduction in governmental financial support. Regarding the strategic costs, as noted, some Chinese strategists in venues such as the CTBT were not in favour of China's signature of that treaty because they perceived it put the country at a strategic disadvantage. For example, Zou Yunhua, a representative of the Commission on Science, Technology, and Industry for National Defence (COSTIND) on the Chinese CTBT delegation, stated that China's technical inferiority in the nuclear weapons field would forever be frozen in the absence of further testing (quoted in Johnston 2008: 107–8).[44]

The MOFA, on the other hand, remained sensitive to the condemnations of Chinese nuclear tests made by most developing countries, middle powers, and the NGO community. The Ministry believed that an unwillingness to sign the treaty would buck a "great international trend" and would damage the international image benefits to China of "participating in one of the pillar treaties of the non-proliferation regime" (Johnston 2008: 115). That argument won out over those of the sceptics, at least as far as signature of the treaty was concerned.

Concern over China's image in relation to international trends had been important in 1992 as well, leading up to China's signature of the NPT. As Johnston notes, one of the reasons for China to sign it was that, when the French announced they would accede, Beijing feared being the last remaining member of the original five NWS outside the treaty (Johnston 2008: 133). Consensus also seems to matter. One Chinese arms control expert in the PLA stated in 1990: "the number of [NPT] signatories continues to grow, making it one of the arms control treaties that enjoy the largest membership" (quoted in Medeiros 2007: 73). Image, and reasonably high levels of distributive fairness, as expressed in widespread signature of international treaties, can be persuasive when China debates whether to adhere to global norms.

External actors were, then, significant in prompting the Chinese institutional innovation that we see as being vital to moving Beijing along a path that supported non-proliferation, demonstrating the interactive

---

[44] Shen Dingli argued in 2009 that China is "increasingly prepared to ratify the treaty" because of "technical considerations" and as it now has "its own version of [a] science-based stewardship program" (2009: 11).

role of domestic and external factors in explaining levels of consistency. The NAM the United States, and transnational arms control groups, together with international institutions such as the IAEA, the UN, and CD at different moments bolstered the arguments emanating from bodies such as the MOFA. These external actors voiced their approval of Chinese actions that could be said to represent responsible statehood, showing how the global normative framework could reverberate among Chinese elites. In addition, external actors often offered the kinds of direct and indirect strategic, political, and economic incentives that could widen the scope of the domestic consensus in favour of the NNPN. The positive incentives included more serious Soviet-American efforts in the early 1990s to reduce nuclear weaponry, important in winning the Chinese military's support for signature of the NPT. A Japanese summit in Beijing in August 1991, the first by any G7 country after the Tiananmen bloodshed of June 1989, together with Tokyo's offer to provide $6 billion in aid, came with some conditions: Chinese membership of the NPT and more active support for non-proliferation. There were also key trade benefits associated with NPT membership: the United States had conditioned a nuclear cooperation agreement with China (initially signed in 1985) on Beijing's membership of that treaty. Such a condition "galvanized support for NPT membership in the Chinese nuclear industry, an industry eager for access to U.S. nuclear technology" (Medeiros 2007: 73–6). The more diffuse incentives were that participation in this normative framework demonstrated China's commitment to building a more peaceful regional and global environment, allowing it to concentrate on its growth priority.

However, a series of events closely connected with US preferences reinforced and exposed other motives behind Chinese policies, and this exposure has contributed to the weakening of the non-proliferation norm (Medeiros 2007: 200; Chu and Rong 2008: 169). Some US actions have also rekindled doubts in Beijing about the norm's efficacy.[45] Chinese behaviour since the late 1990s towards many third parties and rhetoric with respect to the legal components of the non-proliferation regime have shown its general support for preventing horizontal proliferation; however, its reluctance to pressure hard either Pyongyang or Tehran raises

---

[45] Author interviews, Beijing, September 2008. For a detailed discussion of the way that changes in US nuclear strategy, particularly withdrawal from the ABM treaty, the Nuclear Posture Review and National Missile Defence, have influenced China's thinking, see Tompkins (2003), Medeiros (2007: 200–1), and Chu and Rong (2008: 169), together with the discussion in the following section.

doubts about the strength of its commitment when other deeply held interests are in contention with it. With respect to North Korea, China would like to reverse Pyongyang's nuclear programme, and has levelled some sanctions, especially after the North's second nuclear test in May 2009;[46] but it is also determined to prevent a collapse of the regime in Pyongyang and instability on its borders. This has resulted in an unwillingness to sustain tough economic sanctions against the North.[47] Similarly, in the case of Iran, deep and important commercial and energy security interests have underpinned a stance that demonstrates a general and strong reluctance to impose sanctions and in favour of prolonging negotiations. Where Pakistan is concerned, the agreement made in the spring of 2010 for China to build two new civilian nuclear reactors has been interpreted predominantly as a way of compensating its ally Pakistan for the US-India nuclear deal.[48]

In addition, China's own nuclear force modernization programme undercuts the argument that possession of nuclear weapons is neither necessary nor beneficial to the security of the state. Defence White Papers, with sections explaining China's non-proliferation policies, are produced every two years, but the language of these papers is infused with concerns about US unilateralism and strategic gain. It has long linked its reluctance to ratify the CTBT to America's unwillingness to ratify the treaty, behaviour that is reminiscent of its approach in the climate change negotiations.

---

[46] S/RES/1874, 12 June 2009. However, see also China's explanatory statement at SC/9679, 12 June 2009, which weakened the force of that resolution.

[47] Viewed over a longer historical period, China has come a long way with respect to Pyongyang. As the Bush administration's Deputy Assistant Secretary of State for East Asian and Pacific Affairs, Thomas J. Christensen put it: "Almost none of the progress to date in the talks would have been possible without China's active engagement in the process" (Christensen 2009: 93–4). There are also 2009 reports of Chinese customs officials confiscating defence and nuclear-related material en route to North Korea through Chinese territory. See, for example, "China Foils Smuggling of Missile-Use Material to N. Korea," 29 July 2009, http://english.chosun.com/site.data/html_dir/2009/07/29/2009072900407.html, accessed 29 November 2009. However, in October 2009, Premier Wen Jiabao made a "goodwill" trip to the DPRK and agreed several economic and technological cooperation agreements. See CRS Report (2010a: 11).

[48] Tini Tran, "Chinese Leader's Comments Dash Iran Sanction Hopes," *Associated Press*, 16 October 2009. Van Kemenade (2009: 15) notes that China has become Iran's largest trade and investment partner that includes Beijing providing "large quantities of capital goods, engineering services, dams, irrigation systems, thermal power stations, a nuclear power plant, ammunition, various machineries ... cross-border roads, railroads, pipelines etc., all in exchange for Iranian oil, minerals and base materials." See also, "Nuclear Proliferation in South Asia: The Power of Nightmares," *The Economist*, 26 June 2010.

The relationship with the United States is, thus, significant to understanding China's levels of behavioural consistency with respect to this normative framework, a subject to which we now turn.

4 The Bilateral Relationship and Behavioural Consistency

Chinese and American attitudes and policies towards non-proliferation have been intertwined in several of the past decades of the norm's evolution and have had an impact on its strengths and weaknesses. As noted earlier, initial US debates on the position US administrations should take to proliferation hinged to a large degree in the late 1950s and early 1960s on discussion of China's emergence as a nuclear weapons state. Washington most probably would have moved towards an NPT even without a nuclear China, but Beijing's acquisition of the weapon certainly accelerated the process. In 2005, the striking of the US nuclear deal with India in part was related to the George W. Bush administration views that India needed to be developed as a strategic counterweight to a more powerful China.

On the Chinese side, its decision to acquire nuclear weapons rested significantly on the prevalence of US nuclear threats voiced several times during the 1950s, including during the Korean Conflict, and over tensions affecting Indo-China and in the two Taiwan Straits crises. In the early 1960s, both US Presidents Kennedy and Johnson considered launching a preemptive strike against Chinese nuclear facilities.[49] Those threats convinced Beijing of the need to accelerate the development of its nuclear weapons' capacity and in those decades to view non-proliferation goals as designed to perpetuate its and other states' disadvantaged strategic position.

In later years, the United States frequently used both political and economic incentives and disincentives to induce China to expand its non-proliferation commitments and to limit the export of material the US deemed sensitive (Medeiros 2007: 10). On occasion, these carrot-and-stick policies designed to effect China's compliance went beyond the commitments required by the global normative framework (e.g., with respect to China's policy towards Algeria and Iran in the 1990s).

---

[49] The United States was not alone in contemplating such action. As China's relations with the Soviet Union deteriorated in the 1960s, Moscow also threatened to destroy China's burgeoning nuclear capabilities.

Sino-American negotiations over nuclear export controls were particularly contentious in the 1980s and for most of the 1990s. Some in the US Congress were highly critical of certain of the executive branch's attempts to reach agreement with the PRC, and there was no consensus in China at that time on the benefits of non-proliferation.[50] The 1981 consideration of a bilateral nuclear cooperation agreement (NCA) represented the first major opportunity to discuss in some detail nuclear non-proliferation, with the United States focusing particularly on Chinese exports to potential proliferators. The Chinese nuclear industry was keen to get access to US nuclear technology, and US industry was hardly a disinterested observer either, given that China's "moribund ... nuclear industry would be eligible to compete for up to $7 billion in anticipated sales of reactors and associated equipment" (Clausen 1993: 171). Nevertheless, a year later, these talks were suspended. This came as a result of China's refusal to place its exports under international safeguards (Medeiros 2007: 38). The financial motives in conducting this trade were too great for China to resist; moreover, US Congressional legislation constrained the power of the US industrial lobby and the executive branch's preference to strike a deal.

An eventual NCA was placed before the US Congress in July 1985 after China had joined the IAEA, but it met strong Congressional criticism for its vagueness on safeguards. It eventually passed: this time the US nuclear industry's lobbying efforts in favour of the agreement were more successful, the main argument being that the United States would lose out to German and French firms if an agreement failed to be reached (Clausen 1993: 173, n. 33). However, the implementation of the agreement stalled again largely because of suspicions of Beijing's continuing aid to a Pakistani bomb programme.

The United States made further attempts in the early 1990s to get China to limit nuclear trade with Algeria, Iran, and Pakistan more strictly. At this point, the prospects for positive change in China's behaviour had increased with China's signature of the NPT during this period and the security benefits of non-proliferation being better understood. Helpful to this were US efforts in building a professional arms control community in the PRC. However, with respect to China's nuclear trade, the US administration decided to deploy negative incentives and used the threat of denial

---

[50] We are strongly indebted to the analysis provided in Medeiros (2007), especially Chapter 2, in much of what follows, together with supplemental material from interviews in Beijing and Shanghai, September and December 2008. See too the 2009 CRS Report.

of Most-Favoured Nation (MFN) trading status. In addition, as a result of suspicions about Beijing's nuclear relationship with Islamabad, the United States put in place a freeze on Export-Import loans for American projects in China.

The success of US policies was at best partial at this stage as China interpreted its IAEA and other commitments narrowly or in ways that did not accord with US priorities. Beijing argued, for example, that it had signed the nuclear reactor deal with Algeria a year before it had joined the IAEA, and that civilian nuclear cooperation with an NPT member such as Iran was perfectly permissible under the NPT treaty. Where Pakistan was concerned, the relationship was simply too deep and too valuable strategically for China at that stage to tighten up its exports to Islamabad.

By the late 1990s, Chinese and US policies finally came more closely into alignment, the resolution of a major dispute in 1996 over Pakistan and involving the export of ring magnets showing the extent to which the two had converged in this policy area. The United States considers magnets to be dual-use items and once the sale was discovered the US State Department assessed whether to impose sanctions under its 1994 Nuclear Proliferation Prevention Act. Washington came very close to cancelling Export-Import loan guarantees for US companies involved in business in China, in the meantime increasing the credibility of that threat by operating a virtual sanctions policy that involved suspending review of pending Export-Import bank loans.

Direct contacts between the US Secretary of State and the Chinese Foreign Minister resulted in a pledge in May 1996 that China would stop its assistance to unsafeguarded nuclear facilities. China also "reaffirmed" its commitment to non-proliferation and agreed to discuss policy in this area, together with export control requirements, with the US government.[51] That latter agreement pointed to the need for China to gain better control over its companies that were exporting dual-use items under the new freedoms that had been steadily granted them as Chinese trade liberalized. The financial incentives for the Chinese nuclear industry to go out and make profitable deals also remained high. Thus, regaining control over these activities was not going to be straightforward, but the

---

[51] Concerns remain about China's commitment to stop aiding Pakistan. For example, on 5 May 2004, Beijing signed a contract to build a second nuclear power reactor in Pakistan, just before China joined the NSG. The timing means the Pakistani facility is exempted from the NSG's requirement for full-scope safeguards (CRS 2009: 5). In the spring of 2010, it agreed to build Pakistan two further civilian nuclear reactors.

effort was stepped up with the publishing of new export control regulations in 1997.

The US State Department also decided to use the leverage of the unimplemented NCA to gain China's adherence to a range of commitments beyond those that might be reached over Pakistan. The requirements were further tightening of its domestic regulations, Beijing's membership of a multilateral export control body, and curtailment of its nuclear cooperation with Iran.[52] These conditions were to be met, despite the perceived costs to Chinese interests articulated most strongly by members of China's defence industry and military. President Jiang Zemin, keen to emerge from under the shadow of the recently deceased Deng Xiaoping, was determined to hold successful summits first in 1997 in Washington and then in 1998 in Beijing with President Clinton. This boosted the Clinton administration's political leverage at a critical moment, prompting Chinese agreement with the various stipulated conditions, including the banning of several areas of cooperation with Iran.

Further evidence of convergence in positions came in 1998 when the United States and China worked closely together to condemn India and Pakistan's May nuclear tests. China actually took the lead in hosting a P5 meeting of foreign ministers at its Geneva-based UN mission and jointly drafted with Washington UN Security Resolution 1172 that called on the two South Asian states to abandon their programmes and join the NPT and CTBT.

As is obvious then, US actions have been a powerful influence on China's policies in this issue area. US administrations have used a variety of economic and political levers to effect change in China's policy, some of which exposed a Chinese tendency to interpret NPT requirements minimally in cases where its interests were strongly engaged. Nevertheless, US non-proliferation requirements generated debates inside China's domestic institutions about foreign policy priorities and the security consequences of nuclear proliferation. As a result, its behaviour has become

---

[52] Apparently, the Chinese Foreign Minister sent a secret letter to his US counterpart "promising not to begin new nuclear cooperation with Iran, after building a small nuclear research reactor" (CRS 2009: 10). Some Chinese scholars believe the agreement with the United States had long-term negative costs in terms of its energy and political relationship with Iran (author interviews, Shanghai, December 2008). However, this seems unlikely. China has been very successful in signing a number of important energy agreements in recent years. For example, in 2009, Beijing's leading oil companies, Sinopec and CNPC, signed multi-billion-dollar contracts to help with Tehran's oil extraction. See "Chinese Companies Supply Iran with Petrol," *Financial Times*, 23 September 2009.

more consistent with the NNPN, and Washington has played a major part in influencing that change in direction.

However, US policies have been double-edged in their effects – encouraging normative adherence but also raising levels of doubt in China about the extent to which the norm constrains US behaviour and therefore about the extent to which the norm should constrain its own behaviour. Alongside Beijing's normative commitments and the perceived sacrifices of Chinese interest, there remains an enduring sense in China that power politics and the requirements of US national security strongly influence US policy towards the non-proliferation regime. The long-standing US determination to build missile defences and its May 2002 decision actually to abrogate the ABM treaty sparked intense debate in Beijing and reinforced the perceived need for the changes in its nuclear weapons policy that were already in train.[53] Shen Dingli argues that Chinese concerns about its capacity for "effective retaliation" heightened as a result of the attempted development of missile defence, including space-based missile defence capabilities. These threats, plus ever-improving US precision-strike capabilities, prompted Beijing to consider enhancing "both its nuclear basing modes and force penetration capability in order to increase the survivability of its arsenal against a nuclear first strike or precision conventional strike" (Shen 2009: 10). US policies have come, then, to represent a potent challenge to China's security interests, and its minimum deterrence strategy.[54] As Sha Zukang put it in 2000 in response to US NMD and TMD plans: "It is too early to say what we will do. All I can say is that China will do everything possible to ensure its security" (quoted in Medeiros 2007: 203).

Chinese specialists also condemn Washington for its application of double standards.[55] The US-India nuclear deal has reinforced a sense in China that strategic interest not universality is at the basis of US policy in this issue area. As four key arms control and disarmament specialists

[53] Kent provides some telling quotations from high-level officials in China on these matters (2007: 89–90). Twomey (2009: 17) notes moderately slow qualitative improvements in China's arsenal over the last decade or so. Tompkins (2003) puts more emphasis on the acceleration of some trends after 2001. At a summit in April 2006, Presidents Bush and Hu agreed to the establishment of a strategic nuclear dialogue between the two governments (Gill 2007: 98), which is yet to get off the ground above a track 2 level.

[54] Tompkins reports, on the basis of more than 60 not-for-attribution interviews with Chinese officials, arms control experts, military officers, and journalists, conducted in the summer of 2002, that the US missile defence programme would "have the largest impact on Chinese thinking about nuclear weapons" (2003: 5).

[55] Author interviews Beijing and Shanghai, September and December 2008.

noted in a *Renmin Ribao* interview, published in September 2008, the deal "weakens an important plank in the NPT ... effectively condones [India's] nuclear weapons program ... demonstrates that America's nuclear policy is selective and biased ... [and shows that d]ouble standards are everywhere: some countries are demonized and sanctioned for their nuclear weapons programs, others are given tacit consent and even cooperation."[56] These developments reduce Chinese incentives for conformity with the normative framework and encourage arguments in favour of the modernization of its nuclear weapons programme – an action that undercuts common understandings of Article VI of the NPT. The US agreement with India has undercut China's willingness to adopt more punitive approaches towards Iran and the DPRK, particularly since its strategic and economic interests point it towards a more conciliatory stance. The deal also prompts it to compensate its long-time ally, Pakistan.

Of course, China too acquiesced in the NSG waiver agreement for India in September 2008 allowing the deal to go ahead, but the circumstances of its acquiescence reinforced for Beijing the priority that Washington gave to strategic interest over the global norm. One report has suggested a direct telephone call by President George W. Bush to President Hu Jintao, leading the Chinese delegation to withdraw from the negotiations at the final stage so that the agreement could pass by consensus (Srivastava 2008). In addition, several of our interviews in Beijing in September 2008 and in Shanghai in December 2008 elicited the argument that China's refusal to support the deal might have undermined its attempts to improve ties with New Delhi, additionally important in that the Bush administration had put great store in building strategic relations with India as a hedge against China's rise.[57] Indeed, as one interviewee

---

[56] *Renmin Ribao*, Overseas Edition, 15 September 2008, http://news.xinhuanet.com:80/world/2008–09/15/content_10003743.htm, accessed 18 March 2010.
[57] As one published report has put it: "there are still quite a few people in the U.S. political circle who consider the rise of China as a 'threat' to the United States in the long run, and hence are eager to elevate U.S. relations with India in a big way so as to make India an important strategic stronghold to ward off China" (Cheng 2008: 23). However, Cheng also predicts that the India–US relationship is going to be difficult, because India guards its sovereignty closely and differs from the United States on a number of major international issues (2008: 26–7). Christensen in 2006 argued more generally for the view that US resolve prompts China to improve relations with its neighbours. As he put it: "since the mid-1990s relatively assertive U.S. security policies toward Japan, Taiwan, Southeast Asia, and South Asia have helped catalyze the growth of Chinese diplomatic and economic engagement with the PRC's neighbors, and thereby have helped stabilize the region" (Christensen 2006b: 83). China's agreement to the NSG waiver could be viewed in this light.

put it, India's interest in nuclear weapons could not be stopped and a friendly nuclear India was better for China than a non-nuclear enemy.

US and Chinese policies also became intertwined in somewhat unhelpful ways over the CTBT process. US-China negotiations designed to bring about a CTBT were intense at times and important to the resolution of some key issues (Johnston 2008: 106). Both states signed the treaty in 1996. Nevertheless, the US Senate's refusal to ratify reduced the global pressure on China also to ratify that treaty – an outcome similar to the position on climate change after the George W. Bush administration withdrew from the Kyoto process. Furthermore, the US failure to ratify and the eventual dismissal of its worth under Bush reinforced a sense in Beijing that China had been duped into support of it. Some Chinese scholars have thus argued that, if the United States were to restart nuclear testing, China "would have no choice but to follow the U.S. example" (Tompkins 2003: 3).

The outcome in the early twenty-first century is therefore somewhat mixed. To stress the most positive dimensions: we have evidence over the last few years of China's higher levels of adherence to the norm – its more vocal and practical actions on the exports side, in favour of treaty consolidation, and some pressure on the outliers, Iran and North Korea. Beijing's position outlined in its 2005 paper on UN reform, calling for the "international community" to take "effective measures in real earnest to strengthen the universality and authority" of the NPT, remains its public position. Some of its nuclear arms control specialists have called for "strict rules against transfer, a clear differentiation between nuclear and civilian technologies, careful monitoring and regular IAEA inspections." They have also asked that the United States "lead by example by respecting and upholding non-proliferation norms ... exercis[ing] self-restraint."[58] President Hu in September 2009 in a major speech at the UN supported nuclear disarmament, ratification of the CTBT, and negotiation of a FMCT. Although China has not given up its search for a ban on the weaponization of space, Hu dropped China's earlier linkage of progress on the FMCT to the start of negotiations on a treaty preventing an arms race in outer space (PAROS).

The United States, despite evidence of backsliding particularly from the start of the twenty-first century, has also been a key player since the 1960s in building up and extending the non-proliferation norm. It has

---

[58] *Renmin Ribao*, Overseas Edition, 15 September 2008, http://news.xinhuanet.com:80/world/2008–09/15/content_10003743.htm, accessed 18 March 2010.

engaged in international treaty negotiations, participated in the creation of international institutions, and passed domestic legislation that has often constrained exports. The Obama administration has provided leadership on the issue over the last two years and tried to move forward certain core components of this normative framework. This has included a bold pledge about nuclear disarmament – even though the President himself acknowledged that this was unlikely to happen in his lifetime.

From this more positive vantage point, the prospects for Beijing's and Washington's policies coming into closer alignment have somewhat brightened, as have those of the NNPN. However, past Chinese and US behaviour has also demonstrated that, at times, national strategic concerns have overridden the requirements of the normative framework, thus reducing both states' confidence in the framework's capacity to constrain the other.

5 Conclusion

The NNPN framework has been an emblematic part of global order in the period since 1945, and the challenge to its current status raises the spectre that we are on the verge of an era where several new states, and possibly non-state groupings, acquire such weaponry. In the past, moral and legal discourse, at both societal and governmental levels, boosted the strength of that norm, but the behaviour of major NWS in relation to it is also significant to its present and future.

That norm has long held a central place in the US-China relationship, both when the United States viewed China as a threatening proliferator, and when China experienced the United States as a country willing not only to use nuclear threats as a weapon of diplomacy but also later to manipulate political and economic incentives to induce the non-proliferation behaviour it favoured. China itself has used its more circumscribed leverage in this issue area to induce change in US policy towards matters crucial to it, notably North Korea, and in its demands with respect to the framing of UN resolutions designed to promote US counter-proliferation objectives.

Behavioural consistency with the norm has obviously been strongly influenced by this bilateral interaction, but not by this relationship alone. For the United States, external incentives led to norm creation and attempted norm reinterpretation, but domestic ideas and institutions have consistently been important to its fate. US interpretations of the global strategic environment filtered through particular dominant domestic values at elite (rather than broader societal) levels have been crucial to understanding degrees of behavioural consistency. Leadership, notably presidential interest in proliferation questions, has been critical at certain key turning points. Congress's legislative role and constitutional rights in the area of trade regulation and treaty confirmation have also given that branch of government a consistent place in policy making and have sometimes moved the White House into closer norm adherence. The United States' role in norm creation has been important, but its presumed custodial role has also given it a sense that other governments should accept that Washington can reinterpret the norm at times when it perceives strategic costs to have risen to unacceptably high levels. US self-positioning in this issue area has also given it the ability to decide whether an individual country's policies with respect to the norm are adequate or in violation. Nevertheless, while the United States may have given more prominence to counter-proliferation than non-proliferation objectives from the late twentieth century, it has never rejected the NNPN and, under the Obama administration, has tried to move more closely into conformity with it. This demonstrates the power of the framework itself to impose some constraints on action and rhetoric.

For China, a wide range of factors have been important in determining behavioural consistency, reflecting its need both to adapt to a normative structure already in place when it more fully entered into international society, and the leadership's need to build domestic knowledge and consensus behind the non-proliferation idea. Domestic political and economic change in the late 1970s sparked a whole range of new global requirements as we explore in each of the issue areas covered in this book. Exposure to international institutional arrangements unfamiliar to it, as well as to new ideas provoked energetic attempts to understand concepts such as verification and the security consequences of nuclear proliferation. Economic and political incentives, together with international image concerns, operated to provide the necessary momentum behind this new thinking, resulting eventually in the development of policies and domestic legislation broadly consistent with the non-proliferation norm. Some in China have come to believe in the rightness of the norm, that it distributes benefits and costs reasonably fairly and overall provides improvements in global and national security. Others see it as selectively applied on the part of China's major strategic interlocutor, as redolent with double standards, and that it may be used by the United States to benefit Washington at the expense of Beijing. However, the domestic institutionalization of the norm and ongoing concerns about international image help to sustain actual behaviour reasonably consistent with the normative requirements. These levels of support come under greatest strain when US administrations embark on policies that China perceives as having increased its strategic vulnerability, or when the norm conflicts with core interests associated with its domestic goals.

The non-proliferation norm is under challenge, but for the time being it appears to have sufficient legitimacy and to be sufficiently embedded to retain some level of constraint over these two states and many other members of global society. The levels of contestation between China and America in this normative area have broadly declined over time. This is one consequence of the norm's relatively low levels of significance within the domestic societies when compared with other issue areas that we discuss in this book. In addition, the demands that it makes on these two states are reasonably symmetrical. Further consolidation of this normative framework remains a possibility were current rhetorical commitments to its further elaboration to come to fruition. But this is a demanding strategic agenda, made plain in part by the problems that Beijing and Washington have in coordinating policies towards Iran and the DPRK. An inability to resolve these challenges may weaken the basis for cooperation on broader non-proliferation objectives to the detriment of this aspect of global order.

5

Climate Change

This issue speaks to several of our main concerns about the concept and nature of global order. First, climate change – a more accurate and encompassing term than "global warming" – transcends state borders and affects every state in the global system, but it is not easily addressed through a governance framework that rests on a pluralist state-based notion of global order (Hurrell 2007: 118). Second, and related to this, responses to climate change have brought into being complex governance structures involving international organizations, environmental and other NGOs, scientific communities, and businesses that have often worked at cross-purposes and thereby elevated the difficulties of formulating a robust climate protection norm. Third, the US and Chinese positions have been significantly influenced by the stances that each has taken towards climate change negotiations. Both governments have been reluctant to play a substantive role in deepening and strengthening this norm unless the other accepts that it too must play its part. Finally, at the global level, the United States and China are at the heart of the problem: they are the world's largest energy consumers and the two largest producers of greenhouse gases (GHG),[1] currently accounting together for over 40 percent of all global emissions of such gases (Lieberthal and Sandalow 2009: 1). This is dramatically complicated by the fact that China's annual emissions are growing much more rapidly and because of the large asymmetry in their

---

[1] Carbon dioxide (CO_2), the leading GHG, persists in the atmosphere for about 100 years and is only very slowly absorbed by the natural environment. This means that new annual GHG emissions – the "flow" problem – add to an existing "stock" of GHG in the atmosphere that dissipates very slowly.

historic contributions to the atmospheric stock of GHG (Hallding, Han, and Olsson 2009: 24; Pew Center/Asia Society 2009: 18).[2]

The global normative framework for climate protection has distinctive features that have rendered its creation and elaboration particularly problematic, and five, in particular, have made the norm subject to high levels of contestation. First, and unlike some of the other global norms that we investigate in this book, it has high domestic significance and poses a direct challenge to domestic ways of life – including individual and societal decisions about resource use and general expectations of further material improvement. Second, the norm is asymmetric, requiring much of the advanced countries – because of their historical contribution to the problem and stronger capacity to mitigate or adapt to the effects of climate change – and rather little of those formally designated as developing countries, which are often still focused on the alleviation of poverty. This is not a norm that has been dominated in its creation and elaboration entirely by the world's most advanced economies. Third, the levels of acceptance of the norm have been more severely tested over time as it has come to take on a number of specific features that have raised questions about its overall coherence and fairness. Fourth, the United States and China have emerged as being at the heart of this issue and their own relationship has become bound up tightly in it. They are now generally recognized as crucial to a core feature of the norm that affects its ability to be consolidated: the specific content of a common but differentiated responsibility in addressing climate change. Finally, it has taken years to establish a scientific consensus on climate change based on acceptance of its largely anthropogenic origins (and this consensus remains under challenge). This, too, has restrained the progress of the norm and provided greater space and time for these deeper, value-laden contestations to work their way through both domestic and international negotiating forums.

These and other factors will be explored in a chapter that first investigates the main features of this multilayered norm (Falkner 2009) of global climate protection, including its associated voluntary and mandatory

---

[2] One 2008 report estimates that China's share of global emissions will increase to 33% by 2030, overwhelming the 11% share of the United States (Garnaut 2008: 65). The historical contributions of each country are currently diametrically opposed to this, however. The United States was responsible for an estimated 30% of cumulative global emissions from 1850 to 2000, compared to about 7% for China (Eileen Clausen and Elliot Diringer, "U.S. Exceptionalism and Climate Change, Part I", 19 July 2007, www.theglobalist.com/printSotryId.aspx?S, accessed 31 March 2009).

abatement targets. Next, it examines Chinese and US behaviour in reference to these various normative components and assesses the main factors that explain levels of behavioural consistency with the global normative framework. It explores why neither state has been a particularly supportive player in the advancement of the norm, showing how their respective concerns about asymmetry and equity have been enhanced by the priority each gives to economic growth and competitiveness, and by the difficulty of overcoming domestic political obstacles to a problem with such long-term consequences.

1 The Global Norm of Climate Protection

Over the past three decades, climate change has become a prominent issue on the global negotiating agenda being featured in UN and regional diplomacy; at gatherings of the world's climatologists; at meetings of the G7/8, G20, and other more focused groupings; and in bilateral discussion. But it has taken a long time to get to this point of agreement. It was not until the fourth assessment report in 2007 of the Intergovernmental Panel on Climate Change (IPCC) that the Panel could state that evidence of global warming is undeniable: "Warming of the climate system is unequivocal, as is now evident from observations of increases in global average air and ocean temperatures, widespread melting of snow and ice and rising global average sea level" (IPCC 2007: 2).[3] In 2009, the US Department of Defense and US intelligence agencies began to address the potentially dire security consequences of climate change and how to incorporate these challenges into the national security strategy.[4] Beijing's October 2008 White Paper entitled "China's Policies and Actions for Addressing Climate Change" dramatically acknowledged the widespread problems global warming poses for the country, stating that China is "most susceptible to the adverse effects of climate change, mainly in the fields of agriculture, livestock breeding, forestry, natural ecosystems, water resources, and coastal zones."[5]

The 1960s witnessed heightened concern over environmental degradation, leading to the 1972 UN Conference on the Human Environment (UNCHE) held in Stockholm. It marked an important turning point in

[3] Some back-tracking from previous conclusions about the pace of the retreat of the Himalayan glaciers took place in 2010.
[4] John M. Broder, "Predictions of Mayhem as the Globe Gets Warmer," *International Herald Tribune*, 10 August 2009.
[5] *GOV.cn*, 29 October 2008.

global environmental negotiations (Elliott 1998: 7; DeSombre 2002: 8). Stockholm attracted some 1,200 delegates from 114 countries and, in an innovative and far-reaching development, provided for a parallel NGO conference. Only two heads of government thought it necessary to attend – the Swedish (unsurprisingly) and the Indian. Global politics made country representation and enthusiasm for the enterprise somewhat variable. The Soviet-bloc states, ignoring their own frequently disastrous environmental records, declared the problem to be a by-product of capitalism and withdrew. Developing countries were immediately wary that the event would serve to give priority to a developed world concern with the environment over questions of poverty and development, and remained insistent on developed country responsibility for environmental degradation. An attempted bridge in positions came in Article 21, which recognized that states "had the sovereign right to exploit their own resources pursuant to their own environmental policies" but also "the responsibility to insure that activities within their jurisdiction or control do not cause damage to the environment of other[s]." Despite these controversies, three outcomes have been attributed to this gathering: a nonbinding declaration, a plan of action, and an organizational framework centred on the United Nations (Elliott 1998: 12). This paved the way for the UN General Assembly to establish in January 1973 the United Nations Environment Programme (UNEP), a body that "had a role as coordinator and catalyst rather than a specialised agency with an operational mandate" (Elliott 1998: 13).

The Stockholm conference also catalyzed the emergence of an environmental movement, with some of these organizations – such as Greenpeace, the World Wildlife Fund, and Friends of the Earth – able to parlay their substantial resources and expertise to influence subsequent global agendas (Greene 1997: 318). In particular, the actions and reports of epistemic communities of scientists demonstrated the significance of non-state actors in norm creation and development.[6] In 1979 a group of climatologists and others held the first World Climate Conference that investigated the relationship between human activities and global warming. That conference established a programme of research and helped precipitate the creation of the IPCC in 1988. A second World Climate Conference in 1990, together with the production of the IPCC's first assessment report, also helped to frame the debate and prompted the UNGA in December

---

[6] The work of Peter M. Haas (1989 among others) is most often associated with the idea of epistemic communities and their role in policy formation.

1990 to put in place an Intergovernmental Negotiating Committee for a Framework Convention on Climate Change. It was tasked to negotiate a framework convention that would form the basis for future protocols (Harris 2008: 459).[7]

The year 1992 marked the most significant turning point in creating the generalized norm. In the run-up to the opening of the 1992 UN Conference on Environment and Development (UNCED), held in Rio de Janeiro, some 150 countries worked on this Framework Convention on Climate Change (now commonly referred to as the UNFCCC). That convention, formalized at Rio – this time with the attendance of some 135 heads of state – set no mandatory targets or deadlines. But in Article 2(6) it did record the broad aim to stabilize "greenhouse gas concentrations at a level that would prevent dangerous anthropogenic interference with the climate system." It also adopted *Agenda 21*, a detailed 800-page programme with forty chapters promoting the concept of sustainable development, and led to the development of a Commission on Sustainable Development. On 4 June 1992, some 154 countries and the European Community signed the Rio treaty, which came remarkably speedily into force in March 1994, shortly after its fiftieth ratification (Elliott 1998: 70). Although this gave the treaty a degree of legitimacy and universalism rivalling that of the nuclear non-proliferation treaty, its provisions contained only voluntary rather than legally binding commitments and emphasized the need for "flexibility" in implementation. The repercussions were plain: while the developed world collectively had agreed voluntarily to stabilize their emissions at 1990 levels by the year 2000, neither Australia, Canada, Japan, New Zealand, Norway, nor the United States made serious efforts to meet their targets over this period (Gardiner 2004).

Principle 16 of the Rio Declaration accepted the "polluter pays" principle and the "precautionary principle" (that action is required even when there is a degree of scientific uncertainty). Other generalized principles established at Rio have also been of lasting significance, especially the agreement to "common but differentiated responsibilities" embodied in Principle 7 of the Rio Declaration.[8] In its dominant interpretation that

---

[7] The establishment of the IPCC and the holding of international conferences after that time has been credited with moving the European Union from a reactive force to a proactive force (Costa 2008: 533).

[8] Principle 7 of the Rio Declaration reads: "States shall cooperate in a spirit of global partnership to conserve, protect and restore the health and integrity of the Earth's ecosystem. In view of the different contributions to global environmental degradation, States

has been taken to mean that the interests of the developing world in economic development should be protected and the developed countries should bear primary responsibility for stabilizing emissions. Furthermore, the developed countries agreed to provide financial assistance to less-developed countries to grow in a more environmentally sustainable way through the Global Environment Facility. Finally, it was agreed that states would provide regular reports on their current and predicted national GHG emissions. This held out the promise of increasing awareness and expertise in the climate change field, of promoting national targeting, and of embedding the goal of climate protection in domestic institutions and national policies.

Not all states were convinced of the merit of each of the core principles agreed at Rio. Especially challenging has been the idea of common but differentiated responsibilities, because it touches directly on how fairly burdens are distributed. Nevertheless, the norm took on more specific attributes over the course of the 1990s, the next step being the move from non-binding to binding targets. The first of the annual Conference of the Parties (COPs), meeting in Berlin in March 1995, started the negotiations to impose more stringent commitments on the developed countries. By the third COPs in December 1997 in Kyoto, the signatories to the UNFCCC agreed to a protocol that required most developed countries to reduce their emissions to a level 5.2 percent below those of 1990 between the period 2008 and 2012 (DeSombre 2002: 100–1). Developing countries were not given any specific abatement targets and transition economies were permitted to choose their own base year from which to calculate the reductions (DeSombre 2002: 110). Among advanced countries, Australia, Iceland, and Norway were given special dispensation actually to increase their emission rates (Elliott 2004: 24). Nevertheless, the principle of mandatory targets for most of the developed world had been established.

The Kyoto negotiations also gave specificity to the principle of flexibility in implementation, endorsing emissions trading programmes that allowed the buying and selling of credits among the developed countries, the "Joint Implementation" scheme whereby developed countries could earn emissions credits via investment in one another's emission reduction projects, and the Clean Development Mechanism (CDM), which awarded

have common but differentiated responsibilities. The developed countries acknowledge the responsibility that they bear in the international pursuit of sustainable development in view of the pressures their societies place on the global environment and of the technologies and financial resources they command."

developed countries credit for implementing emission reduction projects in developing countries (Harris 2008: 460). In addition, Article 3 of the Kyoto Protocol accepted the idea that carbon sinks, such as forests, could be counted towards reaching a country's emissions targets.

The endorsement of emissions trading programmes at Kyoto showed that there was growing support for the principle that market mechanisms should, where possible, be used so as to promote efficient emissions reduction (Harris 2008: 460; Falkner 2009).[9] This market principle strongly reflected US preferences, but the US Congress and the George W. Bush administration disliked much else in the package. American withdrawal from climate negotiations in 2001 was a signal move in preventing Kyoto from coming into force for several years, since it required ratification by developed countries accounting for 55 percent of 1990 emissions. India and China announced their ratification of the treaty in August 2002 at the Johannesburg World Summit on Sustainable Development, which George W. Bush conspicuously failed to attend, though his administration was quick to point out that Kyoto required neither state to set emissions targets. With Russia's ratification in November 2004, the 55 percent benchmark was reached, and Kyoto came into force in February 2005. Among the G20 countries, this left only the United States, Australia, Saudi Arabia, and Turkey as non-signatories; today, the United States stands alone in this respect.

Despite US hostility during the George W. Bush years, the UN framework had generated its own momentum and some sense of commitment. Indeed, US rejection of Kyoto may have encouraged the EU to work in a more unified way to save the Kyoto process (Costa 2008: 538) and to demonstrate that this was an issue on which it could provide leadership. The EU pioneered an emissions trading system in January 2005 and in 2007 agreed to unilateral EU-wide cuts of 20 percent from 1990 levels by 2020, rising to 30 percent if other developed countries could be persuaded to adopt a similar cutback.[10] The steady drumbeat of IPCC assessment reports aided the EU in its search for agreement, the third report appearing in 2001 and the fourth in 2007. In addition, the Stern Report to the

---

[9] Bernstein (2001, 2002) argues that a norm of "liberal environmentalism" was decisive in the adoption of emissions trading mechanisms, but as we argue later, US promotion of market mechanisms was also crucial.

[10] The EU also agreed to improve energy efficiency by 20% and to make use of renewable sources of energy for 20% of Europe's energy needs by the same target date (*Financial Times*, Special Report, Part II, 16 September 2008: 12).

British government in 2006 on the economics of climate change argued that the likely costs of inaction far outweighed the costs of action.

The unequivocal language of the fourth IPCC report influenced the 13th COPs meeting held in Bali in 2007, a gathering of over 180 countries, plus over 10,000 delegates from intergovernmental organizations (IGOs) and NGOs, and tasked to draw up a "Road Map" for 2012 post-Kyoto arrangements. By then, developing country emissions' growth had moved to centre-stage: without mitigation, total developing country emissions were projected to account for 90 percent or more of all new GHG outputs over the next two decades (Garnaut 2008: 53; IEA 2008: 11). These developments invigorated consideration of what kind of agreement would replace the Kyoto Protocol after 2012. Notably, developing countries agreed in Bali to consider taking future action to reduce the rate of increase in emissions, "a substantial shift from their longstanding policy of refusing to agree to any commitments whatsoever" (Harris 2008: 462). The George W. Bush administration modified its stance at that meeting, the President accepting the need to enter into international negotiations to find a successor to the Kyoto Protocol within the UNFCCC framework.[11] At the G8 meeting on climate change in July 2008 at Hokkaido, Japan, Bush also signed up to "the goal of achieving at least 50% reduction of global emissions by 2050."[12]

This shift in US policy brought it closer to the international mainstream, but the Hokkaido declaration left much unsaid, including whether the baseline for reductions would be 1990 or 2005. It also emphasized the importance of technological innovation in meeting the emissions target and stressed that "this global challenge can only be met by a global response, in particular, by the contributions from all major economies, consistent with the principle of common but differentiated responsibilities and respective capabilities." The G8 stated, in addition, that "[w]e will also help support the mitigation plans of major developing economies by technology, financing and capacity-building." Emerging countries reacted to this thinly veiled demand for binding constraints on their emissions and lack of specificity on aid by arguing that emissions reductions by developed countries of 80 to 95 percent by 2050 compared

---

[11] Prior to that, according to John T. Holdren, the Bush administration had "obstructed progress in the negotiations behind the scenes." See Thijs Niemantsverdriet, *Newsweek Web Exclusive*, 3 December 2007.

[12] G8 Summit Leaders Declaration, 8 July 2008, http://www.mofa.go.jp/policy/economy/summit/2008/doc/doc080714__en.html, accessed 18 September 2009.

with 1990 levels were necessary so as to permit the developing world to continue to increase their emissions.[13]

Given the continuing distrust of the George W. Bush administration's motives and level of commitment to the UN process, Barack Obama's victory in the 2008 US presidential elections was widely seen as a potential turning point in US climate policy. The Obama administration quickly signalled that the United States would move from reluctant participation to active involvement and made an explicit commitment to emissions reductions that the George W. Bush administration had only made in private. Obama's special envoy for climate change in the US State Department, Todd Stern, offered to work for an agreement to reduce emissions by 15 percent from 2005 levels by 2020, and by 80 percent by 2050, provided that emerging countries placed curbs on their growth in emissions.[14] Although this was broadly welcomed, especially abroad, it was also a reminder that the new administration felt unable to accept the kinds of medium term emissions reductions that developing countries demanded, or for that matter the Kyoto treaty. The new administration also retained the Bush position that US cuts would be conditional on greater developing country participation.

Thus, even though the "Bali Road Map" for targets after 2012 was accepted in 2007 as forming the basis for a new agreement to be reached at the COPs in Copenhagen in December 2009, its achievement depended on the resolution of continuing basic differences over targeting, funding, and timing. Copenhagen demonstrated that this resolution was still not within the negotiators' grasp. It was agreed in December 2009 that action should be taken to prevent temperature rises of more than 2°C above pre-industrial levels; however, no legal treaty outlining specific emissions targets could be agreed. Instead, some fifty-five countries, responsible for about 80 percent of global emissions, filed voluntary targets with the UN at the end of January 2010 to curb emissions, some setting out a range of commitments dependent on what other countries offered.[15] Developed

[13] *Financial Times*, Special Report, Part II, 16 September 2008: 6–7.
[14] Press Briefing of the US Delegation UNFCCC Climate Change Talks, Bonn, Germany, 29 March 2009. This commitment turned out to be far ahead of what US domestic politics would bear.
[15] Fiona Harvey, "Big Nations Set Out Emission Cuts Targets," *Financial Times*, 1 February 2010. Commitments, including base year and various voluntary targets, are set out in http://unfccc.int/home/items/5264.php for industrialised countries, and http://unfccc.int/home/items/5265.php for developing countries, 1 February 2010, accessed 20 March 2010.

countries did set a goal at Copenhagen of mobilizing $100 billion a year in funding by 2020 to help with adaptation in the developing world (and $10 billion over each of the next three years), but the details of where this was to come from were sparse. Much as had happened in 1992, both developed and developing countries remained reluctant to put into a global treaty tougher, internationally verifiable, and mandatory emissions goals and timetables.

The attempts to give the more generalized principles greater bite have, then, exposed multiple tensions at the core of this long negotiating process. Countries vary in their assessment of the severity of the problem, how much they contribute to it, their ability to pay for the necessary responses, and their capacities to adapt to the impact of change (Elliott 1998: 64). This influences their perspectives on what needs to be done, whether a mid-term or longer-term goal should be set, and whether the Kyoto baseline of 1990 should be kept or a new one found. In addition, climate protection involves at least two equity issues and the interests of several stakeholders. These contentious matters tend to pit the developed North against the less-developed South. First, there has been disagreement over how to measure levels of responsibility: on a per capita basis, or total output calculation; or on the basis of historic, current, or future emissions levels (Elliott 1998: 64–5). Second, there is a basic conflict between stewardship of the global environment and that of another norm, the right of poor countries to develop. This conflict is especially severe in light of developed world reluctance so far to provide substantial finance for emissions-reduction projects in these countries or to transfer the technologies that will be needed to reduce emissions and to mitigate their effects. Finally, many types of economic activities contribute to global warming – including industry, land use, and agriculture – and many groups continue to lobby hard in support of their interests (DeSombre 2002: 96; Falkner 2008).

Given these disagreements, some argue that there is no norm of global climate protection (Gardiner 2004), or that it is glacial in the pace of its regulatory effects and ability to constrain, with the politics far behind the ever more dire predictions of the scientists (Harris 2008: 455).[16] From

---

[16] Certainly that is the view of those scientists meeting at the International Scientific Congress on climate change in March 2009. Their findings confirmed that "given high rates of observed emissions, the worst-case IPCC Scenario trajectories (or even worse) are being realised," including sea levels rising almost twice as fast as the IPCC assessment report of 2007 had predicted. International Scientific Congress, Copenhagen, Denmark, 12 March 2009, http://climatecongresss.ku.dk/newsroom/congress_key_messages/, accessed 20 March 2009; *The Economist*, 14 March 2009: 82.

this perspective, the comparative vigour of the response by the major developed and developing countries to the global economic crisis of 2008–09 demonstrates that climate protection will remain subordinated to the political imperative of continued economic growth.

Despite these misgivings, however, we have seen that there is a normative framework designed to address the consequences of global warming via the stabilization at an agreed level of GHG concentrations in the atmosphere and some associated implementing principles specifying how the goal of climate protection is to be achieved. These principles include common but differentiated responsibilities in response to the harm caused by anthropogenic emissions, the provision of regular national reports on GHG emissions, and the commitment by developed countries to support financially a shift in the developing world towards environmentally sustainable development models. The principle of common but differentiated responsibilities was built around acceptance of the idea that all countries should be required to limit their emissions but that developed countries should take the lead because of their greater historical contributions to global warming and their higher current levels of economic development.

These principles and even the norm itself are dynamic and multilayered, but they have generally evolved in the direction of increasing specificity (Falkner 2009). In the run-up to the 2009 Copenhagen summit, divisions focused on the appropriate balance and timing of commitments between developed and developing countries, how the contributions of individual countries to the problem and its resolution should be measured, and what levels of funding and technological transfer the developed world should provide for the less developed. Although only some of these issues made any progress in December 2009 and parts of the agenda required a special negotiating session between the US delegation and the BASIC group[17] to advance at all, these divisions do reflect attempts to give the core norm greater specificity rather than to reject it. The Kyoto Protocol had added new layers to the complex bundle that has at its core the climate protection norm, notably binding targets to a particular timetable for the developed world, no equivalent obligation for developing countries, and various flexibility instruments with a market-friendly orientation. By the time of the meeting in Bali in 2007, the developed countries had begun to explore the establishment of new targets to replace those agreed at Kyoto. Immediately before Copenhagen, some major players among the

[17] This group is made up of Brazil, South Africa, India, and China.

non-Annex I countries – such as Brazil, China, India, South Africa, and the Republic of Korea – had committed to voluntary national targets designed to reduce the rate of increase in their emissions. In return, they demanded financial and technical assistance for those less able to bear the burdens in the developing world and refused strong international monitoring of their own commitments. The Obama administration also repeated its earlier pledge to cut its emissions "in the range of 17%" by 2020, 30 percent by 2025, and 83 percent by 2050 over 2005 levels.

In the absence of a post-Kyoto binding global treaty, it is these voluntary national commitments, verifiable through reports every two years to the UN, together with a pledge of funding for the most disadvantaged countries, that form the basic features of the norm in this new decade, with the possibility that these pledges will be turned into a legal international treaty in the months and years to come. As before, much depends on the US and Chinese positions in this debate, and more obviously after December 2009 on the relationship between Washington and a smaller group of emerging countries. This represents a potentially significant watering-down of the previous developed-developing country divide associated with Rio and Kyoto.

2 China and the Climate Protection Norm

Since 2007, China has become the world's largest emitter of GHGs, "rocketing up the emissions curve ... [while] the United States is flattening out." In 1992, China's total annual CO_2 emissions were about 2.5 gigatons, half the US total; by 2009, its emissions exceeded 7 gigatons.[18] This dramatic shift in the relative contributions of the United States and China, which are projected to accelerate over the next two decades, has been driven by three main factors: China's relatively rapid growth and related urbanization of its society, the end of a long period in which the energy intensity of the Chinese economy declined, and its unusually high dependence on coal as an energy source (Garnaut 2008: 57–66; Yang 2010: 9). Coal meets about 70 percent of China's primary energy needs and 80 percent of its electricity production, which accounts for nearly 40 percent of its primary energy output (IEA 2007: 262–5). This weakens the Chinese argument that it is exceptional only in terms of its rapid

---

[18] Todd Stern, "Remarks as Prepared," Center for American Progress, Washington, DC, 3 June 2009. http://www.americanprogress.org/events/2009/06/china.html, accessed 27 July 2009.

growth and large population. China's emissions per capita are already above the world average (although four times less than America's) and its cumulative per capita emissions could be at the world average by 2020 (Hallding et al. 2009: 96). Its industrial sector now accounts for more than 40 percent of its total primary energy consumption, a share that has increased rapidly in recent years. By the early twenty-first century, China produced 35 percent of the world's steel output and 28 percent of its aluminium (Lewis 2007/08: 156). China's emergence as the main global centre of manufacturing contrasts with America's continuing shift towards a service economy.[19]

Conditions, thus, do not seem to be propitious for Chinese norm adherence; and, indeed, Elizabeth Economy reminds us that Deng Xiaoping had nothing to say on environmental protection, stressing only China's need for growth, a position that had and still has an "inviolable" quality for many Chinese officials (Economy 1997: 29). However, the Beijing government has been a regular participant at international environmental conferences from the time of the Stockholm conference in 1972. Its contributions then and in 1992 at the UN Conference on Environment and Development (UNCED) have made it a norm-maker rather than norm taker in what was a new issue area in global negotiations. In addition, UNCED, in particular, has been credited with having had a "profound effect on environmental policies, institutions, and thinking in China" (Economy 2004: 187). Domestic environmental NGOs have been allowed to develop, and domestic institutions and new laws have been created. Reportedly, journalists from fifty Chinese media outlets and volunteers from at least twenty NGOs travelled to Copenhagen in December 2009 for the climate summit.[20] In the first decade of the twenty-first century, Beijing has produced national plans and assessments relating to climate change and designed to reduce the rate of increase in its level of CO_2 emissions. Its January 2007 National Assessment Report outlined in telling detail the temperature rises and disastrous consequences that Chinese will have to endure in the coming decades, including negative impacts on its domestic food security and on the coastal regions that produce such a large proportion of China's total GDP (Hallding et al. 2009: 42–3) Thus,

[19] An economic consultancy concluded in 2008 that China would overtake the United States as the world's largest producer of manufactures by 2009, four years earlier than previously predicted ("China to Overtake US as Largest Manufacturer," *FT.com*, 10 August 2008).

[20] Shi Jiangtao, "Carbon Debate Creates Climate for China's Civil Society to Grow," 9 December 2009, www.scmp.com/climatechange, accessed 20 March 2010.

China's position has evolved as its domestic circumstances have altered, the normative framework has developed, and the underlying scientific findings relating to climate change have become more precise.

When it first began to participate in the international debate in 1972, unsurprisingly its officials were still heavily influenced by a Maoist world view that depicted environmental issues as a problem of the developed capitalist world, given capitalism's rapacious over-exploitation of the world's resources (Schroeder 2008: 510–11). Pollution was the main topic at Stockholm and Beijing joined with New Delhi in claiming "poverty [as] the greatest polluter." However, it also set out ten principles that needed to be considered in the revision of Stockholm's Draft Declaration, including the requirement to differentiate between the responsibilities of the developed and developing worlds, the establishment of an international environmental fund, and the exchange of scientific and technical knowledge on methods of conservation. With respect to the actions of individual governments, it supported the right of states to exploit their own resources, but balanced that by noting state responsibility to develop the domestic measures necessary to the combating of pollution (Kent 2007: 150).

While Beijing's principles were not accepted in the final declaration to a degree it deemed satisfactory (thus, it did not take part in the vote on the final document), these kinds of ideas have featured in environmental negotiations since that time, with Beijing taking a lead in orchestrating others in the developing world behind these negotiating stances. In 1991, a year prior to UNCED, it established a coalition of the "G-77 and China" and convened a "Conference of Developing Countries on Environment and Development." Beijing's goals at this meeting were to line up the forty-one countries in attendance behind a set of principles Chinese officials had agreed upon internally in the spring of 1990, including the idea of developed country responsibility and culpability, the industrialized world's need to provide compensatory financial assistance to the developing world in order to help with implementation of signed agreements and declarations, and the understanding that environmental protection should not lead to the sacrifice of development goals (Economy 1997: 32–3). In 1992 at Rio, China's Premier, Li Peng, signed the UNFCCC and in reiterating these ideas China earned for some a "reputation as one of the most recalcitrant participants in the international political negotiations, advocating the weakest reporting obligations and no concrete measures or timetables for reducing greenhouse gas emissions" (Economy 1998: 246). Despite this seeming recalcitrance, China was clearly influenced by the

Rio experience, publishing in 1994 *China's Agenda 21*, modelled on UNCED's *Agenda 21*.

China's involvement in international negotiations also resulted in changes at the domestic level, despite the conservative stance it had projected abroad. In 1973, for example, Premier Zhou Enlai – in response to both a report brought back by China's Stockholm delegation and environmental crises at home – organized for the first time a national conference on environmental protection. Officials from various ministries, such as industry, health, water conservancy, and agriculture, were brought together to formulate steps necessary to deal with certain of China's environmental problems (Economy 1997: 22) By 1978, a concern for the environment made its way into the country's Constitution. A year later the National People's Congress approved a draft national environmental law, a forerunner to a whole raft of new legislation and guidelines (Economy 1997: 23). By 2001, China had seven environmental laws on the books, with water and air pollution a particular focus, and there were more than 123 associated administrative regulations (Economy 2004: 101; Morton 2009: 38).

While pollution remained the main concern, climate change was not neglected. Beijing established in 1987 a "Chinese National Climate Committee," designed to coordinate the work of the country's scientists and to feed their results into the institutional debate (Schroeder 2008: 511). By 1989, China had a climate change research programme, which was composed of forty projects and involved twenty ministries and five hundred experts. Much of the research – requiring the sharing of computer modelling techniques, the provision of monitoring equipment, and training of environmental officials – was externally funded by international organizations such as the World Bank, the Asian Development Bank, and UNEP. Japan at the governmental level, and the United States at the non-governmental, were major bilateral donors (Economy 2004: 183; Morton 2005). Beijing's eighth five-year plan (1991–95) included its first reference to the term climate change and called for a research project that looked at its long-term effects over twenty to fifty years (Schroeder 2008: 512).

Stockholm also encouraged bureaucratic reorganization, including the establishment in 1974 of a small Environmental Protection Bureau under the State Council (Ross 1999: 298). Ten years later, the State Council established an Environmental Protection Commission, and later upgraded the Environmental Protection Bureau to the level of a national office within the Ministry of Rural Construction and Environmental

Protection. Led by a chemist, Qu Geping, who had participated in the Stockholm Conference and had been China's representative to the UNEP in 1976–77, the national bureau doubled its staff to (a still paltry) 120, eventually gaining independent status in 1988 with the establishment of the National Environment Protection Agency (NEPA). After the Rio conference, NEPA started to issue an annual "Communiqué on the State of China's Environment" (Economy 2004: 96–7, 99). That body in turn gave way in 1998 to the State Environmental Protection Agency (SEPA), which became a full ministry in 2008. Despite this improvement in its status, SEPA still had a battle on its hands in promoting its interests against those of other ministries. Participation at Rio in 1992 also prompted the development of China's own NGOs in this field, starting with "Friends of Nature" in 1994. Official statistics in 2006 report over 3,000 officially registered environmental NGOs (quoted in Morton 2009: 63).

SEPA attracted the support of Premier Zhu Rongji, but it still had to share the international negotiating field with other state bodies and ministries. The State Development and Planning Commission (since 2003 the National Development and Reform Commission [NDRC]), had a powerful remit and was attracted by the international funding that became available through the Clean Development Mechanism (CDM). The NDRC, a body that also serves as the main decision-making venue for economic and energy policy (Yang 2010: 11), spawned the National Coordination Committee on Climate Change, which brought together the Ministry of Foreign Affairs, the Ministry of Science and Technology, and the SEPA to oversee climate change actions (Lewis 2007/08: 158). In 2007, that became a National Climate Change Leading Group, chaired by Premier Wen Jiabao and reporting to the State Council. Shortly after, the MOFA matched this, establishing a similar body in the Foreign Ministry with its own special representative who was tasked in part to demonstrate "the government's active participation in international cooperation on responding to climate change" (quoted in Lewis 2007/08: 159).

Further significant changes were introduced in 2003 when the new Hu-Wen leadership promoted its "Scientific Development Concept" and stated its intention to build a "harmonious society." Harmony required, in part, moving away from the policies of all-out and unbalanced growth that were leading to greater inequities in society, ecological disasters, and energy shortages. These policies were endorsed at the National People's Congress in March 2004 and by 2008 had been incorporated into the Chinese Constitution (Hallding et al. 2009: 47–9). In 2005, SEPA introduced the concept of a "Green GDP," designed to measure the costs to local economies of environmental degradation (Economy 2007: 53), an idea that was also flagged up in China's eleventh five-year plan (2006–10).[21] In this five-year plan, Beijing introduced for the first time "ambitious compulsory targets to reduce energy and pollution intensities from their 2005 levels by 20 and 10 percent respectively" (Hallding et al. 2009: 49). The plan also included the target of developing renewable fuels for 10 percent of its total energy consumption by 2010, rising to 15 percent by 2020.

In June 2007, China released its "National Climate Change Programme"[22] which made China "the first developing country to publish a national strategy addressing global warming" (Hallding et al. 2009: 53). That strategy document states China's aims are to "make significant progress on controlling GHG emission, continue to enhance the national adaptive capacity to climate change, enhance climate change related scientific and technological research to reach a new level, greatly improve public awareness of climate change, and strengthen the organizational and institutional development in the area of climate change" (quoted in Hallding et al. 2009: 53).

According to China's deputy head of the NDRC and Head of the National Climate Change Coordination Committee, Xie Zhenhua, this publication showed "the sincerity and determination of China to actively address climate change and participate in related international cooperations [sic]."[23] It made no promises about the capping of emissions, but it did suggest a serious effort to moderate the growth in these emissions – not an insignificant requirement given that, between 2001 and 2006, China's emissions growth had soared. As Garnaut (2008: 293) noted, these policies were more ambitious than those of a number of advanced countries, though China's cumulative energy intensity reduction through 2008 was only 8 percent, well short of the 20 percent required by 2010 (Howes 2009).[24]

---

[21] 2005 was also the year when Pan Yue, a vice minister at SEPA, announced: "The [economic] miracle will end soon because the environment can no longer keep pace" (quoted in Economy 2007: 38). See also Pan Yue's discussion of scientific development and its links to the idea of ecological civilization, *People's Daily Online*, 13 March 2007, http://english.people.com.cn/200703/13/eng20070313_357107.html, accessed 27 July 2009, and Morton (2009: 32–4).

[22] See http://en.ndrc.gov.cn/newsrelease/P020070604561191006823.pdf, accessed 27 July 2009.

[23] Chinese Embassy, "Official: Chinese Gov't Attaches Importance to Issue of Climate Change," 12 December 2007, http://lr.china-embassy.org/eng/majorevents/t389439.htm, accessed 9 April 2009.

[24] Stephen Howes, "Can China Rescue the World Climate Change Negotiations?," 1 September, 2009, http://www.eastasiaforum.org/2009/09/01/can-china-rescue-the-world-climate-change-negotiations/, accessed 15 September 2009.

That this national programme was released a few months before the high-profile COPs meeting in Bali in December 2007 was probably no coincidence. Indeed, China has in the past made important announcements in this policy field at or just before major international conferences. At Bali, China emphasized that its own efforts at home to reduce the growth of carbon emissions through increases in energy efficiency had made a major contribution through the period 1990 and 2005 (although this was not actually the case for the 2001–05 period), and its future goals in this area were designed to further reduce the pace of the increase in its level of emissions.[25] Beijing also advocated the establishment of nationally appropriate, measurable, reportable, and verifiable (MRV) mitigation targets for developing countries, provided the developed world offered the technology and financing that would make those mitigation efforts feasible and international verification of targets was not required (Hallding et al. 2009: 88–91; Zhang and Morton 2010).

Further progress came when President Hu Jintao, at the specially convened climate change conference at the UN in September 2009, promised an unspecified effort by China to "cut carbon dioxide emissions per unit of GDP by a notable margin by 2020 from the 2005 levels."[26] This idea had been signalled in April 2009 when Su Wei, Director-General of China's Leading Group on Climate Change, spoke optimistically of "easily [translating] our [existing] energy reduction targets to carbon dioxide limitation" (quoted in Buijs 2009: 58). It was on that basis that the State Council announced in November 2009 a goal to reduce its carbon emissions per unit of GDP by 40–45 percent of 2005 levels by 2020.[27] Other reports in 2009 demonstrated that China's officials and scholars had become more open to discussing the period when the country's emissions might actually begin to decline rather than simply reduce the rate of increase.[28] In another of Su's statements, he accepted that "China will

[25] Chinese Embassy, "Official: Chinese Gov't Attaches Importance to Issue of Climate Change," 12 December 2007, http://lr.china-embassy.org/eng/majorevents/t389439.htm, accessed 9 April 2009. Lewis reports: "While the intensity of China's carbon emissions (ratio of energy-related CO2 emissions to GDP) declined 67 percent between 1980 and 2000, its absolute emissions increased by 126 percent over this period." She goes on: "Yet, if China's emissions intensity had remained fixed where it was in 1980, its emissions would be more than double what they are today" (2007/08: 166).

[26] *BBC News*, "UN Climate Summit: Key Quotes," 22 September 2009, http://newsvote.bbc.co.uk/, accessed 22 September 2009.

[27] Shi Jiangtao, "Carbon Pledge on Track with Past Performance," *South China Morning Post*, 28 November 2009.

[28] The years between 2030 and 2040 are most often given as estimates. See *Green Leap Forward* (2009a). See also Buijs (2009: 56) and Zhang (2009b). Hu Angang, an adviser

not continue growing emissions without limit or insist that all nations must have the same per-capita emissions. If we did that, this earth would be ruined."[29]

However, China's leaders also had clearly articulated the quid pro quo for further action at the December 2009 Copenhagen summit: the developed world had to take the lead and commit to a mid-term emission reduction goal for 2020 "of at least 25–40% below the 1990 level," to provide funding to poorer countries, and to transfer the technology necessary to increasing the developing world's capacity to reduce emissions levels (Carnegie meeting, 18 March 2009).[30] Subsequently, in May 2009, and probably as a negotiating gambit, China called on rich countries to make 40 percent reductions by 2020 from 1990 levels and to provide funding of at least 0.5–1.0 percent of their GDP as aid to developing countries.[31] In 2008 US dollars, this would amount to approximately $210 billion to $420 billion per annum, a much larger sum than the $100 billion per year proposed by the British Prime Minister – but not then endorsed by the United States – in September 2009. There were also demands by China, India, and Brazil – unwelcome to industrial groups in the developed world – that advanced countries permit the confiscation of patents on clean technologies via compulsory licensing, a principle already permitted in the WTO in cases of public health emergencies.[32]

At Copenhagen in December 2009, and in the absence of legally enshrined developed world carbon abatement targets, Chinese officials went no further than repeating their commitment to the 40 to 45 percent voluntary reduction in carbon intensity announced prior to the December meeting. However, Beijing did show some limited flexibility on the matter of international monitoring of mitigation pledges, accepting at the last minute that emerging countries had to monitor and report the results of their national efforts to the UN every two years, with "provisions for international consultations and analysis under clearly defined guidelines that will ensure that national sovereignty is respected."[33]

to Wen Jiabao, has set the most ambitious targets, arguing for a reduction in Chinese emissions to 1990 levels by 2030 (Hu 2009).

[29] "China Wary of Being Cast as the Villain if Talks Fail," *FT.com*, 21 September 2009.

[30] "NDRC Vice Chairman Puts Forward Three-point Proposal on Climate Change," Domestic Service in Chinese, *Xinhua*, 12 December 2008; "China Calls for Deeper CO_2 Cuts by Rich Nations," *China Daily*, 13 May 2009.

[31] "China Gets Tough on Climate Talks," *FT.com*, 22 May 2009.

[32] "Patent Spat Looms at Climate Change Meeting," *FT.com*, 13 July, 2009.

[33] See "Copenhagen Climate Change Summit Review," *Financial Times*, 23 December 2009: 4. Lieberthal reports serious contention within the Chinese delegation at

What, then, can we conclude about China's relationship with the climate protection norm and its associated standards and expectations? How coincident have China's positions been with respect to these and how has China interpreted the major agreed principles? At the level of rhetoric, national legislation, and articulated commitments China for most of this period has stayed roughly in step with the demands that this global normative framework makes of it, classified as a developing country. This stance has remained consistent as the norm has hardened over time. The Beijing government has come some way from its obstructive position at the Stockholm conference and belief then that general environmental issues were not a problem that a poor country such as China needed to address. From the time of the 1992 UNCED conference, it came to accept the core principles – which were hardly constraining for China – and moved from a sceptical to more enthusiastic stance towards the CDM and the principle of emissions trading generally, emerging as a leading CDM host country (Lewis 2007/08: 165). However, it strenuously resisted arguments that went beyond the existing global norm.

From the early 2000s, climate change moved up China's domestic and international policy agendas, and its stance modified in consequence, especially as we came closer to the determination of post-Kyoto arrangements. In 2007, the year it produced its own National Climate Change Programme, it agreed that developing countries needed to adopt – if voluntarily and according to their own particular circumstances – a more proactive role in reducing the growth of emissions and in producing nationally verifiable mitigation commitments. In 2009, Beijing accepted the need for it not only to improve energy efficiency but also to reduce its carbon emissions per unit of GDP. At Copenhagen, it repeated this pledge and accepted some limited international role in measuring its results. Moreover, surprisingly it accepted the need to formulate a last-ditch deal between the BASIC group of emerging countries and the United States, thus going beyond its previous commitments to stick closely to negotiating only within the G77 + China coalition. There is nothing so far to

Copenhagen after Premier Wen Jiabao agreed to this compromise language. See his "Climate Change and China's Global Responsibilities" Brookings Institution Web site, 11 January 2010, http://www.brookings.edu/opinions/2009/1222_china_climate_lieberthal, aspx?p=1, accessed 27 January 2010. A Chinese perspective on China's role in the negotiations is provided in Zhao Cheng and Tian Fan (*Xinhua*) and Wei Dongze (*People's Daily*), "Verdant Mountains Cannot Stop Water Flowing; Eastward the River Keeps on Going," 24 December 2009, http://www.fmprc.gov.cn/eng/zxxx/t648096.htm, accessed 20 March 2010.

suggest that it would accept a binding international treaty, but it has lodged its national, voluntary, mitigation targets with the UN, has not ruled out a post-Kyoto UN treaty entirely, and has confirmed its support for the Copenhagen Accord.[34]

However, this iteration of the Chinese position in relation to the normative framework would be seriously incomplete without some reference to the leadership's failure or inability to implement many of the national legislative and discursive commitments it has made in the past. For example, SEPA's Green GDP proposal was quietly shelved a year after its introduction, the Agency's staffing levels have been kept extremely low, and it relies on local Environmental Protection Bureaus (EPBs) for implementation of its directives. These EPBs are reliant on local officials for most of their financial support, officials that "still regard meeting GDP growth expectations as their primary objective" (Lieberthal and Sandalow 2009: 33). One of China's leading environmental lawyers has claimed that "barely ten percent of [the country's] environmental laws and regulations are actually enforced," and the Chinese Academy for Environment Planning found that a scant 1.3 percent of annual GDP earmarked for environmental protection between 2001 and 2005 actually found its way into legitimate environmental projects (Economy 2007: 51–2). Some of the reasons for this failure of implementation will be tackled in the next section, but they do raise serious doubts about the depth of the internalization of the climate protection norm.

In sum, China's position is (as Xie Zhenhua characterized it in March 2009): "reduction, adapt[at]ion, technology, and funds" (Carnegie meeting, 18 March 2009: 6). Reduction in absolute levels of GHG emissions is for the developed world, while China and other developing and emerging countries adapt and draw on new technologies and funding to reduce their rate of increase in emissions. Consistent with this, some international measures, such as the CDM and technology transfer, and consultations on mitigation results, may even provide China with sustainable development benefits and in the past China has shown little hesitancy in accepting these aspects of the global regime.

---

[34] In its formal letter to the UNFCCC Secretariat, China stated that it would "endeavor to lower its carbon dioxide emissions per unit of GDP by 40–45% by 2020 compared to the 2005 level, increase the share of non-fossil fuels in primary energy consumption to around 15% by 2020 and increase forest coverage by 40 million hectares and forest stock volume by 1.3 billion cubic meters by 2020 from the 2005 levels." Letter from Su Wei to Yvo de Boer, 28 January 2010 at http://unfccc.int/press/items.2794.php, accessed 5 February 2010.

Nevertheless, in the failure to implement some of its past commitments, we see evidence of competing policy objectives that help to underpin a conservative stance towards the norm, strong attachment to the UNFCCC and 1997 Kyoto Protocol, and a reluctance to accept strict international monitoring. In the following section, we ask what explains this conservative positioning from 1992 to 2007, and what has driven the somewhat greater flexibility in the twenty-first century in the context of still competing policy priorities?

Explaining Levels of Behavioural Consistency

Three factors are of particular importance in our explanation of China's policies with respect to this normative framework. The first, and most powerful, relates to the primacy accorded to the interrelated domestic values of social stability, economic development, and poverty reduction. The second is the relationship between institutional capacity and domestic interests, which, as they coalesce or compete, have important consequences for the levels of normative consistency. The third refers to international factors, including the global norm, which have acted as both a resource from which China has been able to draw and, over time, a growing source of constraint.

Concerns about climate change in China have always faced an unequal fight when the topic has come up against matters of economic development. As Lieberthal and Sandalow have starkly put it: "All other goals are premised on the basis of maintaining rapid economic growth ... [which] has serious consequences for China's carbon emissions growth curve" (2009: 31). Thus, Beijing has persistently refused to adopt mandatory cuts in emissions of GHGs (neither the UNFCCC nor Kyoto Protocol has required it to do so) and has been lax in implementing those environmental policies that have been perceived to have negative consequences for growth.[35] If double-digit growth has been the saviour of one-Party rule in the PRC and growth of at least 8 percent is perceived as the foundation of social stability, then it is not hard to see why local and central government officials would give priority to meeting these targets. This priority was evident in the government's response to the global economic crisis of 2008–09. The unprecedented fiscal stimulus included large increases in government spending on energy-intensive projects, and the government also adopted a "green passage" policy

---

[35] Indeed, Schroeder (2008: 523) argues that Beijing will only support climate change measures provided they impose no costs on development.

that aimed to speed approval of industrial projects (Lieberthal and Sandalow 2009: 31–2).[36]

Moreover, China's resurgence has meant rapid social change, including "managing perhaps the greatest migratory flow in human history." As it shifts from a rural to an urbanized society, this prompts new demands for energy-intensive urban infrastructure, jobs, and homes. To the extent that environmental concerns have become more important in recent years as a result of this urbanization process, reducing atmospheric and water pollution and ensuring reliable energy supply have been more immediate priorities for these new urban dwellers than addressing climate change (Lieberthal and Sandalow 2009: 31–2).

These social demands and the overriding priority of growth have had serious effects on the capacity of environmental bodies such as SEPA (from 2008 the Ministry of Environmental Protection). That body has been in an unequal struggle with other powerful ministries, particularly the NDRC (Yang 2010: 11), and with powerful local and provincial officials who have often been rewarded for meeting ambitious growth targets. SEPA, for example, after a six month battle found that the National Statistics Bureau would not publish its 2005 calculations of China's "Green GDP" because of an expected "unfavourable reaction from provincial governments" resulting from "pollution data [that] would hurt their performance assessments."[37] Apart from competing institutional and political interests, SEPA's goals can also be thwarted by deeper structural impediments, such as "weak capacities, ... low levels of technological expertise, weak institutional coordination, and poor financial management" (Morton 2005: 3).

How, then, given values that prioritize growth, the relatively weaker capacity of environmentalists to promote and enforce environmental legislation, and the focus predominantly on air and water pollution, do we explain the more activist stance on the matter of climate change in the last half decade? Many argue that Beijing's increased willingness to move forward the global climate protection norm and its associated principles

[36] Hebei province, for example, announced the approval of four new cement plants in one day in January 2009 ("Slump Tilts Priorities of Industry in China," *New York Times*, 19 April 2009).

[37] Beijing News noted that the report would have revealed "losses from pollution and reduction in the GDP indicator even higher than the 2004 report" which itself recorded environmental costs equivalent to $64 billion, or 3.05% of China's GDP ("Environment-China: Jittery Officials Thwart Green GDP Report," *Inter Press Service Agency*, 27 July 2007, http://ipsnews.net/print.asp?idnews=38687 accessed 20 March 2010).

is essentially self-interested and a by-product of other domestic priorities rather than acceptance of a responsibility to contribute to global GHG emissions reductions (Schroeder 2008; Hallding et al. 2009; Lieberthal and Sandalow 2009: 28). This reduced the tension between the growth priority and the global normative framework, broadening the coalition of those who support a more flexible stance in the global negotiations.

For example, the leadership has become increasingly concerned that the negative environmental and social externalities of rapid economic growth and urbanization have become too high, necessitating efforts to reduce air and water pollution and rebalance the economy. The Hu-Wen leadership's adoption of the "Scientific Development Concept" in 2003/04 was a partial response to that realization, even though it chose to emphasize continuing high levels of growth through efficient, sustainable measures rather than a reduction in the rate of growth. To the extent that the effort to reduce local pollution by improving energy and carbon efficiency also reduces the rate of increase in China's GHG emissions, then a useful additional by-product is a new policy in climate change negotiations.

Furthermore, China's rapid development has entailed a growing dependence on foreign-sourced supplies of raw materials and fossil fuels in particular.[38] From 1993, China became an oil importer, with some 45 percent coming from the Middle East (Lieberthal and Herberg 2006; ICG June 2008). In 2001, China's economy grew faster than projected, and its use of energy outstripped that of rises in its GDP. Some of the resource deals it struck to sustain this growth came with costs to its image: for example, the agreements reached with Burma/Myanmar and Sudan. Moreover, a growth in imports of crucial commodities spurred a growing Chinese interest in the security of supplies and of supply routes. The government has encouraged its major energy and commodity firms to give attention to the security of their supplies, in part through diversification, but China has not been able to resolve its growing concern with the security of its sea lanes (Downs 2006; Medeiros 2009: 57–9). To the extent that improving China's energy efficiency and increasing the production of energy from renewable sources could limit this growing dependence on foreign commodity supplies, this would have substantial positive benefits for Chinese resource security.

---

[38] For a recent Chinese perspective on this, see Wang Yanjia (2010), "Energy Security and Climate Change Issues in China." Wang discusses China's setting up an oil stockpile and its attempts to improve energy efficiency and the security of supply routes, among other topics.

Finally, greater energy efficiency would also reduce costs for Chinese producers, many of whom have suffered from rising input costs in recent years. At a time when many advanced countries are moving in a similar direction, greater energy efficiency is likely to be crucial for sustaining industrial competitiveness. The cheap cost of domestic energy has favoured domestic producers and consumers to date, but this has worsened the local pollution and foreign dependence problems noted earlier. In addition, given Beijing's desire to respond to the growing demands of citizens for improved public services and welfare, it is unlikely that the government will be able to continue to afford to provide large effective subsidies of this kind.

Taken together, these three considerations could be said to provide a powerful motivation for the interests of domestic environmental institutions to come closer into alignment with the views of powerful central government leaders, firms, and ministries as all seek pathways to modify China's energy and pollution-intensive pattern of development. To the extent that this has permitted China to adopt a somewhat less obstructionist stance towards the global climate protection agenda, this has alleviated some of its image concerns and potentially benefitted the world's climate. But, in this view, this has been a side-benefit of a policy adopted for reasons other than a perceived need to conform with the normative framework associated with climate change.

However, this predominantly interest-based argument does not explain why these goals have been linked to the normative framework since they could all have been pursued in a way that was largely divorced from it. Neither do they capture the reasons for China's decision to take on a leadership role in these climate change negotiations, nor why its new policy directions have crystallized at certain key moments in the climate change debate. This part of the explanation requires attention to international factors, including the role of the global norm itself.

Indeed, participation in the international negotiations and in other forms of international exchange facilitated the making of that link between global norm and domestic interest. As noted earlier, Beijing's Stockholm delegation in 1972 returned with a report that was instrumental in persuading the Beijing leadership to set up its first national conference on environmental protection and to reorganize its bureaucracy to give greater prominence to environmental issues. In addition, participation at Stockholm brought China into contact with a community of like-minded others with similar interests and concerns. By 1992, the G77 + China were successful in having some of their most crucial aims met in the Rio treaty – predominantly their goal to retain an emphasis on their need for development – and in creating a norm that required little behavioural change from much of the developing world. From the start, China took a lead role as one of the norm makers in this issue area; thus its preferences were not ignored at critical stages of norm creation and development. Instead Beijing (for good or ill, depending on one's perspective) took part in shaping the generalized underlying principles of the global norm outlined in 1992, and its more specific requirements as articulated at Kyoto in 1997.

The side-payments deriving from international participation were also attractive to Beijing and strengthened domestic institutional capacities. Multilateral and bilateral funding from external donors led to the training of domestic experts and the establishment of cognate transnational and domestic research programmes. Many of the scientists and environmentalists that were engaged in this research were influential in the domestic debate in the 1980s and early 1990s – although they did not override the growth imperative – and still contribute policy ideas to Premier Wen's National Leading Group on Climate Change. Finally, after initially being very suspicious of the CDM, Beijing came enthusiastically to embrace its funding, which helped to reduce the cost of adopting new technologies.[39] However, it also participated in this mechanism, according to Lewis, because it showed that "China can be viewed internationally as … proactive on the climate issue" (Lewis 2007/08: 165).[40]

This last point alerts us to the potential influence of international image in explaining China's higher levels of contribution to the debate on climate change over the last few years. We have seen how domestic institutional innovation – the creation in 2007 of a special representative in the MOFA for climate change negotiations – was explained as a way to demonstrate China's active participation in the international discussions, and we noted that Beijing has perceived benefits from making major domestic policy announcements in this issue area at international gatherings. Yu Hongyuan's interviewees from the environmental science bureaucracies put it thus in 2007: "China belongs to the international community and has a responsibility to participate in a positive fashion

[39] By 2008, the NDRC had ratified almost 1,600 CDM projects: that is, nearly 25% of the world's total (Morton 2009: 79).

[40] Note, however, the December 2009 controversy over the country's use of industrial policy to obtain money under the scheme, leading to a suspension of approvals for funding. "UN Halts China Wind Farms Amid Funding Dispute," *Financial Times*, 2 December 2009.

because China is an important player. Good intentions in environmental protection will gain us backing internationally and promote international understanding" (Yu 2007: 157).

That requirement to demonstrate responsible behaviour has become more urgent as China has emerged as the leading source of CO_2 emissions. As both Economy and Kent note, global attention to China's place in the hierarchy of emitters increased over time. Before the 1980s, China's emissions levels were not of much interest to other global actors, but by the late 1980s and early 1990s that began to change. By 1991, the PRC was emitting roughly 10 percent of the world's total carbon dioxide, putting it in third place after the Soviet Union and the United States. By 2002, it had risen to second in rank (Economy 2004: 181; Kent 2007: 146–7), and by 2007 it had finally overtaken the United States to become the world's leading emitter. Its per capita emissions are now higher than the global average.

Some among the G77 began to grow restless in response to this evidence of the emerging economies' growing contributions to the problem of global warming, especially those small island states with serious concerns about rising sea levels. Argentina broke away from the majority G77 position in 1998, agreeing to set voluntary commitments to lower its emissions. For China, this heralded the danger that Argentina's actions would "create a new category of Parties under the FCCC" (quoted in Economy 1998: 249), with Beijing fearful presumably that it would be moved into that new category with all of the associated new and unwelcome demands. Similarly, Bangladesh promoted the idea of differentiated responsibility for large developing countries, "notably China," further suggesting growing differences within the G77 coalition (Hallding et al. 2009: 14). The South Korean government – still classed as another non-Annex 1 developing country – announced in November 2009 a voluntary cut in its emissions target of 4 percent by the year 2020.[41]

At Copenhagen itself, the Association of Small Island States (AOSIS) and forty-nine UN-designated Least Developed Countries called for ambitious, binding, and *universal* cuts in emissions to be agreed upon and for a clause to be inserted into the final agreement that commitments by non-Annex 1 countries to mitigate emissions be independently verified (IISS 2010b). As a leaked Chinese environmental research institute report

[41] "South Korea to Announce Emissions Cut Target before Year End," *Xinhua*, 24 September 2009; "South Korea Promises 4% Emissions Cut," *Financial Times*, 18 November 2009.

complained after Copenhagen: "A conspiracy by developed nations to divide the camp of developing nations [was] a success," making reference in support of this to the AOSIS call for the imposition of mandatory reductions on the BASIC group.[42] Given these fissures developing within its originally supportive coalition, the Beijing government took some steps to reduce the danger of being viewed as an obstacle to agreement rather than as the champion of the less-developed world in these negotiations.

This evidence of growing international concern over China's role in contributing to CO_2 emissions has also led to the topic of climate change constantly being raised in meetings between the Chinese leadership and its foreign interlocutors. As one of Schroeder's Chinese interviewees put it: "Every time foreign leaders come to China, they want to discuss climate change. Every time Hu Jintao goes abroad, foreign leaders want to discuss climate change. It is really getting on his nerves." Indeed, that interviewee went on to claim that the proposal China submitted at the 2007 Bali meeting owed itself to this constant pressure since it led Hu to demand of those charged with attending the international negotiations: "you must do something to reduce the pressure on my shoulders" (quoted in Schroeder 2008: 515). Whether or not that pressure was solely responsible for the Bali proposals (and that seems unlikely), it is clear that concerns about international image have played some role in modifying China's stance in the climate change negotiations.

China's relationship with the normative framework, thus, has depended fundamentally on its concerns to protect growth, to enhance social stability, to reduce pollution, and to improve energy efficiency and thus national security. However, over time, the relationship between these factors and protecting the world's climate has been perceived as being somewhat less competitive than was once the case, thereby increasing the power of those domestic institutional actors that believe that the climate protection norm is worth defending and promoting. Indeed, there is some evidence that sizable majorities of the Chinese public have begun to see climate change as a security threat.[43] While the domestic impact of global

---

[42] Jonathan Watts et al., "China's Fears of Rich Nation 'Climate Conspiracy' at Copenhagen Revealed," 22 February 2010, http://www.guardian.co.uk/environment/2010/feb/11/, accessed 22 February 2010. Premier Wen's efforts to explain the positions his delegation took at Copenhagen, and thereby undercut the negative perceptions of its performance, can be found at http:///www.fmprc.gov.cn.eng/zxxx/t673753.htm, 14 March 2010, accessed 20 March 2010.

[43] A Lowy Institute survey in November 2009 recorded that 76% of the Chinese polled saw climate change as a threat (Hanson and Shearer 2009).

warming has helped draw out the compatibilities, international factors – especially those associated with international image – have also played their part in moving climate change higher up China's policy agenda and by 2007 to a modification in its negotiating position. Also important to China's evolving policy debate has been the role of the United States, a topic we address in the next section.

3 The United States and the Climate Protection Norm

Over the course of the twentieth century, the United States became the exemplar of industrialization and capitalist development. After World War II, government policy aimed to ensure sufficient employment and expanding prosperity for the middle classes at home and national security abroad in the context of the Cold War (Krugman 2008). The rapid expansion of industry, the defence sector, population, and suburbia with its associated car ownership and household goods were consistent with these goals, but they came at the cost of substantial local environmental degradation. By the late twentieth century, US energy efficiency was relatively low and GHG emissions were relatively high compared to other major countries (Table 5.1).[44] The United States emitted about a fifth of the world's GHGs annually with less than a twentieth of its population.

An influential domestic environmental movement emerged in response to localized pollution, with important consequences for national and, much later, global environmental policy. This movement drew on a long tradition in American literature on the threats posed to the wilderness by westward expansion, industrialization, and urbanization, from Henry Thoreau's *Walden* (1854) to Rachel Carson's *Silent Spring* in 1962 (Buell 1995). Important conservation groups emerged well before World War II, including the Sierra Club (1892), the Audubon Society (1905), the Izaak Walton League (1922), and the Wilderness Society (1935), but there was a rapid expansion of the movement in the 1960s culminating in the first Earth Day on 22 April 1970. This produced "a durable national consensus that environmental protection must now be a first-order public concern" (Rosenbaum 2008: 6). Teddy Roosevelt's National

---

[44] As one example, as of 2007, the average fuel efficiency of automobiles in the United States was about half that of Europe. See Sivak and Tsimhoni (2009) and "U.S. 'Stuck in Reverse' on Fuel Economy," *MSNBC*, 28 February 2007. It should be emphasized, however, that per capita GHG emissions vary greatly across US states. As of 2007, for example, per capita emissions in Texas were about 2.5 times higher than in California (these two states are the largest emitters). See EPA (2009).

TABLE 5.1. *Comparative Greenhouse Gas Emissions, 1950–2000, Major Countries/Regions*

	Cumulative CO$_2$ Emissions, 1950–2000		Per Capita Cumulative CO$_2$ Emissions, 1950–2000		GHG Emissions in 2000 (all GHGs, excluding land use change)		Per Capita GHG Emissions in 2000 (all GHGs, excluding land use change)	
	MtCO$_2$	Rank	Tons CO$_2$ per person	Rank	MtCO$_2$	Rank	Tons CO$_2$ per person	Rank
US	184,827	1	623	11	6,846	1	24	7
EU (27)	182,771	2	373	32	4,919	2	10	39
China	108,117	3	83	112	4,818	3	4	98
Japan	41,603	8	326	42	1,313	6	10	37
World	1,091,724		169		33,191		6	

Source: Climate Analysis Indicators Tool (CAIT) Version 6.0, Washington, DC: World Resources Institute, 2009.

Parks programme was among the first policy responses, followed by a variety of New Deal programmes in the 1930s and a slew of local, state, and federal environmental initiatives in the 1960s and 1970s. At the state level, California led in efforts to raise environmental protection standards, notably relating to air and water quality, with important consequences for other states (Vogel 1995; DeSombre 2000). Federal programmes included the Clean Air Act (1963), the Wilderness Act (1964), the National Environmental Policy Act (1969) and the establishment in 1970 of the Environmental Protection Agency (EPA). Presidents Kennedy, Johnson, and Nixon all accepted the political necessity to act on environmental protection, though Nixon was most active and initiated an "environmental decade" in US policy in the 1970s (Rosenbaum 2008: 8).

As in most countries, the national consensus is strongest on issues of local environmental protection, particularly when matters of preserving America's historic natural endowment and human health loom large. Sometimes health concerns can generate support for international collective action to protect the global environment, as in US support for the Montreal Protocol in the late 1980s to reduce the ozone hole. In marked contrast to the ozone case, the threat posed by climate change is longer term, considerably easier for doubters to contest, and mitigation costs are almost certainly many times greater, making it difficult to achieve national agreement that the costs of the proposed remedy are acceptable. This has given the United States a rejectionist reputation regarding the global climate protection norm, which the George W. Bush administration actively reinforced. However, the US stance towards the norm is more complex than this reputation and the rhetoric of the Bush administration suggest.

The George H. W. Bush administration came to office in 1989 promising a more positive stance on environmental protection than during the anti-regulation Reagan era. It is often said that Bush failed to deliver on his claim to be an "environmental President" because of domestic recession, a sceptical business community, and internal policy splits. However, his government did enact some important legislation during 1990–92, notably extending the Clean Air Act to require substantial cuts in some harmful emissions from power plants (Rabe 2004: 9; Rosenbaum 2008: 352). However, Bush failed to tackle seriously the more politically difficult issues of nitrogen oxide emissions from vehicles and GHG emissions generally, preferring a non-binding agreement at Rio in 1992 (Paarlberg 1997; Hopgood 1998: 155–68). Notably, his administration accepted the idea of the special leadership responsibilities of developed countries for climate protection but stated that the United States did "not accept any interpretation of principle 7 that would imply a recognition or acceptance by the United States of any international obligations or liabilities, or any diminution in the responsibilities of developing countries."[45] President Bill Clinton exploited this deep ambivalence and promised that "the United States [would] once again resume the [environmental] leadership that the world expects of us" (Harris 2001: 5–6). His decision to establish the President's Council on Sustainable Development, headed by the environmentalist Vice President Gore, was one signal of this new determination to address environmental problems and climate change in particular more effectively.

The decision to sacrifice Gore's favoured carbon tax proposal in the difficult budget negotiations, despite rapid economic recovery and Democratic majorities in the House and Senate, was an early sign that the Clinton administration would be unable to forge the necessary domestic consensus. The Republican victory in the 1994 Congressional elections further constrained the administration's climate strategy. In 1995, the administration accepted the negotiating principles for a global climate convention established by COP-1 in Berlin, including the principle of common but differentiated responsibilities. But the Senate's Byrd-Hagel resolution of 25 July 1997, which passed 95 votes to zero, declared in clear language that

> [T]he United States should not be a signatory to any protocol to, or other agreement regarding, the United Nations Framework Convention on Climate Change of 1992, at negotiations in Kyoto in December 1997 or thereafter which would: (1) mandate new commitments to limit or reduce greenhouse gas emissions for the Annex 1 Parties, unless the protocol or other agreement also mandates new specific scheduled commitments to limit or reduce greenhouse gas emissions for Developing Country Parties within the same compliance period; or (2) result in serious harm to the U.S. economy.[46]

This unanimous statement did not amount to an outright rejection of the climate protection norm or of the principle of differential responsibilities, but of what was widely portrayed in the United States as a wholly unbalanced agreement. Sentiment in the House of Representatives was the same. It also voted unanimously in favour of "specific scheduled commitments to limit or reduce greenhouse gas emissions for the developing country

---

[45] UNCED (1992), para. 16.
[46] 105th Congress, 1st session, S. Res. 98, 25 July 1997.

parties within the same compliance period" (House Committee 1998: 6). Given developing country opposition even to voluntary emissions cuts, the administration signalled in late 1997 that at best it could support a commitment to stabilize US GHG emissions at 1990 levels over the 2008–12 period (Falkner 2009: 16). In the end, the US delegation to Kyoto, under considerable pressure from the European Union, agreed to a 7 percent reduction in return for an agreement to flexible and market-friendly implementation mechanisms. This indicated the continuing ability of the United States to shape the global deal even though there was no prospect of Senate ratification of the Kyoto Protocol.

The new George W. Bush administration aimed to close the large gap that had emerged between the administration's position and that of Congress by insisting that any global deal must achieve greater "equity" between developed and developing countries. As Bush explained, "I oppose the Kyoto Protocol because it exempts 80 percent of the world, including major population centers such as China and India, from compliance, and would cause serious harm to the U.S. economy."[47] At most, his administration offered to improve energy efficiency (Rabe 2004: 14) – a position that emphasized the priority given to economic growth and competitiveness, and one later replicated by China. Like the Senate before it, the Bush administration avoided rejecting the core climate protection norm outright and remained a party to the UNFCCC, despite the President's own misgivings about the science and reports that his administration tried to "censor" the views of the government's own climate scientists.[48] Instead, it tried to reshape the global consensus on the associated principles of the climate protection regime, especially those concerning equity and flexibility of implementation, so that it would impose no burden on US economic growth (Falkner 2009).

As the scientific consensus hardened and the ranks of its critics swelled, the George W. Bush administration launched new initiatives to engage major emerging countries, above all China. In 2005 it launched the Asia Pacific Partnership on Clean Development and Climate, which included

[47] "Text of a Letter from the President to Senators Hagel, Helms, Craig, and Roberts," 13 March 2001, http://georgewbush-whitehouse.archives.gov/news/releases/2001/03/2001 0314.html, accessed 21 September 2009.

[48] In early 2007, the House Oversight and Government Reform Committee held hearings on allegations of political interference in climate science. The most widely reported allegations came from Dr James Hansen, Director of NASA's Goddard Institute for Space Studies and one of America's most prominent climate scientists. See http://oversight.house.gov/index.php?option=com_content&task=view&id=2607&Itemid=2.

China and other major Asian countries and which emphasized technology transfers and voluntarism as a solution to energy security and climate change problems.[49] In 2007, it convened the Major Economies Forum on Energy Security and Climate Change (MEF), which brought together the world's fifteen major polluters, and attempted to frame this as a contribution to the UNFCCC process.[50] Critics saw these initiatives as diverting attention from historic responsibilities; many also opposed the attempted linking of climate change and energy security. The MEF achieved very little, which is not inconsistent with this interpretation.[51] The depth of international suspicion regarding the administration's true motives was reflected in the reception of the US delegation to Bali in 2007, when it was booed off the stage.

The second term of the Bush administration, particularly its final two years, did see a shift in emphasis. While Bush continued to resist a commitment to specific near-term GHG reductions, he accepted the G8 Hokkaido summit declaration in July 2007 of a 50 percent global cut in emissions by 2050 and language that supported the fourth assessment report of the IPCC and the Bali road map.[52] This shift was also more consistent with a proliferating range of sub-federal climate change policy initiatives. Many US states moved into the political vacuum after the failure to ratify Kyoto and an emerging sub-federal coalition expanded rapidly during the Bush years, adopting policies that were more consistent with the global norm.[53] For example, the regional greenhouse gas initiative (RGGI), established in December 2005 by the governors of seven northeastern and mid-Atlantic states, agreed to a mandatory cap and trade programme for electricity producers from 2009. California and six other western states agreed another regional cap and trade programme in September 2008. The US Mayors Climate Protection Agreement of 2005 initially included mayors from 141 cities and reached 973 mayors from all 50 states by September 2009.[54] All these initiatives demonstrated a

---

[49] http://georgewbush-whitehouse.archives.gov/news/releases/2005/07/20050727–11.html, accessed 21 September 2009.

[50] http://georgewbush-whitehouse.archives.gov/news/releases/2007/09/20070927.html, accessed 8 July 2009.

[51] Author discussions with MEF sherpas, London, November 2009.

[52] G8 declaration on environment and climate change, Hokkaido, Japan, 8 July 2008: http://www.g8.utoronto.ca/summit/2008hokkaido/2008-climate.html, accessed 9 July 2009.

[53] See Rabe (2004), Falkner (2009), Lieberthal and Sandalow (2009: 20–23), and http://www.pewclimate.org/states-regions, accessed 20 March 2010.

[54] http://usmayors.org/climateprotection/agreement.htm, accessed 21 September 2009.

considerable appetite amongst many US political actors to treat Kyoto as a legitimate policy benchmark.

The election of President Obama in November 2008 and the consolidation of Democratic Party control in Congress appeared to accelerate the shift already underway in US federal policy. In his election night speech, Obama spoke of a "planet in peril" and committed his administration to achieving a post-Kyoto global deal.[55] His first budget identified the need "to invest in clean energy, end our addiction to oil, address the global climate crisis, and create new American jobs that cannot be outsourced."[56] It committed the administration to seek emissions reductions "in the range of" 17 percent below 2005 levels by 2020 and 83 percent below 2005 levels by 2050, in part through a cap and trade system in which all emissions permits would be auctioned. Obama appointed prominent scientists and others committed to climate protection to key policymaking positions.[57] The administration also broke new ground in the EPA's formal "endangerment finding" designating GHGs as a threat to human health and thus subject to regulation[58] and in new domestic standards for automobile fuel efficiency and emissions.[59] More generally, the administration committed itself to global leadership on climate issues. In testimony to Congress in September 2009, Todd Stern, the administration's chief climate negotiator, asked rhetorically "what do other countries, whether developed or developing, have a right to expect from us? Frankly, that we stand and deliver. That we apply the global leadership that is our hallmark to an issue of profound, generational meaning."[60]

[55] http://edition.cnn.com/2008/POLITICS/11/04/obama.transcript/, accessed 27 March 2010.

[56] http://www.whitehouse.gov/omb/budget/overview, 26 February 2009, accessed 21 September 2009.

[57] The physicists John Holdren and Steven Chu became the President's chief scientific adviser and energy secretary, respectively, while Carol Browner, former head of the EPA, became chief adviser on climate policy and Todd Stern chief climate negotiator.

[58] A Supreme Court decision required the EPA to begin regulating vehicle emissions, and the Obama administration authorized EPA to regulate emissions from stationary sources (industry and power stations) as well ("Enter the EPA," *The Economist*, 3 October 2009).

[59] The agreement between carmakers, trade unions, and environmental NGOs on a new average fuel economy standard of 35.5 miles per gallon by 2016 was announced in May 2009. Automobile firms were induced to agree after the administration convinced California, which had held out for even higher standards, to join the new national scheme. See "Obama Unveils Fuel Efficiency Alliance," *FT.com*, 19 May 2009.

[60] Todd Stern, Special Envoy for Climate Change, "The Current State of our Negotiations on a New International Climate Agreement," statement to the House Select Committee for Energy Independence and Global Warming, Washington, DC, 10 September 2009.

This ambitious agenda masked important elements of continuity with the international environmental diplomacy of previous administrations, notably the desire to rebalance the principle of common but differentiated responsibilities in a way that would substantially reduce the emphasis on the historic responsibilities of developed countries, above all of the United States. The Obama administration was unwilling to seek the ratification of the Kyoto treaty. It also reconvened the Major Economies meeting (rebranded as the Major Economies Forum on Energy and Climate) in April 2009, fully aware that the deadlock between developed and developing countries remained a key obstacle to a post-Kyoto global deal.[61] Todd Stern argued that major developing countries "must take actions that will significantly reduce their emissions below their so-called 'business-as-usual' path in the mid-term (around 2020), to an extent consistent with what is called for by the science; they must reflect these actions in an international agreement, just as we must reflect our own undertakings; and these actions must be subject to a strong reporting and verification regime."[62]

In short, the Obama administration's emphasis on achieving greater "balance" in a post-Kyoto deal echoed the insistence of previous administrations on shifting the emphasis in the global norm from defining historic responsibilities for cumulative emissions towards collective future responsibilities for emissions reductions. Given developing country resistance to this policy, it raised continuing doubts over whether any plausible global deal would be acceptable to Congress, where there is less evidence of a substantive policy shift. The House's Waxman-Markey comprehensive energy bill, formally known as the American Clean Energy and Security Act (ACES), passed by a narrow majority in June 2009, aimed at the same emissions-reduction targets as the administration, to be achieved through a cap and trade system.[63] These emissions-reduction targets appeared to represent the upper limits of political possibility: they were repeated by the administration before the Copenhagen conference and in the US letter of association with the Copenhagen Accord of January 2010.[64] The

---

[61] "Clinton Says U.S. is Ready to Lead on Climate," *New York Times*, 28 April 2009.

[62] Todd Stern, "The Current State of our Negotiations on New International Climate Agreement," statement to the House Select Committee for Energy Independence and Global Warming, Washington DC, 10 September 2009.

[63] See http://www.opencongress.org/bill/111-h2454/show, accessed 20 March 2010.

[64] "Obama to Attend Summit but Cuts Plan Disappoints," *Financial Times*, 26 November 2009; Todd Stern, letter to Yvo de Boer, Executive Secretary, UNFCCC, 28 January 2010, http://unfccc.int/files/meetings/application/pdf/unitedstatescphaccord_app.1.pdf, accessed 27 March 2010.

2020 target amounted to a 4 percent reduction from 1990, well below the levels offered by the EU, the 20 percent recommended by the IPCC, and those demanded by developing countries. The House bill also envisaged limiting the economic impact of these targets for key interest groups through large hidden subsidies and the use of mandated action rather than price incentives. They raised doubts about the seriousness of the targets themselves and were a departure from the US-sponsored principle of market-based mitigation. The hoped-for Senate version of this bill, the leading sponsor of which was Senator John Kerry, was widely expected to be even weaker and was not ready for the Copenhagen meeting in December 2009. In July 2010 the Democratic leadership in the Senate suspended its efforts to pass such a bill. All of this indicated the enduring domestic constraints on US global climate leadership.

In summary, the United States has played a major role in shaping the global climate protection norm but has remained in a persistent state of tension with it. The important domestic and international contributions of American environmentalists, scientists,[65] and sub-federal politicians have not fully compensated for the unwillingness or inability of the US federal government to lead the global effort on climate protection. The gap between this behaviour and America's status as the largest historical contributor to anthropogenic warming has placed in doubt the United States' commitment to the norm, and the potential for an appropriate global response. Although the US government has never completely rejected the global climate protection norm itself, it has persistently attempted to use its substantial leverage to reshape the norm's implementing principles in a direction that reflected its view of greater "equity."

Explaining Levels of Behavioural Consistency

What accounts for this evolving and difficult US relationship with the global climate protection norm? The general literature on environmental policymaking in the United States emphasizes multiple layers of causality and focuses on the role of the various branches of government, the Constitution, environmentalists, organized producer groups, and scientists

---

[65] Scientists at American universities have long made up the largest contingent within the IPCC and more generally have made a major contribution to the science of climate change. Contributors to Working Group 1 (the core climate science group) of the 2007 IPCC report and their affiliations can be found at: http://www.ipcc.ch/pdf/assessment-report/ar4/wg1/ar4-wg1-annexes.pdf. See also http://www.eecg.utoronto.ca/~prall/climate/AR4wg1_authors_table.html, accessed 1 October 2009.

(e.g., Rosenbaum 2008: 27–109). Rather than assess systematically all the factors that contribute to environmental policy outcomes in the United States, we focus here on the four that are most significant: organized groups, political ideology and policymaker beliefs, political institutions, and international factors (including the global norm itself). We argue that the interaction between domestic values and political institutions on the one hand and US power on the other has been the main reason for US inconsistency with the norm.

The environmental movement, a diverse collection of individual activists and organized groups, has been the main source of demand for change in US domestic environmental policies, actively lobbying politicians and providing information to policymakers. Its influence is reflected in the greater resources government has agreed to devote to environmental legislation, implementation and applied scientific research, and in the periodic appointment of environmentalists to key policy positions (Harris 2001: 24). The leverage of the environmental movement in the policy process has significantly depended on its ability to influence general public opinion, which came to share its broad goal of environmental protection from the 1960s.

In the area of climate change, however, this has been the movement's Achilles heel. It has been unable to make a decisive link between climate protection and public health/wilderness protection, and it has been unable to reassure voters that the economic costs of mitigation will be acceptable. Some US public opinion surveys do find significant public concern about climate change, but this is generally not matched by a willingness to pay significant costs (Rosenbaum 2008: 52–7).[66] Nor do American voters rank climate change as a major concern, in apparent contrast to citizens elsewhere.[67] Since the late 1980s, not much more than a third of respondents to Gallup polls have claimed to have been very worried about global warming (Figure 5.1). These data suggests that the hardening scientific consensus, popularized in Al Gore's film *An Inconvenient Truth* (2006), has not had powerful effects on public perceptions. In mid-2009,

---

[66] "Most Would Pay Higher Energy Bills to Address Climate Change Says Global Poll," http://www.worldpublicopinion.org/pipa/articles/btenvironmentra/427.php?lb=bte& pnt=427&nid=&id=, accessed 16 September 2009.

[67] Gallup, "Little Increase in Americans' Global Warming Worries," 21 April 2008, http:// www.gallup.com/poll/106660/Little-Increase-Americans-Global-Warming-Worries. aspx, accessed 16 September 2009; World Public Opinion, "Assessing Governments on Climate Change," 29 July 2009, http://www.worldpublicopinion.org/pipa/pdf/jul09/ WPO_ClimateChange_Jul09_quaire.pdf, accessed 16 September 2009.

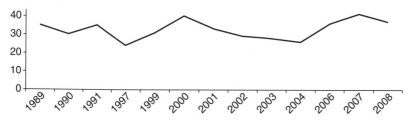

FIGURE 5.1. Percentage of respondents saying that they worry "a great deal" about the "greenhouse effect" or global warming, 1989–2008.
Source: Gallup, "Little Increase in Americans' Global Warming Worries," 21 April 2008.

despite the efforts of the Obama administration, a record 41 percent of those polled thought that the news media generally *exaggerated* the seriousness of the problem.[68]

The softness of public support for climate change mitigation in the face of ongoing concerns about the economic impact of emissions limitation has given business greater influence over US climate policy outcomes than in many others areas of environmental policy. Although US business lobbies have never been unambiguously hostile to climate policy, they have generally opposed policies that would substantially raise costs relative to important competitors. The fossil fuel sector, the electricity generation sector, and energy-intensive manufacturing sectors have been strongly opposed to binding emissions constraints without substantial compensation. For many of these firms, GHG emissions caps are the latest chapter in a sustained and costly long-term regulatory assault on their profitability (Rosenbaum 2008: 17). The Global Climate Coalition, created in 1989 after the first IPCC meeting, was a coalition of the major oil companies, auto firms and other manufacturers firmly opposed to emissions constraints.[69] It engaged in aggressive lobbying and funded anti-IPCC and anti-Kyoto advertising campaigns. Organized labour, heavily concentrated in the manufacturing sector, was also supportive of this position. This pattern is broadly consistent with a general finding that US business supports multilateral agreements only if these internationalize domestic regulations from which business cannot plausibly escape, or if they offer competitive advantages

[68] Gallup, "Increased Number Think Global Warming Is 'Exaggerated,'" 11 March 2009, http://www.gallup.com/poll/116590/Increased-Number-Think-Global-Warming-Exaggerated.aspx, accessed 16 September 2009.

[69] Despite its title and the membership of a few non-US multinational firms, the GCC was dominated by large US firms.

to particular sectors (the Montreal Protocol is a standard example of the latter).[70]

Some go further in arguing that business generally enjoys a "privileged relationship" with government due to its ability to deliver economic growth and employment (Lindblom 1980: 73; Harris 2001: 18). But as Falkner (2008: Chapter 4) shows, although business opposition discouraged the US government from agreeing to binding emissions cuts, the business sector faced countervailing forces and internal conflicts. Some business groups concluded that open hostility to the cause of climate protection was too costly: the major automobile firms, BP, Shell, Texaco, Dow Chemical, and DuPont all withdrew from the GCC in the late 1990s, and the GCC disbanded completely in 2002. Around this time, some major firms moved towards a position more supportive of the UNFCCC and the Kyoto Protocol, including the International Climate Change Partnership (ICCP) and the World Business Council on Sustainable Development (WBCSD).[71] The WBCSD today has more than three dozen American MNCs among its membership, including GCC defectors.

The true motives for these changes in stance are difficult to discern and may be multiple, including the perceived reputational costs of climate change denial, clean energy opportunities, and a desire for greater regulatory certainty at home and abroad. Many US chief executives now see climate change as among the top three factors affecting future profitability, though they still rank it less highly than many of their foreign counterparts (McKinsey & Co. 2007, 2008). Some corporate leaders, notably in the insurance and asset management sectors, now actively support substantive cuts in emissions,[72] and financial firms strongly favour a global carbon trading regime, from which they could also benefit.[73] The small but powerful energy technology sector also perceives large potential gains from the increased demand for clean technologies that could flow from a new global climate deal, provided there is adequate intellectual property (IP) protection.[74]

---

[70] DeSombre (2000) makes this claim for US environmental policy. Other examples of the United States trying to export domestic rules that raise business costs can be found in Basel capital requirements for banks and the OECD anti-bribery convention of 1997.

[71] See http://www.iccp.net/index.html and http://www.wbcsd.org/templates/Template WBCSD5/layout.asp?type=p&MenuId=MQ&doOpen=1&ClickMenu=LeftMenu, accessed 14 September 2009.

[72] The Investor Network on Climate Risk, established in the United States in 2003, included seventy corporate members managing $7 trillion of funds by September 2009 (see: www. incr.com, accessed 17 September 2009).

[73] "Finance Groups Demand Tough Climate Targets," *FT.com*, 17 September 2009.

[74] In May 2009, the US Chamber of Commerce launched the Coalition for Innovation, Employment and Development, whose primary goal is to lobby in favour of the

But the balance of US business opinion continues to oppose costly emissions constraints. The US Chamber of Commerce and the National Association of Manufacturers opposed both cap and trade legislation and EPA regulatory authority over GHG emissions in 2009.[75] Even if business cannot control the evolution of the policy debate, it retains enough power and coherence to ensure that its concerns about costs and competitiveness are taken into account.

The ability of business to do this is also due to the strong value placed on economic growth in American society. This growth priority has been reflected in a deregulatory agenda since the 1980s. President Reagan's vigorous assertion of the need for "regulatory relief" transformed the Republican Party and had powerful longer-term consequences. It placed the formerly ascendant environmental movement on the defensive, bolstered the influence of business in public policymaking, and weakened substantially the already limited capacity of the public policy system to implement existing environmental law (Rosenbaum 2008: 70–1). Climate change became one of the favoured targets of anti-regulation Republicanism, which labelled it as scientifically undemonstrated and as requiring remedies that were unacceptably costly to the American public and business.

Although George H. W. Bush personally favoured a less ideological brand of Republicanism, his administration and that of Bill Clinton accepted important elements of Reagan's anti-regulatory agenda. The revival of radical Republicanism in the Congressional elections of 1994 and the emergence of enduring Republican majorities in both houses until 2001, also constrained the environmental policy ambitions of the Clinton administration. The George W. Bush administration continued this anti-regulatory, pro-business policy agenda despite Bush's earlier professed centrism on environmental issues and the temporary loss of the Republican majority in the Senate during 2001–03. It was also close to the evangelical Christian lobby, which at that stage was relatively hostile to concerns about climate change.

In stressing the role of dominant societal values in US climate policy, we do not mean to argue that the hardening of the scientific consensus on climate change in recent years had no effect. This hardening

maintenance of strong IP protection in the climate change negotiations (see www.thecied. org/portal/cied/default, accessed 17 September 2009).

[75] Some large US firms openly split with this position, including some less coal-dependent electricity generators ("Nike Resigns from Chamber's Board, Citing Climate-Change Differences," *The Hill Blog Briefing Room*, 30 September 2009).

consensus did raise the political risks of climate change denial for prominent politicians,[76] especially among swing or "independent" voters.[77]
Some prominent voices in the evangelical movement, which hitherto had
been strongly associated with conservative Republicanism, also shifted
position and called for measures to prevent global warming.[78] Republican
politicians who were less dependent upon conservative constituencies
have also been willing to move with the evolving scientific consensus,
notably Governor Arnold Schwarzenegger of California. Picking up on
shifting independent-voter sentiment, by the 2008 presidential elections,
all of the main candidates were committed to mandatory national emissions reductions of at least 50 percent by 2050 and to a cap and trade
system.[79] But climate change mitigation policies, especially at a time of
high unemployment, remain vulnerable to the critique that they impose
unacceptable costs on the American public and business and are a recipe
for intrusive government. This ensures that emissions-reduction commitments are strongly biased towards the long term.

The division of powers in the Constitution also gives Congress substantial influence over energy and environmental policy, creates multiple points of access for interest groups, and provides states with an
important role in the policy process. The sensitivity of Congressional
representatives from both major parties to local concerns weakens
their attention to national interests (Paarlberg 1997: 144; Rosenbaum
2008: 34–9, 76–7). Significant numbers of "brown Democrats" from
the midwest and south depend on the votes of blue collar workers
in districts that either produce or use fossil fuels intensively. Energy-
intensive industries also have significant influence in these Congressional
districts and states. Representative Rick Boucher (D) of Virginia, for
example, demanded that any climate bill must "preserve coal jobs, create the opportunity for increasing coal production and keep electricity
rates in regions like Southwest Virginia affordable."[80] Legislators from

---

[76] Vice President Dick Cheney was a prominent exception. See "Exclusive: Cheney on
Global Warming," *ABC News*, 23 February 2007, http://abcnews.go.com/Technology/
story?id=2898539&page=1, accessed 21 September 2009.

[77] Gallup, "Climate-Change Views: Republican-Democratic Gaps Expand," 29 May 2008,
http://www.gallup.com/poll/107569/ClimateChange-Views-RepublicanDemocratic-
Gaps-Expand.aspx, accessed 16 September 2009.

[78] "Evangelical Leaders Urge Action on Climate Change," *NPR.org*, 8 February 2006.

[79] "Braced for Change," *FT.com*, 15 September 2008.

[80] "Boucher: Cap and Trade Deal Preserves Coal Jobs," *Bluefield Daily Telegraph*, 16 May
2009. Coal provides for a quarter of the country's total primary energy demand (compared to 40% for oil), over a half of its total power generation and over a third of its total
CO_2 emissions (IEA 2007: 608).

intensive carbon-producing and consuming states have long been well represented on the important House Energy and Commerce Committee and in Congress generally (Cragg and Kahn 2009). In the ACES bill of mid-2009, provisions to reduce the costs of emissions cuts for energy utilities and manufacturers significantly favoured brown Democrat constituencies; even so, forty-four House Democrats still voted against the bill.[81] The Democrat-controlled Senate overrepresents rural, energy-producing, and industrial states even more than the House.[82]

Similar divisions can be seen among US states. We noted earlier the instances of states, like California, which were conspicuously more "internationalist" on climate policy than the George W. Bush administration. Yet, during 1998–99, sixteen states passed legislation or resolutions criticizing Kyoto or opposing Senate ratification (Rabe 2004: 20).[83] Some of these sixteen states had exceptionally high per capita emissions from power generation (North Dakota, West Virginia, Wyoming), some had large fossil fuel resources (West Virginia), some had heavy concentrations of energy-intensive manufacturing industry (Illinois, Indiana, Michigan, Ohio, Pennsylvania), and some were relatively rural (Alabama, Arizona, Colorado, Idaho, Kentucky, Mississippi, North Dakota, South Carolina, Virginia, West Virginia, Wyoming).[84]

The discussion so far suggests that voter and business preferences and values have combined with the particularities of US institutions to shape American behaviour vis-à-vis the climate protection norm. Does this leave any room for international factors in explaining policy outcomes? Our answer is that the international dimension has been important in three ways. First, US relative power has been crucial in permitting it to resist often substantial international pressure to conform more closely to the climate protection norm and to shape the global climate change framework itself. Second, US perceptions of imbalance in the global climate change framework have resonated strongly with the domestic concerns about the high cost of climate mitigation already mentioned. Third, the growing importance of the bilateral relationship with China has substantially affected US attitudes and behaviour towards the global climate protection norm.

---

[81] Of 219 votes in favour, 211 were Democrat and only 8 were Republican. Of the 212 votes against, 168 were Republican and 44 were Democrat.

[82] "Emissions bill faces tough Senate fight," *FT.com*, 22 May 2009.

[83] Some states, like West Virginia, even prohibited state agencies from taking steps to reduce emissions.

[84] Based on authors' calculations from Energy Information Agency and US Census data.

Some argue that US power has been less important than we claim. In Rosenbaum's (2008: 335) judgement, for example, "worldwide diplomatic pressure virtually compelled the United States to remain involved in global climate warming treaty negotiations" during George W. Bush's tenure. This view, however, underestimates the unique ability of the United States to engage internationally in ways not open to other countries – bilaterally with other key players, in convening new groupings like the MEF, and in the UN framework itself. There have been parallels, for example, between the United States and Australia in the constraints both countries faced at the domestic level, but US ambivalence towards climate protection gave space to such countries to resist conforming that they would otherwise have lacked (Howe 2007). To the extent that foreign pressure did play a role in forcing the George W. Bush administration to shift tack, it primarily did so by reverberating in the US domestic political debate over the administration's record. Bush's international isolation on climate policy went from being a badge of honour to – in some quarters – a domestic political liability, symbolic of the costs of US unilateralism. Events like Hurricane Katrina and the course of the Iraq War undermined the administration's claims to competence, particularly among swing voters. This perception, along with the hardening of the scientific consensus on climate change and the entry into force of the Kyoto treaty in 2005, left the Bush administration looking exposed on climate policy. Many state and local government actors saw this more quickly than the administration itself and shifted position accordingly.

Even so, it would be misleading to assign a determining role to considerations of relative power in the elaboration of US climate change policy. Successive US administrations refrained from arguing explicitly that the United States should resist the principle of common but differentiated responsibilities because its negative relative growth effects would erode US strategic preponderance in the longer term. This was also true of the George W. Bush administration, in which the desire to maintain strategic preponderance was uppermost and which at an early stage identified China as a major potential strategic competitor. Notably, in the two National Security Strategy documents produced during that period (USNSS 2002, 2006), climate change was acknowledged as a problem that required efforts "to stabilize greenhouse gas concentrations associated with ... growth, containing them at a level that prevents dangerous human interference with the global climate" (USNSS 2002: 20). Thus, the administration's public objections to Kyoto rested largely on the unacceptable costs for domestic jobs and growth that it claimed it would entail.

Our argument, then, is that strategic factors help to explain the unique ability of the United States to resist conformity with the emerging global norm and to attempt to reshape its content, but strategic considerations have not been decisive in shaping the content of US climate policy itself. Although no administration can ignore the strategic implications of climate change, there has been no consensus on the relationship between climate change and national security. Indeed, in the final years of the George W. Bush administration, the increasing political, fiscal, and personal costs of the Iraq War and the associated failure of the Bush administration's plans to democratize the Middle East revived old concerns about the costs of growing US oil import dependence. By 2007, oil imports were over 60 percent of annual US petroleum consumption, with about a quarter of this coming from the Middle East, far in excess of the level of import dependence during the oil shocks of the 1970s (Rosenbaum 2008: 256). Military and strategic planners increasingly saw America's "addiction" to fossil fuels as highly costly in defence, foreign policy, reputation, and economic terms.[85] A report by eleven senior retired US admirals and generals in 2007 pointedly argued that US national security planning "cannot wait for certainty" on the impact of climate change and that "the U.S. should commit to a stronger national and international role to help stabilize climate change at levels that will avoid significant disruption to global security and stability" (CNA Corporation 2007: 7). Along similar lines, the Obama administration identified climate change as a direct threat to national security and to the health and safety of US citizens, using this as one argument for US leadership to foster international collective action to mitigate this threat (USNSS 2010: 8, 12, 47). It also tried to reframe the argument for national climate mitigation policies as resting on both economic and security considerations: "The nation that leads the world in building a clean energy environment will enjoy a substantial economic and security advantage" (USNSS 2010: 30).

However, as we have seen, these arguments have not proved to be compelling for the US Congress, in which the consensus view has remained that the costs of greater consistency with the UN climate protection framework are simply too high for the US economy and American voters.

---

[85] "Military Sharpens Focus on Climate Change," *Washington Post*, 15 April 2007; "Climate Change Seen as Threat to U.S. Security," *New York Times*, 8 August 2009.

Thus, the Obama administration was unable to convince a Democrat-controlled Congress, acutely aware of the reluctance of voters and industry to accept costly short-run measures for uncertain long-run benefits, to pass a climate bill commensurate with its own assessment of the severity of the threat.

This reluctance to accept tangible economic costs has been greatly exacerbated in the US case by the perception that the existing distribution of climate mitigation costs under the principle of common but differentiated responsibilities is unreasonable. The primary objection of the Byrd-Hagel resolution was that Kyoto failed to require any serious contribution from the developing world. Here, the limits of American power have been apparent: although US influence over the global framework has been substantial, it has been unable to break the resistance of the developing world to binding limits on their own emissions of the kind that would satisfy Congress. The United States is the largest past contributor to the increase in the stock of GHG in the atmosphere since the industrial revolution, but there is a strong national consensus that it should not be asked to bear a corresponding share of the future costs of mitigation. As we discuss in the next section, US concerns about the unfairness of the existing global deal relate to the major emerging market countries generally, but they have become increasingly focused on China.

4 The Bilateral Relationship and Behavioural Consistency

Both Beijing's and Washington's stances on climate change have been increasingly influenced by their developing bilateral political, economic, and strategic relationship. Their relationship has fed directly into the perceptions that each has held of the legitimacy of the global negotiating process as well as the outcomes reached over the course of the negotiations. The two governments have rightly been characterized as being in a "mutually supportive but ultimately destructive dance" in this policy area (Vandenbergh 2007/08: 905).[86] This mutuality was demonstrated particularly after the signature of the Kyoto Protocol, when each pointed to the other's uncooperative behaviour as a reason not to adopt mandatory limits, thus tempering their willingness actually to press for limits. Analysts of Chinese policy have argued that Bush's withdrawal

---

[86] Chandler put it starkly (2008: 1): "the United States and China seemingly remain locked in a climate suicide pact, each arguing the other is the reason for inaction."

took the pressure off China for eight years (Zhang 2009a). Their bilateral relationship is also increasingly seen as the key to unlocking a global climate deal: if they act to reduce emissions "the rest of the world can more easily coalesce on a global plan." Conversely, "if either fails to act, the mitigation strategies adopted by the rest of the world will fall far short of averting disaster for large parts of the world" (Chandler 2008).

Both countries initially saw the UN as the appropriate forum for addressing global climate protection but came to take very different views on the fairness of the distributive bargain that was eventually reached in the 1990s. From the Chinese perspective, the UN process in the 1990s was seen as highly legitimate in input and output terms, because it placed most of the mitigation burden on those countries, and particularly the United States, that had contributed to the problem. It also did little to threaten China's growth priority or, of course, the goal of those in China who wish to see Beijing's international influence and strategic position improve over time. From the US perspective, this was precisely what made the bargain illegitimate: the perceived unfairness of the distribution of costs of global climate mitigation rendered its output legitimacy low for America. This in turn cast doubt on the process itself, especially during the George W. Bush administration, which tried actively to use different fora as part of a strategy to rebalance the distributional bargain reached at the UN.[87]

The United States signed the 1992 Rio declaration as did China. It was the Kyoto Protocol, with its mandatory targets for the developed world that brought these legitimacy questions directly to bear on the bilateral relationship. As we have seen, both houses of Congress unanimously demanded that any global deal require binding emissions caps on developing countries, emphasizing the damage that a Kyoto-style deal would do to the American economy. Statements made at a House Hearing on the Kyoto Protocol in 1998 particularly singled out China for negative comment, the Chair of the Committee, Benjamin A. Gilman, summarizing the Chinese negotiating position at Kyoto as a policy of the "'Three Nos': no obligations on China, no voluntary commitments by China, and no future negotiations to bind China" (House Committee 1998: 6).

Distributional concerns were clearly higher in Congress than in the executive branch during the Clinton period, with the executive willing to accept the unspecified but "meaningful participation" of the developing

---

[87] This is not to suggest that these perceptions were not contested by other social groups, scientists, and political leaders within these two countries.

world in mitigating the effects of global warming, including use of the CDM, whereas the majority in Congress wanted to equalize the future burdens imposed on the developed and developing worlds. The George W. Bush administration's views on Kyoto were much closer to those of Congress, and it also focused attention on China's lack of commitment to emissions constraint. In March 2001, Bush pulled out of the Kyoto negotiations on the stated grounds that it did not include targets for countries like China, and he repeated this argument as the basis for his refusal to participate on several occasions after that time (Lieberthal and Sandalow 2009: 26), including in February 2005 when Kyoto came into force.

China, then, has figured increasingly prominently in the US political debate on the climate protection norm over several decades, with Beijing strengthening US doubts about the climate change negotiations in ways that relate directly to the distributional bargain reached at Kyoto as well as the respective strategic costs.[88] First, there is the matter of effectiveness: many in the United States have argued that without Chinese agreement to reduce its own absolute level of emissions any efforts that the United States makes will be rendered meaningless.[89] Second, many claim that any such agreement would shift trade, investment, and jobs to developing country economies such as China, with a negative impact on US growth and employment.[90] Third, some claim that unilateral efforts on America's part will reduce its negotiating leverage with China.

In particular, both the United States and China have been reluctant to agree to climate mitigation policies that threaten to reduce economic growth. For both sides, this risk is increasingly seen as inseparable from the actions of the other. China's willingness to agree to an explicit, binding constraint on the growth of its emissions has therefore become a key prerequisite for US agreement to binding constraints – and vice versa.

---

[88] This and the next paragraph rely substantially on Vandenbergh (2007/08), Zhang (2007), and Lieberthal and Sandalow (2009).

[89] Todd Stern put it thus on 3 June 2009: "even if every other country in the world besides China reduced its emissions by 80% between now and 2050...China's emissions under business-as-usual assumptions would alone be so large as to put us on a track to global concentrations of 540 ppm of CO_2, and a 2.7 degree centigrade temperature increase – far above what scientists consider safe." "Remarks as Prepared," Center for American Progress.

[90] Many proposals have been made, including in the major draft climate bills in Congress and by Steven Chu, the Obama administration's energy secretary, for carbon tariffs on goods entering the US market from countries that do not apply carbon taxes of some form (Houser 2009). Most would conflict with the global norm on open trade (Hufbauer et al. 2009).

Thus, the Obama administration, while accepting the principle of differential treatment, has continued to insist that China must make explicit and quantifiable commitments to reduce emissions of the kind found in the Montreal Protocol.[91] The topic of climate change figured prominently in President Obama's summit in Beijing in November 2009, the US-China Joint statement promising that "consistent with their national circumstances," they were resolved to "take significant mitigation actions and recognize the important role the two countries play in promoting a sustainable outcome."[92] Those discussions in Beijing may well have prompted, shortly afterwards, the announcement of the abatement and mitigation targets referred to earlier, but their inability to agree upon specific mandatory targets reflecting the critical "common but differentiated" element of the norm remains obvious.

For China, its reluctance to offer more in climate change negotiations has in part been built on a strong suspicion that the United States has worked to undermine the input and output legitimacy of the climate change deal reached in 1997. These suspicions have only been increased by the reluctance or inability of successive US administrations to ratify Kyoto and by the ease with which many US politicians justify this stance by reference to China's unwillingness to accept similar obligations (Lieberthal and Sandalow 2009: 38). Competitiveness concerns, as with those of strategic balance, are essentially zero-sum: China's are mirror-image of those that are prominent in the United States and are also framed in terms of fairness. The Chinese are understandably sensitive to the fact that the United States, along with other developed countries, has already been through its emissions-intensive phase of urban and industrial development. Moreover, some argue that the rapid growth in China-based manufacturing has been driven in part by the combination of Western firms' production strategies and Western consumers' over-consumption. Officials claim that up to a third of Chinese emissions result from goods produced in China that are exported to and consumed elsewhere, especially to the US market (Jakobson 2009: 6–7).

In addition, Chinese often voice suspicions based on strategic calculations: that the US government's real aims in calling for its participation in Kyoto targets have been to increase its economic costs and thus to block China's rise. Beijing has also expressed the fear that US attempts to deal

---

[91] Todd Stern, "Remarks as Prepared," Center for American Progress, 3 June 2009.
[92] "US-China Joint Statement," Beijing, China, 17 November 2009, The White House, Office of the Press Secretary.

on a bilateral basis with China on climate change issues is part of an attempt to break down the solidarity among the G77, which China has used to deflect attention from itself and to maintain collective pressure on the United States. However, Beijing was unable to prevent the direct negotiations between the BASIC group and the United States that led to the final accord at Copenhagen in December 2009, an outcome later interpreted in China as part of a US and developed world "conspiracy" to divide the developing world.[93]

This mutually destructive dance has been, then, a difficult one to break apart once the normative framework moved beyond the establishment of generalized principles and into the realm of setting targets and timing. The incentive structures embedded in the bilateral relationship have reinforced for both countries the arguments behind non-participation in a scheme that requires mandatory targets. It may even have led to forms of collusion between the two governments, such as when both appeared to work together at negotiations in 2005 (and possibly with India too) to weaken attempts to work out post-Kyoto arrangements (Kent 2007: 196). US and Chinese opponents of Kyoto-like targets have pointed to each other as a reason not to adopt mandatory targets, while concurrently failing to push in the direction of the adoption of such mandatory measures – hence the joint support for the Asia-Pacific Partnership and its voluntary requirements.

These impulses may also explain why Sino-American cooperation and collaboration on scientific and other projects on climate change have tended to be "miscellaneous and episodic rather than sustained," negatively affected by either "insufficient funding, shifting policy priorities, and failure to significantly 'scale-up' promising projects" (Pew Center/ Asia Society 2009: 27).[94]

Yet it would be wrong to ignore the positive potential of Beijing's and Washington's central role in the global climate negotiations. According to

[93] Geoff Dyer, "China Treasures Deal Despite Being Cast as Villain of Piece," *Financial Times*, 22 December 2009. As a spokesperson for China's foreign ministry put it: suggestions that China had ignored the rest of the G77 in reaching this December accord "were untrue and irresponsible comments made out of ulterior motives" (ibid.). See also "Climate Change after Copenhagen: China's Thing about Numbers," *The Economist*, 2 January 2010 and Watts et al., "China's Fears of Rich Nation 'Climate Conspiracy'," http://www.guardian.co.uk/environment/2010/feb/11, accessed 22 February 2010.

[94] This 2009 report provides a long list of such agreements. Chandler, writing in 2008, noted that "budget pressures recently led to the cancellation of U.S. government support for PowerGen," source of a significant project in China to demonstrate carbon capture and sequestration techniques (2008: 4).

Todd Stern, "we [the Obama administration] are focusing on key bilateral relationships, and none is more important than China. China may not be the alpha and omega of the international [climate] negotiations, but it is close."[95] In her first visit to China as Secretary of State in February 2009, Hillary Clinton brought Todd Stern and highlighted the importance of climate change in the bilateral relationship, to the general approval of Chinese commentators at that time who praised the decision not to focus on human rights issues (Glaser 2009: 3). The administration also proposed joint research on a range of clean technologies, and a number of specific agreements in this area were reached during President Obama's visit to Beijing in November 2009.[96]

On balance, however, the prospects for cooperation are not good. The shift in administration attitudes under Obama, combined with continuing Congressional scepticism, has placed more pressure on China to make positive contributions both in the bilateral relationship with the United States and in determining the post-Kyoto arrangements. But it has also increased the pressure on the Obama administration itself, both in terms of domestic politics and global expectations. The continuing lack of domestic support in America for the kind of climate deal that would be acceptable to Beijing (and to other developing country capitals) has serious consequences for broader US-China ties. The Obama administration has signalled that China faces the threat of more protectionist measures from Congress if it does not contribute constructively to a climate change deal.[97] Nor is it likely that large US financial and technology transfers to China will be acceptable in Congress given China's rapid growth, recent increases in military spending, large bilateral trade surpluses, unprecedented foreign exchange holdings, and refusal to adopt large and binding emissions-reduction commitments. In the absence of Congressional agreement to US administration positions, Beijing will continue to argue that America is primarily responsible for holding up progress on a global climate change deal.

5 Conclusion

We have reached an important new stage in international negotiations intended to add a new post-Kyoto layer to the climate change framework.

[95] Todd Stern, "Remarks as Prepared," Center for American Progress, 3 June 2009.
[96] "China, US Must Lead on Clean Energy," *Agence France Presse*, 30 September 2009; "US, China Seek to Join Forces on Electric Cars, Sandalow Says," *Bloomberg*, 30 September 2009; US-China Joint Statement, 17 November 2009; US Asia-Pacific Council (2010).
[97] "China and India Warned Over Emissions," *FT.com*, 15 September 2009.

With an American administration keen to participate in building arrangements for the period after 2012 but unable to generate a domestic consensus behind such policies, and with China's emergence as the leading carbon emitter, both governments are in great contention with the climate protection norm. However, the factors constraining significant shifts in policy remain powerful in both societies, which suggests, at best, more incrementalism rather than a breakthrough in policy positions.

Levels of behavioural consistency with the normative framework have depended fundamentally on the degree of tension between domestic values and the global norm. In the case of China, we have pointed to long-standing conflict between the domestic value accorded to social stability and economic development and limiting GHGs emissions. Levels of contestation have only diminished somewhat from the early 2000s when there was a degree of "grafting" of the global norm onto the local norm (Acharya 2009: 61), and it became more widely accepted in China that the country's growth objectives could more readily be sustained through attention to improvements in energy efficiency. In this coming together of the local and global, we saw how the influence of other domestic level forces could be strengthened. If this resonance between domestic and global continues, Chinese creation of domestic institutions, expertise, and legal frameworks pertinent to the climate protection norm suggest the potential for higher levels of contribution to advancement of the global norm over time. Tempering this optimism is the Chinese government's continuing commitment to high levels of growth and the rapid urbanization of Chinese society with all of its attendant energy demands.

In the case of the United States, there has been a similar concern with protecting the conditions for economic growth and competitiveness, a domestic value bolstered significantly by a political institutional structure that has made Congressional representatives highly sensitive to the concerns of voters and local industries, particularly energy-intensive ones. The desire of successive administrations to protect the position of the United States as the world's sole superpower may sometimes have compounded this growth concern, but the main origins of its climate protection policies lie in domestic politics and society rather than in the global power structure. Although America's greater global power has certainly shaped its response and its ability to resist foreign exhortations for greater behavioural consistency, the main sources of the softening of the US stance on climate policy in the second George W. Bush administration were increasing pressure for change from domestic opponents, sub-federal political actors, and parts of the US business community. The Obama administration raised hopes even more that a breakthrough on a global deal was within reach, yet it has been thwarted by the strength of the underlying values, interests, and institutions that have shaped American climate change policy over the past few decades. These had changed much less than optimists believed and have been bolstered by the global financial crisis of 2008–09, which further strengthened concerns about the negative consequences of climate protection for economic growth.

The core values of both states do not provide much opportunity for the global norm to diffuse within their respective societies. In the US case, that hostility has been exacerbated by the asymmetric features of the norm, including the sense that America's economic competitiveness and perhaps ultimately its strategic position will be challenged by those emerging powers, like China, not subject to the same constraints. For China, the lack of justice in an argument that would require it – a late developer – to make large sacrifices alongside advanced countries like America is difficult to accept. At times, this fundamental disagreement over what would constitute a fair bargain on climate mitigation has threatened to produce a downward spiral that would undermine the global norm and any prospects for a global deal.

Yet, despite the power of these domestic level forces, the global norm of climate protection has placed some constraints on these two countries. The power of the global norm is shown in the US failure to reject the climate protection norm, even while it rejected the Kyoto treaty. This limit to US power may apply generally when global norms have gained some degree of legitimacy via scientific consensus, treaty development and the momentum associated with negotiating timetables. The vocal US rejection of Kyoto even had the unintended consequence of increasing the norm's importance as a focal point for international and domestic debate and pushed Washington into a less hostile position towards the UN process in the final two years of the Bush presidency.

In Beijing's case, the global norm has also played a role in promoting China's more flexible position in the last few years. It has a better understanding of climate science and has recognized the ways in which its domestic and international goals could more readily be linked. It has also recognized the international image costs that can arise from a failure to soften its positions or show sympathy for those developing countries least able to cope with the effects of global warming. China does not want to be perceived as the state that has undermined the UN process that it has long regarded as the legitimate venue for these negotiations – even more so at a time when it has become the leading CO_2 emitter.

Undoubtedly, however, the course of this global norm and its movement from creation to elaboration has been fraught with difficulty. While it is the case that we have a global norm on climate protection, it is far too optimistic to claim that it has been consolidated or has enough stability and legitimacy to ensure eventual success. A bilateral deal on emissions constraints between the United States and China could go a considerable way to unblocking the prospects for a legally binding treaty at the global level; however, that bilateral agreement remains far from certain given the challenge this norm poses in terms of domestic significance, relative strategic cost, and perceived distributional fairness.

6

Financial Regulation

The dilemmas posed by the emergence of cross-border capital flows and global financial firms since the 1960s are emblematic of the difficulties posed in a hybrid global order that had been predicated on national financial regulation and supervision.[1] Financial globalization has been associated with periodic crises of growing frequency and with important cross-border dimensions, prompting efforts to coordinate regulatory approaches. The major developed countries dominated these efforts. They possessed the largest and deepest financial systems and were also the primary beneficiaries of financial integration. The G7 countries were the most important participants, though the slightly larger G10 grouping that established the Basel Committee on Banking Supervision (BCBS) in 1974 was the primary forum for coordination efforts.[2] Along with many other public and private international bodies, the BCBS elaborated a growing body of voluntary international standards concerning supposed best practice principles for financial regulation and supervision. Although this international standard-setting process has for some time been fairly technocratic and hidden from public view, it has become increasingly central to global economic governance. After the global financial crisis of 2008, it rose to the very top of the global economic governance reform agenda.

---

[1] Regulation is the process of rule setting, whereas supervision refers to the process whereby agencies monitor actor compliance with behavioural rules and norms. Throughout, we often use regulation as shorthand for both.

[2] The G10 countries were in fact eleven: Belgium, Canada, France, Germany, Italy, Japan, the Netherlands, Sweden, Switzerland, the United Kingdom, and the United States.

In this chapter, we focus on banking regulation as an area of signal importance in global financial regulatory cooperation both before and after the 2008 financial crisis. The United States, by some distance the most important country that participated in these international coordination efforts, has been especially influential over the shaping of the normative framework and the principles and standards associated with it. China, by contrast, was excluded until very recently from the BCBS and most other international standard-setting bodies in financial regulation. Thus, its historic position has been that of a rule taker, in sharp contrast to that of the United States.

This large asymmetry in the relationship of both countries to the global normative framework makes this area of policy coordination especially interesting for this study. Another reason why this case is important for our study is that, as we elaborate later and in contrast to other cases, the US-China bilateral relationship plays only a small part in how both countries relate to the global normative framework. This is mainly because China's level of financial development – although relatively high compared to many countries at similar levels of economic development – remains much lower than that of the United States. Its financial system is also relatively bank dominated and substantially less open than many other major developing countries, with the large state-owned banks playing a central role (McKinsey Global Institute 2009: 27–9; Barth et al. 2007). These banks are also primarily domestically oriented, in sharp contrast to the more sophisticated and increasingly internationalized G10 banks on which the Basel framework has been heavily focused.

The relative unimportance of the bilateral relationship helps us to isolate the other factors that explain the relationship of the United States and China to the evolving global normative framework of financial regulation. The very different relationship of the two countries to the regime (norm maker vs. norm taker) also permits us to explore what effects this kind of asymmetry has on levels of behavioural conformity with the norms themselves. A priori, one might expect norm makers in a particular policy area to exhibit much higher levels of behavioural conformity with the normative framework than norm takers. In this area, however, we find this expectation does not turn out to be straightforwardly true. By some measures, China's attitudes towards the core norms and associated rules and principles of the Basel framework have been remarkably convergent, whereas the United States has sometimes found it difficult to achieve full behavioural consistency even in areas where its influence on the global framework has been close to decisive.

This finding constitutes the central puzzle around which this chapter is organized. The first section outlines the evolution of the normative framework, focusing mainly on the Basel framework for banking regulation. Although the current scope of global financial regulatory cooperation goes well beyond bank regulation (Davies and Green 2008), this narrowing of scope permits greater analytical depth, greater comparability across time (since banking regulation was the main focus of early cooperation and has remained its centrepiece) and a more meaningful comparison between these two countries (since Basel standards are most relevant to China's bank-dominated financial system). The second and third sections, respectively, consider how the United States and China relate to the normative framework for global bank regulation, before assessing how their levels of behavioural conformity with it can be explained. Section 4 briefly addresses why their bilateral relationship has little impact on their behaviour in this policy area. Section 5 concludes with a comparison of the two countries' evolving relationship with the global banking regulatory framework.

1 The Global Banking Regulatory Framework

The BCBS has been for more than three decades the primary forum in which regulators from the developed countries have met to agree principles and standards for banking regulation and supervision. The BCBS initially consisted of representatives of the central banks of the G10 countries, most of whom also had regulatory and supervisory responsibilities for banks, but it soon expanded to include other relevant national agencies when these differed from the central bank. Its country composition reflected the heavy European bias of the G10, a bias that was later reinforced when Luxembourg and Spain were added to the group.

The activities of the BCBS can be seen as being motivated by an attempt by national authorities in the most financially developed countries to deal with the regulatory and supervisory consequences of the globalization of the banking sector. The main practical expression of this phenomenon in the 1970s was the "Euromarkets," a wholesale interbank market in which US-based banks played a prominent role. The Basel Committee's main initial concern, driven by the failure of an internationally active German bank in 1974, was to ensure that offshore branches of member country banks operating in the Euromarkets did not escape adequate supervision (Davies and Green 2008: 35). The Basel "Concordat" of 1975 assigned primary supervisory responsibility to home country authorities (that in which the parent bank was located).

The main work of the BCBS, however, has been negotiating and agreeing upon voluntary standards on minimum bank capital rules.[3] Over time, the increase in global banking activity raised concerns that large national variations in bank capital requirements were producing two significant problems: competitive inequalities in global capital markets and the potential for a regulatory "race to the bottom" in which financial business gravitated towards the least stringently regulated jurisdiction. The particular problem for US and some European banks and regulators in the 1980s was Japan's relatively lowly capitalized banks, which were less affected by the Latin American debt crisis in the 1980s than their Western counterparts. The US Congress was concerned to increase the capital of money centre banks that were highly exposed to Latin American governments, not least to demonstrate that large IMF loans to these governments did not amount to an indirect bailout of Wall Street by American taxpayers (Singer 2007: chapter 4). US regulators and banks were reluctant to accept significantly higher minimum capital requirements unless similar requirements were also adopted by regulators in competitor jurisdictions, including Japan (Kapstein 1994; Reinicke 1995; Oatley and Nabors 1998; Tarullo 2008: chapter 3). To resolve this political dilemma, the senior US money centre bank regulator, the Federal Reserve (Fed), first negotiated a new bilateral capital standard with the Bank of England. These two authorities then effectively threatened to deny non-compliant banks from other jurisdictions access to the key financial centres of New York and London, encouraging their Japanese and other BCBS counterparts to agree a modified version of the US–UK deal. This became known as the Basel Capital Adequacy Accord, or "Basel I."

The central component of this accord was that all internationally active banks headquartered in Basel Committee countries should hold capital to the value of at least 8 percent of their "risk-weighted" assets by the end of 1992.[4] There were two basic objectives: "to strengthen the soundness and

---

[3] In general terms, regulatory "capital" is the minimum amount of "risk capital" that banks must hold to conduct business – often, as we shall see, this is defined as shareholders' equity plus other forms of "quasi-equity" capital.

[4] Defining capital was highly contentious but eventually achieved by a political compromise between those who preferred a narrow equity-based definition (e.g., Germany) and those who wished to include other non-equity instruments (e.g., Japan). To satisfy the former, it was agreed that "Tier 1" (mostly equity) capital had to be at least 4% of total risk-weighted assets, with "Tier 2" capital (comprising other capital instruments) making up the rest. Basel I also used a very blunt approach to risk determination by assigning risk weights ranging from 0% to 100% to broad categories of assets (e.g., the debt of OECD governments attracted a 0% risk weighting, credit lines with a maturity of more than one

stability of the international banking system" and "to have a high degree of consistency in its application to banks in different countries with a view to diminishing an existing source of competitive inequality among international banks" (BCBS 1988: 1). Regulators were unable to offer a clear rationale for an 8 percent minimum capital adequacy ratio (CAR), but according to some experienced practitioners it "was judged to be the kind of level that would allow well-run banks to stay out of trouble most of the time" (Davies and Green 2008: 38). Regulators in the major financial centres usually encouraged banks to hold capital somewhat above the Basel minima as a kind of safety buffer (McDonough 1998a).

The two main norms of the Basel framework were thus: first, minimum capital requirements for internationally active banks to ensure reasonable system stability and, second, common implementation of these minima across the major economies to ensure approximate competitive equality. These norms were agreed explicitly only by BCBS regulatory representatives and the associated capital standards were intended to apply mainly to their own internationally active banks. But as the G10 countries represented a very large proportion of all international financial activity and then comprised the world's three major international financial centres (New York, London, and Tokyo), Basel standards became, by default, global standards and spread rapidly in the 1990s. Banks wishing to establish branches in the major global financial centres were effectively barred from doing so if their home countries were not reasonably Basel-compliant; the more costly alternative for banks from non-compliant countries was to establish separately capitalized local subsidiaries. Network effects increased the incentives of both governments and domestic banks to adopt Basel standards: that is, the more jurisdictions that adopted them, the greater the reputational costs for non-convergent actors.[5] Many countries, notably in the European Union, also applied the capital rules to all their banks, not just internationally active ones. Inevitably, given the increasingly global reach of Basel standards, some non-member countries felt that the Committee's narrow membership raised concerns about its representativeness and legitimacy. The BCBS deflected such arguments by pointing out that its membership encompassed the bulk of global financial activity and that

year 50%, and all corporate loans 100% irrespective of the condition of the borrower). Off-balance sheet commitments were also included.
[5] Substantive behavioural convergence was another matter, however (Walter 2006b, 2008).

Basel standards were voluntary; implementation even for Committee members was on a "best efforts" basis.

Paradoxically, as Basel I spread globally, support for it among banks and regulators in the most advanced financial centres waned considerably. The Basel Committee had always intended that the accord would be periodically updated to reflect changes underway in the banking system (McDonough 1998a), but it underestimated the practical difficulties of achieving this. The major global banks felt that Basel I was increasingly inappropriate and constraining given the rapid expansion of trading in financial assets, of securitization,[6] and the development of new sophisticated internal risk management models. Basel risk weights were very crude and produced regulatory capital requirements that diverged substantially from these banks' own judgements about the desirable level of "economic capital," or the amount of capital they would prefer to set aside for each asset depending on their estimates of its riskiness. Regulators in the major international financial centres, particularly in New York and London, largely accepted this critique and argued that sophisticated banks should be permitted greater scope to manage their own risks. Officials at the US Federal Reserve in particular openly argued that financial innovation had made Basel CARs increasingly less meaningful (Tarullo 2008: 88). The crude risk-weighting scheme of Basel I, by opening up a large gap between regulatory and economic capital, also encouraged banks to engage in regulatory arbitrage by issuing new financial products aimed at minimizing required capital.[7] Alan Greenspan, US Fed Chairman since 1987, argued as early as 1994 that the old approach to financial regulation, exemplified in Basel I, needed to give way to a new approach in which financial institutions would be largely "self-regulated," a view he claims most Fed officials shared.[8] By self-regulation, Greenspan meant greater reliance on both internal bank controls and external monitoring by third-party creditors facilitated by greater transparency about internal risk management processes (Greenspan 2007: 489–92).

---

[6] Securitization refers to the process of pooling assets (such as mortgages or corporate loans) and issuing new securities – which can be sold and traded – backed by the cash flows that accrue to the pool.

[7] The best examples were the rapid development of the collateralized debt obligation (CDO) and credit default swap (CDS) markets from the late 1990s. These allowed banks to remove capital-costly loans from their balance sheets and to insure those that remained on-balance sheet (with the agreement of regulators in advanced countries, such insurance also reduced capital requirements). See McDonough (1998a, 1998b) and Tett (2009).

[8] "Fed Chief Sees Need for Self-Regulation," *Financial Times*, 9 June 1994, and Greenspan (2007: 373–6).

The first victory of this major bank and regulator coalition was the Market Risk Amendment (MRA) to Basel I in 1996. Trade organizations such as the American Bankers Association (ABA) and the Institute of International Finance (IIF) lobbied strongly in the mid-1990s for regulators to permit the use of quantitative "value-at-risk" (VaR) models to calculate "market risks" and hence capital requirements on their trading books (where banks held assets for short to medium term trading purposes rather than holding the assets to maturity).[9] The Fed, led by Greenspan and other senior officials, promoted the argument for VaR within the BCBS despite the initial scepticism of other BCBS members (Tarullo 2008: 63ff). Residual scepticism was, however, sufficiently strong for the BCBS to apply a "multiplication factor" of three times the bank's estimated VaR for purposes of capital calculation.

For the major banks and regulators, the MRA was insufficient to rectify the fundamental shortcomings of Basel I because it left the system of capital calculation for *credit* (i.e., default) risks untouched. Major banks and regulators who favoured a move towards market-based regulation thought that the principle behind the MRA should be extended to credit risks as well. In June 1998, Federal Reserve Bank of New York (FRBNY) President William McDonough took over as chair of the BCBS, so the Fed was in a stronger position to get its way.[10] The following month the BCBS agreed to launch a major review of the Basel capital accord. McDonough's view was that "the development of credit risk modeling [ought] to be the catalyst for a complete rethinking of the theory and practice of credit risk management" (McDonough 1998a). A revised Basel framework specifically should

include an approach to quantitative capital requirements that offers the possibility of translating our expectations for all types of financial institutions across countries; integrating the quantitative capital requirements with a set of qualitative expectations for banks in managing their risk and evaluating their capital needs; and relying as much as possible on market discipline, with emphasis on transparency and disclosure. (McDonough 1998b)

The Basel Committee recognized that heavy reliance on internal risk management models was only appropriate for the most sophisticated

---

[9] VaR models calculate the probabilistic risk of loss on a given portfolio of assets in a particular trading period. "Market" risk on trading portfolios stemmed from movements in the prices of these assets.

[10] The FRBNY is the primary regulator of the main US money centre banks based in New York.

banks. For the less sophisticated, the Committee proposed a revised "standardized approach" to capital calculation that would use the third-party credit ratings for borrowers provided by credit ratings agencies to determine appropriate credit risk weightings for most assets. It also proposed a new capital charge for "operational" risk (the risk of loss from failures in processes, people, or systems) to apply to all banks, as well as enhanced market discipline via greater bank transparency (BCBS 1999). In addition, it suggested tentatively that "for some sophisticated banks ... an internal ratings-based [IRB] approach could form the basis for setting capital charges" (BCBS 1999: 5). Some international banks and the IIF criticized this initial proposal as insufficiently radical, but Greenspan and McDonough emphasized that they needed to work with the BCBS to develop these proposals further. By mid-2000, advocates of a generalized move to an IRB approach seemed to have gained the upper hand in the Committee (Tarullo 2008: 99, 103–4). However, a second consultative proposal of January 2001 satisfied few constituencies in the private or the public sector, propelling the Committee into a complicated, iterative process of gathering public comments, conducting impact assessment exercises, discussions with banks, and internal renegotiations and calibrations.

Six years after the process of revision was launched, the BCBS announced agreement on a revised capital framework, commonly called Basel II. It provided a menu of three different approaches to capital calculation in "Pillar 1" of the agreement (BCBS 2004: Part 2). The first option in Pillar 1 was the advanced IRB (A-IRB) approach, in which banks would adopt a model-based approach to the calculation of credit and operational risks. The second option was a simpler "foundational" (F-IRB) approach, which envisaged greater input from supervisors on credit loss exposures. The third, most basic option was a "standardized" approach closer to Basel I but which encouraged the use of external credit risk ratings to assign risk weights for credits to governments, firms and other banks. Pillar 2 of the new accord provided supervisors with the tools and responsibility to review banks' overall risk management processes and strategy and to levy additional discretionary capital charges on banks deemed to have sub-optimal internal risk management frameworks. Pillar 3 aimed to promote market discipline as a complement to internal risk management and supervisory review via a set of disclosure requirements intended to allow market participants better to assess a bank's risk profile against its capital.

The shift from Basel I to Basel II thus reflected, albeit imperfectly, an emergent third norm of greater reliance on market self-regulation that had begun to take hold in the early 1990s. This third norm was promoted vigorously by key actors in the US Fed, with support from regulators in the United Kingdom and much encouragement from large complex financial institutions themselves. It was strongly associated with the growing faith in the self-stabilizing nature of deregulated financial markets, something that Greenspan, during this period the world's most influential central banker and bank supervisor, had long accepted. It also reflected the view that a greater reliance on market mechanisms could promote efficiency and stability simultaneously. It should be noted that the primary emphasis of Basel II was to encourage more sophistication in risk assessment and management; the definition and level of required capital in Basel I was retained, demonstrating considerable inertia in this key component of the framework.

The growing strength of this new norm was reflected in the Basel Committee's preference for the A-IRB approach to capital calculation. The two other options were intended to apply to less sophisticated banks and, by implication, to most developing countries. Those regulators favouring greater reliance on market-based regulation had argued that Basel II should provide incentives for banks and regulators to move towards the IRB approach over time. This accorded with the demand by some major banks that they should be permitted to hold *less* capital if their internal models demonstrated that this was both efficient and safe. More cautious regulators felt that overreliance on banks' internal models might be dangerous. A built-in incentive for banks and regulators to migrate towards an IRB approach was also inconsistent with the norm of establishing a level competitive playing field. In developed countries, including notably in the United States and Germany, smaller banks argued that this would give an unfair advantage to larger competitors.

For developing countries generally, there was a concern that if Basel II favoured advanced country banks it would inhibit their overall financial and economic development (Powell 2004). Even the "basic" standardized approach was evidently developed for G10, not developing country banks, and would involve major implementation costs and the additional capital charge for operating risk at a time when many developing countries were still in the process of adopting Basel I. Its emphasis on the use of external ratings also seemed to ignore the widespread criticisms of the performance of ratings agencies in recent emerging market crises, as well as the small number of developing country banks and firms with credit ratings. Finally, many countries feared that Basel II would raise the capital cost of international bank lending to emerging markets.

The final outcome reflected a balance between these competing arguments, though Basel II reflected the growing importance of the third norm of market self-regulation.[11] Pillar 1 retained the minimum 8 percent CAR of Basel I and the basic definition of eligible capital, implying a floor to capital relief for sophisticated banks (BCBS 2006: 12). Even the A-IRB approach compromised on a pure IRB model by requiring banks to use their internal models to calculate inputs to the Basel Committee's own regulatory model (Herring 2007: 415–16). However, Pillar 2 permitted supervisors on a discretionary basis to provide some capital relief to the most sophisticated banks. It explicitly aimed "to encourage banks to develop and use better risk management techniques in monitoring and managing their risks" (BCBS 2004: 158). Pillar 3's promotion of market discipline was intended to incentivize banks to improve internal risk management processes and to migrate towards the IRB approach over time. The potential that Basel II would favour more sophisticated banks therefore remained. As we will see, this substantially politicized both the negotiation and the implementation process in the United States, but much less so in China.

It was also unclear whether Basel II could achieve similar levels of global adoption to Basel I. The new agreement was greeted without enthusiasm in much of the developing world; many developing countries were still in the process of implementing Basel I and saw the new approach as inappropriate to their circumstances. The BCBS had made some efforts to increase the perceived input legitimacy of the revised agreement by publishing its initial proposals and asking for comments from interested parties from all countries. The Core Principles Liaison Group (now the International Liaison Group or ILG) was also established to improve consultation with non-members, though it included only a few emerging market countries. Even within this group, the extent of real consultation was narrow and focused heavily upon implementation issues.[12]

---

[11] Basel II also turned out to be a great deal more complex and prescriptive than its main proponents had initially hoped. One indication of this is that while Basel I (as updated through 1998) was only 25 pages long, Basel II reached 239 pages by June 2004 and 333 pages in its more comprehensive version of June 2006; it continues to grow.

[12] These countries consisted of Argentina, Brazil, Hungary, India, Indonesia, Korea, Malaysia, Poland, and Singapore. The expanded ILG consisted of representatives from France, Germany, Italy, Japan, the Netherlands, Spain, the United Kingdom, and the United States, sixteen non-Basel Committee members (Argentina, Australia, Brazil, Chile,

On the eve of the 2008 global financial crisis, the core norms of the Basel framework were thus threefold. The first norm was that financial stability should be promoted in an increasingly integrated world economy through international agreement on supervisory responsibility and core prudential standards. The second norm was that prudential standards should be harmonized where possible to ensure that regulation was not a major source of competitive inequality. The third norm was that financial stability could be best promoted by increased reliance on market-based regulation and discipline, both within firms and in the financial marketplace more generally.

There have always been tensions and tradeoffs between these norms. Basel I in reality paid more attention to achieving rough competitive equality than to promoting financial stability (FSA 2009: 55). Basel II reflected a desire to tilt the regulatory framework in favour of relatively sophisticated international banks without significantly changing the total amount of required capital in the banking system. The third norm was the last to emerge, achieving growing prominence in the Basel framework from the mid-1990s, though it was always more contested than the first two norms. After the global financial crisis of 2008, which revealed serious failures of risk management in some of the world's most sophisticated banks, it became widely seen as incompatible with the stability norm. The most famous expression of these new doubts was provided by Alan Greenspan in his testimony to Congress in October 2008, when he said that recent events had revealed "a flaw" in his philosophy: "Those of us who have looked to the self-interest of lending institutions to protect shareholders' equity, myself included, are in a state of shocked disbelief."[13] Adair Turner, Chairman of the UK's Financial Services Authority (FSA), also testified in early 2009 to a Parliamentary committee that "before the current crisis prompted a deep rethink of regulation, FSA staff had not considered whether banks' business models were sufficiently robust because the watchdog had left that to industry and did not consider that its job."[14]

China, the Czech Republic, Hong Kong, India, Korea, Mexico, Poland, Russia, Saudi Arabia, Singapore, South Africa, and the West African Monetary Union), the European Commission, the International Monetary Fund, the World Bank, the Financial Stability Institute, the Association of Supervisors of Banks of the Americas, and the Islamic Financial Services Board.

[13] "Greenspan Concedes Error on Regulation," *New York Times*, 23 October 2008, http://www.nytimes.com/2008/10/24/business/economy/24panel.html.

[14] "UK Banks to Face Tougher Rules," *FT.com*, 25 February 2009. For a similar statement by Jean-Claude Trichet, President of the European Central Bank, see his interview with *China Finance*, 16 February 2009, http://www.bis.org/review/r090219a.pdf.

This rethink prompted a reexamination of the Basel framework. There is now a broad consensus that both Basel I and II permitted excessive levels of financial leverage[15] and left banks seriously undercapitalized, unable to withstand the kind of systemic loss of confidence that occurred in late 2008.[16] The retention of the Basel I capital definitions in Basel II reflected considerable complacency amongst regulators and banks as the latter engaged in extensive regulatory arbitrage (sometimes openly abetted by regulators themselves), as leverage in the sector increased, and as the securitization trend accelerated. The risks that became concentrated in banks' trading books were poorly accounted for by VaR models, and capital requirements were especially thin in this area. The framework's focus on capitalization also placed insufficient emphasis on bank liquidity and leverage (FSA 2009). These were indictments of Basel I as much as Basel II; indeed, Basel II was not fully implemented in many countries before the crisis and so cannot easily be blamed for it.[17] But the crisis cast considerable doubt on the basic rationale and approach behind the MRA and Basel II because it revealed that market participants, not just regulators, were unable to determine appropriate levels of capitalization, liquidity, and leverage over the cycle. The framework's growing reliance on market assessments of financial risk even amplified the credit cycle, since market actors demonstrate a systematic tendency to underestimate risk during periods of financial stability (Brunnermeier et al. 2009). This meant that an element of destabilizing "pro-cyclicality" was built into MRA and Basel II-style capital requirements.

Although the crisis therefore placed the third norm of market self-regulation in considerable doubt, it reinforced the priority of the first norm that financial stability should be pursued through international regulatory harmonization. In London in April 2009, G20 leaders agreed

to establish the much greater consistency and systematic cooperation between countries, and the framework of internationally agreed high standards, that a global financial system requires. Strengthened regulation and supervision must promote propriety, integrity and transparency; guard against risk across the

[15] Financial leverage is generally defined as the extent to which an entity borrows to purchase assets, though in the financial sector it is often defined as an entity's total liabilities (or total assets) as a proportion of shareholders' equity or of Tier I capital.

[16] See G20 Leaders Statement, paragraph 13, Pittsburgh Summit, 24–25 September 2009, http://www.pittsburghsummit.gov/mediacenter/129639.htm, accessed 5 November 2009.

[17] As discussed later, Basel II had not been implemented in the United States and China; in the European Union, it was implemented for most banks from the beginning of 2008.

financial system; dampen rather than amplify the financial and economic cycle; reduce reliance on inappropriately risky sources of financing; and discourage excessive risk-taking.[18]

In this new climate, lingering support for the view that the Basel framework should provide capital relief to the most sophisticated banks (which are often also the largest and most global) had evaporated – on the contrary, many proposals would require the largest and most complex banks to hold more capital than average so as to reduce the risk to taxpayers. As the balance shifted back to the first norm, however, concerns in the banking sector and among governments about the need for approximate competitive equality reemerged.

Both of these developments ensured that although the legitimacy of the Basel framework was in some doubt by late 2008, the BCBS itself remained indispensable. Under pressure from G20 leaders, the Basel Committee initiated a "comprehensive strategy" aiming to rectify the serious weaknesses in the Basel framework. This included considerably higher capital requirements for credit and market risks,[19] a reversal of the pro-cyclical bias of the framework, higher quality capital (meaning more common shareholders' equity rather than "hybrid" capital), and the generalized introduction of simple prudential leverage and liquidity ratios as backstops to a complex risk-weighted capital framework.[20] The BCBS envisaged that these more stringent requirements would be agreed by the end of 2010 and phased in gradually so as not to hamper economic recovery. General implementation was initially scheduled for the end of 2012, but this was subsequently pushed back to 2019. In London in April 2009, the G20 also placed the Financial Stability Board (FSB)[21] in a more prominent position of coordinating and monitoring progress in regulatory standard setting.

---

[18] G20 Leaders' Statement, "Global Plan for Recovery and Reform," London, 2 April 2009.

[19] How much higher remained a matter of debate as of mid-2010, but the BCBS had already agreed in mid-2009 to impose substantially higher capital requirements on riskier activities such as trading and securitization exposures (BCBS 2009a, 2009b).

[20] BCBS, "Comprehensive Strategy to Address the Lessons of the Banking Crisis Announced by the Basel Committee," 20 November 2008, http://www.bis.org/press/p081120.htm, accessed 15 October 2009. This was followed by more detailed proposals in December 2009 (BCBS 2009c) and in July 2010 (BCBS 2010).

[21] The Financial Stability Forum was established by G7 finance ministers and central bank governors in 1999. In April 2009 it was renamed the FSB after an agreement at the G20 London summit.

But in spite of this broad agreement on the necessary direction of reform, many crucial and controversial details remained to be negotiated, amidst indications that aggressive bank lobbying was successfully forcing regulators to retreat on some of their initial proposals.[22] Another consequence of the crisis, the increased economic and political diversity within the BCBS itself, also increased uncertainty. In June 2009, all remaining G20 countries were given full BCBS membership.[23] This meant that for the first time countries with very different levels of financial development and regulatory/supervisory capacity would be negotiating the details of the new proposals. The very different post-crisis economic trajectories of the major developed and developing countries adds to the difficulty of achieving consensus, as concerns about the competitive and macroeconomic impacts of the new proposals are multiple and widespread. Even among the most advanced countries, there were signs of growing unilateralism in financial reform in early 2010, which threatened to undermine the G20 commitment to coordinate new financial regulation: new bonus taxes in the United Kingdom and France; proposals from the US administration for a bank financial levy that would penalize large, risky banks; and new US restrictions on banks engaging in proprietary trading.[24] In short, even though the two core norms of the Basel framework remain intact, the details of global banking regulatory standards are likely to remain in flux for some time to come.

2 The United States and the Basel Framework

This section begins by investigating the evolving relationship of the United States to the Basel capital framework and to the three main norms identified earlier. It focuses on the level of behavioural consistency with these norms and the principles and standards associated with them. We show that despite the leading position of the United States in the Basel process, it has exhibited a decreasing degree of consistency with the

---

[22] "Basel-Dazzle," *FT.com*, 27 July 2010.

[23] The BCBS initially agreed in March 2009 to expand its membership to a handful of mainly large emerging market countries (Australia, Brazil, China, India, Korea, Mexico, and Russia). This limited expansion soon proved politically unsustainable and only three months later it announced that it would open membership to all other countries in the G20 (this added Argentina, Indonesia, Saudi Arabia, South Africa, and Turkey. See BCBS, "Basel Committee Broadens Its Membership," 10 June 2009, http://www.bis.org/press/p090610.htm, accessed 15 October 2009).

[24] "Big Banks in Call for Greater Coordination," *FT.com*, 26 January 2010.

framework because of domestic contestation over the relative priority of regulatory norms and the growing politicization of implementation. As already noted, American regulatory officials, especially from the Fed, played a crucial role in initiating and negotiating both Basel I and II – as they had in the Basel Concordat on supervisory responsibilities in the mid-1970s. This, as well as the leading global position of US financial markets and large American banks, especially those based in New York, ensured that the Basel framework would be shaped significantly by US preferences. But the fragmented architecture of US financial regulation meant that the US Treasury's Office of the Comptroller of the Currency (OCC), the Federal Deposit Insurance Corporation (FDIC), and the Office of Thrift Supervision (OTS) were also BCBS members, making the formal US delegation to Basel the largest of any country. Despite rising levels of sectoral concentration in recent years, the US banking sector also remains highly diverse and fragmented, with thousands of small local and regional banks competing alongside about twenty banking giants. As we discuss later, this institutional and industry fragmentation refracted and sometimes amplified domestic contestation over regulatory norms.

As previously noted, in the mid-1980s the major US money centre banks strongly objected to Congressional proposals to increase capital in the US banking sector unless these regulatory requirements were internationally harmonized. Various authors explain US leadership in the negotiation of Basel I as a means of reconciling these divergent political interests by avoiding a unilateral increase in regulatory capital. Singer (2007) argues, for example, that domestic financial regulators pursue international capital regulation when the stability and competitiveness of the financial sector are threatened and when legislatures propose solutions that threaten regulator autonomy. Oatley and Nabors (1998) claim that the effects of this agreement were primarily redistributive, reflecting coercive US hegemonic power (by pushing most of the costs onto relatively lowly capitalized Japanese banks who were threatened with exclusion from New York and London). Although others (e.g., Kapstein 1994) argue that Basel I was a more balanced agreement in which all sides gained something, there is a consensus that US leadership was an essential ingredient and that American banks, legislators, and regulators were beneficiaries of the first capital accord.[25]

---

[25] US bank assets and profitability rose after the accord was agreed, though they fell temporarily during the recession of 1990–92 (US Federal Reserve 1996).

In the case of Basel II, US regulators, particularly the Fed, also took a leading role in initiating the negotiations. However, Singer's and other similar explanations do not apply as easily to this case as to Basel I. There were no serious threats to US bank competitiveness or financial sector stability in the late 1990s. The failure of the Long Term Capital Management (LTCM) hedge fund and various emerging market financial crises pointed to some underlying vulnerabilities, but these did not motivate US initiatives to modify the capital adequacy framework for banks. Basel II was launched and negotiated during a period of continuing high bank profitability and stability and when Greenspan's Fed was riding high.[26] Nor were regulators responding to credible threats to their autonomy from Congress. Rather, US regulators seem to have enjoyed substantial autonomy in launching a revision of the Basel accord. The Fed especially was driven by a growing concern that the existing bank capital framework was ill-suited to the risks entailed by modern banking, and by an ideological presumption that market actors were better positioned than regulators to manage financial risk.

This is not to say that this ideological presumption was fully shared by the Fed's fellow domestic regulators or that the balance between financial stability and competitiveness was unimportant in the Basel II negotiations. Rather, the Federal Reserve appeared to be using the Basel process to achieve a unity of purpose among competing domestic bank regulators who had divergent concerns about the implications of the new proposals for domestic financial stability. The OCC and FDIC had serious reservations about the IRB proposal and, implicitly, about Fed leadership on this issue (Tarullo 2008: 89–91, 119–20). Yet the Fed was first among equals at the BCBS. William McDonough was BCBS Chairman and was strongly supported by Greenspan and Roger Ferguson, Vice Chairman of the Federal Reserve Board and Chairman of the Financial Stability Forum, also based in Basel. Other Federal Reserve officials would also subsequently make important contributions to the technical details of the Basel II framework (Herring 2007: 411–12). Although many compromises in the detail were made along the way, the overall shape of the final agreement closely reflected the kind of agreement that McDonough (1998a, 1998b) had sketched out at the beginning. This reflected the considerable support provided to the Fed's position by the major US and

---

[26] US bank profitability rose rapidly after the economic recovery in 1992–93 and remained at consistently high levels from 1993 to 2004. It was not seriously dented by the 2000–01 downturn (US Federal Reserve 2005).

global banks, who believed that they would benefit substantially from a revised capital accord that permitted them to use their own internal models to manage their risks and to set aside appropriate levels of capital. But, as we argue later, although the Fed largely won its battle to put market-based regulation at the heart of the Basel framework, its opponents were able to fight a rearguard action in the subsequent battle over domestic implementation.

The Basel process itself facilitated the influence of this US regulator and industry coalition. In contrast to many intergovernmental negotiations, it permits regulatory officials a prominent role in the development of global norms and associated standards. The technical complexity of many of the issues also provides them with some insulation from domestic political interference, though this has diminished over time. US regulators could deploy their leadership positions at Basel to further their cause and benefitted from a continuing working alliance with British representatives, who shared the prestige and expertise that accrued from London's and New York's positions as the world's major financial centres. Finally, the views and expertise of the major international banks were explicitly sought by the Committee. It would be too strong to describe this as straightforward regulatory capture by a dominant industry lobby, since the major banks lost some key battles (e.g., over the decision to put a floor on capital relief). But in Basel II, the regulatory framework had moved in a direction that these banks had favoured, and it held out the prospect of additional future modifications.

After the 2008 financial crisis, the rising prominence of the third norm of self-regulation suffered a serious setback in US regulatory and political circles as it did elsewhere. As Ben Bernanke, Greenspan's successor as Fed Chairman since February 2006, is reported to have said to colleagues in the depth of the crisis in September 2008, "there are no atheists in foxholes and no ideologues in financial crises."[27] In a now Democrat-controlled Congress, many politicians turned with a vengeance against the philosophy of market-based regulation that had played an increasingly influential role in the Greenspan years. The large public sector bailouts of leading Wall Street banks and the political furore over financial sector compensation practices also undermined the legitimacy of the Fed–money centre bank coalition that was now widely seen as having dominated regulatory outcomes over the previous decade.

---

[27] "A Professor and a Banker Bury Old Dogma on Markets," *New York Times*, 21 September 2008.

In this new climate, the regulatory initiative shifted back to the Presidency and Congress. The Treasury's proposals of June 2009 stressed the need for a significant strengthening of prudential rules, especially substantial increases in bank capital requirements, but it also emphasized that this could only be done through international regulatory cooperation that achieved a "level regulatory playing field."[28] The main justification for the need for international coordination was prudential in nature (i.e., the potential that global banks could escape effective supervision if less stringent regulations were maintained in some countries),[29] though concerns about the international competitiveness of the US financial sector remain prominent.[30] Almost all of the administration's main proposals in the area of prudential rules specified the need for agreement within the BCBS (US Treasury 2009a: 80–8, 2009b). The US Treasury also pushed for increased international surveillance and peer review, primarily though the FSB and the IMF, of the implementation of international regulatory agreements (US Treasury 2009a: 85–6). This reflected a shift in US policy from that of the George W. Bush administration, which had resisted the external assessment of Washington's own compliance with international financial standards, even though they had seen such assessments as important for other countries.[31]

The Democrats in Congress were more concerned to tighten regulatory oversight and prudential controls over the largest financial firms in ways that went beyond the Basel process. In March 2010, the prospects improved for the Senate Banking Committee's draft Restoring American Financial Stability Act, which envisaged a range of reforms to the architecture and content of US financial regulation. One core component of the bill, broadly consistent with developments in the BCBS, was that all US financial groups deemed to be systemically important, including non-banks, would face a range of more stringent prudential controls, including higher capital ratios than in Basel I and II and higher leverage and liquidity ratios. But it went beyond the current Basel framework

---

[28] See the Treasury's factsheet on "Improving International Regulatory Standards and Cooperation," issued in June 2009 (US Treasury 2009b).

[29] US Treasury (2009a: 80).

[30] See Aubrey B. Patterson, American Bankers Association, testimony to Senate Committee on Banking, Housing and Urban Affairs, 24 March 2009, 13.

[31] Assessments of compliance with international standards and codes are conducted primarily through the joint IMF-World Bank Financial Sector Assessment Programme (FSAP) (see Walter 2008: chapter 1). The Bush administration finally agreed to an FSAP for the United States in 2008, which was published in July 2010.

in making these prudential controls an increasing function of bank size and complexity and in adopting the "Volcker rule," also advanced by the Obama administration, which would require US banks to divest their proprietary trading businesses. In the 2,300 page "Dodd-Frank" Wall Street Reform and Consumer Protection Act that was finally passed by the US Senate in July 2010, important details were left to the future discretion of regulators and to the uncertain ongoing negotiations in the Basel Committee and elsewhere.[32] In particular, the new bill directed a newly established interagency Financial Stability Oversight Council to, among other things, "make recommendations to the Board of Governors concerning the establishment of heightened prudential standards for risk-based capital, leverage, liquidity, contingent capital, resolution plans and credit exposure reports, concentration limits, enhanced public disclosures, and overall risk management for nonbank financial companies and large, interconnected bank holding companies supervised by the Board of Governors."[33] The desire to take future developments in the BCBS into account reflected a desire to prevent regulatory arbitrage and the continuing importance of competitiveness concerns.

It has been in the implementation phase of banking regulation where domestic political conflict has often been most apparent, although the emphasis in the United States on statutory regulatory law gives the legislature control over the domestic implementation process as well as some influence during the negotiation phase. The implementation of Basel I in the United States was comparatively straightforward and uncontroversial. The FDIC Improvement Act of 1991 implemented the key elements of the Basel agreement for all US deposit-taking institutions insured by the FDIC. Banks were required to meet the minimum 8 percent CAR by the beginning of 1992, consistent with the BCBS's own timetable for implementation. After the nadir of 1987, US banks had been able to restore their equity capital, and the Basel minima proved unconstraining for most. Even through the recession of 1990–92, average Basel CARs for US banks remained well above the required minimum. The Tier 1 capital ratio alone exceeded 8 percent by 1991 and by the end of 1993, 80 percent of all US banks were classified as "well-capitalized" (with CARs above 10 percent).[34]

---

[32] "Congress Passes Financial Reform Bill," *Washington Post*, 16 July 2010.

[33] Wall Street Reform and Consumer Protection Act, HR.4173, 111th Congress, Sec. 112.a.2.I. In this bill, the Fed is granted regulatory authority over systemically important non-banks.

[34] US Federal Reserve (1994: 494). The FDIC Improvement Act of 1991 specified that well-capitalized banks must have risk-based capital ratios of at least 10%, Tier 1 ratios

In the case of Basel II, by contrast, domestic implementation was much more politicized and controversial – and by comparison with most other countries (Tarullo 2008: 127). The effects of this domestic politicization became evident well before the final agreement was reached in 2004. In 2003, the Fed announced, to the dismay of most of its Basel partners who well understood how much the United States had gained in the negotiations, that the new framework would not be implemented across the US banking sector. Only America's top twenty "global banks" (those with assets greater than $250 billion or with international exposures of more than $10 billion) would be required to implement the A-IRB approach. All other banks would be required to comply with a simpler "Basel IA" framework that would differ from the standardized approach of Basel II, though the IRB approaches would remain as an option for them. This differed greatly from the approach of the EU, which had already indicated that it would apply Basel II to all banks and on a timetable consistent with the Basel Committee's own announced schedule of implementation.[35]

The Fed's justification for this modified stance was that the Basel framework only applied in principle to internationally active banks, that the advanced approaches constituted the main benefit of Basel II, and that the costs of implementation probably outweighed the benefits for smaller US banks (Ferguson 2003). In fact, this reflected a climb-down in the face of frenzied lobbying from smaller banks and their Congressional allies. The change of tack also jeopardized the Fed's ability to keep the major US banks onside in the battle for domestic implementation.

Soon after the agreement on Basel II in mid-2004, signs emerged that the US authorities would also delay domestic implementation. On 29 April 2005, US regulatory authorities announced that they would delay the issuance of a formal notice of proposed rule-making (NPR) concerning Basel II implementation while they awaited the results of a fourth round of quantitative impact assessments of the new framework. The results of these assessments increased existing concerns among some US

of at least 6%, and leverage ratios (Tier 1 capital to total assets) of at least 5% (see FDIC Law, Regulation, Related Acts: 2000 – Rules and Regulations, http://www.fdic. gov/regulations/laws/rules/2000–4500.html, accessed 23 December 2009).

[35] In July 2004, the European Commission released proposals that would implement most of the provisions of the new framework for all banks by the end of 2006 (and end of 2007 for the A-IRB approach). See "Commission Proposes New Capital Requirements for Banks and Investment Firms," 14 July 2004, http://europa.eu/rapid/pressReleasesAction. do?reference=IP/04/899&language=en&guiLanguage=en, accessed 21 October 2009. The European Parliament passed the Capital Requirements Directive on 28 September 2005.

regulators, especially in the FDIC, that Basel II might lead to excessive reductions in required capital for IRB banks.[36] The FDIC did not object in principle to an internal model-based approach to capital adequacy, but it felt that this should be supplemented by simple floors for minimum capital requirements and by retaining the simple leverage ratio. These demands eventually produced a new compromise among US regulators that further delayed and modified implementation. In September 2005, US authorities announced that they would extend the BCBS-agreed implementation deadline of January 2007 for another year to allow banks more time to make necessary changes, and an additional three-year transition period during which the regulators could apply limits on the amount by which required capital could decline under the Basel II framework (down to a minimum of 85 percent of existing levels of capital by 2011).[37] After 2011, regulators would make a decision on whether to remove the floor on a bank-by-bank basis, holding out the prospect of considerable future capital relief for IRB banks. The prudential leverage ratio would also be retained after Basel II implementation, much to the disappointment of the major banks and the Fed. Even so, Fed Governor Susan Schmidt Bies still insisted that the agencies believed that "the primary responsibility for assessing capital adequacy lies with banks."[38]

These concessions to other domestic regulators and to smaller banks threatened the domestic coalition for Basel II with collapse (Herring 2007: 424–5). Larger banks felt that the net benefits of adopting the advanced approach were shrinking and that it would place them at a competitive disadvantage vis-à-vis foreign and investment bank competitors.[39] Four major banks even requested permission to implement the standardized approach. The Fed and OCC continued to insist that the advanced capital calculation approach would be mandatory for core

---

[36] See Sheila C. Bair, Chairman, Federal Deposit Insurance Corporation; "Remarks before the Global Association of Risk Professionals," New York, 26 February 2007: http://www.fdic.gov/news/news/speeches/archives/2007/chairman/spfeb2607.html.

[37] See Board of Governors of the Federal Reserve System, Federal Deposit Insurance Corporation, Office of the Comptroller of the Currency, and Office of Thrift Supervision, "Banking Agencies Announce Revised Plan for Implementation of Basel II Framework," 30 September 2005, http://www.federalreserve.gov/boarddocs/press/bcreg/2005/20050930/default.htm, accessed 8 January 2009.

[38] Susan Schmidt Bies, "An Update on Basel II Implementation in the United States," Remarks to the Global Association of Risk Professionals, New York, 26 February 2007.

[39] Investment banks would be required to adopt a version of Basel II but would not be subject to the leverage ratio (which had been removed by the US Securities and Exchange Commission in 2004) or the transitional capital floors.

banks, but the FDIC and OTS at this point were much more sympathetic to the simpler and less model-dependent standardized approach.

In the end, the concern that reopening the issue would lead to a further delay in US implementation and result in unacceptably high compliance problems for the largest banks pushed the regulators towards a compromise that left the 2005 bargain largely intact. On 7 December 2007, the four federal regulators announced that core banks would be required to implement the A-IRB approach and that other qualifying banks would be permitted to do so.[40] Core banks had to submit implementation plans to regulators by 1 October 2008, with a first transitional floor start date of no later than 1 April 2011.[41] The foundational IRB approach was not permitted as an option for US banks. The formerly touted Basel IA was also scrapped and a new joint NPR on the standardized approach was issued on 29 July 2008.[42]

Thus, although the United States initially veered away from implementation of Basel II, domestic regulators eventually reached agreement to implement its main provisions by 2011 (shorn of the F-IRB option). This allowed the United States to accept the G20 agreement at Pittsburgh in September 2009 to adopt Basel II by 2011. But significant uncertainties remain. The difficulty of achieving agreement on key issues in the BCBS means that the question of domestic implementation in the United States may yet be reopened. Even at the time of the agreement among US bank regulators in December 2007, the FDIC insisted that a major review of the advanced approach be undertaken at the end of the second transitional year and that any "material deficiencies" must be addressed by regulatory changes. It now seems unlikely that the transitional floors to have been applied over the period to 2011 will be removed; they are more likely to be raised and retained. Any lingering political support for the eventual removal of the leverage ratio also evaporated after the crisis. In short, despite the passage of the Dodd-Frank Act, uncertainty about the content and implementation of new prudential rules will persist for the foreseeable future.

[40] 72 FR 69288 (7 December 2007).

[41] "Interagency Statement – U.S. Implementation of Basel II Advanced Approaches Framework, Qualification Process," 8 July 2008, http://www.federalreserve.gov/board-docs/srletters/2008/SR0804a1.pdf, accessed 8 February 2009.

[42] In order to satisfy smaller banks that they will not be placed at a disadvantage there was an expectation that lower capital requirements in some asset classes, notably residential mortgages, would be permitted (Tarullo 2008: 188–9). Given events in US mortgage markets since 2008, this deal appears unsustainable.

Explaining Levels of Behavioural Consistency

As previously described, although there is little indication that US influence over the Basel process significantly declined from the mid-1980s to the mid-2000s, the domestic implementation of Basel II proved much more difficult, contested, and uncertain than Basel I. Financial sector interests, bureaucratic interests, and ideology all played their part in this outcome. Ideology was relatively unimportant in motivating US initiatives in Basel I, but over time, the growing belief of key Fed officials in the superiority of market-based regulation played an important role in motivating and shaping the subsequent revisions of the framework. These revisions greatly complicated the politics of implementation. This battle was primarily a product of domestic distributional politics and the limited ability of the Federal Reserve to persuade its co-regulators and other important domestic audiences that its preferred approach to regulation was desirable.

Domestic distributional conflict inevitably spilled over into key Congressional committees with an interest in the issue. The Senate Banking Committee, for example, held a series of hearings on the negotiation and implementation of Basel II in which proponents and critics of the framework were heard (Tarullo 2008: 127). Members of Congress are very sensitive to the concerns of the many thousand small local and state banks that lobbied hard against some of the initial proposals of the Fed and their major bank supporters. Smaller banks saw this agenda as an attempt to sacrifice their interests and to foster a consolidation of the banking sector. This prompted a series of revisions that reduced the differential impact on banks of the IRB and standardized approaches. Even before the 2008–09 crisis, members of Congress were also sensitive to arguments that large bank failures could be highly costly for taxpayers. The failure in 1998 of LTCM, a sophisticated hedge fund to which many major banks lent large sums, was used by Basel II's opponents to cast doubt on the desirability of relying more heavily upon market self-regulation.[43]

Similar concerns were uppermost in the minds of some of the other major bank regulators, notably the FDIC. Sheila Bair, the Bush appointee as chair of the FDIC since June 2006, was especially critical of a system

---

[43] For an example of legislator concerns of this kind, see "The Failure of Long-Term Capital Management: A Preliminary Assessment," by James A. Leach, Chairman, House Banking and Financial Services Committee, before the House of Representatives, 12 October 1998 (http://financialservices.house.gov/banking/101298le.htm, accessed 8 November 2009).

that in her view threatened to deliver double-digit percentage reductions in regulatory capital requirements for large US banks. The FDIC, with statutory responsibility to intervene in failing banks at lowest cost to the taxpayer, was more naturally concerned with the potential costs of such deregulation (Herring 2007: 427). Obtaining agreement among the main federal regulators was very difficult, and lingering concerns on the part of the OCC and FDIC with the IRB approach led to further compromises, notably the retention of the 1991 FDIC Act backstops and the transitional floors on capital reductions.

Partisan factors appear to have been relatively unimportant in explaining evolving US attitudes towards the international regulatory framework. The Reagan administration's deregulatory agenda foundered (in the area of banking and finance) on the rocks of the Latin American debt crisis and the Savings and Loan crisis in the 1980s, both of which proved very costly for US taxpayers. As we have seen, key US regulatory agencies had considerable autonomy to pursue international agreements in this area, and the George H. W. Bush administration supported revisions to US statutes that implemented Basel I for all US banks.

After 1992, the long-term trend towards an acceleration of the deregulation of finance achieved considerable support across the US political spectrum. Alan Greenspan, appointed by Reagan in 1987 as Fed Chairman, was much more ideologically predisposed towards market solutions than his predecessor, Paul Volcker. Key figures in the Clinton administration were very tolerant of this approach and respectful of Greenspan's growing reputation. Treasury Secretary Robert Rubin and his deputy and eventual successor Larry Summers generally sided with Greenspan's Fed in favouring financial deregulation and resisting proposals to regulate new financial instruments.[44] Both the administration and Congress were broadly convinced by the argument of the major US commercial banks that the Basel I framework put them at a serious competitive disadvantage vis-à-vis their investment bank competitors, who were much less constrained by regulations than were deposit-taking institutions and who were subject to only very light touch supervisory oversight from the SEC. This concern was especially relevant after the Gramm-Leach-Bliley Act of 1999 abolished the depression-era Glass-Steagall separations between commercial and investment banking.

[44] "What Went Wrong," *Washington Post*, 15 October 2008.

That this was not simply a product of the growing influence of pro-market ideas is revealed by the fact that the financial sector was consistently the largest contributor among all economic sectors to federal election financing and the biggest spender on federal political lobbying in the late 1990s (commercial banks spent particularly heavily on lobbying in 1998).[45] The lead position of the financial sector in such political activity was retained in the 2000s. During 1990–2010, 45 percent of all financial sector federal election campaign contributions went to Democrats and 55 percent to Republicans, though in the first half of the 1990s such contributions were evenly balanced between both parties. This money seems to have been well spent. As one Fed governor has summarized, "by the turn of the [21st] century, the Depression-era cluster of restrictions on commercial banks had been replaced by a regulatory environment in which they could operate nationally, conduct a much broader range of activities, and affiliate with virtually any kind of financial firm."[46] Major Wall Street firms also enjoyed exceptional profitability in the decade before 2008.

Since 2008, the undermining of the third Basel norm of market-based regulation has further strengthened the position of critics such as Sheila Bair and necessitated a retreat by the Fed. Bair noted that both the US government and the BCBS had converged towards the FDIC's viewpoint on key issues such as the continuing usefulness of a simple leverage ratio.[47] Even so, considerable philosophical differences remain among the key regulatory agencies. The Fed's Supervisory Capital Assessment Program (better known as the "stress tests" to determine whether the top nineteen US bank holding companies had sufficient capital under alternative economic scenarios) was begun in February 2009 and revealed that major banks often lacked the information necessary to manage risk effectively (US Federal Reserve 2009). In the light of this, the Fed's declared intention was not to rely less on banks' internal risk management processes, but rather to improve them: "[by] placing increased emphasis on the ability of firms to assess their own capital needs, particularly in periods of stress, both to supplement minimum capital requirements and to ensure that

[45] See the statistics compiled from Federal Election Commission records on http://www.opensecrets.org, accessed 22 March 2010.

[46] Daniel K. Tarullo, "Financial Regulatory Reform," speech to the annual US Monetary Policy Forum, University of Chicago Booth School of Business, New York, 26 February 2010.

[47] Statement of Sheila C. Bair, Chairman, FDIC, "The Causes and Current State of the Financial Crisis," before the Financial Crisis Enquiry Commission, 14 January 2010, p. 33.

relevant information on firm risks is readily available to supervisors."[48] Meanwhile, there was substantial support in Congress and in the Obama administration for a different approach that would aim at reducing the overall level of risk in the banking sector (and, by implication, to the government and taxpayers).

The argument that domestic politics has primacy in the implementation phase does not mean that international factors had no effect on the level of US behavioural consistency with the Basel framework. This is not because international institutions – either in the form of Basel's Accord Implementation Group or the IMF and World Bank – possess any significant leverage over the United States in this regard. Nor has the idea that the United States has a broader obligation to adhere to international standards that it has helped to establish played a significant part in the domestic US debate over implementation. Rather, the debate has been highly instrumental in the focus on the net costs and benefits for the United States and its economy. Competitiveness concerns were a key motivation in US efforts first to negotiate then to implement Basel I. Concerns that substantial behavioural departures from the Basel II framework would seriously disadvantage US commercial banks in global markets – and vis-à-vis their US investment bank rivals – was an important reason why, eventually, partial implementation of the framework in the United States was brought back on track (Tarullo 2008: 129). US investment banks were subject to a highly favourable regulatory regime at home and the A-IRB option was the best option on offer for most US money centre banks; it also held out the possibility of future convergence between the regulatory frameworks applied to deposit-taking institutions and investment banks. Globalized banks also emphasized the costs that they would face in dealing with different forms and schedules of implementation across the different jurisdictions in which they operate. The clear intention of the European Union and other major jurisdictions to implement Basel II in a mostly unmodified form would create serious costs for major US banks if the United States did not follow suit. The European Union's action thus points to the limits of US power: having played a crucial role in the launching of the Basel II negotiations, the US could not prevent its spread elsewhere. This in turn raised the costs of non-convergence for major US banks.

---

[48] Daniel K. Tarullo, "Financial Regulatory Reform," speech to the annual US Monetary Policy Forum, University of Chicago Booth School of Business, New York, 26 February 2010.

3 China and the Basel Framework

For most of the reform period, the Basel framework was largely irrelevant for China, with its state-controlled and domestically oriented banking system. From the mid-1990s, however, the Chinese leadership began to see the Basel framework as a useful set of benchmarks for reforming the highly inefficient and mostly insolvent domestic banking sector. In contrast to the United States, competitiveness issues were not initially an important motivator for China's growing convergence with the Basel framework. Instead, Basel became a useful source of political leverage for reformers wishing to clean up and modernize China's banking system, since they faced powerful vested interests that resisted financial sector reform.

China signalled that it would follow the broad trend among developing countries to adopt the Basel framework in its acceptance of the minimum 8 percent CAR in article 39 of the law of the People's Bank of China of 1995 (Brehm and Macht 2004: 322). This was relatively late by the standards of some other East Asian countries, but the delay was unsurprising given the relatively underdeveloped state of China's banking system and regulatory infrastructure. Nevertheless, by this stage the costs of adoption of the Basel framework for the government and for Chinese banks were limited. The voluntary nature of the Basel framework permitted substantial autonomy in the process of implementation. China's financial system was dominated by large, state-owned banks and most of the focus of reform – and on the implementation of the Basel framework in particular – was on these large banks rather than on the thousands of smaller rural and city banks. At this stage, no Chinese banks had significant international operations – in this sense, the Chinese government, like those of many developing countries, went beyond the Basel framework, which applied only to internationally active banks. The Basel framework also permitted the Chinese government to maintain control over its banking system and to continue to prevent significant foreign competition for Chinese banks. For the banks themselves, adoption was acceptable because the enforcement of the new rules and of related loan accounting and other standards was weak (Brehm and Macht 2004; Brehm 2008).[49] The central bank was also the main regulator until 2003, and its approach reflected the relatively low priority placed by the

---

[49] This was also consistent with another trend in developing Asian countries (Walter 2008).

government on prudential regulation in the high growth era.[50] Over time, rapid growth allowed the government to recapitalize the major banks to push them above the minimum Basel capital ratios – though it took until the end of 2008 for almost all Chinese banks to meet this minimum standard.

The initially limited approach to the implementation of Basel standards began to change in the late 1990s as the restoration of the solvency of China's major banks became a key leadership priority. Zhu Rongji, who became Premier in March 1998, launched a series of financial reforms that indicated a stronger intention to adopt and implement Basel standards. The first phase of reform focused on the recapitalization of the major state-owned commercial banks (SOCBs) and the disposal of their high levels of nonperforming loans (NPLs). The second phase, from 2003, focused on the reorganization of these banks, the adoption of modern management practices, new governance structures, and foreign share listings (Luo 2008). Recapitalization was premised on a greater willingness to enforce the minimum 8 percent CAR for the major banks. New rules on loan classification similar to those being adopted elsewhere in Asia were also introduced in 1998, and new accounting and loan loss provisioning rules were introduced in 2001 and 2002, respectively (Angklomkliew et al. 2009: 73–4).

Wen Jiabao continued this reform path from 2003. The creation in 2003 of the China Banking Regulatory Commission (CBRC), which took over from the PBOC as China's principal bank regulator, was intended to force China's banking system onto a more commercial footing so as to ensure that it was no longer the Achilles heel of the economy.[51] The law establishing the CBRC drew heavily on the Basel Core Principles for Effective Banking Supervision, of which the capital adequacy regime is one part, and from other rules prevailing in the advanced countries, especially the United States. The composition of the CBRC's International Advisory Council is also intended to send a strong signal of the regulatory

---

[50] For an analysis of the damaging relationship between factional politics and the tendency of the Chinese system to create large amounts of bad loans, see Shih (2008). On the eve of the Asian financial crisis in mid-1997, the level of nonperforming loans in the Chinese banking sector was among the highest in Asia despite China's exceptional growth performance. The political elite had required the banking system to bear much of the burden of the restructuring of state-owned enterprises (SOEs). The banks were relieved of existing NPLs in the mid-1990s and had capital injections from the PBOC, but efforts to encourage them to move to a more commercial, profit-oriented footing largely failed.

[51] The PBOC retains a substantial supervisory role so that the Chinese model in this respect occupies an intermediate position between the US and UK systems.

authorities' intentions to converge upon what at the time were essentially Western standards of banking regulation and supervision.[52]

Hong Kong, a relatively sophisticated financial centre with one of the most Westernized approaches to financial regulation in the region, was an important source of regulatory innovation for the mainland during this phase. Andrew Sheng, the former Chairman of the Hong Kong Securities and Futures Commission, played an important role as convenor of the CBRC's International Advisory Board (now *Council*) and later became the CBRC's Chief Adviser. David Carse, former Chief Executive of the Hong Kong Monetary Authority, also became a member. For the major SOCBs themselves, Hong Kong listings were an important step in their internal reorganizations and gave them access to foreign capital and managerial expertise. At the same time, the mainland Chinese authorities retained the flexibility to implement Basel and other international standards at a more gradual pace than Hong Kong, including for the SOCBs.

Luo Ping, then in the International Department of the CBRC, stated bluntly in November 2003 that "[b]esides [their] low capital base and asset quality, banks in China also suffer from poor corporate governance and internal controls and a lack of adequate risk management skills" (Luo 2003: 4). Even according to official figures, banking system NPLs in 2003 were still 18 percent of total loans, albeit down from 30 percent in 2001 (unofficial estimates were often much higher). During 2003–04, the CBRC signalled an ambitious timetable for full Basel I implementation by the beginning of 2007, introduced the same five-tier system of loan classification as had other Asian countries, and moved NPLs to state-owned asset management companies.[53] In 2004, new legislation slightly revised the main banking regulations, combining most of the capital requirements of Basel I with the supervisory review and disclosure aspects (pillars two

---

[52] In 2007, members of this advisory body were Jaime Caruana, Director, IMF Monetary and Capital Markets Department and former Chairman, BCBS; Gerald Corrigan, Managing Director, Goldman Sachs and former President, FRBNY; Andrew Crockett, President, JP Morgan International and former Manager, Bank for International Settlements; Howard Davies, former Chairman, Financial Services Authority (UK); Edward George, former Governor, Bank of England; Masamato Yashiro, former President, Shinsei Bank. By 2009, George had died and Caruana had left; new members included Roger Ferguson, former Vice Chairman of the US Federal Reserve Board and former Chairman of the Financial Stability Forum, and Tom de Swaan, a former Dutch regulator and former Chair of the Basel Committee.

[53] This loan accounting required banks to classify loans as Normal, Special Mention, Substandard, Doubtful, and Loss (in declining order of quality). See Walter (2008).

and three) of Basel II.[54] Chinese officials referred to this selective approach to international convergence as "Basel 1.5." Although this fell short of a clear intention to move to adopt Basel II, it should be remembered that the US position was not entirely dissimilar at this time.

Since 2004, some of the gaps in behavioural conformity with the Basel framework have been reduced. According to the CBRC (2008: 146), the proportion of banking system assets in banks compliant with Basel I was a mere 0.6 percent in 2003; by early 2008 the figure was just over 80 percent and by its end 99.9 percent. This indicates substantial progress towards convergence on Basel I, though it also indicates that convergence remains elusive for many smaller Chinese banks (Davies 2008; Luo 2008). Some argue that the IMF had tried but failed to convince the CBRC to follow through on a threat that banks that could not meet Basel I minima by the end of 2006 would be closed, but it would have been very difficult to do this in the absence of a bank resolution or deposit insurance system.[55] Weaker banks are also often controlled by local authorities, some of whom refused to inject the necessary capital. Nevertheless, on the eve of the 2008 global financial crisis, the improvement at the major SOCBs, with the exception of Agricultural Bank of China (ABC), was impressive (Table 6.1).[56]

The perceived success of this banking sector reform programme and the growing strength of China's major banks led eventually to a more ambitious though still partial approach to convergence on Basel II. A senior CBRC official argued in April 2006 that

As a major milestone for banking supervision, Basel II is the way forward for all supervisors globally. But the timing for adoption is to be determined by non-G10 countries in light of their own market conditions. Emerging markets should capitalize on Basel II in jumping up the learning curve for better risk management.[57]

---

[54] See Liu Mingkang, "Setting A New Stage in China's Banking Supervision and Regulation," 11 March 2004, http://www.cbrc.gov.cn/english/module/viewinfo.jsp?infoID=530; Brehm and Macht (2004: 316–17).

[55] Author interviews, Washington, DC, and London, April 2009.

[56] It is worth noting that the large SOCBs have also adopted the more advanced International Financial Reporting Standards (IFRS) system of loan classification, provisioning and reporting as part of their international listing strategy. This system is being extended to all other Chinese banks and is now broadly in line with best practice elsewhere in Asia. International Accounting Standard (IAS) 39 on loan loss accounting and provisioning was implemented for all listed banks on 1 January 2007 and for all other banks in 2009; banks were also encouraged to raise the ratio of provisions to NPLs to at least 150% by end-2009 (Angklomkliew et al. 2009: 73–4).

[57] Luo Ping, "Financial Regulation in Emerging Markets: A Case Study of China, an Emerging Market and an Economy in Transition," presentation to Second Annual Future of Financial Regulation Conference, London School of Economics, 6–7 April 2006.

TABLE 6.1. *Major Chinese State-Owned Banks, Asset Quality Indicators, 2007*

	Total Assets (RMB mn)	NPLs as % of Total Loans	Special Mention Loans as % of Total Loans	Loan Loss Reserves as % of NPLs	Tier I CARs (%)	CARs (%)	Long-Term Deposit Ratings (Fitch Ratings)	Individual Ratings (Fitch Ratings)
SOCBs								
ICBC	8,301,167	3.3	7.0	81.3	11.8	13.7	A	D
ABC	5,343,943	23.4		5.1				E
BOC	5,833,891	3.6	6.5	103.9	11.3	13.4	A	D
CCB	6,117,791	3.0	7.3	90.7	9.4	11.3	A	D
BOCOM	2,135,880	2.1	5.8	85.3	10.1	14.2	A–	D
Policy Banks								
CDB	2,314,267	0.7	0.22	191.0		8.1	A+	n.a.
EIBC	258,297	3.5		34.2			A+	n.a.
ADBC	932,562	7.7		13.1	4.3	6.2	A+	n.a.

Note: Figures are for the first half of 2007 unless otherwise indicated. "Special Mention" loans are those that are in danger of deteriorating but are not currently classified as NPLs.

Source: Fitch Ratings, "Chinese Banks – Annual Review and Outlook," 30 January 2008, www.fitchratings.com.

China's approach to Basel II has been a bifurcated one. This contrasts with the formal approach, if less the reality, of Basel I implementation in China. The government proposed that major SOCBs with an international presence would be required to implement the IRB approach, with the A-IRB approach the preferred option, before the end of 2010, with other banks following on a voluntary basis. In February 2007, the CBRC issued "Guidance on the Implementation of the New Capital Accord by the China Banking Industry." This set out the plan for implementation, though it referred to the need to do so "based on China's realities" (CBRC 2007: 70). The standardized approach would be available to banks that did not qualify for the IRB approach, but they would be required to draw up a plan to adopt the IRB approach within three years (i.e., no later than 2013) (CBRC 2007: 72). In the meantime, these banks would be required to implement China's Basel 1.5, eventually moving onto Basel II some years later. Implementing banks were required to submit their first quarterly compliance assessment reports to the CBRC by the end of 2008 and to provide plans to rectify areas of non-compliance. By 2008, seven major commercial banks had become the focus of regulatory efforts for Basel II implementation (CBRC 2008: 73). These banks were required to improve data and information systems and to train board members, senior management, and staff in business lines and risk management to ensure adequate implementation. Although doubts remain about the ability of Chinese regulators fully to implement Basel II for the major SOCBs, similar doubts apply to many countries.

How, if at all, have China's attitudes to the Basel regime changed in response to the crisis of 2008–09? The early response of the authorities was to insist that Basel II implementation in China remained on track and that the crisis revealed not so much weaknesses in Basel II but in the United States' failure adequately to regulate mortgages, securitization, the shadow banking sector, and off-balance sheet financing vehicles generally (Luo 2008). Chinese officials also emphasized that Basel II could not be blamed for the crisis as the build-up of vulnerabilities predated its implementation.[58] In October 2008, CBRC even brought forward the deadline for Basel II implementation by the IRB banks by one year.[59] This timetable lagged a number of advanced countries (including Hong Kong

---

[58] Author interviews, Beijing, October 2008.
[59] KPMG Risk Advisory Services, "China Boardroom Update: Regulatory Developments," January 2009, http://www.kpmg.com.cn/en/virtual_library/Risk_advisory_services/China_Boardroom/CBU0901.pdf.

and the European Union) but was similar to that of the United States.[60] From September to December 2008, the CBRC maintained the pace of implementation of Basel II. On 23 September, it issued five supervisory guidance papers relating to the implementation of Pillar 1 of Basel II. On 11 December, it issued a further eight draft papers for public comment relating to all three pillars (the now standard practice of more advanced countries of issuing draft regulations for public comment is another that has been adopted in China).[61]

As the global crisis worsened and the Basel regime became subject to increasing criticism in the advanced countries, China's position adapted. Some Chinese officials started to voice more direct criticism of the Basel regime.[62] Behind the scenes, Vice-Premier Wang Qishan is said to have asked in mid-2008 whether he should continue to take his Wall Street teachers' lessons seriously now that their own authority and credibility was in question (Davies 2008). However, these criticisms largely echoed those made by government and regulatory officials in the major countries (e.g., FSA 2009; US Treasury 2009a). As in the United States, the crisis led Chinese officials to call into question the third Basel norm of market-based regulation, but they did not reject openly the other two norms or the Basel framework in general. The financial stability norm remains crucial for China, and it accepts the G20 consensus that the Basel framework must be reformed along the lines laid out in the G20 summits since November 2008.

China's support for this reformist stance was confirmed when it accepted the offer of membership in the BCBS in March 2009. Since then, the authorities pushed ahead with Basel II implementation and with further regulatory adjustments in line with recommendations of the G20 and associated work in the FSB, of which China is now also a member (FSB 2009). For example, in October 2009, CBRC issued new guidelines on liquidity risk management, and it directed Chinese banks to undertake quarterly stress tests to identify key risks and to improve risk management practices – again, following similar tests in the advanced

---

[60] The Chinese SOCBs listed on the Hong Kong Stock Exchange are already subject to local disclosure requirements. Hong Kong's Monetary Authority required all local banks to comply with Basel II (with the A-IRB approach optional) from 1 January 2007, but it did not require the SOCBs to do so.

[61] CBRC (2008: 131–3); "The CBRC seeks comments on eight Basel II related rule-making documents," 11 December 2008, http://www.cbrc.gov.cn/english/info/news/index_more.jsp?current=5, accessed 15 December 2009.

[62] Author interviews, Beijing and London, September 2008 and February 2009.

countries.[63] Along with all other FSB members, China has also agreed to engage in an ongoing process of peer review aimed at promoting the implementation of FSB standards, which include Basel standards (FSB 2009: 9). Although China is generally resistant to a review process that results in "naming and shaming" as some have proposed, along with the United States it has accepted the need for the G20 to lead the implementation of modifications to the Basel framework.[64] This reflects growing self-confidence in China's own financial reforms and in the strength of its financial sector.

Despite this evidence of growing commitment on the part of the authorities to the Basel framework, the Chinese approach has been one of adaptation of Basel standards to domestic circumstances and gradual implementation. There are also remaining questions concerning compliance and enforcement of the formal rules at the domestic level. Despite the impressive capital ratios, profitability, and low NPLs of the major banks, international analysts generally rated their stand-alone financial strength as relatively poor.[65] That is, the major banks still depend heavily on implicit state financial support, though they share this characteristic with most of their Western counterparts. Unlike Western banks, they also remain under state control despite foreign listing and the related injection of foreign private capital, with their boards still dominated by state and Party representatives.[66] Bank heads are vice-governors within the government, and in 2009 four out of five of those of the large SOCBs sat on the Party's Central Committee. The Party thus remains the dominant player in senior managerial and board appointments, limiting the impact of CBRC oversight, strategic investor stakes, and market constraints. The CBRC itself, like the PBOC, is of course also subordinated to the State Council. As long as competition remains limited, state ownership and Party control predominates, lending decisions remain politicized, and

---

[63] "The CBRC issued the Guidance on Liquidity Risk Management of Commercial Banks," 29 October 2009, http://www.cbrc.gov.cn/english/info/news/index_more.jsp, accessed 15 December 2009; eStandards Forum, *Weekly Report*, 10 (7), 19–26 October 2009, 4.

[64] Author interviews, London, February 2010.

[65] See Table 6.1. Fitch (2008) gave independent financial strength ratings of D for most major Chinese banks and E for ABC (A being the highest possible rating). The independent strength rating does not take into account the probability of state support for banks, which of course is close to 1 in China.

[66] In addition to the SOCBs, there are listed joint stock banks, which accounted for nearly 14% of total banking sector assets by the end of 2007, but these are mainly owned by local governments and SOEs. Foreign banks controlled a mere 2.4% of total assets (CBRC 2007: 139).

bank staff incentives are oriented towards political priorities rather than economic risk management (Dobson and Kashyap 2006; Brehm 2008).

There are also continuing doubts about the reporting of NPLs by SOCBs despite the evident improvement of recent years. Levels of reported fraud in the financial system remain high, although enforcement has also improved.[67] Until recently, officially reported figures almost certainly substantially underestimated the true levels of NPLs – even official regulators admitted this (Luo 2003: 3; Ernst & Young 2006; Fitch 2006). There are also doubts about the capacity of banks to provision effectively for distressed assets and to sustain high profits given their high dependence on corporate loan business, high taxes, and rising competition (Fitch Ratings 2008: 3–6). The extraordinary growth in bank credit during 2008–09, driven by the government's need to implement much of the economic stimulus package through the banking sector, has also increased the risk of new NPLs in the future.[68] This risk has been recognized by the CBRC, which tightened supervisory oversight after the crisis and called on banks to increase their loan loss provisioning ratios (CBRC 2008: 9). It remains unclear whether these initiatives will be sufficient to prevent a sharp rebound in levels of NPLs in the Chinese banking system, though an officially commissioned report estimated in July 2010 that Chinese banks faced serious default risks on more than 20 percent of their loans to local government financing vehicles.[69] Even so, given projections of extraordinary asset write-downs for developed Western financial systems (on the order of $1,000 billion for US banks and $1,600 billion for European banks during 2007–10),[70] it is doubtful that China's financial system is distinctively dysfunctional.

In sum, the political economy of the adoption of Basel standards in China has been very different from that in the United States. Whereas the

---

[67] The Chinese National Audit Office (CNAO) is responsible for auditing the major institutions of the central government, including the PBOC and SOCBs. Established by the State Council and responsible to the Premier's office, it has undertaken a series of audits since 1999 that have exposed the continuing problem of illegal lending and substantial fraud in government generally and some of the major banks in particular (including China Development Bank and Agricultural Bank of China). Whether these are good estimates of the full extent of poor lending practices is unclear. For example, in the case of CDB, a development bank that lends for politically important projects, the CNAO found that CDB made RMB 9.1bn ($1.3bn) in illegal loans in 2007 (3.7% of new loans) and that RMB 24.6bn of its loans had been embezzled (10% of new loans). See "Illicit Loan Scandal Threatens CDB Plans," *FT.com*, 29 August 2008.

[68] "China's Banks Lend with Communist Zeal," *FT.com*, 8 July 2009.

[69] "Chinese Banks Face State Loans Turmoil," *FT.com*, 26 July 2010.

[70] IMF (2009b:10) estimates as of October 2009.

negotiation and especially the implementation process were openly politicized in the United States, in China implementation has been remarkably calm and consistent. This reflects to a considerable degree the very different political systems in the two countries. In the United States, most of the political battles must be fought prior to decisions about implementation because of the relatively robust legal and regulatory framework of enforcement. In China, government decisions to adopt Basel standards have not always signalled the end of the implementation game because enforcement has been much less effective. Behavioural inconsistencies in both countries are institutionally context-dependent.

Explaining Levels of Behavioural Consistency

We argue that the main reason for the Chinese government's positive attitude towards the Basel framework is that the leadership continues to see advantages in the importation of financial regulatory and managerial "technology" from the advanced countries. As a result, it has so far resisted attempts to destabilize and discredit the regime. International considerations have also played a part, and probably a greater one than in the US case. These motivations are also essentially pragmatic rather than ideological, which is broadly true of the Chinese leadership's approach towards financial reform in general.[71]

There are three main factors that explain the Chinese leadership's view that positive benefits can be obtained from a broad acceptance of the Basel framework. First, although China's SOCBs now rank among the world's largest and most profitable, China's banking sector remains relatively backward in comparison with the largest banks from advanced countries and their restructuring and reform is unfinished business. This gives banks and regulators a strong incentive to import regulatory and managerial technologies from abroad. The Basel framework has the considerable advantage that China can do this without compromising state control over the banking sector, which remains an essential part of Chinese development strategy. Second, the regulatory agencies, the CBRC and the PBOC, have a strong bureaucratic interest in using global standard setting to leverage their limited autonomy in the domestic policy process. Third, the political system has permitted the government

---

[71] Thus, for example, China continues to use capital controls despite an historically unprecedented current account surplus; it has amassed large foreign exchange reserves as a precaution against financial crisis; and it has permitted only a very gradual and limited entry of international banks into the domestic market.

to limit the politicization of banking sector reform. In this respect, the relative robustness of Chinese banks during the 2008–09 crisis has helped considerably in ensuring that the government has not needed to engage in a further round of costly bailouts of banks (in contrast to the United States).

The belief that China's financial system can benefit from importing foreign managerial and regulatory technology provides the most important motivation (CBRC 2008: 48). In this regard, the Asian financial crises of 1997–98 were an important watershed, as they alerted China's leadership to the economic and political dangers posed by an unreformed financial sector.[72] Although it is likely that there was considerable disagreement within the Chinese leadership over the relevance and implications of the Asian crisis for China, it had two important effects. First, it strengthened the hand of Zhu and his allies by providing an additional reason for tackling financial reform more seriously. Second, crises in other Asian developing countries and Japan undermined any viable Asian alternative to Western standards in financial regulation. Discussion among policy elites before the Asian crisis about the possibility of China adopting aspects of the Korean regulatory framework ceased after 1997.[73] This left the Western approach, exemplified by that in the United States, as the only credible benchmark for Chinese reformers. This view was not unreasonable given the resilience of the US economy and its financial system during the emerging market crises of the 1990s and the LTCM and the dot.com collapses.

This tactic of using international institutions to overcome domestic resistance to reform has often been deployed by the Chinese leadership (Bergsten et al. 2008: 13). Basel norms and standards and the unrivalled legitimacy claims of US (and to some extent UK) regulators provided a powerful weapon which Chinese reformers, as elsewhere in Asia, used to sideline opponents of reform (Walter 2008: 18–27). This tactic is thus primarily pragmatic rather than ideological. The voluntary status of Basel standards is also an important consideration, as it has permitted the Chinese leadership to pick and choose what it needed from Western financial regulatory models, to adapt them to Chinese domestic circumstances, and to maintain a gradualist approach to reform. The contrast between China's tolerant attitude towards Basel and its increasingly

---

[72] Author interviews, Beijing, London, and Washington, DC, September 2008 to April 2009.
[73] Author interviews, Beijing, September 2008.

difficult relationship with the IMF macroeconomic surveillance regime is revealing in this regard. It is also noteworthy that IMF-intervened Indonesia, Korea, and Thailand saw dramatic increases in levels of foreign ownership of their domestic banking sector after 1997 (by 2006, majority foreign-owned banks controlled about one-third of banking system assets in these countries), whereas for China, foreign ownership remains low (at less than 3 percent).[74]

This also implies that although the Chinese leadership largely accepted the first Basel norm concerning the need for international standards to promote financial stability, it is less clear whether it has accepted the competitive equality norm. In fact, an explicit goal of Basel implementation in China is to improve the competitiveness of Chinese banks (CBRC 2007: 71; Luo 2008: 5). The competitiveness of the five major SOCBs has been of particular importance to the Chinese leadership, since they account for half of total banking sector assets (CBRC 2008: 33) and have absorbed enormous amounts of state aid in the past. "Financial repression" in the form of low deposit rates has benefitted the major banks that are flush with deposits at the expense of joint stock banks and depositors (Lardy 2008). Earlier non-compliance with Basel had the drawback for Chinese banks wishing to operate in more developed jurisdictions of requiring them to take the relatively costly route of establishing separately capitalized local subsidiaries (rather than branches). Perhaps more importantly, given the still low degree of internationalization of Chinese banks, this limitation was also a visible signal of lower international status for Chinese banks.[75] The CBRC's annual report in 2008 noted both the milestone reached in October 2008, when China Merchants Bank became the first ever Chinese bank to open a New York branch, and the achievement of global top ten status for Industrial and Commercial Bank of China (ICBC) and Bank of China (BOC).[76]

The second factor, that China's key regulatory agencies have a strong interest in promoting the legitimacy of Basel norms and standards, is related to the first. The CBRC has strong incentives to portray Basel standards to its domestic audiences as technocratic, externally validated, best practice regulatory benchmarks. This stance has helped to maintain pressure on the banks to raise their capital, reduce their NPLs and improve

---

[74] CBRC (2008: 47).

[75] We thank Howard Davies for this point.

[76] CBRC (2008: 49, 51). ICBC and BOC were ranked eighth and tenth, respectively, among all global banks by total Tier 1 capital by *The Banker* magazine in July 2008 (they had both ranked in the top ten for the first time in 2007).

their asset allocation skills. It has also helped the CBRC to carve out a greater (though still limited) degree of operational autonomy vis-à-vis local political authorities, the banks, and the large state-owned enterprises that remain dependent on them. The Chinese political leadership had an interest in supporting this bureaucratic quest for greater operational autonomy, since it distances the leadership from politically difficult decisions about individual banks.

This helps to explain why government officials saw little to gain from calling the legitimacy of the Basel framework into question after the 2008–09 crisis. Chinese banking remains fairly traditional in nature, mostly recycling domestic savings to firms as loans. Securitization is relatively underdeveloped in China and derivatives markets are still small. Basel standards proved particularly inadequate in these areas, but these shortcomings are less costly for China. The Chinese authorities have also retained more traditional prudential controls alongside the more advanced Basel regulations they have been introducing, a decision which in retrospect looks sensible. For example, Chinese banks can only loan up to 75 percent of their deposit base, and home buyers can only borrow up to 70 percent of the value of their property (60% in the case of second homes). As Liu Mingkang, CBRC Chairman, remarked at an IIF conference in Beijing in June 2009, "Basel II is problematic; traditional ratios are still useful; small is beautiful and old is beautiful as well."[77]

In actuality, the CBRC's attempt to foster a culture of financial conservatism in China came under severe pressure from October 2008. The rapid expansion of bank lending as part of the government's fiscal stimulus package not only placed banks' capital ratios under pressure[78] but also signalled a return to government-directed lending (total loan growth more than doubled from 2008 to 2009). By late 2009 there were signs of growing alarm in the CBRC, PBOC, and the leadership that the rapid growth of bank lending could produce a new wave of NPLs and economic overheating. The PBOC raised banks' reserve requirements and reduced lending quotas, and the CBRC issued a series of warnings that banks needed both to restrain lending and ensure that adequate risk assessment procedures were in place.[79] Worryingly for the authorities, these moves did little to reduce actual lending growth in the first quarter of 2010.

---

[77] "China's Bank Regulation Offers Needed Reassurance," *Wall Street Journal*, 30 November 2009.

[78] "China Banks Said to Submit Capital Raising Plans," *Bloomberg.com*, 24 November 2009.

[79] "China Raises Bank Reserve Requirements," *FT.com*, 12 January 2010.

The third factor that helps to explain the Chinese leadership's willingness and ability to sustain a gradualist approach to Basel convergence is the relatively low levels of politicization of banking regulation in China. The very nature of international standards has permitted less politicization: they have allowed the retention of Chinese sovereignty, and they had the important advantage that they were not urged upon China by the IMF or the United States (in contrast to the controversial issues of RMB revaluation and financial liberalization above and beyond China's WTO commitments). The fact that the rest of Asia was moving in the same direction from the late 1990s provided additional domestic political cover. It is possible that the agreement of China to participate in an FSAP review of its financial regulatory framework and the G20 agreement to assign the FSB the responsibility of conducting peer reviews of member implementation of international standards will threaten this in the future. At present, China's willingness to accept this monitoring indicates its growing self-confidence in this policy area and the relative lack of concern that China's financial regulatory reforms give other major countries.

Perhaps the most important contributor to low levels of politicization is the domestic political system. Although the more vigorous adoption of Basel standards since the late 1990s has been costly for some banks and related borrowers, the nature of the Chinese political system means that such opposition is more likely to be played out as informal non-compliance rather than as open objections to the government's policy. Such opposition included powerful factional elements within the Party-state apparatus that benefited from a system in which access to bank credit was determined by national and local political interests (Shih 2008). After the crisis of 2008–09, the decision not to emphasize the flaws of the Basel framework reflected the desire to maintain the pace of financial reform in the face of such opposition, which almost certainly intensified as economic growth fell.

This explanation of Chinese official attitudes towards the Basel framework emphasizes the primary importance of domestic economic and political objectives for the government and its regulatory agencies. As in the US case, however, international factors were not irrelevant. In fact, the role of international factors is almost certainly of greater importance for China than for the United States. The role of the Asian crisis of the late 1990s in motivating China's leadership to tackle financial reform more seriously is one indication of this. The concern of many developing countries that Basel II might constrain their ability to borrow abroad is not a drawback for China, whose government wishes to avoid any dependence on external borrowing. The pragmatic strategy of importing Western-style financial regulatory standards is also consistent with China's commitment to other international agreements, particularly the agreement under its negotiated WTO entry in 2001 to liberalize, though only very partially, its financial sector.

More important has been the growing significance of international markets for China's own major banks. Five of these are listed in Hong Kong, and although their international presence is currently limited, this may well expand rapidly in the future. In the meantime, adherence to Basel standards has made it easier for them to attract private investors and foreign managerial and risk management expertise. The SOCBs and some of the joint stock banks have in fact been very keen on the adoption of Basel II and IFRS, as well as raising their international profile by joining international banking organizations such as the IIF.[80] These banks have also been able to improve their credit ratings and increase their attractiveness vis-à-vis domestic competitors. Although it is unclear how much Basel II implementation will affect the cost of funding, ratings agencies do claim to take Basel II adoption into account when rating banks. The major Chinese banks also have relatively low leverage and are highly liquid, so that new Basel standards in these areas are unlikely to affect negatively their international competitiveness.[81] Their relative resilience through the global crisis of 2008–09 also suggests that they will be able to generate (through profits) or raise through new share issuance additional core equity capital without too much difficulty. In the end, however, these international factors have been important for China but not as significant as domestic motivations in explaining rising levels of behavioural consistency with Basel norms and standards.[82]

4 The Bilateral Relationship and Behavioural Consistency

The bilateral US-China relationship has played relatively little role in affecting the behavioural stance of either country towards the Basel

---

[80] On the now significant Chinese bank membership of the IIF, see IIF (2009: 49).

[81] "China's Bank Regulation Offers Needed Reassurance," *Wall Street Journal*, 30 November 2009.

[82] The Chinese case is thus inconsistent with accounts that emphasize the importance of external pressures on developing countries to adopt international standards (e.g., Soederberg, Menz, and Cerny 2005).

framework. For both sides, Basel standards are a relatively narrow and technical area of policy that to date has not been seen as important for their bilateral relationship. This has not been true for other financial issues, including Chinese official purchases of US Treasury debt and the sensitive issue of the access of US firms and capital to China's domestic financial market. Both issues have often been raised in bilateral dialogues.[83]

The comparatively low importance of Basel issues in the bilateral relationship is perhaps less true as regards the external assessment of compliance with international standards. As noted earlier, both countries had refused to submit to an external review of their compliance with international standards in the form of an IMF-World Bank FSAP, but both agreed to do so in 2008. They reaffirmed this in the G20 summits after the outbreak of the crisis, as well as their willingness to accept peer review and oversight of implementation by the FSB. Thus, on the issue of multilateral surveillance of national compliance with international standards, it seems likely that US non-participation in the FSAP programme – while it lasted – also reduced China's willingness to participate.

For the United States, the primary concern in the past has been the question of the adherence of other developed country banks to similar prudential regulations. Basel I was directed in particular at the Japanese and to some extent French banks, whereas the main concern of American banks in Basel II was that European banks be subject to broadly similar rules. Most recently, after the 2008–09 crisis, key debates over new international rules on increased levels of minimum capital and on limits on bank leverage appear mainly to have raised concerns about the relative effects on US and European banks. In this policy area, Chinese banks have not yet been perceived as sufficiently competitive to warrant much concern. But it seems likely that this will become less true over time.

For China, the picture is slightly different since from the late 1990s through 2007 the US financial regulatory system was seen as the exemplar towards which the Chinese financial system should gradually converge. This emulation strategy had little to do with the bilateral relationship as such, though US difficulties in achieving full implementation of Basel II probably also made it less urgent for China to be seen to be adopting Basel II. The Chinese halfway house of "Basel 1.5" outlined in 2004 sounded very similar to the Basel IA option being touted for smaller banks at the time in the United States, and the delayed US implementation schedule may also have given China more room for manoeuvre.

---

[83] Author interviews, Washington, DC, April 2009.

But the main motivation of the Chinese leadership has been to view the Basel framework on its own merits, primarily in terms of the pragmatic benefits it can bring to Chinese economic reform. These perceived net benefits remained even as faith in the superiority of American regulatory approaches was greatly eroded during 2008–09. Fang Xinghai, head of financial services regulation in Shanghai, said in late 2009 that the main difference between China's and America's approaches to financial regulation was that "in the US, the regulators don't believe in regulation to begin with."[84] As we have seen, this was probably an outdated view of US regulatory philosophy. But the lack of US commitment to adequate financial regulation in the past had proven to be dangerous for itself, the world economy, and thus for China, giving the latter a strong incentive to promote stronger regulation in the developed world through institutions like the G20, FSB, and BCBS. The irony of this new emerging country stance should not be lost on US officials, who only a decade ago saw global institutions primarily as a means of promoting stronger financial regulation in emerging countries (Walter 2008; Helleiner 2010).

5 Conclusion

For both the United States and China, initial decisions to adopt the Basel framework on banking regulation were initially motivated by relatively pragmatic considerations. Basel I provided a level playing field for all US banks and helped to resolve a difficult trade-off between financial stability and competitiveness objectives. For both, the costs of implementation were also limited, in the US case because banks had returned to profitability and in the Chinese case because of the flexibility of implementation. Over time, the increasing attachment of key US officials and banks to the third norm of market-based regulation increased the difficulty of implementation for the United States. Basel II is a case study in how the beliefs of some regulators enjoying a privileged position in an international forum of experts like the BCBS can produce an international agreement for which there is limited domestic political support. For China, this has not been a major drawback, since it has generally used the Basel framework – even though it played no role in its elaboration – more pragmatically as a means of promoting the reform of its major banks.

---

[84] "China's Bank Regulation Offers Needed Reassurance," *Wall Street Journal*, 30 November 2009.

Contestation over adoption and domestic implementation of international banking standards has been played out in China and the United States in very different ways. For China, the politicization of Basel has been very limited, but banking sector reform remains highly politically sensitive because of its direct relevance to the priority of growth and to concerns about its sustainability. The incompatibility between new bank regulations and the interests of key actors in the Chinese financial system, from local Party officials to large banks and SOEs, initially produced major implementation failures. These have diminished in scale and scope over time but they persist, as the response to the 2008–09 crisis demonstrated. In the case of the United States, political contestation is for the most part played out prior to formal adoption and implementation because of the much greater enforcement capacity of regulators, the courts and even the banks themselves. In the case of Basel II, this produced a long and drawn out battle over implementation that is far from over. This is not to say that regulatory avoidance is absent in the US case. American regulators still remain highly dependent upon most banks' voluntary convergence upon revisions to the Basel framework in coming years.[85] Without this, there is a real danger that these banks will simply find new ways to innovate around the rules.

The 2008–09 crisis was a major blow to the credibility and legitimacy of the Basel framework and to the US approach to financial regulation. It left the US banking system – and that of many other countries – seriously undercapitalized in ways that were never predicted by most proponents of model-based regulation. Only deft footwork on the part of the BCBS prevented it from being discredited altogether, and it remains to be seen whether the negotiation and implementation of new rules will be as difficult and contested as they have been in the past. The crisis was also a blow to the credibility of the Federal Reserve as both monetary policymaker and as senior bank regulator. Many members of Congress, including many Democrats, argued that its failures in the latter area strengthened the case for it to be stripped of its regulatory responsibilities entirely.[86] Both the Bush and Obama administrations, however, wished to

---

[85] Ayres and Braithwaite (1992) emphasize that effective regulation must rely on and provide strong incentives for voluntary compliance by regulated actors.

[86] The November 2009 version of the Senate Banking Committee's regulatory reform bill was the clearest example of this, though it contrasted with the Obama administration's and the House Financial Services Committee's proposals ("US Banks Bill Seeks to Strip Fed of Powers," *FT.com*, 10 November 2009). The Senate Committee later dropped this provision.

avoid this outcome and argued for a substantial enhancement of the Fed's system-wide regulatory powers and responsibility (US Treasury 2008a, 2009a). This view eventually prevailed, but critics of the framework were brought into the regulatory process, and criticisms that were expressed well before the crisis broke became mainstream.[87] Paradoxically, China emerged as a defender of the Basel framework and insisted that it is on track for implementation in spite of its own desperate efforts to maintain growth through an unprecedented expansion of bank lending.

---

[87] Governor Daniel K. Tarullo, "Modernizing Bank Supervision and Regulation," testimony before the Committee on Banking, Housing, and Urban Affairs, US Senate, Washington, DC, 19 March 2009.

7

Conclusion

*Behavioural Consistency and Its
Implications for Global Order*

This final chapter draws together our findings across the five issue areas, so as to determine the role that both China and the United States play in relation to global order. The first part provides a brief overview of the levels of behavioural consistency across the five global normative frameworks. The second part discusses how levels of behavioural consistency are best explained. The third part addresses the implications of our empirical findings and our analytical framework for the scholarly debate on norms and actor behaviour. The fourth and final part assesses the implications of our analysis for our understanding of the contemporary global order and its prospects.

1 Main Findings on Levels of Behavioural Consistency

Summarizing the main patterns of behavioural consistency is not straightforward given the complex and often substantial variations that we have described in the preceding five chapters. In order to identify the most important patterns in this complex picture, we outline here broad behavioural patterns first by country and second across issue areas. It should be emphasized that in this section we put to one side the often considerable level of domestic debate and contestation regarding national policy choices as well as many of the nuances of national behaviour. Our main goal is to generalize about dominant behavioural tendencies rather than to return to the complexities of national policy choices that received more attention in the previous five chapters. We do, however, return to this domestic contestation in the next section. Table 7.1 provides a summary of these dominant behavioural patterns for each of our five issue areas. It reveals a very mixed picture for both countries.

Since the reform era, China has moved from a position of generally low behavioural consistency towards gradually higher levels in the majority of the areas covered in this study. In no area is China's level of consistency comparable to the very highest levels of conformity found in international society. Beijing, for example, has been unwilling to place denuclearization in Iran and the DPRK consistently over other interests of direct importance to it. Nevertheless, the broad trend from a low starting point remains striking. Sometimes this higher level of conformity with global norms has come relatively cheaply and has reflected the low demands placed by particular global frameworks on China (the Kyoto Protocol being the clearest example). At other times, however, it has been more costly for important sections of Chinese society and politics.

The one main exception to the generalization of gradually improving behavioural consistency – macroeconomic policy surveillance – has seen levels of Chinese consistency fall from already moderate levels as the surveillance framework has become both more relevant and more constraining for China's domestic policy choices. This contrasts with the outcome in the other area of economic policy covered in our study, financial regulation, where levels of Chinese consistency have increased substantially over time as domestic reformers have chosen to use global norms strategically in their efforts to reform China's domestic financial system.

There has been no similar trend towards rising levels of behavioural consistency in the case of the United States, where the picture is much more mixed. The United States has continued to be an important source of norm elaboration and innovation in some areas: in the introduction of market mechanisms into climate protection, in constraining the operational remit of R2P, and in recent initiatives in financial regulation and multilateral economic surveillance. Sometimes, its behavioural consistency has been relatively high in part because it has come relatively cheaply (Basel I and parts of the international macroeconomic surveillance framework are examples). From an early stage, however, the United States has also exhibited a persistent tendency to depart periodically from global norms that it has helped to establish.

This long run inconsistency in US international behaviour is observable in a range of areas, both during and after the Cold War: the United States has sometimes chosen to exercise force unilaterally, to overlook the

TABLE 7.1. *Summary of Behavioural Patterns Across Five Issue Areas*

	Use of Force	Macroeconomic Policy	Nuclear Non-Proliferation	Climate Change	Financial Regulation
What are Global Norms?	1. No use of force except in self-defence; UN SC overriding role in response to use. 2. R2P: states' responsibility to protect citizens from gross violations; intervention (not necessarily military) can occur if the state manifestly fails to protect.	1. International surveillance over macro policy choices, especially exchange rates. 2. Balance in adjustment responsibilities between surplus and deficit countries.	1. Prescribed roles for nuclear and non-nuclear weapons states. 2. Export standards. 3. Inspection and regulatory regime. 4. Peaceful use of nuclear energy.	1. General agreement of anthropogenic harm 1992. 2. 1997 Kyoto: mandatory targets for advanced countries, national plans for developing countries. 3. Use of market mechanisms where possible.	1. Financial stability norm (minimum bank capital standards). 2. Competitiveness norm (level playing field). 3. Decentralized, market-based regulation.
Main features of the normative framework	1. UN Charter Articles 2(4) and 51 but subject to interpretation. 2. Framed at UN in 2005 World Summit outcome document and July 2009 debate where crimes specified and possible responses outlined. Still developing as norm. Vague on responses to gross violations.	1. Increasingly binding rules against unfair exchange rate policies; soft principles in other areas. 2. Highly contested exchange rate rules; weak enforcement. 3. Persuasion and peer pressure through multiple forums.	1. Made up of treaties, UN resolutions, inspection, restrictions on trade, domestic regulations. 2. Contested between NWS and NNWS as unequal bargain. 3. IAEA powers weak. 4. UN resolutions mandatory but difficult to enforce.	1. UN-based. 2. Soft at first; more specific from 1997 for developed world. 3. Highly contested distributive aspects. 4. Weak enforcement.	1. Soft, voluntary, increasingly specific, technocratic standards; third norm more contested. 2. Decentralized, weak enforcement. 3. Near-universal formal convergence (Basel 1); menu of options and differential implementation (Basel 2).

Levels of US consistency	Low (1); mixed on (2).	Low (1); higher on (2), primarily as regards other surplus countries.	Relatively high but periodically inconsistent (Pakistan, India, Israel).	Low generally; becoming higher in post-2006 period, but not Kyoto-compliant.	High on Basel I, moderate and partial on Basel II (delayed implementation).
Levels of Chinese consistency	Gradually higher consistency, especially since reform era (1). Conservative view of R2P but not blocking (2).	Initially moderate but not constraining; declining as constraints increase (1). Irrelevant until 2000s, now low (2).	Low initially, now higher with good domestic regulations, strong rhetoric. Reluctant to sanction: e.g., Iran and DPRK.	Little required of China, but has introduced domestic legislation, especially since 2007. 2009 promised a carbon mitigation strategy.	Low but rapidly improving on Basel I; gradual, partial implementation of Basel II on similar timetable to United States.

nuclear weapons capacities of friendly states, or to ignore IMF advice to reduce its fiscal deficits. In recent decades, it has withdrawn initial commitments to implement financial regulatory or climate protection agreements that it played an important part in shaping. This tendency was especially prominent in the post-9/11 years, and there was an identifiable tendency towards declining behavioural consistency across a number of issue areas during the George W. Bush period. But an over-emphasis on either 1990 or 2001 as major historical disjunctures would miss a broader and persistent tendency in US behaviour since at least 1945. The US stance towards global norms has been marked by selectivity as well as inconsistency. Selectivity has been evident in climate protection (compare US acceptance of the Montreal Protocol but rejection of Kyoto), macroeconomic policy surveillance (strong insistence on surplus country responsibilities but low willingness to accept adjustment costs itself), and humanitarian intervention/R2P (used to justify intervention in some countries but not others).[1]

In pointing to this time-inconsistency and selectivity in the US stance towards global normative frameworks, we are not claiming that America has been distinctively hypocritical. We do, however, reject the view that this identifiable tendency is noticeable simply because global regimes – and many other states and social groups – require more of the United States than of any other country. Even if expectations of US behaviour are often high, the formal constraints imposed by global normative frameworks on the United States are generally no greater than those that apply to other developed countries, most of which do not enjoy America's global influence. In some important areas, constraints are also broadly symmetrical for both developed and developing countries. For example, the formal normative constraints that apply to the United States are similar to those that apply to China and other developing countries as regards the use of force, nuclear non-proliferation, and Basel I.[2] Certainly, in areas like climate protection, global frameworks often do impose greater than average constraints upon the United States.[3] But in some other areas, such as

---

[1] Perhaps the best example of selectivity lies outside of our five cases: the United States promoted the principle of economic openness in the major post-war economic regimes, but it chose not to apply this principle to agriculture and textiles in the 1950s, became a heavy user of "administrative protection" from the 1970s, and still insisted that other countries reduce protective barriers that disadvantaged American firms and workers.

[2] This is also largely true in the area of the protection of human rights and in many aspects of global trade agreements.

[3] Some GATT and WTO obligations also apply the principle of special and differential treatment, which accords lower responsibilities to developing countries.

macroeconomic policy surveillance, the constraints on the United States have been considerably lower than for many countries.

As regards the degree of behavioural consistency of both states across different issue areas, it is important first to be clear about where no discernable patterns exist. There is no observable general tendency for behavioural consistency across issue areas to differ systematically according to whether they are primarily economic or primarily security related,[4] whether they exhibit greater rather than lesser longevity,[5] whether they exhibit greater or lesser symmetry of obligation for different states,[6] or whether they have higher or lower levels of content specificity.[7] There also appears to be no direct relationship between behaviour and frameworks that impose relatively binding obligations with centralized enforcement mechanisms. For example, Chinese and US levels of consistency with binding nuclear non-proliferation obligations have sometimes been relatively high, but this can also be said of their stance towards non-binding financial regulatory standards. There is also, importantly, no general tendency towards an inverse relationship between the two countries' respective stances towards global norms.

There is, however, a tendency for levels of behavioural consistency to be lower in areas that are of higher domestic social and political significance, an outcome that challenges the assumption that economic and security globalization inexorably leads to the imposition of severe constraints on domestic policy choices. This lack of consistency is especially clear as regards macroeconomic policy surveillance and climate protection, where both sides have strongly resisted commitments that would substantially constrain their domestic policy autonomy or impose significant economic costs on them. Although it might appear at first glance that financial regulation, which can have high domestic significance, is an important counterexample to this generalization, we argue in the next section that this is not the case.

To summarize, we have found that neither China nor the United States exhibit consistently high levels of behavioural conformity across

---

[4] For example, behavioural consistency is on average higher in international trade, financial regulation, nuclear non-proliferation, and the use of force than in macroeconomic policy surveillance.

[5] For example, consistency is relatively high in some frameworks that are long-standing (nuclear non-proliferation) and in some of relatively recent origin (financial regulation).

[6] For example, consistency has been relatively high in some symmetrical frameworks (Basel I) but lower in others (use of force).

[7] For example, consistency is low for the United States in one relatively specific framework (Kyoto) and higher in others (the WTO, Basel).

a range of global normative frameworks relevant to important areas of foreign and domestic policy. The stances of both countries towards such frameworks often differ substantially, though not inversely. Instead, for China, there has been a broad trend towards gradually rising levels of behavioural consistency, but with some important exceptions. For the United States, there has been no equivalent trend in either direction, but instead a general tendency towards important behavioural inconsistencies at particular times, accompanied by a willingness to defend these as justified whilst insisting that other countries abide more strictly by global behavioural norms. There is also a broad tendency for both countries to exhibit lower levels of behavioural consistency in areas of high domestic social and political significance. The next section investigates in more detail the factors that account for these results.

2 Explaining Levels of Behavioural Consistency

We argue that three factors have consistently been of greatest importance in producing the variation in the levels of behavioural consistency that we have summarized in the preceding section. These factors often interrelate and overlap, but for analytical purposes they can be seen as distinct. They are the level of domestic social and political significance that the framework has for each country; the extent to which it is perceived as procedurally legitimate and provides for a reasonably fair distribution of costs and benefits across countries; and the extent to which this distribution is perceived to affect the global power hierarchy, within which the bilateral relationship between China and the United States has become increasingly integral. The first factor addresses how global normative frameworks relate to domestic values, interests, and institutions, including whether the distributive aspects of these frameworks impose costs that are seen as acceptable *within* countries. The second and third factors also relate to the balance of costs and benefits, measured in both material and social terms, that are perceived to flow from the normative framework, but in particular *between* countries, not least between the United States and China themselves. We address each of these three factors.

The Level of Domestic Social and Political Significance

As already noted, global norms that have relatively high levels of domestic social and political significance are often associated with lower levels of behavioural consistency. This should not be surprising, since in such areas governments are often obliged to balance the incentives to follow global norms and associated rules against the constraints that domestic politics can impose. These constraints can easily create incentives to defect from global norms and rules. This is particularly likely to be the case if powerful domestic opponents can portray global norms as "intrusive," as conflicting with important domestic values and behavioural norms, or as imposing excessively high costs on particular groups or society as a whole. However, high domestic significance need not always be an obstacle to behavioural consistency, particularly if the latter allows the government to resolve domestic political conflicts or to achieve net benefits that are valued by particular interest groups or society at large. A corollary of this argument is that in the case of global frameworks that do not impose substantive costs on domestic society and institutions and do not have strong enforcement capacity, governments have greater autonomy to make behavioural choices based on other considerations, including the perceived appropriateness of the norm, its recognized legitimacy, and the strategic advantages that may flow from norm adherence.

This argument is reasonably straightforward, but we need to show how it is manifested in different ways for China and the United States, both in the empirical areas that we have covered in this study and in other important areas of global governance. We also need to account for two obvious potential anomalies, financial regulation and international trade (the latter not covered in depth in this study), both of which have high domestic significance but are associated with comparatively high consistency on both sides.[8] We begin with the United States because of the higher transparency of its political system and the greater degree of separation between social interests and political institutions there, before moving on to discuss the Chinese case.

Widely shared and deeply embedded domestic values can be powerful drivers of US political behaviour. The strong belief in the special legitimacy of US political institutions and processes can produce a deep reluctance to submit to constraint by international institutions and associated normative frameworks, even in cases where the United States has played a leading role in their establishment. This reluctance is especially strong for global norms that have high levels of domestic significance,

---

[8] Another possible partial anomaly exists in the more traditional foreign policy area relating to the limited use of force, which is characterized by relatively low domestic significance and (in the US case) uneven behavioural consistency. We take up this issue in the section on "Distributional Issues and the Global Power Hierarchy."

since it is in precisely these policy areas that Americans are most likely to believe that their own institutional processes – imbued with a high level of formal checks and balances – should have primacy. In these cases, global norms, often embodied in and enforced by international institutions that by US standards operate with much lower levels of democratic legitimacy, thus easily become, almost by definition, "intrusive" and of doubtful moral value.

This point, it should be noted, is complementary with but goes beyond the common institutionalist argument that domestic institutional processes characterized by high checks and balances can be an obstacle to international cooperation (Milner 1997; Tsebelis 2002). Congressional oversight and legislative functions, together with its openness to lobbies, have certainly made Congress critical in all our issue areas. Bureaucratic power and interest have been important in the creation of the non-proliferation framework (the ACDA), in the use of force decisions (the Defense Department), and in financial regulation (the Federal Reserve and Treasury). But Congress remains a key institutional actor and has often acted to reduce behavioural consistency in areas like climate change and international macroeconomic policy surveillance. This institutional complexity by itself is often a barrier to behavioural consistency, but we see it as especially important because of the high moral legitimacy accorded the US Constitution and separation of powers. In short, this is not simply a matter of resonance with local norms but also a recognition that those domestic values often interact with institutions in ways that limit the ability of the US government to commit credibly to global norms and associated rules.

This helps to resolve one of the paradoxes of the American relationship with global normative frameworks: that the time-inconsistency and selectivity noted previously is visible even for global frameworks that have been shaped in considerable part by US power. This is perhaps especially clear as regards global norms with direct ethical importance. America has long been known to be reluctant to permit jurisdiction to international human rights legislation within its own domestic laws (Ignatieff 2005). But it is also evident in other policy areas with high domestic significance, notably macroeconomic policy, which is also characterized by high institutional fragmentation. This makes it very difficult for the executive branch to reopen domestic policy bargains in international fora like the G7/8, G20, or IMF, though the United States is hardly unique in this respect (Webb 1995). What makes the United States different from Japan, Germany, and China is that even in situations of internal conflict over macroeconomic policy, domestic actors in the United States have much less incentive to try to use international constraints as a means of tipping the domestic policy debate in their favour.[9] This is partly due to America's unique power to force macroeconomic adjustment costs onto others, which we discuss later, but also because US politicians often find little domestic political advantage in playing "the international card" openly.[10]

There are similar tendencies in areas like climate protection, though in this case there has also been a lack of resonance between this global norm and the domestic norm of wilderness protection. This has meant that economic concerns, especially that strict and binding emissions constraints would threaten incomes and jobs, have often had primacy in domestic debates and have been an important constraint on the US government's ability to accept internationally negotiated targets – even when the executive branch has been committed to the UN process. The access of business groups that oppose such commitments to the federal policy process, and the ability of these and other opponents to appeal to other widely shared values (notably, the values of progress and enrichment through market-based economic growth) have reinforced such constraints.

We noted earlier that potential counterexamples to this argument can be found in financial regulation and international trade, where US behavioural consistency has been relatively high. We also argued, however, that high domestic significance need not be an obstacle to high consistency if consistency allows the government to resolve domestic political conflicts or to achieve net benefits for key interest groups or society as a whole. Although US politicians find it difficult explicitly to use international constraints as a means of resolving domestic political conflicts, they have often used them to achieve this in a less open way, especially when this offers substantial net benefits for important groups. In the area of international financial regulatory standard setting, the benefits to large US financial firms (reducing the costs of foreign financial competition and, in Basel II, promoting an approach to risk management they favoured) and to taxpayers (raising levels of capital in Basel I) were substantial. The same can be said of US attitudes towards reciprocal and binding

---

[9] For discussions of how Helmut Schmidt used external pressure to reshape German domestic economic policy in the late 1970s and how Japanese politicians have more often done the same, see Putnam (1988), Funabashi (1989), Schoppa (1993), and Webb (1995).

[10] Arguments that international commitments that effectively tie the hands of US policy-makers in areas like fiscal policy would be in the country's long run interest seem to ignore this difficulty (Bergsten 2009).

commitments in international trade, which have enabled politicians to mobilize pro-export interests, the main beneficiaries of such deals. This has provided an important counterbalance to protectionist domestic interests and enabled politicians to deliver cheaper imports that have raised voters' living standards.

It should also be noted that commitments to global frameworks have often also been attractive to US politicians and firms when they have been seen as constraining foreigners more than themselves. This view relates to the external counterpart of the authority accorded to US domestic institutions and policy processes: the idea of the United States as custodian and promoter of a just international order that prevents unjust war, protects against existential threats, promotes civil and political rights, and so on.[11] In relation to the use of force, for example, the United States was prominent in shaping that part of the UN Charter that defines the circumstances under which force can legitimately be used. Congress, too, at times legislated in ways that were intended to constrain South Asian countries from acquiring nuclear materials, with the consequence of raising levels of US behavioural consistency in nuclear non-proliferation. But the greater moral authority accorded to America's own political processes, and the tendency to see its own custodial role as permitting periodic deviations from international rules, have more often contributed to a mixed record of consistency on the use of force and nuclear non-proliferation. This also helps to explain why US political leaders have often seen their own actions as both legally compliant with and supportive of international rules in these areas, even when many outsiders have taken a very different view. Thus, important domestic political values and institutions have also interacted to promote selectivity and time-inconsistency in areas of relatively low direct political significance. As we show later, however, domestic factors are not always the dominant cause of inconsistency in these areas.

For China, domestic values and interests have sometimes also been a powerful constraint on behavioural consistency with global norms, but more often than in the US case they have promoted a rising though still incomplete level of consistency. The leadership's operating assumption is that the policy priority of economic growth is a broadly held societal

---

[11] It follows from this that global norms that lack a high level of US input are particularly likely to be deemed illegitimate. Kyoto was often portrayed by its domestic opponents as a European plot; during the Reagan years, parts of the UN system were seen as captured by a coalition of undemocratic developing countries (Krasner 1985).

value, as is the preference for social and political stability. This presumed value consensus is strongly supported by business and connected interests that have benefitted substantially from the economic opportunities provided in the reform era. This can sometimes limit China's behavioural consistency with global norms, as in the case of UN-mandated sanctions against valued economic partners like Iran. A particular conception of domestic interest has also clearly affected Chinese governmental behaviour in the area of human rights: signature of the core international treaties has not led to norm-consistent behaviour because the maintenance of the one-Party state has been given precedence over other concerns. In some areas, levels of behavioural consistency have fallen over time. This is clearest in international macroeconomic policy surveillance, which by 2005 was increasingly perceived as a threat to the growth priority.

However, this case of waning consistency has been exceptional. In other areas of high domestic significance, the growth priority has promoted rising behavioural conformity over time. The importance of this factor can be seen both in areas of global governance that constrain China little – the Kyoto treaty – as well as in areas that constrain it more substantially – the global trade and financial regulatory regimes. In these latter two areas, the perceived growth benefits of raising the efficiency and competitiveness of Chinese firms and of importing superior foreign industrial and regulatory technologies has been a crucial plank in the reformist strategy, even though this has been costly for some domestic interests (this tactic, as already noted, has not been open to most US politicians). The growth priority has also raised the incentives of the Chinese leadership to conform more closely to global norms in areas of lower domestic significance, including the use of force and nuclear non-proliferation. Fostering the perception that China's international intentions are benign and that partnership with China offers substantial mutual benefits is entirely consistent with this growth priority, as is the promotion of a more peaceful and stable global and regional environment. In all of these areas, however, China has not achieved full consistency and has often resisted attempts on the part of other actors to push it further and faster.

Domestic interests and institutions can also play a constraining role in China, particularly at the level of implementation. Weaknesses in domestic institutional frameworks have created considerable implementation gaps in financial regulation, climate change, trade liberalization, property and other rights protections, and the national treatment principle (the commitment to treat domestic and foreign firms on an equal footing). Sometimes these implementation failures are driven less by institutional weakness than by domestic institutional conflict. For example, as regards attitudes towards humanitarian intervention and in the commitment to the nuclear non-proliferation framework, the level of behavioural consistency has depended significantly on the power of the MOFA to override sometimes competing military and commercial interests. Such conflicts arise particularly when there is no elite consensus in support of the norm.

Domestic implementing institutions can be particularly challenged in cases where normative frameworks have high levels of content specificity. Such institutional weakness (as in the early stages of nuclear export controls in China), which substantially reduces the prospects for implementation, can be endogenous to the domestic political process. This can be because powerful actors are unconvinced about the legitimacy of the global framework and resist allocating resources and enforcement capacity to implementing agencies. Sometimes, such institutional weakness can result more from deeper institutional fragmentation and decentralization. This is clear in the decentralized US political system, but also in China where there are many opportunities for veto players to block progress and where national leaders must corral various levels of government to achieve policy consistency.

Global Normative Frameworks: Distributional Fairness and Legitimacy

We noted in Chapter 1 that much of the debate about norms and actor behaviour has revolved around the issue of whether norm-consistent behaviour is driven by instrumental cost-benefit calculations, by involuntary coercion (in cases where actors perceive negative net benefits), or by actors who perceive norms and associated rules as morally legitimate. We accepted the point made by Culpepper (2008) that these distinctions might be overly tight and that there was no a priori reason to presume that actors would *not* take material costs and benefits into account when making judgements about the moral legitimacy of norms and associated rules. Indeed, we allowed for the possibility that "the material benefits that may flow from behavioural consistency can reinforce this process of cognitive adaptation – we see no reason why social learning should not often be encouraged and accompanied by such material inducements."

We argue in this section that this possibility is much more than merely theoretical and that, in practice, it is impossible to separate Chinese and

US perceptions of the "appropriateness" of particular global normative frameworks from distributional considerations. We are not arguing that the perceived substantive distributive fairness of global normative frameworks is the only factor that determines whether their rules are seen as acceptable by domestic actors. The specificity of framework content, the extent to which global norms resonate with domestic norms and values, and the perceived legitimacy of framework procedures and enforcement mechanisms can all be important. Often, however, difficulties in these areas sharpen actor perceptions that in their substantive content, global normative frameworks are distributively unfair. Our empirical analysis leads us to conclude that it is in fact generally the case that global frameworks that are perceived to be very unfair in their distributional consequences are much less likely to induce behaviour that is consistent with the norm.

Our rationalization of this finding is that there will almost always be actors within countries like China or the United States who argue in favour of the proposition that global norms and rules with legal status or virtually universal acceptance deserve to be obeyed on the largely non-instrumental grounds that this will make the world a better place. But equally, there will almost always be others who argue on more narrowly instrumental grounds that the net costs of norm-consistent behaviour are too high. And this argument is more likely to be persuasive in a domestic context where there is a strong perception that the global framework does indeed distribute costs and benefits unfairly. Thus, distributional issues – including "material facts" – are integral to judgements about legitimacy and the distinction between instrumental cost-benefit motivations and "norm-driven" behaviour is a false one.

We can see this point more clearly in two cases where China and the United States have both exhibited relatively low levels of behavioural consistency. For the Chinese leadership, the international macroeconomic surveillance regime was seen by 2005–06 to impose an unacceptably large proportion of the costs of global adjustment on China. These costs were directly related to the perceived effects that substantial RMB revaluation would or could have on the leadership's priority of domestic income and employment growth. At the same time, the surveillance regime imposed few costs on other countries; in particular, it was noticeably ineffective in encouraging America to reduce its large fiscal deficit more quickly. To the extent that China decided in mid-2005 to accept moderate revaluation, it was gradual (so as to limit the risks this posed to growth) and instrumentally motivated in the sense that the decision was taken under the credible threat of a protectionist response from the major developed countries. China's vote against the 2007 Decision on Bilateral Surveillance, which it perceived as a Western attempt to target and stigmatize China's own policy choices, was also a strong signal that it saw the distributional bias of the regime as unfair, and that its associated procedures and enforcement mechanisms were unjust. Behavioural inconsistency in this case was therefore closely related to concerns about distributional and procedural unfairness, and that the United States and other developed countries were using the IMF as a tool to push adjustment costs onto China.[12]

The US position on climate change is similar to this case. The distributional bargain of the 1990s, as embodied in the Kyoto treaty, was perceived as highly unfair by Congress and large sections of American society. This perception was so strong because the norm conflicted with deeply held domestic values in favour of growth, because it did not resonate closely with the domestic norm of wilderness protection, and because it placed few constraints on countries whose emissions were growing most rapidly. The Clinton administration may not have shared this perception, but it was unable to persuade other important actors in the US domestic policymaking process that this distributional concern should be set aside on the *moral and instrumental* grounds that global catastrophe beckoned if US leadership on climate mitigation was not forthcoming. In this case, there was little that the international community could do to force US compliance except by proceeding with ratification as part of a dual strategy of moral shaming and trying to raise the material costs of rejection for particular American actors (primarily international business). Such efforts often sharpened the view of opponents in the United States that the UN framework was substantively unfair and procedurally illegitimate.

As these instances demonstrate, actor perceptions of fairness in distribution are closely related to perceptions of procedural legitimacy and symmetry of obligations and enforcement. Difficult questions of material fact are also very important in these kinds of moral judgement: how much do RMB undervaluation and US fiscal deficits contribute to global imbalances?; is China intentionally holding down its currency to promote export-led growth?; are coercive sanctions rather than positive incentives

---

[12] To give another example: in the case of China's signature in 1996 of the CTBT, it took hard argumentation to overcome expert opinion that if China stopped testing, it would cement China's subordinate position and the unfair strategic advantages enjoyed by the two major nuclear weapons states.

more likely to induce cooperative behaviour in non-compliant states?; are human-made emissions responsible for global warming?; how should historic contributions to the stock of greenhouse gases be measured?; how much will emissions constraint reduce growth?; and so on. Greater content specificity of normative frameworks can also heighten concerns about the provenance of the norm and whether it has procedural or substantive legitimacy. US concerns of this kind with the global climate protection framework were heightened by the very specific emissions limit that Kyoto would have imposed on it.

In cases where actors perceive the distribution of costs and benefits to be reasonably fair, they are more likely to be persuaded that norm-consistent behaviour is acceptable. In such situations, the moral argument that norm-consistent behaviour will produce a more secure and better world has greater chance of being persuasive, though it may take time for significant political actors to reach this understanding. We can see this in areas such as nuclear non-proliferation, where China initially signed up for a variety of instrumental reasons, but now has implemented a series of domestic regulations and institutional reforms that suggest greater internalization of the more solidarist arguments against nuclear proliferation. Such arguments have also been compelling at certain times for key actors in the US policy process, even when the administration has chosen to set them aside and depart from the norm. The arguments for setting the norm aside have often obliged the government (as, for example, in the US-India nuclear deal in 2005–06) to explain why this would in fact contribute to rather than detract from global order.

Distributional Issues and the Global Power Hierarchy
In our discussion so far, we have considered how actor behaviour is related to perceptions of the distributive and procedural fairness of global normative frameworks. This discussion has been largely confined to how such frameworks distribute costs in order to obtain certain public benefits (e.g., is the assignment of costs in the Kyoto treaty likely to produce both a fair and an effective climate protection regime?). We need to widen the discussion at this point because actors assess the distributive consequences of global frameworks not only in these terms. They also assess how the distributive implications of normative frameworks affect their social position generally.

Here, we are not arguing that states are primarily concerned with how the distributional consequences of any global bargain affect their relative power (cf. Grieco 1990). We have already argued that for these two powerful states, domestic values, interests, and institutions matter greatly in explaining levels of behavioural consistency with global norms and that their perceptions of the distributional fairness of these norms are often crucial. However, the positions of China and the United States in the global power hierarchy – positions that may be determined by a combination of material power as well as reputational, image, and legitimacy concerns – also shape their stances towards global normative frameworks. This is especially true in areas where their governments have higher levels of autonomy from domestic social and political constraints.

America's position at the peak of this hierarchy is an important factor in explaining the tendency towards time-inconsistency and selectivity that we have observed. We argued earlier that this is partly due to its domestic values (exceptionalism and its counterpart of global custodianship) and its domestic institutions (checks and balances, interest group access to the policymaking process). But it is important to understand how these domestic-level pressures on US policymakers interact with America's power position to produce strong incentives to step outside of multilateral frameworks to achieve instrumental goals and, sometimes, to reshape these frameworks. The unrivalled ability of the United States to exert substantial leverage over other countries through bilateral negotiations (including the SED), to shift costs onto other countries in existing groupings such as the G7, to exert influence within multilateral institutions (from the UN to the IMF), and to convene new groupings for international or domestic political advantage (e.g., the MEF and G20) gives it a range of options available to no other country. Sometimes, domestic legislation requires the US government to utilize these options to achieve national advantage even at the expense of multilateralism and associated behavioural norms (the 1988 Trade and Competitiveness Act is the classic example).

In more traditional foreign policy areas like the use of force for limited purposes and nuclear non-proliferation, the US executive branch often has somewhat greater autonomy from these domestic constraints. This is far from complete, of course: the rise of terrorist threats and then the actual attacks of September 2001 on America's own territory reinforced the executive branch's moves towards counter-proliferation and preventive uses of force. Nevertheless, overall in these areas the executive is relatively more autonomous. Yet even here this autonomy has sometimes been a source of behavioural inconsistency and selectivity. When the United States has chosen to depart from global norms and rules, for reasons of instrumental self-interest and/or higher reasons of global custodianship, it has mattered greatly that unlike almost all other countries it also possesses the relative power to do this. The difficulty other actors have in constraining the United States increases America's incentive to depart from global norms.

Indeed, given the combination of America's unrivalled global power position and the strong pressures exerted by its domestic political processes, it is perhaps surprising that we see as much behavioural consistency as we do from the United States. Here, we argue that concerns over reputation do limit US ambivalence towards global rules in important normative areas. These reputational constraints are simultaneously global and domestic. Many Democratic members of Congress, and both main Democratic contenders in the 2008 Presidential elections, spoke of the need to restore America's damaged reputation as a means of putting the United States once again at the forefront of global leadership. Their advocacy of soft or smart power reflected the view that America could achieve more – and perhaps that it could once again help to achieve a better world – if it had willing followers convinced of America's moral and legitimate authority. These arguments resonate strongly with America's self-image as a moral actor and force for good in the global system. As the effect of the George W. Bush administration's initial climate change policies on local and regional political actors also demonstrated, America's pluralist political system can produce domestic countermovements that can also promote greater consistency with global norms. This example also demonstrates, however, that these reputational constraints have generally been insufficient to prevent periodic behavioural lapses.

For China, with its strong perception of its rising but still secondary status within the global hierarchy, there are more powerful incentives to avoid gaining a reputation for selectivity and time-inconsistency. This is not just a matter for China of obtaining relatively immediate and direct benefits from international cooperation. China's leadership has an evident desire to be perceived by others as a peaceful, non-threatening country and a responsible great power. Its involvement in UN PKOs, its signature of the NPT and CTBT, and its acceptance of the UN Charter and the 2005 World Summit Outcome document as authoritative texts are examples of this signalling and suggest that concerns about international image have been strong prompts behind China's commitment to many global order norms.

All this is entirely consistent with the view that China's actions are motivated mainly by a mixture of "specific" and "diffuse" instrumentalism: that behavioural consistency can provide both direct and indirect benefits. Being seen as a responsible great power will help China to gain space for its economic development, to discourage others from attempting to destabilize its political system or to constrain its choices, and to improve its own status and legitimacy – both in the eyes of its own citizens and in the eyes of others. Generally, gaining a reputation for rule abidance might facilitate positive reciprocation by other actors in different areas and at different times.[13] Such diffuse instrumentalism need not require complete consistency with global norms and rules; indeed, the acquisition of a general reputation for responsibility and norm-consistent behaviour might permit some behavioural divergence in particular areas. At times, the government appears straightforwardly willing to diverge from particular rules that are seen as unfair and excessively damaging to key Chinese interests, sometimes using its developing status as a tool to deflect external demands and to reduce the reputational and other costs divergence entails. Increasingly, it has emphasized the consistency between its own policy priorities, notably growth, and the requirements of global order.[14] The fact that other great powers, particularly the United States, have far from perfect reputations in this respect also reduces the bar that China needs to reach to achieve these reputational benefits.

Diffuse instrumentalism need not be the only reason for a growing tendency for norm-consistent behaviour. As mentioned already, in any country there will always be those who argue that global norms and rules should be observed because they are legitimate and because this underpins global order – and there is no reason why both kinds of motivation might not be relevant to political decisions. As General Pan Zhenqiang put it in 2008, the immorality and illegality of nuclear weapons were important underpinnings of the non-proliferation norm and of the need for strong export controls (Pan 2008: 68–9). It is unlikely, however, that solidarist arguments of this kind are decisive within the Chinese leadership any more than in America's; generally, they will fail unless bolstered by others of a more instrumentalist kind.

This is in part because there are also those – not least within the military in both countries – that have come to assess the distributional

---

[13] This relates to what has been called "diffuse," as opposed to "specific," reciprocity (see Keohane 1986). For a discussion of how this is conceptually distinct from norm-driven behaviour, see Buchanan and Keohane (2006: 409–12).

[14] In 2009, the Chinese leadership emphasized the contribution of Chinese growth and RMB stability to global economic stability. As Quah (2010) argues, the first claim has become increasingly plausible.

consequences of global norms, and the question of whether they should be abided by, in increasingly bilateral terms. This bilateral focus can induce considerable suspicion about the motives of the other and harm the prospects for norm-consistent behaviour on both sides. The increasingly bilateral focus of climate and macroeconomic policy has inhibited cooperation and norm building in these areas, sometimes providing an easy excuse for domestic opponents to oppose such action. Even in cases of norm-consistent behaviour, important voices on both sides interpret the other's motives as purely instrumental and as including the objective of shifting the bilateral power balance in their favour. Periodic behavioural lapses by the other further erode the legitimacy of global norms and increase the tendency to judge their merits in instrumental terms.

Of course, there are exceptions to this: the growing importance of the bilateral relationship does not always act to erode global normative frameworks and the willingness to cooperate. First, for the United States, the bilateral relationship with China is only one consideration among many in economics and in more traditional foreign policy matters. China might be viewed as the potential main long-term strategic competitor by the Pentagon, but the pressing reality of other threats – particularly those relating to terrorist attack – have undercut the dominance of this perspective. Second, even when China has been the main concern, the United States has sometimes responded to what it has seen as recalcitrant Chinese behaviour by strengthening global normative frameworks (the nuclear non-proliferation treaty, nuclear export regulations, and the 2007 Decision on Bilateral Surveillance are examples, though in the latter case at least it deterred higher Chinese consistency).

Third, the bilateral relationship has become one of complex interdependence, which has given each side incentives to maintain a reasonable degree of consistency with global norms and to offer quid pro quos across issue areas. Trade is one standard example of such interdependence, but so too is macroeconomics: America's rising dependence on Chinese financing in recent years and the growing dependence of US firms on Chinese sourcing has made the government more reluctant to press China aggressively on revaluation and encouraged the Bush and Obama administrations to rely more heavily than they might otherwise have done on the international surveillance framework. The US desire for Chinese support for its anti-terrorist campaign made Washington more reluctant to allow Taiwan to rock the boat by pushing its independence agenda.

The bilateral relationship often has operated differently for China given its secondary status and because the United States has always loomed much larger for China than vice versa. Even so, it has sometimes also promoted cooperative behaviour by China, or as expressed in the strategic guideline encouraged it to "develop cooperation and avoid confrontation" (quoted in Medeiros 2009: 98). The strong perception of US superpower status (at least until the global economic crisis of 2008–09) has often made China more willing to emulate American practices and to pursue policies that permit it to import US technology. On the use of force, Chinese perceptions of US superiority and America's strategic depth in Asia have also been a reason to retain a pacific stance – though it has also encouraged China to build a military capacity that will restrict US strategic options. China's asymmetric dependence on the US export market remains sufficiently large that it has incentives to cooperate in a range of other areas (from currency politics to nuclear non-proliferation). Again, there is evidence here of positive spillover from one issue area to another.

Nevertheless, while these kinds of exceptions need to be borne in mind, on balance, the growing importance of the bilateral relationship has probably eroded the willingness of both to accept global normative frameworks as legitimate standards of appropriate behaviour. This in turn can reduce the legitimacy of global norms for other actors with potentially important implications for global order – a point we take up in Section 4. The relationship can also provide incentives for non-cooperative behaviour on both sides, which can lead to negative spillover into other issue areas. Furthermore, the incentives for cooperation created by complex bilateral interdependence have been too weak to date to resolve key global order problems from climate change to macroeconomic coordination.

To conclude this discussion of the factors that drive behavioural convergence with global norms for our two states, do domestic or international factors matter most? Our answer is that this depends substantially on the scope and content of global order norms and that, in fact, there is a complex and unavoidable relationship between the two levels. The highest levels of behavioural *in*consistency are found when there is a combination of high domestic societal costs, relative strategic loss, and low levels of international distributive fairness (as in the cases of macroeconomic surveillance and climate change). In issue areas where the domestic implications are more diffuse (as in use of force and nuclear non-proliferation) behavioural consistency is higher when approximate conformity does not raise perceptions of fairness and strategic cost to unacceptable levels.

3 Norms and Actor Behaviour: The Scholarly Debate

What do our empirical findings and our explanatory framework add to the scholarly debate about the importance of norms in global politics and economics? Certainly for the two important countries that we have considered in this book, norms and actors in the global system are mutually constitutive. Norms can be reinterpreted or contested and thereby evolve over time. This inevitably limits the extent to which they are constraining on the most powerful actors, particularly great powers, who have more scope than others to shape their evolution and interpretation. Nevertheless, norms are not infinitely malleable and their associated international rules and standards can be difficult for any single actor to change or dislodge. This creates a strong element of inertia in the global normative order such that even the strongest states will find that their preferences in particular situations will diverge from the norms, rules, and standards that they help to shape. For this reason, it is sensible to ask how much they are constrained by global norms.

Our exploration of five important issue areas does not lead us to the simple conclusion that norms cause certain behavioural outcomes. What it does show, however, is that global norms remain an inescapable and important part of the decision-making environment, even on issues where we show domestic factors have been decisive in shaping the behaviour of these two states. We thus disagree with the argument that the most powerful states – above all the United States – are able to stand entirely outside of global normative constraints because of their material power. Even for the most important actors, norms often serve as benchmarks or as framing devices around which domestic and international interactions and negotiations revolve. Actors also use norms strategically and for purposes for which they were not directly designed (to enhance social status and international image, for example). They use them to rebuke the behaviour of others and to cast doubt on the legitimacy of their words or deeds.

For example, the United States' attempts to reinterpret norms in areas like climate change and the use of force during the George W. Bush administration failed because other actors – both international and domestic – were able to defend global norms, to compel the administration to provide justifications that addressed them, and ultimately to force the United States to embark on courses of foreign policy action that demonstrated its lack of substantial international support. In the case of China, the social power of norms as signalling tools has heightened the influence of, for example, NAM opinion on Beijing in relation to the nuclear non-proliferation norm. China's self-identification as a responsible great power has led to presentational and behavioural changes in reference to R2P, UN peacekeeping, and even climate change. Its strong rhetorical support for the UN Charter is sometimes used as a weapon to criticize US behaviour it views as inconsistent with global norms – Kosovo in 1999 being one example. Much of this type of behaviour increases cynicism about norms, both among scholars and in global politics, and may reduce their moral authority. But the fact that states still see value in using norms for these various purposes suggests they retain considerable social importance in the global system.

Nevertheless, in broad terms, Brooks and Wohlforth (2008) are right to point to the limits of the constraining effects of global norms, particularly for the United States. Global norms may be an inescapable reality even for the most powerful states, but they are not sufficient in themselves to produce behavioural conformity. For example, global norms will tend to be trumped where deeply held domestic societal values do not resonate with them, and they will be more influential in constraining great power behaviour when they are adapted by norm entrepreneurs to fit with existing domestic norms and societal values (Cortell and Davis 2005: 23–4; Acharya 2009). When both governments came to be more concerned about energy efficiency and energy independence, both became somewhat more flexible in climate change negotiations. For Beijing, financial regulatory frameworks were acceptable because domestic banking reform resonated with the growth priority.

Our argument also leads us to the conclusion that the procedures and enforcement mechanisms attached to most global normative frameworks are not the key to understanding the sources of behaviour that produce global order, as some realists would claim. Rather, behavioural consistency is more dependent on the extent to which actors perceive global norms, rules, and procedures as legitimate. Such legitimacy in turn depends to a considerable extent on questions of representativeness, on fairness in procedure, and on the distribution of costs and benefits. In areas where global normative frameworks have high domestic social and political significance, it is often difficult for governments to escape the constraints that domestic distributional considerations can entail.

Behavioural convergence in such cases will require governments to compensate losers or to override them.[15] In more traditional areas of foreign policy, distributional fairness is more often perceived in interstate terms, but it remains important.

The importance of distributive fairness also makes it more difficult to distinguish in practice than in theory between moral and instrumental motivations for norm-following, or between norms and material facts (Hurrell 2005: 16; Buchanan and Keohane 2006: 409). Normative frameworks have unavoidable material and social distributional consequences, whether these are primarily domestic in nature or international. Governments are compelled to listen to complaints from well-organized domestic interest groups who may lose from norm-following, or from military or foreign policy elites who fear their consequences for national autonomy and global influence.

This, it seems to us, is often more important than the question of whether particular actors are norm makers or norm takers. For China, more often in the position of being a norm-taker than a norm-maker, the questions of distributive fairness, legitimate procedure, and consistency with domestic policy norms and priorities have been much more important than whether it had substantive input into the process of norm creation. The United States has historically been unwilling to abide by rules and norms set by others, but it has also been unwilling to abide consistently by rules that it played a central role in establishing, the nonproliferation of nuclear weapons being one example.

4 Global Order and Its Prospects

We have argued that the United States and China are both crucial to global order, despite the large asymmetries in their relative power and in the roles they have played respectively in generating or constituting global normative frameworks. The US role in constituting global order has been especially important, particularly since 1945. But the enhancement of China's importance has rested in part on the distinctive rapidity of China's growth, the centrality that the United States and China have come to accord to each other, and their evident constitutive relationship with several key global order norms. For example, as we have

---

[15] An attempted example of the former is the 2009–10 emissions reduction legislation promoted by the Democratic political leadership in the House and Senate, which envisaged large subsidies to energy-intensive sectors.

shown, neither can fundamentally address climate change without taking the other into account, and other actors believe that if both commit to addressing the problem of temperature rise another critical layer to the global norm of climate protection could be added. In the area of macroeconomic surveillance, if the two states were to follow through on their November 2009 agreed statement to "pursue policies of adjusting domestic demand and relative prices to lead to more sustainable and balanced trade and growth,"[16] this could have important and positive consequences for the future stability of the global economy.

Although we have emphasized areas of inconsistency in these two states' behaviour with respect to global norms, we have also shown that these norms form an unavoidable part of the global political landscape and that these two states cannot stand outside of these frameworks. Global norms address real and unavoidable problems in global governance. As we have additionally argued, the central issue with respect to the ordering function of these norms in global society relates to their perceived legitimacy. Thus, two important conditions for the consolidation of global norms are widespread perceptions of procedural legitimacy and of fairness in the distribution of costs and benefits. Even where a global norm may be perceived as intrinsically representative of rightful behaviour, since legitimacy can be understood as shared understanding, procedure and distributive consequences inevitably matter. As regards the latter, perceived fairness within and between countries is important. Furthermore, we have also found that there is a third important condition of normative legitimacy: the ability of political actors to perceive, or to be willing to help graft, a relationship between global and domestic norms.

Those political actors that can be said to contribute to global order, on the basis of this finding, are those that pay attention to these aspects of legitimate procedure and fairness of burden. But it is also essential that they be attentive to the possibilities for correspondence between their own interests and global norms in ways that appeal to societies beyond their own. In the circumstances where these three aspects are attended to, global norms will strengthen and global order is more likely to operate in ways that allow us to "live together relatively well in one planet."[17] On the other hand, global norms will be damaged where the bases of contestation are not addressed, where more parochial strategic interests

---

[16] "U.S.-China Joint Statement, Beijing, China," 17 November 2009, The White House, Office of the Press Secretary.

[17] In the formulation of Raymond Aron, quoted in Hurrell (2007: 2).

regularly overwhelm the global normative requirements, or where the nature of the global norm is created and elaborated in ways that favour the values of an individual or narrow coalitions.

In this regard, these two crucial states – for different reasons – create particular challenges for the maintenance and enhancement of global order. The United States has sometimes led, sometimes blocked, but almost always influenced the development and elaboration of global order norms since the early twentieth century. Many still look to it for leadership despite the travails of recent years. This reliance arises mainly from its material wealth but also from what might be termed habit and expectation: the United States has been a predominant power and enjoyed periods of hegemonic leadership since 1945, especially in the Cold War years and with respect to its allies. But its preponderance and its confidence in the resonance between its domestic values and those of global society have often made it inattentive to the three features relating to legitimacy referred to earlier. Many global institutional procedures and distributive outcomes are still associated by others with American domi-nance, and the reluctance to recognize the validity of competing values has also limited the global legitimacy of US initiatives. Thus, although there is a powerful solidarist tradition in US foreign policy, its domi-nant form has often alienated rather than won over those actors who are naturally suspicious of its values and its power.

Strikingly, given that many still see the contemporary global order as associated with American values and power, China's generally rising lev-els of behavioural consistency within it have been driven by a reasonably strong association between domestic values and some global norms. This has been prompted to a large extent by the willingness of reformers in the Chinese leadership to reshape and refocus domestic societal and political values in ways that are more consistent with existing global order norms (exceptions to which include the areas of civil and political rights and democratic forms of domestic governance). The success of this adaptation process to date has been extraordinary for poverty reduction in China and for global growth, but its effects on global order are ambiguous, and sometimes damaging. The multiple imbalances in China's growth model are recognized by the leadership but it appears to lack effective solutions to them. Beijing has often defined its contributions to global order in relatively parochial ways and has shown a preference for conservative incrementalism in order to test out the implications of normative crea-tion and evolution for its own concerns. It has not yet readily embraced a leadership role in relation to global order problems. Neither, however, does its conservatism form a basis for a radical rewriting of the rules of global order – and relatively few would want to see China engage in this radical rewriting. Its overall approach may certainly affect the direction and speed of travel for global norms – and these directions are likely to become plainer as it becomes more powerful. But its preference for adaptation will also continue to constrain any attempt to launch an outright challenge to global order norms for some time to come.[18]

Yet for neither state can we leave the discussion here. Both operate within a global society of far greater complexity than a focus on the bilateral relationship or the individual state's relationship with global norms conveys. While the United States adjusts to China's resurgence, there are also other newly resurgent or rising states that are capable to varying degrees of mounting economic or strategic challenges to both Washington and Beijing. The European Union has shown a capacity not only to shape the course of global trade negotiations but also to set the regulatory standards in areas as diverse as climate change, food security, industrial technology, and privacy protection. And non-state groupings and processes – from extremist groups to human rights organizations and financial markets – at one level imply a diffusion of power in global society, but at another level that these two states have to mediate a range of events and pressures difficult to comprehend let alone to control.

For China, its global ordering preference might rest on the survival of a pluralist society of sovereign states; however, much of its recent experience has forced it to move beyond that understanding. Thus, although it might prefer to protect the principle of non-intervention in domestic affairs, a flood of Burmese and North Korean refugees into its own territory, an increased need for UN peacekeeping, and a demand for a response to a humanitarian disaster overseas have all required innovation and adaptation in reference to this principle. The importance of exports, foreign capital, and technology in its growth model has forced China to commit itself to a range of global economic agreements and rule out a return to autarky. Climate change is ineluctably affecting the human security of its citizens and thus impinging on its core interests in stability and growth. Pluralism, then, has adapted when up against real world

---

[18] As Wen Jiabao put it in September 2008 in reply to Fareed Zakaria's question as to why China did not play a more active role in managing world problems: "China is NOT a superpower [but] remains a developing country ... To address our own problems, we need to do a great deal ... That's why we need to focus on our own development." "Transcript of Interview with Chinese Premier Wen Jiabao," http://www.cnn.com/2008/WORLD/asiapcf/09/29/chinese.premier.transcript/index.html, accessed 27 March 2010.

order problems, but often in ways that suggest great caution: China's inherent conservatism leaves it in a halfway house that creates tensions in domestic society and politics and that provides unsatisfactory answers to some pressing global problems.

For the United States, too, even though it has been more attracted to solidarist conceptions of global order than China, it has found that preponderant material power is insufficient to promote its conceptions and address certain of its core interests. Maintaining freedom of strategic action has not been an effective solution to such concerns as countering nuclear proliferation, terrorism, or criminal drug networks and it has come at the cost of eroding the legitimacy of global norms and institutions. The policy adjustments in George W. Bush's second term, together with the election of Barack Obama appeared to be in part an implicit acknowledgement that unilateralism had failed and that US primacy had to be wedded to legitimacy in order to tackle complex global governance issues. In the more globalized post–Cold War era, an America wielding "smarter" power seemed to stand a better chance of persuading a far larger grouping of political actors to address collective problems. Yet the long historical legacy of US selectivity and inconsistency is proving difficult to erase and, as we have seen, has its roots in enduring aspects of domestic US politics and society.

As we have also argued, there are certain ways in which the US-China bilateral relationship can facilitate or constrain a more cosmopolitan understanding of global order. There is, for example, a degree of emulation in play that can operate positively in addressing global governance problems. At one level, this is how we could interpret President Hu Jintao's decision to become in September 2009 the first Chinese President ever to address the UN General Assembly – and his topic was climate change – as well as President Obama's chairing, also for the first time ever by a US President, of a 2009 UN Security Council session on nuclear non-proliferation and nuclear disarmament. Complex economic interdependence has also encouraged both governments to utilize the relevant norms in trade and finance as a way of mediating disputes. The cases of Iran and North Korea and their putative and actual nuclear weapons programmes, though resolved to neither the United States' or China's satisfaction so far, has generated a more intense debate between them about the threats that actual proliferation in neighbourhoods of significance to both actors actually pose.

From an optimistic reading, these common experiences and interests could provide the basis for enhancing global order. They rely on an understanding that the challenges of global governance will not lessen and that these respective states' rhetoric in reference to these challenges – that we share a common fate and that one group cannot prosper at the expense of the other – have to be acted upon. This will require a willingness on the United States' side to rewrite past unequal bargains that have become entrenched and a willingness on the Chinese side to accept that incrementalism and parochialism can be an obstacle to meeting global challenges. There are two main alternatives. One is a continued erosion of more solidarist conceptions of legitimacy and a focus on the specific and diffuse instrumental benefits that can be obtained from ad hoc cooperation. This option is attractive to many influential actors in both countries but is likely to become increasingly frustrating to outsiders and to significant segments of domestic society. A second alternative is also possible and even less appealing: a global order based on a narrow conception of strategic rivalry at a time of perceived political and economic transition. The perception in some quarters that the global and bilateral power balance is shifting rapidly raises the likelihood of this outcome. If this perception becomes more widespread, the negative spiral this could set in train would further impoverish and endanger global society and deny resolution of the major collective action problems that confront us all.

Bibliography

Acharya, Amitav. 2009. *Whose Ideas Matter? Agency and Power in Asian Regionalism*. Ithaca, NY: Cornell University Press.

Alagappa, Muthiah. 2003. "The Study of International Order: An Analytical Framework." *In*: Muthiah Alagappa (ed.) *Asian Security Order: Instrumental and Normative Features*. Stanford, CA: Stanford University Press, 33–69.

2008. "Introduction: Investigating Nuclear Weapons in a New Era." *In*: Muthiah Alagappa (ed.) *The Long Shadow: Nuclear Weapons and Security in 21st Century Asia*. Stanford, CA: Stanford University Press, 1–34.

Albright, David and Paul Brannan. 2008. "Indian Nuclear Export Controls and Information Security: Important Questions Remain." Institute for Science and International Security, *ISIS Report*, 18 September.

Albright, David and Andrea Stricker, 2010. "After the 2010 NPT Review Conference: Advancing the Non-Proliferation Pillar." Institute for Science and International Security, *ISIS Report*, 15 July.

Albright, David, Paul Brannan, and Andrea Scheel Stricker. 2009. "Self-Serving Leaks from the A.Q. Khan Circle." Institute for Science and International Security, *ISIS Report*, 9 December.

Andreani, Gilles. 1999–2000. "The Disarray of US Non-Proliferation Policy." *Survival* 41(4), 42–61.

Angklomkliew, Sarawan, Jason George, and Frank Packer. 2009. "Issues and Developments in Loan Loss Provisioning: The Case of Asia." *BIS Quarterly Review*, December, 69–83.

Annan, Kofi A. 1999. *The Question of Intervention: Statements by the Secretary-General*. New York: United Nations Department of Public Information.

Anthony, Ian. 2008. "Civilian Nuclear Cooperation: An Indian Exemption?" *European Security Review* 40, September, 16–21.

Anthony, Ian, Christer Ahlstrom, and Vitaly Fedchenko. 2007. *Reforming Nuclear Export Controls: The Future of the Nuclear Suppliers Group*. Oxford: Oxford University Press for SIPRI.

Arend, Anthony Clark and Robert J. Beck. 1993. *International Law and the Use of Force*. London: Routledge.

Aron, Raymond. 1974. *The Imperial Republic*. Englewood Cliffs, NJ: Prentice Hall.

Ayres, Ian and John Braithwaite. 1992. *Responsive Regulation: Transcending the Deregulation Debate*. New York: Oxford University Press.

Barth, James R., Gerard Caprio, Jr., and Ross Levine. 2007. "Banking Regulation and Supervision Database." World Bank, July. http://go.worldbank.org/SNUSW978P0.

BCBS (Basel Committee on Banking Supervision). 1988. *International Convergence of Capital Measurement and Capital Standards*. Basel: BCBS, July.

　1999. *A New Capital Adequacy Framework. Consultative Paper*. Basel: BCBS, June.

　2004. *Basel II: International Convergence of Capital Measurement and Capital Standards: a Revised Framework*. Basel: BCBS, June.

　2006. *International Convergence of Capital Measurement and Capital Standards: A Revised Framework, Comprehensive Version*. Basel: BCBS, June.

　2009a. *Enhancements to the Basel II Framework*. Basel: BCBS, July.

　2009b. *Revisions to the Basel II Market Risk Framework*. Basel: BCBS, July.

　2009c. *Strengthening the Resilience of the Banking Sector: Consultative Document*. Basel: BCBS, 17 December.

　2010. "Annex" to "The Group of Governors and Heads of Supervision Reach Broad Agreement on Basel Committee Capital and Liquidity Reform Package." BCBS Press Release. Basel: BCBS, 26 July.

Bellamy, Alex J. 2006. "Whither the Responsibility to Protect? Humanitarian Intervention and the 2005 World Summit." *Ethics and International Affairs* 20(2), 143–69.

　2008a. "Conflict Prevention and the Responsibility to Protect." *Global Governance* 14(2), 135–56.

　2008b. "R2P and the Problem of Military Intervention." *International Affairs* 84(4), 615–40.

Bergsten, C. Fred. 2008. "A Partnership of Equals: How Washington Should Respond to China's Economic Challenge." *Foreign Affairs* 87(4), 57–69.

　2009. "The Dollar and the Deficits." *Foreign Affairs* 88(6), 20–9.

Bergsten, C. Fred, et al. 2008. *China's Rise: Challenges and Opportunities*. Washington, DC: Peterson Institute for International Economics.

Bernanke, Ben. 2005. "The Global Saving Glut and the US Current Account Deficit." Sandridge Lecture, Virginia Association of Economics, Richmond, VA. 10 March. http://www.federalreserve.gov/boarddocs/speeches/2005/200503102/default.htm.

Bernstein, Steve. 2001. *The Compromise of Liberal Environmentalism*. New York: Columbia University Press.

　2002. "Liberal Environmentalism and Global Environmental Governance." *Global Environmental Politics* 2(3), 1–16.

Bobbitt, Philip. 2008. *Terror and Consent: The Wars for the Twenty-First Century*. London: Penguin/Allen Lane.

Bolton, John. 2007. *Surrender Is Not an Option: Defending America at the United Nations and Abroad*. New York: Threshold Editions.

Boughton, James M. 2001. *Silent Revolution: International Monetary Fund, 1979–1989*. Washington, DC: IMF.

2002. "Why White, Not Keynes? Inventing the Postwar International Monetary System." *IMF Working Paper*, WP/02/52, March.

Boutros-Ghali, Boutros. 1992. *An Agenda for Peace: Preventive Diplomacy, Peacemaking and Peace-Keeping*. Report of the Secretary-General pursuant to the statement adopted by the Summit Meeting of the Security Council on 31 January 1992. New York: United Nations.

Brehm, Stefan. 2008. "Risk Management in China's State Banks – International Best Practice and the Political Economy of Regulation." *Business and Politics* 10(1), 1–29.

Brehm, Stefan and Christian Macht. 2004. "Banking Supervision in China: Basel I, Basel II and the Basel Core Principles." *Zeitschrift für Chinesisches Recht* 4, 316–27.

Brender, Anton and Florence Pisani. 2010. *Global Imbalances and the Collapse of Globalised Finance*. Brussels: Centre for European Policy Studies.

Broder, Jonathan. 2009. "Power Playing with Others." *CQ Weekly*. 20 April, 1–8.

Brookings Institution Panel. 2007. "Darfur at a Crossroads: Global Public Opinion and the Responsibility to Protect." Washington, DC, 5 April.

Brooks, Stephen G. and William C. Wohlforth. 2008. *World Out of Balance: International Relations and the Challenge of American Primacy*. Princeton, NJ: Princeton University Press.

Broz, Lawrence. 2002. "Political System Transparency and Monetary Commitment Regimes." *International Organization* 56(4), 861–87.

Brunnermeier, M. K., A. Crockett, C. A. Goodhart, A. Persaud, and H. S. Shin. 2009. *The Fundamental Principles of Financial Regulation*. London: Centre for Economic Policy Research/Geneva Reports on the World Economy.

Buchanan, Allen and Robert O. Keohane. 2006. "The Legitimacy of Global Governance Institutions." *Ethics and International Affairs* 20(4), 405–37.

Buell, Lawrence. 1995. *The Environmental Imagination: Thoreau, Nature Writing, and the Formation of American Culture*. Cambridge, MA: Belknap Press of Harvard University.

Buijs, Bram. 2009. *China, Copenhagen and Beyond: The Global Necessity of a Sustainable Energy Future for China*. Clingendael International Energy Programme, Netherlands Institute of International Relations. September.

Burr, William and Jeffrey T. Richelson. 2000–01. "Whether to 'Strangle the Baby in the Cradle': The United States and the Chinese Nuclear Program, 1960–64." *International Security* 25(3), 54–99.

Busby, Joshua William. 2007. "Bono Made Jesse Helms Cry: Jubilee 2000, Debt Relief, and Moral Action in International Politics." *International Studies Quarterly* 51(2), 247–75.

Caporaso, James. 1992. "International Relations Theory and Multilateralism: The Search for Foundations." *International Organization* 46(3), 599–632.

Carlson, Allen. 2006. "More than Just Saying No: China's Evolving Approach to Sovereignty and Intervention." *In*: Alastair Iain Johnston and

Robert S. Ross (eds.) *New Directions in the Study of China's Foreign Policy*. Stanford, CA: Stanford University Press, 217–41.

Carnegie Meeting. 2009. "U.S.-China Climate Change Cooperation." Carnegie Endowment for International Peace and Security. Transcript with Xie Zhenhua and US Senator Maria Cantwell, Washington, DC, 18 March.

Carranza, Mario E. 2007. "From Non-Proliferation to Post-Proliferation: Explaining the US-India Nuclear Deal." *Contemporary Security Policy* 28(3), 464–93.

Carter, Ashton B. and William J. Perry. 1999. *Preventive Defense: A New Security Strategy for America*. Washington, DC: Brookings Institution Press.

Cass, Deborah Z., Brett G. Williams, and George Barker (eds.). 2003. *China and the World Trading System: Entering the New Millennium*. Cambridge: Cambridge University Press.

CBRC (China Banking Regulatory Commission). 2007. *Annual Report 2007*. Beijing: CBRC.

 2008. *Annual Report 2008*. Beijing: CBRC.

Celasun, Oya and Geoffrey Keim. 2010. "The U.S. Federal Debt Outlook: Reading the Tea Leaves." *IMF Working Paper*, WP/10/62, March.

Chan, Steve. 1999. "Chinese Perspectives on World Order." *In*: T. V. Paul and John A. Hall (eds.) *International Order and the Future of World Politics*. Cambridge: Cambridge University Press, 197–212.

 2008. *China, the U.S., and the Power-Transition Theory: A Critique*. London: Routledge.

Chandler, William. 2008. "Breaking the Suicide Pact: U.S.-China Cooperation on Climate Change." *Policy Brief* 57. Washington, DC: Carnegie Endowment for International Peace.

Chayes, Abram and Antonia Handler Chayes. 1993. "On Compliance." *International Organization* 47(2), 175–205.

Checkel, Jeffrey T. 2001. "Why Comply? Social Learning and European Identity Change." *International Organization* 55(3), 553–88.

Cheng Ruisheng. 2008. "Trend of India's Diplomatic Strategy." *China International Studies* 10(1), 20–40.

Chin, Gregory and Wang Yong. 2010. "What's in a Speech?" *China Security* (16), http://www.chinasecurity.us.

China's Defense White Paper. 2006. "China's National Defense in 2006." http://english.peopledaily.com.cn/whitepaper/defense2006/defense2006forward.html.

 2009. "China's National Defense in 2008." http://www.gov.cn/english/official/2009–01/20/content_1210227.htm. Beijing. January.

China's Position Paper. 2005. "Position Paper of the People's Republic of China on the United Nations Reforms." 9 June. http://na.china-embassy.org/eng/xwdt/t199361.htm.

Choubey, Deepti. 2008. *Are New Nuclear Bargains Attainable?* Washington, DC: Carnegie Endowment for International Peace.

 2009. *Restoring the NPT: Essential Steps for 2010*. Washington, DC: Carnegie Endowment for International Peace.

Christensen, Thomas J. (Deputy Assistant Secretary for East Asian and Pacific Affairs). 2006a. "China's Role in the World: Is China a Responsible Stakeholder?" remarks before the U.S.-China Economic and Security Review Commission, Washington, DC, 3 August 2006, http://www.state.gov/p/eap/rls/rm/69899.htm.

2006b. "Fostering Stability or Creating a Monster? The Rise of China and U.S. Policy toward East Asia." *International Security* 31(1), 81–126.

2006c. "Windows and War: Trend Analysis and Beijing's Use of Force." *In*: Alastair Iain Johnston and Robert S. Ross (eds.) *New Directions in the Study of China's Foreign Policy*. Stanford, CA: Stanford University Press, 50–85.

2009. "Shaping the Choices of a Rising China: Recent Lessons for the Obama Administration." *The Washington Quarterly* 32(3), 39–104.

Chu Shulong and Rong Yu. 2008. "China: Dynamic Minimum Deterrence." *In*: Muthiah Alagappa (ed.) *The Long Shadow: Nuclear Weapons and Security in 21st Century Asia*. Stanford, CA: Stanford University Press, 161–87.

Chwieroth, Jeffrey M. 2010. *Capital Ideas: The IMF and the Rise of Financial Liberalization*. Princeton, NJ: Princeton University Press.

Clark, Ian. 2001. *The Post-Cold War Order: the Spoils of Peace*. Oxford: Oxford University Press.

2007. *International Legitimacy and World Society*. Oxford: Oxford University Press.

Clausen, Peter A. 1993. *Nonproliferation and the National Interest: America's Response to the Spread of Nuclear Weapons*. New York: Harper Collins.

CNA Corporation. 2007. *National Security and the Threat of Climate Change*. Alexandria, VA: CNA Corporation.

Cooper, Richard N. 2005. "Living with Global Imbalances: A Contrarian View." *Policy Brief No. 05-3*. Peterson Institute for International Economics, November.

Cortell, Andrew P. and James W. Davis, Jr. 2000. "Understanding the Domestic Impact of International Norms: A Research Agenda." *International Studies Review* 2(1), 65–87.

2005. "When Norms Clash: International Norms, Domestic Practices, and Japan's Internalisation of the GATT/WTO." *Review of International Studies* 31(1), 3–25.

Cortright, David. 2007. "Overcoming Nuclear Dangers." *Policy Analysis Brief*, Stanley Foundation, November.

Costa, Oriol. 2008. "Is Climate Change Changing the EU: The Second Image Reversed in Climate Politics." *Cambridge Review of International Affairs* 21(4), 527–44.

CRS (Congressional Research Services). 2007. "Nuclear Weapons in U.S. National Security Policy: Past, Present, and Prospects." By Amy F. Woolf. RL34226. 29 October.

2009. "China and Proliferation of Weapons of Mass Destruction and Missiles: Policy Issues." By Shirley A. Kan. RL31555. 26 May and 23 December.

2010a. "China-North Korea Relations." By Dick K. Nanto et al. R41043. 22 January.

2010b. "U.S. Nuclear Cooperation with India: Issues for Congress." By Paul K. Kerr. RL33016. 4 February.

Cui Liru. 2008. "The Absence of a Model." *China Security* 4(2), Spring.

Culpepper, Pepper D. 2008. "The Politics of Common Knowledge: Ideas and Institutional Change in Wage Bargaining." *International Organization* 62(1), 1–33.

Daalder, Ivo H. 2007. (ed.) *Beyond Preemption: Force and Legitimacy in a Changing World*. Washington, DC: Brookings Institution Press.

Davies, Howard. 2008. "China and Financial Reform." Lecture delivered at the London School of Economics and Political Science, 15 October.

Davies, Howard and David Green. 2008. *Global Financial Regulation: The Essential Guide*. Cambridge, MA: Polity Press.

Deng Xiaoping. 1987. *Fundamental Issues in Present Day China*. Beijing: Foreign Languages Press.

Deng, Francis et al. 1996. *Sovereignty as Responsibility: Conflict Management in Africa*. Washington, DC: Brookings Institution.

Deng, Yong. 2001. "Hegemon on the Offensive: Chinese Perspectives on US Global Strategy." *Political Science Quarterly* 116(3), 343–65.

2006. "Reputation and the Security Dilemma: China Reacts to the China Threat Theory." *In*: Alastair Iain Johnston and Robert S. Ross (eds.) *New Directions in the Study of China's Foreign Policy*. Stanford, CA: Stanford University Press, 186–214.

DeSombre, Elizabeth R. 2000. *Domestic Sources of International Environmental Policy: Industry, Environmentalists, and U.S. Power*. Cambridge, MA: MIT Press.

2002. *The Global Environment and World Politics*. New York: Continuum.

Dobson, Wendy and Anil K. Kashyap. 2006. "The Contradiction in China's Gradualist Banking Reforms." *Rotman Institute for International Business Working Paper Series* 08, University of Toronto.

Dooley, Michael P., David Folkerts-Landau and Peter Garber. 2003. "An Essay on the Revived Bretton Woods System." *NBER Working Paper*, No. 9971, September.

2009. "Bretton Woods II Still Defines the International Monetary System." *NBER Working Paper*, No. 14731, February.

Downs, Erica. 2006. *China*. Washington, DC: Brookings Institution Press, December.

Downs, George W., David M. Rocke, and Peter N. Barsoom. 1996. "Is the Good News about Compliance Good News about Cooperation?" *International Organization* 50(3), 379–406.

Doyle, Michael. 2008. *Striking First: Preemption and Prevention in International Conflict*, edited and introduced by Stephen Macedo. Princeton, NJ: Princeton University Press.

Dunaway, Steven. 2009. *Global Imbalances and the Financial Crisis*. New York: Council on Foreign Relations.

Dunne, Tim. 2007. "'The Rules of the Game are Changing': Fundamental Human Rights in Crisis after 9/11." *International Politics* 44(2/3), 269–85.

Economy, Elizabeth. 1997. "Chinese Policy-Making and Global Climate Change: Two-Front Diplomacy and the International Community." *In*: Miranda A. Schreurs and Elizabeth C. Economy (eds.) *The Internationalization of Environmental Protection*. Cambridge: Cambridge University Press, 19–41.

1998. "The Impact of International Regimes on Chinese Foreign Policy-Making: Broadening Perspectives and Policies ... but Only to a Point." *In*: David M. Lampton (ed.) *The Making of Chinese Foreign and Security Policy*. Stanford, CA: Stanford University Press, 230–53.

2004. *The River Runs Black*. Ithaca, NY: Cornell University Press.

2007. "The Great Leap Backward? The Costs of China's Environmental Crisis." *Foreign Affairs* 86(5), 38–59.

Eichengreen, Barry J. 1992. *Golden Fetters: The Gold Standard and the Great Depression, 1919–1939*. Oxford: Oxford University Press.

Elliott, Lorraine. 1st edn. 1998 and 2nd edn. 2004. *The Global Politics of the Environment*. Basingstoke: Palgrave/Macmillan.

Emmott, Bill. 2008. *Rivals: How the Power Struggle Between China, India and Japan Will Shape Our Next Decade*. London: Allen Lane.

EPA (US Environmental Protection Agency). 2009. *Energy CO2 Emissions by State*. Washington, DC: EPA. http://www.epa.gov/climatechange/emissions/state_energyco2inv.html.

Ernst & Young. 2006. "Global Nonperforming Loan Report." Global Real Estate Center.

European Chamber of Commerce in China. 2009. *Overcapacity in China: Causes, Impacts and Recommendations*. European Chamber of Commerce in China, in association with Roland Berger Strategy Consultants.

European Commission. 2007a. *Evaluation of the European Commission's Co-Operation and Partnership with the People's Republic of China: Country Level Evaluation, Final Synthesis Report*. Brussels: European Commission, April.

2007b. *China: Country Strategy Paper 2007–2013*. Brussels: European Commission.

EU (European Union). [no date]. *Eurostat Database*: http://epp.eurostat.ec.europa.eu/portal/page/portal/eurostat/home/Brussels: European Commission.

Falkner, Robert. 2008. *Business Power and Conflict in International Environmental Politics*. Basingstoke: Palgrave/Macmillan.

2009. "The United States and the Global Climate Norm: Who's Influencing Whom?" Paper presented at the Annual Convention of the International Studies Association, New York City, 15–18 February.

Ferguson, R. W., Jr. 2003. "Basel II: Scope of Application in the United States." Remarks before the Institute of International Bankers, 10 June.

Finnemore, Martha. 1996. *National Interests in International Society*. Ithaca, NY: Cornell University Press.

2003. *The Purpose of Intervention: Changing Beliefs about the Use of Force*. Ithaca, NY: Cornell University Press.

Fitch Ratings. 2006. "China: Taking Stock of Banking System NPLs." China Special Report, www.fitchratings.com.

2008. "Chinese Banks – Annual Review and Outlook." 30 January 2008. www.fitchratings.com.

Foot, Rosemary. 1995. *The Practice of Power: US Relations with China since 1949.* Oxford: Oxford University Press.

2000. *Rights Beyond Borders: The Global Community and the Struggle over Human Rights in China.* Oxford: Oxford University Press.

2006. "Chinese Strategies in a US-Hegemonic Global Order: Accommodating and Hedging." *International Affairs* 82(1), 77–94.

2007. "Modes of Regional Conflict Management: Comparing Security Cooperation in the Korean Peninsula, China-Taiwan, and the South China Sea." *In*: Amitav Acharya and Evelyn Goh (eds.) *Reassessing Security Cooperation in the Asia-Pacific: Competition, Congruence, and Transformation.* Cambridge, MA: MIT Press, 93–112.

2009a. "Selective or Effective Multilateralism? Chinese Perspectives on a US-Led Proliferation Security Initiative." Unpublished MS.

2009b. "The Responsibility to Protect (R2P) and China: Is This a Nontraditional or Traditional Security Issue for Beijing?" Unpublished MS.

Fordham, Benjamin O. 2004. "A Very Sharp Sword: The Influence of Military Capabilities on American Decisions to Use Force." *Journal of Conflict Resolution* 48(5), 632–56.

Fordham, Benjamin O. and Christopher C. Sarver. 2001. "Militarized Interstate Disputes and United States Uses of Force." *International Studies Quarterly* 45(3), 455–66.

Frankel, Jeffrey A. and Shang-Jin Wei. 2007. "Assessing China's Exchange Rate Regime." *Economic Policy* 22(51), 575–627.

Fravel, M. Taylor. 2005. "Regime Insecurity and International Cooperation: Explaining China's Compromises in Territorial Disputes." *International Security* 30(2), 46–83.

2007/08. "Power Shifts and Escalation: Explaining China's Use of Force in Territorial Disputes." *International Security* 32(3), 44–83.

2008a. *Strong Borders Secure Nation: Cooperation and Conflict in China's Territorial Disputes.* Princeton, NJ: Princeton University Press.

2008b. "China's Search for Military Power." *The Washington Quarterly* 31(3), 125–41.

FSA (Financial Services Authority). 2009. *The Turner Review: A Regulatory Response to the Global Banking Crisis.* London: FSA.

FSB (Financial Stability Board). 2009. *Progress since the Pittsburgh Summit in Implementing the G20 Recommendations for Strengthening Financial Stability: Report of the Financial Stability Board to G20 Finance Ministers and Governors.* Basel: FSB, 7 November.

Fu Ying. 2003. "China and Asia in a New Era." *China: An International Journal* 1(2), 304–12.

Funabashi, Yoichi. 1989. *Managing the Dollar: From the Plaza to the Louvre.* Washington, DC: Institute for International Economics.

Gaddis, John Lewis. 1982. *Strategies of Containment: A Critical Appraisal of Postwar American National Security Policy.* Oxford: Oxford University Press.

GAO (United States Government Accountability Office). 2005. *International Trade: Treasury Assessments Have Not Found Currency Manipulation, but Concerns about Exchange Rates Continue.* Washington, DC: GAO-05-351, April.

Gardiner, Stephen M. 2004. "The Global Warming Tragedy and the Dangerous Illusion of the Kyoto Protocol." *Ethics and International Affairs* 18(1), 23–39.

Gardner, Richard N. 1980. *Sterling-Dollar Diplomacy in Current Perspective.* New York: Columbia University Press, 3rd edition.

Garnaut, Ross. 2008. *The Garnaut Climate Change Review.* Cambridge: Cambridge University Press.

Garrett, Geoffrey and Barry R. Weingast. 1993. "Ideas, Interests, and Institutions: Constructing the EC's Internal Market." *In*: J. M. Goldstein and R. O. Keohane (eds.) *Ideas and Foreign Policy: Beliefs, Institutions, and Political Change.* Ithaca, NY: Cornell University Press, 173–206.

Gavin, Francis J. 2004/05. "Blasts from the Past: Nuclear Proliferation and Rogue States before the Bush Doctrine." *International Security* 29(3), 100–35.

2010. "Nuclear Proliferation and Non-Proliferation." *In*: Melvyn P. Leffler and Odd Arne Westad (eds.) *Cambridge History of the Cold War*, Vol. II. Cambridge: Cambridge University Press, 395–416.

Gill, Bates. 2007. *Rising Star: China's New Security Diplomacy.* Washington, DC: Brookings Institution.

Gill, Bates and Chin-Hao Huang. 2009. "China's Expanding Peacekeeping Role: Its Significance and the Policy Implications." *SIPRI Policy Brief.* Stockholm, February.

Gilpin, Robert. 1981. *War and Change in World Politics.* Cambridge: Cambridge University Press.

Glaser, Bonnie. 2009. "U.S.-China Relations: A Good Beginning is Half Way to Success." *Comparative Connections* 11(April), http://csis/org/files/media/csis/pubs/090/qus_china.pdf.

Glaser, Bonnie S. and Evan S. Medeiros. 2007. "The Changing Ecology of Foreign-Policy Making in China: The Ascension and Demise of the Theory of 'Peaceful Rise'." *The China Quarterly* 190, 291–310.

GCR2P (Global Centre for the Responsibility to Protect). 2009. "Implementing the Responsibility to Protect. The 2009 General Assembly Debate: An Assessment." New York, August.

Goldstein, Judith L. 1993. *Ideas, Interests, and American Trade Policy.* Ithaca, NY: Cornell University Press.

Goldstein, Morris. 2004. "Adjusting China's Exchange Rate Policies." Revised version of the paper presented at the International Monetary Fund's seminar on China's Foreign Exchange System, Dalian, China, 26–27 May.

2007. "A (Lack of) Progress Report on China's Exchange Rate Policies." *Working Paper Series*, WP 07–5. Peterson Institute for International Economics. Washington, DC.

Goldstein, Morris and Nicholas Lardy. 2007. "China's Exchange Rate Policy: An Overview of Some Key Issues." Paper presented at the Conference on China's Exchange Rate Policy, Peterson Institute for International Economics, Washington, DC, 19 October.

GOV.cn. 2008. "China's Policies and Actions for Addressing Climate Change." 29 October. http://english.gov.cn/2008–10.29/content_1134544.htm.

Gowa, Joanne. 1983. *Closing the Gold Window: Domestic Politics and the End of Bretton Woods*. Ithaca, NY: Cornell University Press.

Gray, Christine. 2000. *International Law and the Use of Force*. Oxford: Oxford University Press.

2008a. *International Law and the Use of Force*. 3rd edn. Oxford: Oxford University Press.

2008b. "The Charter Limitations on the Use Of Force: Theory and Practice." *In*: Vaughan Lowe, Adam Roberts, Jennifer Welsh and Dominik Zaum (eds.) *The United Nations Security Council and War*. Oxford: Oxford University Press, 86–98.

Green Leap Forward. 2009a. "China Softens Climate Rhetoric." 6 August. http://greenleapforward.com/2009/08/06/.

2009b. "China to Adopt 'Binding' Goal to Reduce CO2 Emissions Per Unit GDP by 40 to 45% of 2005 levels by 2020." 26 November. http://greenleap-forward.com/2009/11/26/.

Greenspan, Alan. 2007. *The Age of Turbulence: Adventures in a New World*. London: Allen Lane.

Greene, Owen. 1997. "Environmental Issues." *In*: John Baylis and Steve Smith (eds.) *The Globalization of World Politics*. Oxford: Oxford University Press, 387–414.

Grieco, Joseph M. 1990. *Cooperation Among Nations*. Ithaca, NY: Cornell University Press.

Haas, Peter M. 1989. "Do Regimes Matter? Epistemic Communities and Mediterranean Pollution Control." *International Organization* 43(3), 377–403.

Hadley, Stephen. 2008. "Arms Control and Non Proliferation, Remarks by the National Security Advisor to the Center for International Security and Cooperation." Stanford, 8 February.

Hallding, Karl, Guoyi Han, and Marie Olsson. 2009. *A Balancing Act: China's Role in Climate Change*. Stockholm: The Commission on Sustainable Development, May.

Hanson, Fergus and Andrew Shearer. 2009. *China and the World: Public Opinion and Foreign Policy*. Sydney: Lowy Institute, http://www.lowyinstitute.org/Publication.asp?.pid=1193.

Harris, Paul G. 2001. "International Environmental Affairs and U.S. Foreign Policy." *In*: Paul G. Harris (ed.) *The Environment, International Relations, and U.S. Foreign Policy*. Washington, DC: Georgetown University Press, 3–41.

2008. "Introduction: The Glacial Politics of Climate Change." *Cambridge Review of International Affairs* 21(4), 455–64.

Hassner, Pierre. 2007. "Who Killed Nuclear Enlightenment?" *International Affairs* 83(3), 455–67.

Helleiner, Eric. 2010. "What Role for the New Kid in Town? The Financial Stability Board and International Standards." Paper prepared for workshop "New Foundations for Global Governance." Princeton University, 8–9 January.

Henning, C. Randall. 2007. "Democratic Accountability and the Exchange-Rate Policy of the Euro Area." *Review of International Political Economy* 14(5), 774–99.

Herring, Richard J. 2007. "The Rocky Road to Implementation of Basel II in the United States." *Atlantic Economic Journal* 35(4), 411–29.

Hogan, Michael J. 1998. *A Cross of Iron: Harry S. Truman and the Origins of the National Security State, 1945–1952.* New York: Cambridge University Press.

Holliday, Ian. 2009. "Beijing and the Myanmar Problem." *The Pacific Review,* 22(4), 479–500.

Hopgood, Stephen. 1998. *American Foreign Environmental Policy and the Power of the State.* Oxford: Oxford University Press.

House Committee on International Relations. 1998. "The Kyoto Protocol: Problems with U.S. Sovereignty and the Lack of Developing Country Participation." 13 May. http://commdocs.house.gov/committees/intlrel/hfa49425.000/hfa49425_0.htm.

Houser, Trevor. 2009. "Why Carbon Tariffs Are a Bad Idea – For Now." Originally posted on the Argument at ForeignPolicy.com, consulted 26 March at http://www.petersoninstitute.org/publications/opeds/.

Howe, Wendy. 2007. "Australia's Climate Change Regime: An Alternative Approach to Climate Change." *Macquarie Law Working Paper,* 13 November.

Howes, Stephen. 2009. "Can China Rescue the World Climate Change Negotiations?" 1 September. http://www.eastasiaforum.org/2009/09/01/.

Hu Angang. 2009. "A New Approach to Copenhagen." *Chinadialogue.net.* 6 April.

Hufbauer, Gary Clyde, Steve Charnovitz, and Jisun Kim. 2009. *Global Warming and the World Trading System.* Washington, DC: Peterson Institute for International Economics.

Hurd, Ian. 2007. "Breaking and Making Norms: American Revisionism and Crises of Legitimacy." *In:* Christian Reus-Smit and Ian Clark (eds.) Special Issue. *International Politics* 44(2/3), 194–213.

2008. "Constructivism." *In:* Christian Reus-Smit and Duncan Snidal (eds.) *The Oxford Handbook of International Relations.* Oxford: Oxford University Press, 298–316.

Hurrell, Andrew. 1998. "Society and Anarchy in the 1990s." *In:* B. A. Roberson (ed.) *International Society and the Development of International Relations.* London: Pinter, 17–42.

2005. "Legitimacy and the Use of Force: Can the Circle Be Squared?" *Review of International Studies* 31, 15–32.

2006. "Hegemony, Liberalism and Global Order: What Space for Would-Be Great Powers?" *International Affairs* 82(1), 1–19.

2007. *On Global Order: Power, Values, and the Constitution of International Society*. Oxford: Oxford University Press.

IAEA (International Atomic Energy Agency). 2008. "Reinforcing the Global Nuclear Order for Peace and Prosperity: the role of the IAEA to 2020 and Beyond." May. http://www.iaea.org/NewsCenter/News/PDF/2020report0508.pdf.

ICG (International Crisis Group). 2008. *China's Search for Oil*. Brussels: Asia Report No. 153, June.

2009. *China's Growing Role in UN Peacekeeping*. Brussels: Asia Report No. 166, April.

IEA (International Energy Agency). 2007. *World Energy Outlook 2007*. Paris: OECD/IEA.

2008. *World Energy Outlook 2008*. Paris: OECD/IEA.

IEO (Independent Evaluation Office, IMF). 2007. *Report on the Evaluation of the IMF Exchange Rate Policy Advice, 1999–2005*. Washington, DC: IEO, SM/07/132, 18 April.

Ignatieff, Michael (ed.). 2005. *American Exceptionalism and Human Rights*. Princeton, NJ: Princeton University Press.

IIF (Institute of International Finance). 2009. *Annual Report 2008*. New York: IIF.

IISS (International Institute for Strategic Studies). 2010a. *The Military Balance*. London: Routledge.

2010b. *Strategic Comments*: "Copenhagen Accord faces first test." Vol. 16, Comment 1, January. London: International Institute for Strategic Studies.

Ikenberry, G. John. 1992. "A World Economy Restored: Expert Consensus and the Anglo-American Postwar Settlement." *International Organization* 46(1), 289–321.

2001. *After Victory: Institutions, Strategic Restraint, and the Rebuilding of Order after Major Wars*. Princeton, NJ: Princeton University Press.

2005. "Power and Liberal Order: America's Post War World Order in Transition." *International Relations of the Asia-Pacific* 5(2), 133–52.

IMF (International Monetary Fund). 2000. "IMF Concludes 2000 Article IV Consultation with the People's Republic of China." *Public Information Notice* (PIN) No. 00/71, 1 September.

2001. "IMF Concludes 2001 Article IV Consultation with the People's Republic of China." *Public Information Notice* (PIN) No. 01/91, 24 August.

2003. "IMF Concludes 2003 Article IV Consultation with the People's Republic of China." *Public Information Notice* (PIN) No. 03/136, 18 November.

2004a. "IMF Concludes 2004 Article IV Consultation with the People's Republic of China." *Public Information Notice* (PIN) No. 04/99, 25 August.

2004b. "People's Republic of China: 2004 Article IV Consultation – Staff Report; Staff Statement; and Public Information Notice on the Executive Board Discussion." *Country Report* No. 04/351, 5 November.

2005a. *World Economic Outlook: Globalization and External Imbalances, May 2005*. Washington, DC: IMF.

2005b. "IMF Concludes 2005 Article IV Consultation with the People's Republic of China." *Public Information Notice* (PIN) No. 05/122, 12 September.

2005c. "People's Republic of China: 2005 Article IV Consultation – Staff Report; Staff Statement; and Public Information Notice on the Executive Board Discussion." *Country Report* No. 05/411, 17 November.

2006a. "Article IV of the Fund's Articles of Agreement: An Overview of the Legal Framework." International Monetary Fund, Legal Department, Washington, DC, 28 June.

2006b. "People's Republic of China: 2006 Article IV Consultation – Staff Report; Staff Statement; and Public Information Notice on the Executive Board Discussion." Washington, DC: IMF, October.

2006c. *Article IV of the Fund's Articles of Agreement: An Overview of the Legal Framework*. Washington, DC: IMF, 28 June.

2007. "The Multilateral Consultations on Global Imbalances." Washington, DC: IMF, April, http://www.imf.org/external/np/exr/ib/2007/041807.htm.

2008. *2008 Triennial Surveillance Review – Overview Paper*. Washington, DC: IMF, 2 September.

2009a. "United States: 2009 Article IV Consultation – Staff Report; Staff Supplement; and Public Information Notice on the Executive Board Discussion." Washington, DC: *Country Report* No. 09/228, July.

2009b. *Global Financial Stability Report, October: Navigating the Financial Challenges Ahead*. Washington, DC: IMF.

2009c. "IMF Executive Board Concludes 2009 Article IV Consultation with the People's Republic of China." Washington, DC: *Public Information Notice* (PIN) No. 09/87, July 22.

2009d. *Bilateral Surveillance Guidance Note*. Washington, DC: IMF, 27 October.

[no date]. *World Economic Outlook Database*: http://www.imf.org/external/pubs/ft/weo/2010/01/weodata/index.aspx. Washington, DC: IMF.

IPCC (Intergovernmental Panel on Climate Change). 2007. *Synthesis Report. Summary for Policymakers*. Geneva: IPCC.

ICISS (International Commission on Intervention and State Sovereignty). 2001. "The Responsibility to Protect." December. http://www.iciss.ca/report2-en.asp.

International Organization. 1982. Special Issue, edited by Stephen Krasner. 36.

International Politics. 2007. Special Issue, edited by Ian Clark and Christian Reus-Smit. 44(2/3).

Jacobson, Harold J. and Michel Oksenberg. 1990. *China's Participation in the IMF, the World Bank, and GATT: Toward a Global Economic Order*. Ann Arbor: University of Michigan Press.

Jakobson, Linda. 2009. "China and Climate Change Negotiations." *The World Today* 65(5), 4–7.

James, Harold. 1996. *International Monetary Cooperation Since Bretton Woods*. Washington, DC: Oxford University Press.

Jiang Zemin. 2002. "Build a Well-off Society in an All-Round Way and Create a New Situation in Building Socialism with Chinese Characteristics." 8 November, http://english.peopledaily.com.cn/200211/8/eng20021118_106983.shtml.

Johnson, Rebecca. 2009. "Enhanced Prospects for 2010: An Analysis of the Third PrepCom and the Outlook for the 2010 NPT Review Conference." June, http://www.armscontrol.org.

——— 2010. "Rethinking the NPT's Role in Security: 2010 and Beyond." *International Affairs* 86(2), 429–45.

Johnston, Alastair Iain. 1995. *Cultural Realism: Strategic Culture and Grand Strategy in Chinese History*. Princeton, NJ: Princeton University Press.

——— 1996. "Cultural Realism and Strategy in Maoist China." *In*: Peter J. Katzenstein (ed.) *The Culture of National Security: Norms and Identity in World Politics*. New York: Columbia University Press, 216–68.

——— 1998. "China's Militarized Interstate Dispute Behaviour 1949–1992: A First Cut at the Data." *The China Quarterly* 153, 1–30.

——— 2003. "Is China a Status Quo Power?" *International Security* 27(4), 5–56.

——— 2008. *Social States: China in International Institutions, 1980–2000*. Princeton, NJ: Princeton University Press.

Joseph, Jofi. 2009. "Renew the Drive for CTBT Ratification." *The Washington Quarterly* 32(2), 79–90.

Joyner, Daniel H. 2005. "The Proliferation Security Initiative: Nonproliferation, Counterproliferation, and International Law." *Yale Journal of International Law* 30(2), 507–48.

Kapstein, Ethan B. 1994. *Governing the Global Economy*. Cambridge, MA: Harvard University Press.

Katzenstein, Peter J. (ed.) 1996. *The Culture of National Security: Norms and Identity in World Politics*. New York: Columbia University Press.

Keck, Margaret E. and Kathryn Sikkink. 1998. *Activists Beyond Borders: Advocacy Networks in International Relations*. Ithaca, NY: Cornell University Press.

Keidel, Albert. 2008. "China's Economic Rise – Fact and Fiction." *Carnegie Endowment for International Peace Policy Brief* No. 61, July.

Kent, Ann. 1999. *China, the United Nations, and Human Rights: the Limits of Compliance*. Philadelphia: University of Pennsylvania Press.

——— 2007. *Beyond Compliance: China, International Organizations, and Global Security*. Stanford, CA: Stanford University Press.

Keohane, Robert O. 1984. *After Hegemony: Cooperation and Discord in the World Political Economy*. Princeton, NJ: Princeton University Press.

——— 1986. "Reciprocity in International Relations." *International Organization* 40(1), 1–27.

Keohane, Robert O. and Joseph S. Nye. 1977. *Power and Interdependence: World Politics in Transition*. Boston: Little Brown and Company.

Khong, Yuen Foong. 2008. "Neoconservatives and the Domestic Sources of American Foreign Policy: The Role of Ideas in Operation Iraqi Freedom." *In*: Steve Smith, Amelia Hadfield, and Tim Dunne (eds.) *Foreign Policy: Theories, Actors, Cases*. Oxford: Oxford University Press, 251–67.

Kim, Samuel S. 2009. "China and Globalization: Confronting Myriad Challenges and Opportunities." *Asian Perspective* 33(3), 41–80.

Kimball, Daryl. 1999. "CTBT in Crisis: How the US Senate Rejected CTBT Ratification." *Disarmament Diplomacy*. 40: September/October, http://www.acronym.org.uk/dd/dd40/40wrong.htm.

Kitfield, James. 2010. "Wanted: Dead," and "Are Drone Strikes Murder?" *National Journal Magazine*. 9 January. At NationalJournal.com.

Kleine-Ahlbrandt, Stephanie and Andrew Small. 2008. "China's New Dictatorship Diplomacy." *Foreign Affairs* 87(1), 38–56.

Klotz, Audie. 1995. *Norms in International Relations: The Struggle Against Apartheid*. Ithaca, NY: Cornell University Press.

Kowert, Paul and Jeffrey Legro. 1996. "Norms, Identity, and Their Limits: A Theoretical Reprise." *In*: Peter J. Katzenstein (ed.) *The Culture of National Security*. New York: Columbia University Press, 451–97.

Kramer, Anne E. 2007. "What the World Thinks." *In*: Ivo H. Daalder (ed.) *Beyond Preemption: Force and Legitimacy in a Changing World*. Washington, DC: Brookings Institution, 96–136.

Krasner, Stephen D. 1985. *Structural Conflict: The Third World Against Global Liberalism*. Berkeley: University of California Press.

Krause, Joachim. 2007. "Enlightenment and Nuclear Order." *International Affairs* 83(3), 483–99.

Krugman, Paul R. 2008. *The Conscience of a Liberal: Reclaiming America from the Right*. London: Allen Lane.

Kurlantzick, Joshua. 2007. *Charm Offensive: How China's Soft Power Is Transforming the World*. New Haven, CT: Yale University Press.

Lampton, David M. 2007. *The Three Faces of Chinese Power: Might, Money, and Minds*. Berkeley: University of California Press.

Lardy, Nicholas. 1994. *China in the World Economy*. Washington, DC: Institute for International Economics.

   2002. *Integrating China into the Global Economy*. Washington, DC: Brookings Institution.

   2008. "Financial Repression in China." *Peterson Institute Policy Brief* 08-8.

Leffler, Melvyn P. 1992. *A Preponderance of Power: National Security, the Truman Administration, and the Cold War*. Stanford, CA: Stanford University Press.

   2005. "9/11 and American Foreign Policy." *Diplomatic History* 29(3), 395–413.

Levy, Adrian and Catherine Scott-Clark. 2007. *Deception: Pakistan, the United States and the Global Nuclear Weapons Conspiracy*. London: Atlantic Books.

Lewis, Jeffrey G. 2007. *The Minimum Means of Reprisal: China's Search for Security in the Nuclear Age*. Cambridge, MA: MIT Press.

Lewis, Joanna I. 2007/08. "China's Strategic Priorities in International Climate Change Negotiations." *The Washington Quarterly* 31(1), 155–74.

Li Shaojun. 2003. "International Regimes of Nuclear Nonproliferation and China." *In*: Wang Yizhou (ed.) *Construction within Contradiction: Multiple Perspectives on the Relationship between China and International Organizations*. Beijing: China Development Publishing House, 47–72.

Lieberthal, Kenneth and Mikkal Herberg. 2006. *China's Search For Energy Security: Implications for U.S. Policy*. Washington, DC: National Bureau of Asian Research, Vol. 17, No. 1. April.

Lieberthal, Kenneth and David Sandalow. 2009. *Overcoming Obstacles to U.S.-China Cooperation on Climate Change*. Washington, DC: Brookings Institution, January.

Lindblom, Charles A. 1980. *The Policy Making Process*. Englewood Cliffs, NJ: Prentice-Hall, 2nd edition.

Luck, Edward C. 2006. "Article 2(4) on the Nonuse of Force: What Were We Thinking?" *In*: David P. Forsythe, Patrice C. McMahon, and Andrew Wedelman (eds.) *American Foreign Policy in a Globalized World*. London: Routledge, 51–80.

    2008. "The United Nations and the Responsibility to Protect." *Policy Analysis Brief*, The Stanley Foundation, August.

    2009. "Sovereignty, Choice, and the Responsibility to Protect." *Global Responsibility to Protect* 1(1), 10–21.

Luo Ping. 2003. "Challenges for China's Banking Sector and Policy Responses." China Banking Regulatory Commission, paper delivered to conference on India's and China's Experience with Reform and Growth, New Delhi, 14–16 November.

    2008. "Implications of Basel II for Emerging Markets and China's Approach to Basel II." China Banking Regulatory Commission, paper delivered to 2008 Basel II Summit, Singapore, 4 March.

MacFarlane, S. Neil and Yuen Foong Khong. 2006. *Human Security and the UN: A Critical History*. Bloomington: Indiana University Press.

Mackby, Jennifer and Walter Slocombe. 2004. "Germany: The Model Case, A Historical Imperative." *In*: Kurt M. Campbell, Robert J. Einhorn, and Mitchell B. Reiss (eds.) *The Nuclear Tipping Point: Why States Reconsider Their Nuclear Choices*. Washington, DC: Brookings Institution, 175–217.

Mahoney, James and Gary Goertz. 2006. "A Tale of Two Cultures: Contrasting Quantitative and Qualitative Research." *Political Analysis* 14(3), 227–49.

Mayall, James. 2004. "Humanitarian Intervention and International Society: Lessons from Africa." *In*: Jennifer M. Welsh (ed.) *Humanitarian Intervention and International Relation*. Oxford: Oxford University Press, 120–41.

McCown, T. Ashby, Patricia Pollard, and John Weeks. 2007. "Equilibrium Exchange Rate Models and Misalignments." *Occasional Paper*, 7, Office of International Affairs, March.

McDonough, William J. 1998a. "Issues for the Basel Accord." Remarks by William J. McDonough, President, Federal Reserve Bank of New York and Chairman, Basel Committee on Banking Supervision, at the Conference on Credit Risk Modeling and Regulatory Implications, London, 22 September.

    1998b. "Credit Risk and the 'Level Playing Field'." Remarks by William J. McDonough, President, Federal Reserve Bank of New York and Chairman, Basel Committee on Banking Supervision at Conference on the Challenge of Credit Risk, 24 November.

McDougall, Walter. 1997. *Promised Land, Crusader State*. New York: Houghton Mifflin.

McKinsey & Co. 2007. "Assessing the Impact of Societal Issues: A McKinsey Global Survey." November, http://www.mckinseyquarterly.com/Strategy/ Strategy_in_Practice/Assessing_the_impact_of_societal_issues_A_ McKinsey_Global_Survey_2077?pagenum=3#Exhibit4.

    2008. "How Companies Think about Climate Change: A McKinsey Global Survey." February, http://www.mckinseyquarterly.com/How_companies_ think_about_climate_change_A_McKinsey_Global_Survey_2009.

McKinsey Global Institute. 2009. *Global Capital Markets: Entering a New Era.* San Francisco: MGI, September.

Medeiros, Evan S. 2007. *Reluctant Restraint: The Evolution of China's Nonproliferation Policies and Practices, 1980–2004.* Stanford, CA: Stanford University Press.

2009. *China's International Behavior: Activism, Opportunism, and Diversification.* Santa Monica: Rand Corporation.

Milner, Helen V. 1997. *Interests, Institutions, and Information.* Princeton, NJ: Princeton University Press.

Morton, Katherine. 2005. *International Aid and China's Environment.* London: Routledge.

2009. *China and the Global Environment.* Lowy Institute Paper 29. Sydney.

Mussa, Michael. 2007. "IMF Surveillance over China's Exchange Rate Policy." Paper presented at the Conference on China's Exchange Rate Policy, Peterson Institute for International Economics, Washington, DC, 19 October.

Nye, Joseph S. 2004. *Soft Power: The Means to Success in World Politics.* New York: Public Affairs.

Oatley, Thomas and Robert Nabors. 1998. "Market Failure, Wealth Transfers, and the Basel Accord." *International Organization* 52(1), 35–54.

Obstfeld, Maurice and Kenneth Rogoff. 2004. "The Unsustainable US Current Account Position Revisited." *NBER Working Paper*, No. 10869, October.

Paarlberg, Robert. 1997. "Earth in Abeyance: Explaining Weak Leadership in U.S. International Environmental Policy." *In*: Robert J. Lieber (ed.) *Eagle Adrift: American Foreign Policy at the End of the Century.* New York: Longman, 135–62.

Pan Zhenqiang. 2008. "Chinese Perspectives on the Strategic Context of Nuclear Weapons." *In*: Christopher Twomey (ed.) *Perspectives on Sino-American Strategic Nuclear Issues.* New York: Palgrave/Macmillan, 57–72.

Pang Zhongying. 2008. "China: Partner – or Ward?" *Internationale Politik* 9(3), 42–7.

Pant, Harsh V. 2009. "The US-India Nuclear Pact: Policy, Process, and Great Power Politics." *Asian Security* 5(3), 273–95.

Paul, T. V. 2009. *The Tradition of Non-Use of Nuclear Weapons.* Stanford, CA: Stanford University Press.

Paul, T. V. and Mahesh Shankar. 2007/08. "Why the US-India Nuclear Accord Is a Good Deal." *Survival* 49(4), 111–22.

Paulson, Henry M., Jr. 2008. "The Right Way to Engage China." *Foreign Affairs* 87(5), 59–77.

Pearson, Margaret M. 1999. "China's Integration into the International Trade and Investment Regime." *In*: Elizabeth Economy and Michael Oksenberg (eds.) *China Joins the World: Progress and Prospects.* New York: Council on Foreign Relations, 161–205.

Pew Center on Global Climate Change/Asia Society. 2009. "Common Challenge, Collaborative Response: A Roadmap for US-China Cooperation on Energy and Climate Change." Report, New York.

Pomper, Miles. 2009. "Mitigating the Proliferation Risks of the Anticipated Worldwide Growth in Nuclear Energy." Paper given at conference on "Effective Multilateralism" University of Oxford, 17–19 December.

Potter, William C. 2005. "India and the New Look of US Non-Proliferation Policy." *NonProliferation Review* 12(2), 242–54.

Powell, Andrew. 2004. "Basel II and Developing Countries: Sailing Through the Sea of Standards." *World Bank Policy Research Working Paper* No. 3387.

Power, Samantha. 2002. *A Problem from Hell: America and the Age of Genocide.* New York: New Republic Books.

Prasad, Eswar S. 2007a. "Monetary Policy Independence, the Currency Regime, and the Capital Account in China." Paper presented at the Conference on China's Exchange Rate Policy, Peterson Institute for International Economics, Washington, DC, 19 October.

2007b. "Is the Chinese Growth Miracle Built to Last?" Unpublished paper, 26 November. http://prasad.aem.cornell.edu/doc/new_papers/ChinaGrowth.Nov07.pdf.

2010. "The U.S.-China Economic Relationship: Shifts and Twists in the Balance of Power." Paper prepared for testimony to the U.S.-China Economic and Security Review Commission, hearing on "U.S. debt to China: implications and repercussions." 25 February (revised 10 March).

Putnam, Robert D. 1988. "Diplomacy and Domestic Politics: The Logic of Two-Level-Games." *International Organization* 42(3), 427–60.

Quah, Danny. 2010. "Post-1990s East Asian Economic Growth: The Inexorable Rise and Influence of China." *In:* Takatoshi Ito (ed.) *The Rise of China and Structural Challenges in Korea and Asia.* Cheltenham: Edward Elgar.

Rabe, Barry G. 2004. *Statehouse and Greenhouse: The Emerging Politics of American Climate Change Policy.* Washington, DC: Brookings Institution.

Reinhart, Carmen M. and Vincent R. Reinhart. 2008. "Capital Inflows and Reserve Accumulation: The Recent Evidence." *NBER Working Paper*, No. 13842.

Reinhart, Carmen M. and Kenneth S. Rogoff. 2002. "The Modern History of Exchange Rate Arrangements: A Reinterpretation." *NBER Working Paper* No. 8963.

Reinicke, Wolfgang H. 1995. *Banking, Politics and Global Finance: American Commercial Banks and Regulatory Change, 1980–1990.* Washington, DC: Brookings Institution.

Reisman, W. Michael. 1999–2000. "The United States and International Institutions." *Survival* 41(4), 62–80.

Reiss, Mitchell B. 1988. *Without the Bomb: The Politics of Nuclear Non-proliferation.* New York: Columbia University Press.

2006. "A New Nuclear Bargain: Atoms for Peace 2.0?" Paper prepared for a National Bureau of Asian Research Workshop, December.

Rengger, Nicholas and Caroline Kennedy-Pipe. 2008. "The State of War." *International Affairs* 84(5), 891–901.

Riedel, Bruce. 2008. "South Asia's Nuclear Decade." *Survival* 50(2), 107–26.

Risse, Thomas. 2000. 'Let's Argue!': Communicative Action in World Politics." *International Organization* 54(1), 1–39.

Roberts, Adam. 2004. "The United Nations and Humanitarian Intervention." *In:* Jennifer M. Welsh (ed.) *Humanitarian Intervention and International Relations.* Oxford: Oxford University Press, 71–97.

2008. "Proposals for UN Standing Forces: A Critical History." *In*: Vaughan Lowe, Adam Roberts, Jennifer Welsh, and Dominik Zaum (eds.) *The United Nations Security Council and War*. Oxford: Oxford University Press, 99–130.

Roberts, Adam and Dominik Zaum. 2008. *War and the United Nations Security Council since 1945*. Adelphi Paper 395. London: Routledge.

Rodrik, Dani. 2008. "The Real Exchange Rate and Economic Growth." *Brookings Papers on Economic Activity* 2, 365–412.

Rosenau, James N. 1997. *Along the Domestic-Foreign Frontier: Exploring Governance in a Turbulent World*. Cambridge: Cambridge University Press.

Rosenbaum, Walter A. 2008. *Environmental Politics and Policy*. Washington, DC: CQ Press, 7th edition.

Ross, Lester. 1999. "China and Environmental Protection." *In*: Elizabeth Economy and Michel Oksenberg (eds.) *China Joins the World: Progress and Prospects*. New York: Council on Foreign Relations, 296–325.

Ross, Robert S. 2000. "The 1995–1996 Taiwan Strait Confrontation: Coercion, Credibility, and the Use Of Force." *International Security* 25(2), 87–123.

2009. "China's Naval Nationalism: Sources, Prospects, and the U.S. Response." *International Security* 34(2), 46–81.

Rublee, Maria. 2009. *Non-Proliferation Norms: Why States Choose Nuclear Restraint*. Athens: University of Georgia Press.

Ruggie, John Gerard. 2005. "American Exceptionalism, Exemptionalism, and Global Governance." *In*: Michael Ignatieff (ed.) *American Exceptionalism and Human Rights*. Princeton, NJ: Princeton University Press, 304–38.

Ruhle, Michael. 2007. "Enlightenment in the Second Nuclear Age." *International Affairs* 83(3), 511–22.

Sands, Philippe. 2005. *Lawless World: America and the Making and Breaking of Global Rules*. London: Allen Lane.

Sanford, Jonathan E. 2006. *China, the United States and the IMF: Negotiating Exchange Rate Adjustment*. Washington, DC: Congressional Research Service, April.

Scharpf, Fritz W. 1999. *Governing in Europe: Effective and Democratic?* Oxford: Oxford University Press.

Schell, Jonathan. 2007. *The Seventh Decade: The New Shape of Nuclear Danger*. New York: Metropolitan Books.

Schoppa, Leonard J. 1993. "Two Level Games and Bargaining Outcomes: Why Gaiatsu Succeeds in Japan in Some Cases and Not Others." *International Organization*, 47(3), 353–86.

Schroeder, Miriam. 2008. "The Construction of China's Climate Politics: Transnational NGOs and the Spiral Model of International Relations." *Cambridge Review of International Affairs* 21(4), 505–25.

Scobell, Andrew. 2003. *China's Use of Military Force*. Cambridge: Cambridge University Press.

Seaborg, Glenn T. and Benhamin S. Loeb. 1987. *Stemming the Tide: Arms Control in the Johnson Years*. Lexington, MA: DC. Heath.

Shambaugh, David (ed.) 2005. *Power Shift: China and Asia's New Dynamics*. Berkeley: University of California Press.

Shen Dingli. 2009. "Toward a Nuclear Weapons Free World: A Chinese Perspective." Report for the Lowy Institute. Sydney: November.

Shih, Victor C. 2008. *Factions and Finance in China: Elite Conflict and Inflation.* Cambridge: Cambridge University Press.

Shue, Henry and David Rodin (eds.). 2007. *Preemption: Military Action and Moral Justification.* Oxford: Oxford University Press.

Simmons, Beth A. 2001. "The International Politics of Harmonization: The Case of Capital Market Regulation." *International Organization* 55(3), 589–620.

Singer, David. 2007. *Regulating Capital: Setting Standards for the International Financial System.* Ithaca, NY: Cornell University Press.

SIPRI (Stockholm International Peace Research Institute). 2008. *SIPRI Yearbook 2008.* Oxford: Oxford University Press.

    2009. *SIPRI Yearbook 2009.* Oxford: Oxford University Press.

    2010. *SIPRI Yearbook 2010.* Oxford: Oxford University Press.

Sivak, Michael and Omer Tsimhoni. 2009. "Fuel Efficiency of Vehicles on US Roads: 1923–2006." *Energy Policy* 37(8), 3168–70.

Skidelsky, Robert. 2000. *John Maynard Keynes: Fighting for Britain.* London: Macmillan.

Sobel, Mark and Louellen Stedman. 2006. "The Evolution of the G7 and Economic Policy Coordination." *Department of the Treasury, Office of International Affairs Occasional Paper,* No. 3, July.

Soederberg, Susanne, Georg Menz, and Philip G. Cerny (eds.) 2005. *Internalizing Globalization: the Rise of Neoliberalism and the Decline of National Varieties of Capitalism.* Basingstoke: Palgrave Macmillan.

Solomon, Robert. 1982. *The International Monetary System, 1945–1981.* New York: Harper & Row.

Srivastava, Anupam. 2008. "NSG Waiver for India." *PacNet* No. 46. Honolulu: Pacific Forum CSIS, 8 September.

Steinberg, Donald. 2006. "America and the Responsibility to Protect: Examining the Underlying Assumptions." Address delivered at the Chicago Council on Global Affairs, November 15. Published on International Crisis Group website: http://www.crisisgroup.org/home/index.cfm?id=4561&l=1.

Steinberg, James B. 2009. "East Asia and the Pacific: Administration's Vision of the U.S.-China Relationship." Keynote address at the Center for a New American Security, Washington, DC, 24 September.

Stern, Nicholas. 2009. *The Global Deal: Climate Change and the Creation of a New Era of Progress and Prosperity.* New York: Public Affairs.

Stern, Todd and William Antholis. 2007/08. "A Changing Climate: the Road Ahead for the United States." *Washington Quarterly* 31(1), 175–88.

Sudan Strategy. 2009. "Sudan: A Critical Moment, A Comprehensive Approach." Office of the Spokesman, Washington, DC, 19 October. http://www.state.gov/r/pa/prs/ps/2009/oct/130672.htm.

Suzuki, Shogo. 2008. "Seeking 'Legitimate' Great Power Status in Post-Cold War International Society: China's and Japan's Participation in UNPKO." *International Relations* 22(1), 45–63.

Tannenwald, Nina. 2007. *The Nuclear Taboo: The United States and the Non-Use of Nuclear Weapons Since 1945.* Cambridge: Cambridge University Press.

Tarullo, Dan. 2008. *Banking on Basel: The Future of International Financial Regulation*. Washington, DC: Peterson Institute for International Economics.

Taylor, John B. 2007. *Global Financial Warriors: The Untold Story of International Finance in the Post-9/11 World*. New York: W. W. Norton.

Teitt, Sarah. 2008. "China and the Responsibility to Protect." Brisbane: Asia-Pacific Centre for the Responsibility to Protect, 19 December.

2009. "Assessing Polemics, Principles and Practices: China and the Responsibility to Protect." *Global Responsibility to Protect* 1(2), 208–36.

Tellis, Ashley J. 2005. "The US-India 'Global Partnership': How Significant for American Interests?" Testimony before the House Committee on International Relations, 16 November. http://www.carnegieendowment.org/publications/index.cfm?fa=view&id=17693.

Tett, Gillian. 2009. *Fool's Gold: How Unrestrained Greed Corrupted a Dream, Shattered Global Markets and Unleashed a Catastrophe*. London: Little, Brown.

Thakur, Ramesh and Thomas G. Weiss. 2009. "R2P: From Idea to Norm – and Action?" *Global Responsibility to Protect* 1(1), 1–32.

Thayer, Carlyle A. 2007. "China's International Security Cooperation with Southeast Asia." *Australian Defence Forces Journal* 172, 16–32.

Thompson, Drew. 2009. "Border Burdens: China's Response to the Myanmar Refugee Crisis." *China Security* 5(3), 11–20.

Tompkins, Joanne. 2003. "How U.S. Strategic Policy is Changing China's Nuclear Plans." January–February, http://www.armscontrol.org/act/2003_01-02/tompkins_janfeb03.

Tsebelis, George. 2002. *Veto Players: How Political Institutions Work*. Princeton, NJ: Princeton University Press.

Twomey, Christopher P. 2008. "Dangers and Prospects in Sino-American Nuclear Relations." *In*: Christopher P. Twomey (ed.) *Perspectives on Sino-American Strategic Nuclear Issues*. New York: Palgrave/Macmillan, 3–12.

2009. "Chinese-U.S. Strategic Affairs: Dangerous Dynamism." *Arms Control Today* 39(1), 17–20.

U.S. Asia-Pacific Council. 2010. "Global Issues Take Center Stage in U.S.-China Relations: Interview with Dr Kenneth Lieberthal." Vol. 1, January.

UNCED (United Nations Conference on Environment and Development). 1992. Report of the United Nations Conference on Environment and Development, A/CONF.151/26/Rev.1, Vol. II, Proceedings of the Conference. Geneva: United Nations, 3–14 June 1992.

UNGA (United Nations General Assembly) Document. 2004. A/59/565. *A More Secure World: Our Shared Responsibility*. Report of the Secretary General's High Level Panel on Threats, Challenges, and Change. 2 December. http://www.un.org/secureworld/

2005. A/RES/60/1. *World Summit Outcome*. 24 October.

2009. A/63/677. *Implementing the Responsibility to Protect: Report of the Secretary-General*. 12 January.

Underdal, Arild. 1998. "Explaining Compliance and Defection: Three Models." *European Journal of International Relations* 4(1), 5–30.

Uppsala Conflict Data Program. [no date]. http://www.pcr.uu.se/research/UCDP/, Uppsala University.

US DOD (US Department of Defense). 2006. *Quadrennial Defense Review Report*. Washington, DC: Department of Defense, 6 February. http://www. defenselink.mil.qdr/report/Report20060203.pdf.

2009. *Military Power of the People's Republic of China, Annual Report to Congress*. http://www.defenselink.mil/pubs/pdfs/China_Military_Power_ Report_2009.pdf.

2010. *Quadrennial Defense Review Report*. February. http://www.defense.gov/ qdr/QDR%20as%20of%2026JAN10%200700.pdf.

US Energy Information Administration. [no date]. *International Energy Statistics*: http://tonto.eia.doe.gov/cfapps/ipdbproject/IEDIndex3.cfm?tid= 90&pid=44&aid=8. Washington, DC: Energy Information Administration.

US Federal Reserve. 1994. "Profits and Balance Sheet Developments at U.S. Commercial Banks in 1993." *Federal Reserve Bulletin*, June, 483–507.

1996. "Profits and Balance Sheet Developments at U.S. Commercial Banks in 1995." *Federal Reserve Bulletin*, June, 483–505.

2005. "Profits and Balance Sheet Developments at U.S. Commercial Banks in 2004." *Federal Reserve Bulletin* 91, 143–74.

2009. *The Supervisory Capital Assessment Program: Overview of Results*. Washington, DC: Federal Reserve, 7 May.

USNSS (US National Security Strategy). 2002. "The National Security Strategy of the United States of America." Washington, DC: The White House, September.

2006. "The National Security Strategy of the United States of America." Washington, DC: The White House, March.

2010. "National Security Strategy." Washington, DC: The White House, May.

US Treasury. 2007. *Report to Congress on International Economic and Exchange Rate Policies*. Washington, DC: Department of Treasury, December.

2008a. *Blueprint for a Modernized Financial Regulatory Structure*. Washington, DC: US Treasury.

2008b. *Report to Congress on Implementation of the International Monetary Fund's 2007 Decision on Bilateral Surveillance over Members' Policies*. Washington, DC: US Treasury, August.

2009a. *Financial Regulatory Reform, A New Foundation: Rebuilding Financial Supervision and Regulation*. Washington, DC: US Treasury.

2009b. "Factsheet: Improving International Regulatory Standards and Cooperation." Washington, DC: US Treasury, 17 June.

2009c. *Report to Congress on International Economic and Exchange Rate Policies*. Washington, DC: Department of Treasury, October.

Valencia, Mark J. 1995. *China and the South China Sea Disputes*. Adelphi Paper 298. International Institute of Strategic Studies. Oxford: Oxford University Press.

2005. *The Proliferation Security Initiative: Making Waves in Asia*. Adelphi Paper 376. Oxford: Oxford University Press.

Van Kemenade, Willem. 2009. *Iran's Relations with China and the West: Cooperation and Confrontation in Asia*. Clingendael Diplomacy Papers, No. 24, The Hague. November.

Vandenbergh, Michael P. 2007/08. "Climate Change: The China Problem." *Southern California Law Review* 81, 905–933.

Vines, David. 2006. "Comments on 'Global Imbalances and Emerging Markets'," In: Alan Ahearne (ed.) *European and Asian Perspectives on Global Imbalances*. Asia Europe Economic Forum, 40–51.

Vogel, David. 1995. *Trading Up: Consumer and Environmental Regulation in a Global Economy*. Cambridge, MA: Harvard University Press.

Walker, William. 2004. *Weapons of Mass Destruction and International Order*. Adelphi Paper 370. Oxford: Oxford University Press.

2007. "Nuclear Enlightenment and Counter-Enlightenment." *International Affairs* 83(3), 431–53.

Walter, Andrew. 1993. *World Power and World Money: The Role of Hegemony and International Monetary Order*. New York: St Martin's Press/Harvester Wheatsheaf.

2006a. "Leadership Begins at Home: Domestic Sources of International Monetary Power." *In*: David M. Andrews (ed.) *International Monetary Power*. Ithaca, NY: Cornell University Press, 51–71.

2006b. "From Developmental to Regulatory State? Japan's New Financial Regulatory System." *The Pacific Review* 19(4), 405–28.

2008. *Governing Finance: East Asia's Adoption of International Standards*. Ithaca, NY: Cornell University Press.

Wang Yanjia. 2010. "Energy Security and Climate Change Issues in China." January. http://www.globalcollab.org/Nautilus/.

Webb, Michael C. 1995. *The Political Economy of Policy Coordination*. Ithaca, NY: Cornell University Press.

Welsh, Jennifer M. 2008. "The Security Council and Humanitarian Intervention." *In*: V. Lowe et al. (eds.) *The United Nations Security Council and War*. Oxford: Oxford University Press, 535–62.

Wheeler, Nicolas. 2000. *Saving Strangers: Humanitarian Intervention in International Society*. Oxford: Oxford University Press.

2004. "The Humanitarian Responsibilities of Sovereignty: Explaining the Development of a New Norm of Military Intervention for Humanitarian Purposes in International Society." *In*: J. M. Welsh (ed.) *Humanitarian Intervention and International Relations*. Oxford: Oxford University Press, 29–51.

Wheeler, Nicholas J. and Frazer Egerton. 2009. "The Responsibility to Protect: 'Precious Commitment' or a Promise Unfulfilled?" *Global Responsibility to Protect* 1(1), 114–32.

Whiting, Allen S. 2001. "China's Use of Force, 1950–1996, and Taiwan." *International Security* 26(2), 103–31.

Williamson, Ambassador Richard W. 2009. "Sudan and the Implications for Responsibility to Protect." *Policy Analysis Brief*, Stanley Foundation, October.

Wittner, Lawrence S. 1997. *Resisting the Bomb: A History of the World Nuclear Disarmament Movement, 1954–1970*. Stanford, CA: Stanford University Press.

Wolf, Martin. 2008. *Fixing Global Finance*. Baltimore: Johns Hopkins University Press.

Woods, Ngaire. 2006. *The Globalizers: The IMF, the World Bank and Their Borrowers*. Ithaca, NY: Cornell University Press.

World Public Opinion.org. 2007. "Publics Around the World Say UN Has Responsibility to Protect Against Genocide." http://www.worldpublicopinion.org/.

WTO (World Trade Organization). [no date]. *International Trade and Tariff Data*: http://www.wto.org/english/res_e/statis_e/statis_e.htm. Geneva: WTO.

Yang Yi. 2010. "Domestic Constraints and International Forces: Exploring China's Position on International Climate Change Policy." 26 January, http://www.globalcollab.org/Nautilus/cc-workshops/seoul/workshop-papers/Exploring_Chinas_Position_on_International_Climate_Change_Policy.pdf.

Yu Xintian. 2008. "Soft Power Enhancement and China's External Strategy." *China International Studies* 12, 20–35.

Yu Hongyuan. 2007. *Global Warming and China's Environmental Diplomacy*. MS in authors' possession.

Yu Yongding. 2006. "Global Imbalances: China's Perspective." Paper prepared for conference on European and Asian Perspectives on Global Imbalances, Beijing, 12–14 July.

Yuan, Jing-dong. 2001. "Assessing Chinese Nonproliferation Policy: Progress, Problems and Issues for the United States." Prepared statement for the U.S.-China Security Review Commission Hearing on China's Proliferation Policies. Washington, DC, 12 October.

——— 2007. "Arms Control Regimes in the Asia-Pacific: Managing Armament and WMD Proliferation." *In*: Amitav Acharya and Evelyn Goh (eds.) *Reassessing Security Cooperation in the Asia-Pacific*. Cambridge, MA: MIT Press, 177–94.

Zacher, Mark W. 2001. "The Territorial Integrity Norm: International Boundaries and the Use of Force." *International Organization* 55(2), 215–50.

Zhang Haibin and Katherine Morton. 2010. "China and International Climate Change Negotiations." *In*: Katherine Morton (ed.) *Between Traditional and Non-traditional Security: Sino-Australian Perspectives on the Region*. Forthcoming.

Zhang Tuosheng. 2010. "On China's Concept of the International Security Order." *In*: Robert S. Ross, Oystein Tunsjo, and Zhang Tuosheng (eds.) *US-China-EU Relations: Managing the New World Order*. London: Routledge, 26–47.

Zhang Yunling and Tang Shiping. 2005. "China's Regional Strategy." *In*: David Shambaugh (ed.) *Power Shift: China and Asia's New Dynamics*. Berkeley: University of California Press, 48–68.

Zhang Zhongxiang. 2007. "China, the United States and Technological Cooperation on Climate Control." *Environmental Science and Policy* 10, at http://ssrn.com/abstract=953292.

2009a. "How Far Can Developing Country Commitments Go in an Immediate Post-2012 Climate Regime?" *Energy Policy* 37(5), 1753–7.

2009b. "In What Format and Under What Time Frame Would China Take on Climate Commitments? A Roadmap to 2050." Honolulu: *East–West Center Working Paper*, No. 66. June.

Zoellick, Robert. 2005. "Whither China: From Membership to Responsibility." Remarks to the National Committee on U.S.-China Relations, 25 November 2005, U.S. Department of State. http://www.state.gov/s/d/former/zoellick/rem/53682.htm.

Index